ADVANCED ROBUST AND NONPARAMETRIC METHODS IN EFFICIENCY ANALYSIS

METHODOLOGY AND APPLICATIONS

Studies in Productivity and Efficiency

Series Editors:

Books in the series:

Fox, Kevin J.:
Efficiency in the Public Sector
Ball, V. Eldon and Norton, George W.:
Agricultural Productivity:
Measurement and Sources of Growth
Färe, Rolf and Grosskopf, Shawna:
New Directions:
Efficiency and Productivity
Daraio, C. and Simar, L.:
Advanced Robust and Nonparametric Methods in Efficiency Analysis:
Methodology and Applications

ADVANCED ROBUST AND NONPARAMETRIC METHODS IN EFFICIENCY ANALYSIS

METHODOLOGY AND APPLICATIONS

by

Cinzia Daraio
Institute of Informatics and Telematics (CNR), Pisa
and
Department of Electrical Systems and Automation,
School of Engineering, University of Pisa

Léopold Simar
Institute of Statistics
Université Catholique de Lovain, Louvain la Neuve, Belgium

Springer

e-ISBN 0-387-35231-7
ISBN-13: 978-1-4419-4197-8 e-ISBN-13: 978-0387-35231-1

Printed on acid-free paper.

Softcover reprint of the hardcover 1st edition 2007

9 8 7 6 5 4 3 2 1

springer.com

Ai miei genitori
Luisa e Innocenzo Daraio

À ma famille

Contents

Dedication v
List of Figures xi
List of Tables xv
Preface xvii
Acknowledgments xxi

1. INTRODUCTION 1
    1.1 What this work is about 1
    1.2 Improving the nonparametric approach in frontier analysis 4
    1.3 An outline of the work 8

Part I Methodology

2. THE MEASUREMENT OF EFFICIENCY 13
    2.1 Productivity and Efficiency 13
    2.2 A short history of thought 16
    2.3 The economic model 19
    2.4 A taxonomy of efficient frontier models 25
    2.5 The nonparametric frontier approach 30
        2.5.1 Data Envelopment Analysis (DEA) 31
        2.5.2 Free Disposal Hull (FDH) 33
    2.6 Recent developments in nonparametric efficiency analysis 39

3. STATISTICAL INFERENCE IN NONPARAMETRIC FRONTIER ESTIMATION 43
    3.1 Statistical foundation 43
    3.2 Introducing stochastic noise in the model 45

3.3 Asymptotic results 47
3.3.1 Consistency 47
3.3.2 Sampling distributions 49
3.4 Bootstrap techniques and applications 50
3.4.1 Bootstrap in frontier models 52
3.4.2 Correcting the bias 54
3.4.3 Bootstrap confidence intervals 55
3.4.4 Is the bootstrap consistent? 56
3.4.5 Applications of the bootstrap 63
3.4.6 Bootstrapping FDH estimators 64

4. NONPARAMETRIC ROBUST ESTIMATORS: PARTIAL FRONTIERS 65
4.1 A re-formulation based on the probability of being dominated 66
4.2 Order-m frontiers and efficiency scores 68
4.3 Order-α quantile-type frontiers 72
4.4 Properties of partial frontier estimators 77
4.4.1 Statistical properties 77
4.4.2 Robust estimators of the full frontier 77
4.4.3 Advantages of using partial frontiers 78
4.4.4 Detection of outliers 79
4.5 Summary of the results for the output oriented case 81
4.6 Parametric approximations of robust nonparametric frontiers 85
4.6.1 Two stage methods 87
4.6.2 The bootstrap algorithms 89
4.7 Multivariate parametric approximations 90
4.7.1 Generalized Cobb-Douglas parametric model 91
4.7.2 Translog parametric model 93

5. CONDITIONAL MEASURES OF EFFICIENCY 95
5.1 Explaining efficiency in the literature 96
5.2 Introducing external-environmental variables 100
5.2.1 Conditional full frontier measures 100
5.2.2 Conditional order-m measures 101
5.2.3 Conditional order-α measures 103
5.2.4 Summary for the output oriented case 105
5.3 Bandwidth selection 108
5.3.1 Univariate case 109
5.3.2 Multivariate case 110

5.4 An econometric methodology 113
5.4.1 Global effect of Z on the production process 113
5.4.2 A decomposition of conditional efficiency 119
5.5 Simulated illustrations 121
5.5.1 Univariate Z 122
5.5.2 Multivariate Z 124

Part II Applications

6. ECONOMIES OF SCALE, SCOPE AND EXPERIENCE IN THE ITALIAN MOTOR-VEHICLE SECTOR 135
6.1 Introduction 135
6.2 Data description 139
6.2.1 Definition of outputs and inputs 142
6.2.2 An exploratory investigation 145
6.2.3 Aggregation of inputs and outputs 148
6.3 Testing returns to scale and bootstrapping efficiency scores 151
6.4 Economies of scale 157
6.5 Economies of scope 160
6.6 Economies of experience 163
6.7 Conclusions 164

7. AGE, SCALE AND CONCENTRATION EFFECTS IN A PUBLIC RESEARCH SYSTEM 167
7.1 Introduction 167
7.2 Data description 176
7.3 Scale and concentration effects 178
7.4 Age effects on CNR scientific productivity 181
7.5 Robust parametric approximation of multioutput distance function 186
7.6 Conclusions 191

8. EXPLORING THE EFFECTS OF MANAGER TENURE, FUND AGE AND THEIR INTERACTION 193
8.1 Introduction 193
8.2 Data description 196
8.3 Impact of mutual fund manager tenure on performance 199
8.4 Interaction between manager tenure and fund age 208

8.5 Conclusions 216

9. CONCLUSIONS 217

References 221

Topic Index 243

Author Index 245

List of Figures

2.1	An overview of the literature on efficient frontier estimation.	27
2.2	Input and Output slacks.	33
2.3	FDH and DEA estimation of $C(y)$ and $\partial C(y)$.	36
2.4	FDH and DEA estimation of $P(x)$ and $\partial P(x)$.	36
2.5	Influence of outliers.	38
4.1	Input order-m frontier in the bivariate case.	69
4.2	Input order-α frontier in the bivariate case.	73
4.3	An illustration of α^{input} measure of efficiency in the bivariate case.	76
4.4	Illustration of full and partial frontiers in the input orientation.	76
4.5	Illustration of full and partial frontiers in the output orientation.	85
5.1	The Boiler case. Z favorable.	116
5.2	The Fridge case. Z unfavorable.	118
5.3	The Fridge case with outliers. Full frontier case	119
5.4	The Fridge case with outliers. Partial frontiers case	119
5.5	Simulated example with univariate Z. Likelihood CV criterion.	123
5.6	Simulated example with univariate Z. Plots of the percentages.	123
5.7	Simulated example with univariate Z. Smoothed non-parametric plots.	125
5.8	Simulated example with multivariate Z. Likelihood cross validation plot.	126
5.9	Density of Z and its Contour plot.	127
5.10	Simulated example with multivariate Z. Plots of the percentage of points outside partial frontiers.	128

5.11 Simulated example with multivariate Z. Surface. 128

5.12 Simulated example with multivariate Z. Plots. 129

5.13 Density of Z and its Contour plot. Z_1 and Z_2 are correlated. 129

5.14 Simulated example with multivariate Z. Z_1 and Z_2 are correlated. 130

5.15 Simulated example with multivariate Z and 5 outliers. Full frontier. 131

5.16 Simulated example with multivariate Z and 5 outliers. α-frontier. 132

6.1 Nominal rate of growth by line of business. 140

6.2 Real rate of growth by line of business. 140

6.3 Projection of the variables for the Italian Motor-vehicle insurers dataset. 147

6.4 Projection of individual insurers. 147

6.5 Output factor versus Input factor and DEA frontier for the Italian Motor-vehicle dataset, year 2000. 152

6.6 Output factor versus Input factor and DEA frontier for the Italian Motor-vehicle dataset, year 2000: a zoom. 153

6.7 Boxplots of the input Shephard efficiency scores. 156

6.8 Economies of scale in the Italian motor-vehicle insurance business. Full frontier case 159

6.9 Economies of scale in the Italian motor-vehicle insurance business. Partial Frontiers case 159

6.10 Economies of experience in the Italian motor-vehicle insurance business. 164

7.1 Estimation of the density of Z, CNR institutes. 180

7.2 Scale and concentration effects on CNR institutes. Surface. 182

7.3 Scale and concentration effects on CNR institutes. Plots of Q^z. 183

7.4 Scale and concentration effects on CNR institutes. Plots of Q^z_α. 183

7.5 Scale and concentration effects on CNR institutes. Plots of Q^z_m. 184

7.6 Age effects on CNR institutes: FDH, order-α and order-m estimates. 185

8.1 Scatterplot matrix of inputs (X) and output (Y) for Aggressive Growth Mutual Funds. 200

8.2 Scatterplot matrix of output and external factors for Aggressive Growth Mutual Funds. Z_1 is manager tenure and Z_2 is Fund age. 200
8.3 Scatterplot matrix of external factors and Inputs for Aggressive Growth Mutual Funds. 201
8.4 Influence of manager tenure on the performance of Aggressive Growth Mutual Funds. 201
8.5 Influence of manager tenure on the performance of Aggressive Growth Mutual Funds. A zoom. 201
8.6 Influence of fund age on the performance of Aggressive Growth Mutual Funds. 208
8.7 Influence of fund age on the performance of Aggressive Growth Mutual Funds. A zoom. 209
8.8 Influence of manager tenure and fund age on the performance of Aggressive Growth Mutual Funds. Surface. 210
8.9 Influence of manager tenure (Z_1) and fund age (Z_2) on the performance of Aggressive Growth Mutual Funds. Plots. 210
8.10 Influence of manager tenure (Z_1) and fund age (Z_2) on the performance of Aggressive Growth Mutual Funds. Density of Z and its contour plot. 211

List of Tables

1.1	Limitations and Advancements of nonparametric methods in frontier analysis.	7
3.1	Summary of the bootstrap principle.	54
5.1	Summary of efficiency measures with references.	106
6.1	Definition of Nominal and Real rate of growth.	141
6.2	Definition of rate of growth by line of business.	141
6.3	Definition of Inputs, Outputs and External Factors.	144
6.4	Descriptive statistics on inputs, outputs and external factor considered in the analysis. Italian motor vehicle insurers.	144
6.5	Correlations matrix. Italian motor vehicle insurers.	145
6.6	Eigenvalues and percentages of variances explained. Italian motor vehicle insurers.	146
6.7	Correlations of the first two pc's with the original variables (Factors loadings). Italian motor vehicle insurers.	146
6.8	Input Factor inertia. Italian motor vehicle insurers.	149
6.9	Eigenvectors of the matrix $X'X$. Italian motor vehicle insurers.	149
6.10	Correlations between the input factor (F_{in}) and inputs. Italian motor vehicle insurers.	149
6.11	Output Factor inertia. Italian motor vehicle insurers.	150
6.12	Eigenvectors of the matrix $Y'Y$. Italian motor vehicle insurers.	150
6.13	Correlations between the output factor (F_{out}) and outputs. Italian motor vehicle insurers.	150
6.14	Bootstrap results: Italian motor-vehicle insurers.	154

6.14 (Continued) 155

6.15 Some descriptive statistics on Age and size (Mktshare) of Italian motor-vehicle insurers. 162

7.1 Research areas. 176

7.2 Definition of variables. 177

7.3 Definition of Inputs and Outputs. 178

7.4 Average values of Inputs and Outputs by research area. 179

7.5 CNR institutes - Descriptive statistics on inputs, outputs and external factors considered in the analysis. 179

7.6 Definition of inputs and outputs used for the translog estimation of CNR output distance function. 187

7.7 Output distance function parameter estimates for CNR research institutes. 188

7.8 Bootstrapped confidence intervals for order-α frontier translog approximation. 189

7.9 Bootstrapped confidence intervals for order-m frontier translog approximation. 190

8.1 Descriptive statistics on inputs, output, external factors for Aggressive Growth mutual funds. 198

8.2 Unconditional measures of efficiency, and various indicators, Aggressive Growth Mutual Funds. 202

8.3 Conditional measures of efficiency and various indicators (Z is manager tenure), by groups of Aggressive Growth Mutual Funds. 204

8.4 Some descriptive statistics by group of funds with different impact of manager tenure. Z manager tenure. 205

8.5 Rank of AG mutual funds with $Q_m^z > 1$ ordered by INCR. Z is manager tenure. 206

8.6 Rank of AG mutual funds with $Q_m^z < 1$ ordered by DECR. Z is manager tenure. 207

8.7 Some descriptive statistics on efficiency measures and indicators by group of funds with different impact of manager tenure. Multivariate Z. 212

8.8 Some descriptive statistics by group of funds with different impact of manager tenure. Bivariate Z. 213

8.9 Rank of AG mutual funds with $Q_m^z < 1$ ordered by DECR. Bivariate Z. 214

8.10 Rank of AG mutual funds with $Q_m^z > 1$ ordered by INCR. Bivariate Z. 215

Preface

The topic of production efficiency has attracted attention since Adam Smith's pin factory and even before. However, a rigorous analytical approach to the measurement of efficiency in production originated with the work of Koopmans (1951) and Debreu (1951), empirically applied by Farrell (1957). Farrell's seminal work gave rise to a considerable amount of studies.

The basic idea of efficiency analysis is to make a comparison among a group of firms or branches or among Decision Making Units (DMUs), in order to evaluate how the resources (or inputs) are used to obtain (produce) the products (services or outputs). This evaluation process is based on the estimation of a benchmark frontier against which the DMUs are assessed, using DMUs' inputs and outputs. The level of efficiency of each DMU is gauged as the distance from the estimated ('efficient') frontier.

In literature on efficiency analysis, the nonparametric approach has received a considerable amount of interest, both from a theoretical and an applied perspective. This mainly because it does not require many assumptions and particularly because it does not need the specification of a functional form for the frontier. Hence, the parameters of the functional form of the frontier do not have to be estimated in this approach, from which the name 'nonparametric' approach derives, whereas in the parametric approach, the parameters of the efficient frontier must be estimated. Data Envelopment Analysis (DEA) and Free Disposal Hull (FDH) are among the most known and applied nonparametric techniques for the measurement of the efficiency in production and service activities (see *e.g.*, Cooper, Seiford and Tone, 2000, for about 1,500 references of their applications). Nevertheless, this traditional nonparametric approach (DEA/FDH based) presents some severe limitations that are not always taken into account by researchers who apply it in empirical works. These limits should be carefully considered in order to provide a correct interpretation of the obtained results.

To summarise, the main drawbacks of the traditional nonparametric approach are known to be:

- Deterministic and non-statistical nature;
- Influence of outliers and extreme values;
- Lack of parameters for the economic interpretation;
- Unsatisfactory techniques for the introduction of environmental or external variables in the measurement (estimation) of the efficiency.

The main objective of this book is to provide a systematic and comprehensive treatment of recent developments in efficiency analysis in order to overcome these drawbacks.

In Part I of the book (Methodology), we introduce a complete set of tools for measuring the efficiency of firms (or production units, or Decision Making Units) and for explaining the observed efficiency differentials. This is a general and flexible toolbox that does not make any assumption on the behaviour of the units under analysis. Therefore, it can be used in theories that generalise the neoclassical theory of production as well as alternative ones (as is the case of the evolutionary theory of production).

The Methodology presents, in an intuitive, rigorous and self-contained way, the state-of-the-art on 'advanced' frontier models based on techniques that do not impose any functional specification of the frontier (nonparametric methods) and are not affected by extremes and outliers in the data (robust methods).

The following issues are dealt with in detail and further developed:

- *Statistical inference in nonparametric frontier estimation.* Here, we introduce stochastic elements in nonparametric frontier models, and we present the application of the bootstrap in efficiency analysis (Simar and Wilson, 1998, 2000b, 2006a), including: estimation of bias and confidence intervals of efficiency estimates; hypothesis testing; comparison of groups' efficiency.

- *Robust estimators of frontiers.* Order$-m$ frontiers (Cazals, Florens and Simar, 2002; Daraio and Simar, 2005a) and α-quantile frontiers (Daouia and Simar, 2004), do not envelop all data points and for that are not influenced by extreme values. They are also characterised by useful statistical properties and interesting economic interpretations.

- *Parametric approximation of nonparametric and robust frontiers.* These approximations, introduced by Florens and Simar (2005) and Daouia, Florens and Simar (2005), provide 'robust' estimates of parameters usable for economic interpretation. These techniques are extended, in this book, to the full multi-input multi-output setup.

- *Nonparametric and robust conditional frontier models.* These models, recently introduced by Daraio and Simar (2005a, 2005b), are able to capture and measure the effect of external environmental variables on the efficiency, in a way that overcomes most drawbacks of previous methods.

This book has been specifically designed for applied economists who have an interest in the advantages of traditional nonparametric methods (DEA/FDH) for efficiency analysis, but are sceptical about adopting them because of the drawbacks they present.

In Part II of the book (Applications), we propose three empirical illustrations taken from different economic fields: insurance sector, scientific research and mutual funds industry. These applications perfectly illustrate how the tools we propose can be used to analyse economies of scale, economies of scope, dynamics of age and agglomeration effects, trade-offs in production and service activities, groups comparison as well as help explain efficiency differentials. These extensively treated empirical applications, based on real data, show the usefulness of our approach in applied economics. Through these applications we illustrate how various statistical tools can be combined to shed light on the key features of the studied production process.

Moreover, this book has also been written for researchers with a background in Operations Research (OR) and/or Management Science (MS), who would like to deepen their knowledge of these new robust and nonparametric techniques, which have been recently presented at specialised conferences and have appeared on the scientific journals in recent years. In this book they will find a readable, synthetic but also accurate presentation of these recent advances - without the burden of technicalities and formal demonstrations - together with an extensive illustration of their use in empirical works.

Acknowledgments

This book is the result of a scientific collaboration between the two authors started in 2000 during the Ph.D. of Cinzia Daraio at the Scuola Superiore Sant'Anna of Pisa, Italy, and reinforced by her Master of Arts in Statistics attended at the Université Catholique de Louvain, Belgium, in 2001-2002. Within this research collaboration a series of papers, published or forthcoming, as well as several joint research projects have been realized or are in progress. This book can be viewed as a milestone of this still continuing and active synergy.

The research activity from which this book originated has been funded by various national and international research funds. In particular the financial support of the following projects is gratefully acknowledged:

- The AQUAMETH (Advanced Quantitative Methods for the Evaluation of the Performance of Public Sector Research) Project within the European Network of Excellence PRIME;

- The Interuniversity Attraction Pole, Phase V (No. P5/24) from the Belgian Government (Belgian Science Policy);

- The Italian national project (iRis) Reorganizing the Italian Public Research system to foster technology transfer: governance, tools and implementation;

- The Italian national project (MIUR 40% - prot. 2004132703) System spillovers on the competitiveness of Italian economy: quantitative analysis for sectoral policies.

We would like to thank all our colleagues and friends who encouraged us in the writing of this book. In particular we are grateful to Carlo Bianchi, Andrea Bonaccorsi, Hal Fried, Giampiero M. Gallo, Shawna Grosskopf, Jacques Mairesse, Henk Moed, Paula Stephan, Robert Russell and Paul Wilson.

Finally, special thanks go to Sean Lorre, Springer editor, and to Deborah Doherty, Springer author support, for their kind cooperation.

Chapter 1

INTRODUCTION

1.1 What this work is about

Theoretical mainstream production analysis has always focused on production activity as an optimization process. In conventional microeconomic theory, it is assumed, in fact, that producers optimize by not wasting resources in a systematic way: producers operate somewhere on the boundary of their production possibility sets. However, consistent empirical evidence shows that not all producers succeed in all circumstances. Hence, it is important to analyse the degree to which producers fail to optimize and the extent of departures from technical and economic efficiency.

On the other hand, empirical production analysis has concentrated on central tendency, or "average" or "most likely" relationship constructed by intersecting data with a function rather than surrounding data with a frontier. There have been attempts to reconcile the two fields by developing quantitative techniques for surrounding rather than intersecting data.

The approach of production frontiers is an effort to define empirically an envelopment of production data. This approach combines the construction of production frontiers with the measurement and interpretation of efficiency relative to the constructed frontiers.

The structure of economic frontiers is of interest in itself: it is important to know whether, for example, technologically efficient production is characterised by economies of scale or scope. The structure of production frontiers can differ from the structure of average production functions constructed from the same data. Best practice is not just better than average practice, it may also be structurally different, and it is important to know whether the structure of efficient production differs from the structure of average production. Best practices (captured by the frontier approach) may be better than average practices (measured in a regression-based framework) in the sense that they exploit available substitution possibilities or scale opportunities that average practices do not. Public policy based on the structure of best practice frontiers may be very different from policy based on the structure of average practice functions.

The distance between production frontiers and observed producers is of obvious policy interest. It is important to know how inefficient observed production is, what types of producers are most and least efficient, and what type of inefficiency is most prevalent. It is also important to know whether inefficient firms (or Decision Making Units) are working in presence of economies (diseconomies) of scale or scope and the extent of trade-offs in the production or service activities.

Interest in the general topic of productivity and efficiency has grown greatly in recent years. There are in fact "efficiency" studies in virtually every country and about virtually every market or non-market production or service activity.

The general area of production economics is not the only discipline interested in frontiers and efficiency. Attention from economists in frontiers was reawakened in the 1970s when the works of Debreu (1951), Koopmans (1951, 1957) and Farrell (1957) were rediscovered.

The approach developed by Shephard (1953, 1970, 1974) in production analysis represents an important contribution, mainly because it is based on distance functions that are intimately related to the measurement of the efficiency. As a matter of fact, a lot of subsequent works are based on Shephard's distance functions.

A valuable body of works has emerged in the Operations Research (OR) and in the Management Science (MS) fields. The OR/MS approach has its own orientation, and relies heavily on linear programming techniques. Extending ideas of Farrell (1957), the OR discipline has developed the popular Data Envelopment Analysis approach (DEA, Charnes, Cooper and Rhodes, 1978) to the estimation of production frontiers and efficiency measurement which employs linear programming techniques. On the other hand, in a more economic framework, the Free Disposal Hull estimator (FDH, Deprins, Simar and Tulkens, 1984) of frontier was introduced. Nevertheless, the linear programming approach came to be accepted as a computational method for measuring efficiency in different kinds of economic decision-making problems since the work by Dorfman, Samuelson and Solow (1958).

FDH and DEA are the most known nonparametric approaches in efficiency analysis. FDH can be seen as a more general nonparametric estimator of frontiers than DEA, or as a non-convex version of DEA. In fact, FDH relies on the free disposability of inputs and outputs (*i.e.*, the possibility of not using or destroying goods -inputs, outputs- without costs) which define the production possibility set; whilst, DEA relies on the free disposability and on the convexity of the production set (convexity implies that if two observations are possible, then all the linear combinations that lie between them are also possible).

The preference of the nonparametric approach over the parametric approach (based on the functional specification of the frontier), is due to the small amount of assumptions required and mainly to the fact that we do not have to specify the functional form of the relation inputs-outputs and we do not need to specify a distributional form for the inefficiency term.

Nonetheless, traditional nonparametric estimators based on envelopment techniques (*i.e.* DEA /FDH types) were for a long time limited by several drawbacks: deterministic (meaning that all deviations from the efficient frontier are considered as inefficiency, and no noise is allowed) and non statistical nature; influence of outliers and extreme values; lack of parameters for the economic interpretation; unsatisfactory techniques for the introduction of environmental or external variables in the measurement of the efficiency.

Our work treats at length recently introduced robust and nonparametric approaches in efficiency analysis which overcome most traditional limits of the nonparametric approach listed above. In doing so, we provide computationally feasible methods of calculation (both of the efficient frontier and of the distance from it) and explanation of efficiency differentials.

We believe that the robust and nonparametric approach in frontier analysis has reached a level of generality and has overcome most of its limits, so that it can be considered as being *more flexible* and more suitable for the evaluation of complex production and service activities, with respect to other approaches, like the parametric approach.

The economic model underlying our robust and nonparametric frontier approach is very general: it does not make any assumptions about the behaviour of the firms (or DMUs) and does not introduce prices of factors which are considered as the link of DEA-based models with the neoclassical theory of production (Ray, 2004). Moreover, in a lot of empirical applications prices are not available (as is the case for scientific research, several no-profit services, and so on).

Our book is designed to fill a gap in the literature by systematically proposing the recent developments of the nonparametric approach and illustrating its usefulness for empirical research through three full economic applications. We propose an intuitive and readable, but in the meantime rigorous presentation of advanced nonparametric and robust methods in efficiency analysis, without the burden of technicalities and demonstrations. This methodology does not impose any assumption on the behavior of firms and therefore, it is a general and flexible tool suitable for applications both in theories of production that generalize the neoclassical theory, and in alternative approaches.

The material contained in this work offers a background for researchers of different disciplines.

It can be used following different *reading paths*:

- Applied economists may be interested in the whole book, both the Methodology and the Applications parts.
- Researchers with OR background could be more interested in the Methodological part, and may perhaps skip Part II (Applications).
- Researchers in MS may well start their reading with the Applications, and then go back to the Methodology, for a better understanding of the applied techniques.

This book could also be adopted for specialised courses in efficiency analysis, for graduate students or undergraduate students of the last years.

1.2 Improving the nonparametric approach in frontier analysis

The main purpose of this book is to propose a general and comprehensive approach for the measurement and explanation of firms' (or DMUs') efficiency differentials by using advanced robust and nonparametric frontier models. In fact, some recent developments in efficiency analysis are able to overcome most drawbacks of the traditional nonparametric approach (DEA/FDH based).

One traditional limitation of the nonparametric approach is its *deterministic* nature and the *difficulty* in making statistical inference. In this setting, it is assumed that all deviations from the efficient frontier are due to inefficiencies. The problem of handling noise in this framework is due to the fact that the model is *not identified*, unless some restrictions are assumed. Aigner, Lovell and Schmidt (1977) consider approaches that assume a parametric function for the frontier; Kneip and Simar (1996) analyse the case of panel data. More general results for handling noise in nonparametric frontier models have been introduced by Hall and Simar (2002) and by Simar (2003b). In Section 3.2 we comment this literature as well as recently introduced approaches based on local maximum likelihood techniques (Kumbhakar, Park, Simar and Tsionas, 2004). In the nonparametric approach, moreover, *statistical inference* is not easy, due to the complex nature of the estimation which is based on very few assumptions. Nevertheless, advances have been made, and statistical inference is available by using asymptotic results (Simar and Wilson, 2000a) or by applying the bootstrap (Simar and Wilson, 1998, 2000, Kneip, Simar and Wilson, 2003). We present this literature in Chapter 3, together with the available hypothesis testing procedures.

The problem of *extremes or outliers* can be treated by applying methods to detect them, and using estimators which are robust to them. This is achieved by *partial frontiers* of order-m or α which are developed in Chapter 4. These frontiers do not envelop all data points and for that are less affected, and hence more *robust*, to extreme values and outliers in the data.

These frontiers do not also suffer of the so called *curse of dimensionality*, typical of nonparametric methods (DEA/FDH), which requires a large amount of observations in order to avoid large bias and imprecise estimation (*i.e.*, huge confidence intervals). Partial frontiers are estimators that approach the "true" frontier as fast as parametric estimators (*i.e.*, the speed of convergence of order-m and α frontiers is root$-n$ where n is the number of firms or DMUs analysed). Whereas DEA estimators have a speed of convergence of $n^{2/(p+q+1)}$- where p is the number of the inputs and q is the number of the outputs used in the analysis. The rate of convergence of FDH is $n^{1/(p+q)}$. This indicates for the DEA/FDH estimators the necessity of increasing the number of observations when the dimension of the input-output space increases to achieve the same level of statistical precision. The dimensionality problem does not apply for these robust frontier estimators: this is an important property because most of the empirical applications relies on small samples and the collection of an increasing number of data is difficult and sometimes almost impossible.

Several authors show formally how DEA efficiency scores are affected by sample size; they demonstrate that comparing measures of structural inefficiency between samples of different sizes leads to biased results. This *sample size* problem can be easily overcome using the robust nonparametric approach based on partial frontiers. In this setting, the parameters m or α may be chosen equal for two or more groups of observations, and their average performance can then be compared.

Another limitation of traditional nonparametric techniques is the more difficult *economic interpretation* of the production process in terms of elasticities of substitution, marginal products, partial elasticities, and so on, due to the lack of parameters. To overcome this drawback Florens and Simar (2005) and Daouia, Florens and Simar (2005) propose the full theory for parametric approximation of nonparametric frontiers, which applies also for robust order-m and order-α frontiers. This topic will be treated and developed in Chapter 4.

Finally, the conventional techniques for explaining efficiency in the nonparametric frontier setting are unsatisfactory. In fact, two main approaches have been proposed in literature but both are flawed by restrictive *prior* assumptions on the Data Generating Process (DGP) and/or on the role of these external factors on the production process. The first family of models is based on a *one-stage* approach (see *e.g.* Färe, Grosskopf and Lovell, 1994, p. 223-226), where these factors are considered as free disposal inputs and /or outputs which contribute to define the attainable set but which are not active in the optimization process defining the efficiency scores. An external-environmental factor is considered as an input if it is favorable to efficiency and as an output if it is detrimental to efficiency. The drawback of this approach is twofold: first we have to know *a priori* what is the role of the factor on the production process, and secondly we assume the free disposability (and eventually convexity, if DEA is used) of the corresponding attainable extended production set. The second family of models is based on a *two-stage* approach. Here the estimated efficiency scores are regressed, in an appropriate limited dependent variable parametric regression model (like truncated normal regression models) on the environmental factors. Recently, some models in this family propose also three-stage and four-stage analysis as extension of the two-stage approach (Fried, Schmidt, and Yaisawarng, 1999; Fried, Lovell, Schmidt, and Yaisawarng, 2002).

However, as pointed out by Simar and Wilson (2003), also these models, like the others in the two-stage family, are flawed in that usual inference on the obtained estimates of the regression coefficient is not available. They state: "none of the studies that employ two-stage approaches have described the underlying data-generating process. Since the DGP has not been described, there is some doubt about what is being estimated in the two-stage approaches", and "A more serious problem in all of the two-stage studies that we have found arises from the fact that DEA efficiency estimates are serially correlated; consequently, standard approaches to inference [...] are invalid". Simar and Wilson (2003) then propose two bootstrap-based algorithms to obtain a more accurate inference. However, even this bootstrap-based approach, through more correct, shares some of the inconveniences of the two-stage based approaches. Firstly, it relies on a *separability* condition between the input $\times$ output space and the space of values of the external-environmental variables: *i.e.*, the value of external-environmental variables does not influence the position of the frontier of the attainable set. Secondly, the regression in the second stage relies on some *parametric* assumptions (like linear model and truncated normal error term).

Daraio and Simar (2005a, b) propose a full nonparametric and robust approach to evaluate the influence of external-environmental variables which overcomes most of the drawbacks of earlier approaches. This topic will be treated in detail in Chapter 5.

In this work, we propose a readable and rigorous description of the most recent developments in robust and nonparametric efficiency models that overcome the main traditional limitations of the nonparametric approach (see Table 1.1) and an extensive illustration of its usefulness for applied economics, through several applications with real data, in different economic fields (scientific research, insurance industry, mutual funds).

The combination of the advancements in statistical inference, robust methods and improvements in the explanation of efficiency differentials is used in the

Table 1.1. Limitations and Advancements of nonparametric methods in frontier analysis.

LIMITATIONS OF NONPARAMETRIC METHODS	PROPOSED ADVANCEMENTS
Deterministic nature and no easy inference	*Noise* - Hall and Simar, (2002); Simar (2003b).
	Statistical properties - Simar and Wilson, (2000a); Kneip, Simar and Wilson, (2003).
	Bootstrapping - Simar and Wilson, (1998, 2000b, 2006a); Kneip, Simar and Wilson, (2003).
	Hypothesis testing - Simar and Wilson, (2001, 2002).
No parameters for economic interpretation	*Parametric approximation of nonparametric frontiers* - Florens and Simar (2005);
	Daouia, Florens and Simar (2005) and this book.
Sensitive to extremes / outliers	*Robust order-m frontiers*
Curse of dimensionality	Cazals, Florens and Simar (2002);
Sample size bias in comparison	Daraio and Simar (2005a);
	Robust order-α frontiers
	Daouia and Simar (2004)
Unsatisfactory methods for explaining efficiency	*Problems of two-stage approaches* Simar and Wilson (2003).
	Probabilistic approach
	Daraio and Simar (2005a, b) and this book.

Applications Part of this book to analyse confidence intervals of efficiency scores as well as efficiency distributions, economies of scale and scope, trade-offs in production and service activities together with comparison of groups' efficiency in the fields of scientific research, mutual funds industry and insurance sector.

1.3 An outline of the work

The book is structured in two parts.

Part I describes the state-of-the-art of robust and nonparametric methods in efficient frontiers estimation.

Part II applies the comprehensive approach proposed in Part I to three different topics: insurance industry, scientific research and mutual funds.

In particular, Part I is organized as follows.

Chapter 2 introduces the measurement of efficiency. In Sections 2.1 and 2.2 some basic definitions and a short history of thought are reported, while in Section 2.3 the economic model underlying the frontier estimation is described. Section 2.4 is dedicated to make an introduction on the several efficient frontier models available and, finally, Section 2.5 introduces the nonparametric approach (DEA/FDH based) in efficiency analysis.

Chapter 3 focuses on the last developments of the statistical inference in the nonparametric setting. Section 3.1 illustrates the statistical foundation of nonparametric frontier estimation. In Section 3.2 some stochastic elements are introduced, while Section 3.3 summarizes the main asymptotic properties of nonparametric estimators. Finally, Section 3.4 introduces the available applications of the bootstrap in nonparametric frontier models.

Chapter 4 introduces robust nonparametric measures based on partial frontiers. Section 4.1 presents a probabilistic formulation of the frontier estimation setting. Section 4.2 is devoted to robust order-m frontiers (input oriented case), while Section 4.3 introduces robust order-α frontiers (input oriented case) as well as some measures of efficiency. The main properties of partial frontiers are described in Section 4.4. In Section 4.5 the various output oriented cases are outlined. The general framework of the parametric approximation of nonparametric and robust frontiers is offered in Section 4.6, while the generalization to the multi-input multi-output parametric approximation is reported in Section 4.7 where the cases of the Generalized Cobb-Douglas and of the Translog functions are detailed.

Chapter 5 is devoted to conditional measures of efficiency and the explanation of efficiency differentials. In Section 5.2 we propose a unifying description of all conditional efficiency measures, and introduce a new probabilistic conditional indicator, while Section 5.3 illustrates the practical data-driven selection of the bandwidth in this framework. The econometric methodology to evaluate the impact of external factors on the performance is presented in Section 5.4 where also a decomposition of the conditional measure is offered, aiming at disentangling the effect of the external factors on the performance. Finally, Section 5.5 offers several simulated examples, with univariate and multivariate external factors, which show the power of conditional measures and how to practically implement the econometric methodology and interpret the obtained results.

In Part II, the three applications have a similar structure. The introductory section presents the relevant literature on the topic treated and states the main research questions addressed in the chapter. Then, the description of the used dataset is presented in a second section, where some descriptive statistics are reported. In particular, in Section 6.2 also an exploratory Principal Component Analysis is reported as well as a procedure to aggregate inputs and outputs. After that, the various methods described in Part I are applied in the different fields and the empirical results are commented. Finally, the concluding section reported at the end of each chapter summarizes and formulate policy implications on the main results obtained.

Specifically, Chapter 6 deals with the Italian insurance industry. It focuses on the motor vehicle sector. It provides tests on returns to scale, bootstrapped confidence intervals for the efficiency estimates, and empirical evidence on economies of scale, scope and experience.

Chapter 7 analyses a public research system: the research institutes of the Italian National Research Council (CNR). Economies of scale, agglomeration and age effects on scientific productivity are investigated, evaluating in particular the interaction between scale and agglomeration effects. A robust scale elasticity is also estimated using the newly introduced multi-output parametric approximation of robust nonparametric frontiers.

Finally, Chapter 8 focuses on US Aggressive Growth mutual funds. It examines how manager tenure and funds age affect the performance of mutual funds. The interaction of manager tenure and age of funds is also assessed providing detailed results on groups of best and worst performers.

The last chapter sums up the main points and concludes the book.

PART I

METHODOLOGY

Chapter 2

THE MEASUREMENT OF EFFICIENCY

This chapter is about the measurement of efficiency of production units. It opens with a section concerning basic definitions of productivity and efficiency. After that, an historical and background section follows, reporting some of the most important contributions until around '90s. Then, the axiomatic underpinning of the Activity Analysis framework used to represent the production process is described in the economic model section. Afterwards, efficient frontier models are classified according to three main *criteria*: specification (or not) of the form of the frontier; presence of noise in the estimation procedure; type of data analyzed (cross-section or panel data). The presentation of the most known nonparametric estimators of frontiers (*i.e.*, Data Envelopment Analysis (DEA) and Free Disposal Hull (FDH)) is subsequently. Finally, a section summarizing recent developments in nonparametric efficiency analysis concludes the chapter.

2.1 Productivity and Efficiency

According to a classic definition (see *e.g.* Vincent 1968) *productivity* is the *ratio* between an output and the factors that made it possible. In the same way, Lovell (1993) defines the *productivity* of a production unit as the ratio of its output to its input.

This ratio is easy to compute if the unit uses a single input to produce a single output. On the contrary, if the production unit uses several inputs to produce several outputs, then the inputs and outputs have to be aggregated so that productivity remains the ratio of two scalars.

We can distinguish between a *partial* productivity, when it concerns a sole production factor, and a *total factor* (or global) productivity, when referred to all (every) factors.

Similar, but not equal, is the concept of efficiency. Even though, in the efficiency literature many authors do not make any difference between productivity and efficiency. For instance, Sengupta (1995) and Cooper, Seiford and Tone (2000) define both productivity and efficiency as the ratio between output and input.

Instead of defining the efficiency as the ratio between outputs and inputs, we can describe it as a distance between the quantity of input and output, and the quantity of input and output that defines a frontier, the best possible frontier for a firm in its cluster (industry).

Efficiency and productivity, anyway, are two cooperating concepts. The measures of efficiency are more accurate than those of productivity in the sense that they involve a comparison with the most efficient frontier, and for that they can complete those of productivity, based on the ratio of outputs on inputs.

Lovell (1993) defines the efficiency of a production unit in terms of a comparison between observed and optimal values of its output and input. The comparison can take the form of the ratio of observed to maximum potential output obtainable from the given input, or the ratio of minimum potential to observed input required to produce the given output. In these two comparisons the optimum is defined in terms of production possibilities, and efficiency is technical.

Koopmans (1951; p. 60) provided a definition of what we refer to as *technical efficiency*: an input-output vector is technically efficient if, and only if, increasing any output or decreasing any input is possible only by decreasing some other output or increasing some other input.

Farrell (1957; p. 255) and much later Charnes and Cooper (1985; p. 72) go back over the empirical necessity of treating Koopmans' definition of technical efficiency as a relative notion, a notion that is relative to best observed practice in the reference set or comparison group. This provides a way of differentiating efficient from inefficient production units, but it offers no guidance concerning either the degree of inefficiency of an inefficient vector or the identification of an efficient vector or combination of efficient vectors against which comparing an inefficient vector.

Debreu (1951) offered the first measure of *productive efficiency* with his *coefficient of resource utilization*. Debreu's measure is a radial measure of technical efficiency. Radial measures focus on the maximum feasible *equiproportionate* reduction in all variable inputs, or the maximum feasible equiproportionate expansion of all outputs. They are independent of unit of measurement.

Applying radial measures the achievement of the maximum feasible input contraction or output expansion suggests technical efficiency, even though there may remain *slacks* in inputs or *surpluses* in output. In economics the notion of efficiency is related to the concept of Pareto optimality. An input-output bundle is not Pareto optimal if there remains the opportunity of any net increase in outputs or decrease in inputs. Pareto-Koopmans measures of efficiency (*i.e.*, measures which call a vector efficient if and only if it satisfies the Koopmans definition reported above, coherent with the Pareto optimality concept) have been analysed in literature. See *e.g.*, Färe (1975), Färe and Lovell (1978) and Russell (1985, 1988, 1990) among others.

Farrell (1957) extended the work initiated by Koopmans and Debreu by noting that production efficiency has a second component reflecting the ability of producers to select the "right" technically efficient input-output vector in light of prevailing input and output prices. This led Farrell to define overall productive efficiency as the product of *technical* and *allocative* efficiency. Implicit in the notion of allocative efficiency is a specific behavioral assumption about the goal of the producer; Farrell considered cost-minimization in competitive inputs markets, although all the behavioral assumptions can be considered. Although the natural focus of most economists is on markets and their prices and thus on allocative rather than technical efficiency and its measurement, he expressed a concern about human ability to measure prices accurately enough to make good use of allocative efficiency measurement, and hence of overall economic efficiency measurement. This worry expressed by Farrell (1957; p. 261) has greatly influenced the OR/MS work on efficiency measurement. Charnes and Cooper (1985; p. 94) cite Farrell concern as one of several motivations for the typical OR/MS emphasis on the measurement of technical efficiency.

It is possible to distinguish different kind of efficiency, such as scale, allocative and structural efficiency.

The *scale efficiency* has been developed in three different ways. Farrell (1957) used the most restrictive technology having constant returns to scale (CRS) and exhibiting strong disposability of inputs. This model has been developed in a linear programming framework by Charnes, Cooper and Rhodes (1978). Banker, Charnes and Cooper (1984) have shown that the CRS measure of efficiency can be expressed as the product of a technical efficiency measure and a scale efficiency measure. A third method of scale uses nonlinear specification of the production function such as Cobb-Douglas or a translog function, from which the scale measure can be directly computed (see Sengupta, 1994 for more details).

The *allocative efficiency* in economic theory measures a firm's success in choosing an optimal set of inputs with a given set of input prices; this is distinguished from the technical efficiency concept associated with the production frontier, which measures the firm's success in producing maximum output from a given set of inputs.

The concept of *structural efficiency* is an industry level concept due to Farrell (1957), which broadly measures in what extent an industry keeps up with the performance of its own best practice firms; thus it is a measure at the industry level of the extent to which its firms are of optimum size *i.e.* the extent to which the industry production level is optimally allocated between the firms in the short run. A broad interpretation of Farrell's notion of structural efficiency can be stated as follows: industry or cluster A is more efficient structurally than industry B, if the distribution of its best firms is more concentrated near its efficient frontier for industry A than for B. In their empirical study, Bjurek, Hjalmarsson and Forsund (1990) compute structural efficiency by simply constructing an average unit for the whole cluster and then estimating the individual measure of technical efficiency for this average unit. On more general aggregation issues, see Färe and Zelenyuk (2003) and Färe and Grosskopf (2004, p. 94 ff).

2.2 A short history of thought

The theme of productive efficiency has been analysed since Adam Smith's pin factory and before[1]. However, as we have seen in the previous section, a rigorous analytical approach to the measurement of efficiency in production originated only with the work of Koopmans (1951) and Debreu (1951), empirically applied by Farrell (1957).

An important contribution to the development of efficiency and productivity analysis has been done by Shephard's models of technology and his distance functions (Shephard 1953, 1970, 1974). In contrast to the traditional production function, direct input and output correspondences admit multiple outputs and multiple inputs. They are thus able to characterize all kinds of technologies without unwarranted output aggregation prior to analysis. The Shephard direct input distance function treats multiple outputs as given and contracts inputs vectors as much as possible consistent with technological feasibility of contracted input vector. Among its several useful properties, one of the most important is the fact that the *reciprocal* of the direct input distance function has been proposed by Debreu (1951) as a coefficient of resource utilization, and by Farrell (1957) as a measure of technical efficiency. This property has both a theoretical and a practical significance. It allows the direct input distance function to serve two important roles, simultaneously. It provides a complete characterization of the structure of multi-input, multi-output efficient production technology, and a reciprocal measure of the distance from each producer to that efficient technology.

The main role played by the direct input distance function is to gauge technical efficiency. Nevertheless, it can also be used to construct input quantity indexes (Tornqvist, 1936; Malmquist, 1953) and productivity indexes (Caves, Christensen, and Diewert, 1982). Similarly, the direct output distance function introduced by Shephard (1970) and the two indirect distance functions of Shephard (1974) can be used to characterize the structure of efficient production

[1] This section is based on Färe, Grosskopf and Lovell (1994), pp. 1-23; and Kumbhakar and Lovell (2000), pp. 5-7.

technology in the multi-product case, to measure efficiency to that technology, and to construct output quantity indexes (Bergson,1961; Moorsteen, 1961) and productivity indexes (Färe, Grosskopf, and Lovell, 1992).

Linear programming theory is a milestone of efficiency analysis. The work of Dantzig (1963) is closely associated with linear programming since he contributed to the basic computational algorithm (the simplex method) used to solve this problem. Charnes and Cooper (1961) made considerable contributions to both theory and application in the development of linear programming, and popularize its application in DEA in the late 70s (see Charnes, Cooper and Rhodes, 1978). Forsund and Sarafoglou (2002) offer an interesting historical reconstruction of the literature developments subsequent to Farrell's seminal paper that lead to the introduction of the DEA methodology.

The use of linear programming and activity analysis can be found in the work of Leontief (1941, 1953) who developed a special case of activity analysis which has come to be known as input-output analysis. Whereas Leontief's work was directed toward constructing a workable model of general equilibrium, efficiency and productivity analysis is more closely related to the microeconomic production programming models developed by Shephard (1953, 1970, 1974), Koopmans (1951, 1957) and Afriat (1972). In these models observed activities, such as the inputs and outputs of some production units, serve as coefficients of activity or intensity variables forming a series of linear inequalities, yielding a piecewise linear frontier technology.

The work of Koopmans and Shephard imposes convexity on the reference technology, therefore, the DEA estimator relies on the convexity assumption. The Free Disposal Hull (FDH) estimator, that maintains free disposability while relaxes convexity, was introduced by Deprins, Simar and Tulkens (1984).

By enveloping data points with linear segments, the programming approach reveals the structure of frontier technology without imposing a specific functional form on either technology or deviations from it.

Frontier technology provides a simple means of computing the distance to the frontier - as a maximum feasible radial contraction or expansion of an observed activity. This means of measuring the distance to the frontier yields an interpretation of performance or efficiency as maximal-minimal proportionate feasible changes in an activity given technology. This explanation is consistent with Debreu's (1951) coefficient of resource utilization and with Farrell's (1957) efficiency measures. However, neither Debreu nor Farrell formulated the efficiency measurement problem as a linear programming problem, even though Farrell and Fieldhouse (1962) envisaged the role of linear programming. The full development of linear programming techniques took place later. Boles (1966), Bressler (1966), Seitz (1966) and Sitorius (1966) developed the piecewise linear case, and Timmer (1971) extended the piecewise log-linear case.

Linear programming techniques are also used in production analysis for non-parametric 'tests'[2] on regularity conditions and behavioral objectives. Afriat (1972) developed a series of consistency 'tests' on production data by assuming an increasing number of more restrictive regularity hypotheses on production technology. In so doing he expanded his previous work on utility functions (Afriat 1967) based on the revealed preference analysis (Samuelson, 1948).

These 'tests' of consistency, as well as similar 'tests' of hypotheses proposed by Hanoch and Rothschild (1972), are all based on linear programming formulations. Diewert and Parkan (1983) suggested that this battery of tools could be used as a screening device to construct frontiers and measure efficiency of data relative to the constructed frontiers. Varian (1984, 1985, 1990) and Banker and Maindiratta (1988) extended the Diewert and Parkan approach. In particular, Varian seeks to reduce the "all-or-nothing" nature of the tests - either data pass a test or they do not - by developing a framework for allowing small failures to be attributed to measurement in the data rather than to failure of the hypothesis under investigation.

All these studies use nonparametric linear programming models to explore the consistency of a dataset, or a subset of a dataset, with a structural (*e.g.* constant return to scale) or parametric (*e.g.* Cobb-Douglas) or behavioral (*e.g.* cost minimization) hypothesis. These tools, originally proposed as screening devices to check for data accuracy, provide also guidance in the selection of parametric functional forms as well as procedures useful to construct frontiers and measure efficiency. The problem of nonparametric exploration of regularity conditions and behavioral objectives has been treated also by Chavas and Cox (1988, 1990), Ray (1991), and Ray and Bhadra (1993).

Some works have *indirectly* influenced the development of the efficiency and productivity analysis. Hicks (1935, p.8) states his "easy life" hypothesis as follows: "people in monopolistic positions [...] are likely to exploit their advantage much more by not bothering to get very near the position of maximum profit, than by straining themselves to get very close to it. The best of all monopoly profits is a quite life". The suggestion of Hicks, *i.e.* the fact that the absence of competitive pressure might allow producers the freedom to not fully optimize conventional objectives, and, by implication, that the presence of competitive pressure might force producers to do so, has been adopted by many authors (see *e.g.* Alchian and Kessel, 1962, and Williamson, 1964).

Another field of work, related to efficiency literature, is the property rights field of research, which asserts that public production is inherently less efficient than private production. This argument, due originally to Alchian (1965), states that concentration and transferability of private ownership shares create

---

[2]Here and below when we use the word test between quotation mark we mean qualitative indicators that are not real statistical test procedures.

an incentive for private owners to monitor managerial performance, and that this incentive is diminished for public owners, who are dispersed and whose ownership is not transferable. Consequently, public managers have wider freedom to pursue their owns at the expense of conventional goals. Thus Niskanen (1971) argued that public managers are budget maximizers, de Alessi (1974) argued that public managers exhibit a bias toward capital-intensive budgets, and Lindsay (1976) argued that public managers exhibit a bias toward "visible" inputs. However, ownership forms are more varied than just private or public. Hansmann (1988), in facts, identifies investor-owned firms, customer-owned firms, worker-owned firms, as well as firms without owners (nonprofit enterprisers). Each of them deals in a different way with problems associated with hierarchy, coordination, incomplete contracts and monitoring and agency costs. This leads to the expectation that different ownership forms will generate differences in performance.[3]

As a more micro level is concerned, Simon (1955, 1957) analyzed the performance of producers in the presence of bounded rationality and satisfying behavior. Later Leibenstein (1966, 1975, 1976, 1978, 1987) argued that production is bound to be inefficient as a result of motivation, information, monitoring, and agency problems within the firm. This type of inefficiency, the so called "X-inefficiency" has been criticized by Stigler (1976) and de Alessi (1983) among others since it reflects an incompletely specified model rather than a failure to optimize.

The problem of model specification - including a complete list of inputs and outputs, and perhaps conditioning variables as well, a list of constraints, technological, and other (*e.g.* regulatory) is a difficult issue to face. Among others, Banker, Chang and Cooper (1996) analyse the effects of misspecified variables in DEA. Simar and Wilson (2001) propose a statistical procedure to test for the relevance of inputs/outputs in DEA models.

This literature suggests that the development of efficiency analysis is particularly useful if and when it could be used to shed empirical light on the theoretical issues outlined above.

2.3 The economic model

In this paragraph we describe the main axioms on which the economic model underlined the measurement of efficiency is based on.[4]

Much empirical evidence suggests that although producers may indeed attempt to optimize, they do not always succeed. Not all producers are always so successful in solving their optimization problems. Not all producers succeed

[3]This expectation is based on a rich theoretical literature. See *e.g.* the "classical" survey by Holmstrom and Tirole (1989).

[4]See also Färe and Grosskopf (2004), pp.151-161.

in utilizing the minimum inputs required to produce the outputs they choose to produce, given the technology at their disposal. In light of the evident failure of at least some producers to optimize, it is desirable to recast the analysis of production away from the traditional production function approach toward a frontier based approach. Hence we are concerned with the estimation of frontiers, which envelop data, rather than with functions, which intersect data.

In this setting, the main purpose of productivity analysis studies is to evaluate numerically the performance of a certain number of firms (or business units or Decision Making Units, DMU) from the point of view of *technical efficiency*, *i.e.* their ability to operate close to, or on the boundary of their production set. The problem to be analyzed is thus set in terms of physical input and output quantities.

We assume to have data in cross-sectional form, and for each firm we have the value of its inputs and outputs used in the production process. Measuring efficiency for any data set of this kind requires first to determine what the boundary of the production set can be; and then to measure the distance between any observed point and the boundary of the production set.

Given a list of p inputs and q outputs, in economic analysis the operations of any productive organization can be defined by means of a set of points, Ψ, *the production set*, defined as follows in the Euclidean space $\mathcal{R}_+^{p+q}$:

$$\Psi = \{(x, y) \mid x \in \mathcal{R}_+^p,\ y \in \mathcal{R}_+^q, (x, y) \text{ is feasible}\}, \tag{2.1}$$

where x is the input vector, y is the output vector and "feasibility" of the vector (x, y) means that, within the organization under consideration, it is physically possible to obtain the output quantities $y_1, ..., y_q$ when the input quantities $x_1, ..., x_p$ are being used (all quantities being measured per unit of time). It is useful to define the set Ψ in terms of its *sections*, defined as the images of a relation between the input and the output vectors that are the elements of Ψ. We can define then the *input requirement set* (for all $y \in \Psi$) as:

$$C(y) = \{x \in \mathcal{R}_+^p | (x, y) \in \Psi\}. \tag{2.2}$$

An input requirement set $C(y)$ consists of all input vectors that can produce the output vector $y \in \mathcal{R}_+^q$.

The *output correspondence set* (for all $x \in \Psi$) can be defined as:

$$P(x) = \{y \in \mathcal{R}_+^q | (x, y) \in \Psi\}. \tag{2.3}$$

$P(x)$ consists of all output vectors that can be produced by a given input vector $x \in \mathcal{R}_+^p$.

The production set Ψ can also be retrieved from the inputs sets, specifically:

$$\Psi = \{(x, y) \mid x \in C(y),\ y \in \mathcal{R}_+^q\}. \tag{2.4}$$

Furthermore, it holds that:

$$(x,y) \in \Psi \Leftrightarrow x \in C(y), y \in P(x), \tag{2.5}$$

which tells us that the output and input sets are equivalent representations of the technology, as is Ψ.

The isoquants or efficient boundaries of the sections of Ψ can be defined in radial terms (Farrell, 1957) as follows. In the input space:

$$\partial C(y) = \{x | x \in C(y), \theta x \notin C(y), \forall \theta, 0 < \theta < 1)\} \tag{2.6}$$

and in the output space:

$$\partial P(x) = \{y | y \in P(x), \lambda y \notin P(x), \forall \lambda > 1\}. \tag{2.7}$$

The axiomatic approach to production theory (Activity Analysis framework) assumes that the technology (production model) satisfies certain properties or axioms. These properties can be equivalently stated on Ψ, $P(x)$, $x \in \mathcal{R}_+^p$, $C(y)$, $y \in \mathcal{R}_+^q$.

Some economic axioms (EA) are usually done in this framework (on these concepts see also Shephard, 1970).

EA1: NO FREE LUNCH. $(x,y) \notin \Psi$ *if* $x = 0, y \geq 0, y \neq 0$.[5]
This axiom states that inactivity is always possible, *i.e.*, zero output can be produced by any input vector $x \in \mathcal{R}_+^p$, but it is impossible to produce output without any inputs.

EA2: FREE DISPOSABILITY. *Let* $\tilde{x} \in \mathcal{R}_+^p$ *and* $\tilde{y} \in \mathcal{R}_+^q$, *with* $\tilde{x} \geq x$ *and* $\tilde{y} \leq y$, *if* $(x,y) \in \Psi$ *then* $(\tilde{x},y) \in \Psi$ *and* $(x,\tilde{y}) \in \Psi$.
This is the *free disposability* assumption, named also the 'possibility of destroying goods without costs', on the production set Ψ.

The *free disposability* (also called *strong* disposability) of outputs can be stated as follows: $y_1 \in P(x), y_2 \leq y_1$ then $y_2 \in P(x)$ or equivalently $y_1 \leq y_2$ then $C(y_2) \subseteq C(y_1)$. The *free disposability* of inputs can be defined as below: $x_1 \in C(y), x_2 \geq x_1$ then $x_2 \in C(y)$ or equivalently $x_1 \leq x_2$ then $P(x_1) \subseteq P(x_2)$.

The free disposability of both inputs and outputs is as follows:

$$\forall (x,y) \in \Psi, \text{ if } x' \geq x \text{ and } y' \leq y \text{ then } (x',y') \in \Psi.$$

We have also a *weak* disposability of inputs and outputs:

---

[5]Here and throughout inequalities involving vectors are defined componentwise, *i.e.* on an element-by-element basis.

- Weak disposability of inputs:

$$x \in C(y) \Rightarrow \forall \alpha \geq 1,\ \alpha x \in C(y) \ \text{ or } \ P(x) \subseteq P(\alpha x);$$

- Weak disposability of outputs:

$$y \in P(x) \Rightarrow \forall \alpha \in [0,1],\ \alpha y \in P(x) \ \text{ or } \ C(\alpha y) \subseteq C(y).$$

The weak disposability property allows us to model congestion and overutilization of inputs/outputs.

EA3: BOUNDED. *$P(x)$ is bounded* $\forall x \in \mathcal{R}^p_+$.

EA4: CLOSENESS. *Ψ is closed, $P(x)$ is closed,* $\forall x \in \mathcal{R}^p_+$, *$C(y)$ is closed,* $\forall y \in \mathcal{R}^q_+$.

EA5: CONVEXITY. *Ψ is convex. The convexity of Ψ can be stated as follows:*

$$\textit{If } \ (x_1, y_1), (x_2, y_2) \in \Psi, \quad \textit{then } \forall \alpha \in [0,1] \textit{ we have}:$$

$$(x, y) = \alpha(x_1, y_1) + (1 - \alpha)(x_2, y_2) \in \Psi.$$

EA6: CONVEXITY OF THE REQUIREMENT SETS. *$P(x)$ is convex* $\forall x \in \mathcal{R}^p_+$ *and $C(y)$ is convex* $\forall y \in \mathcal{R}^q_+$.
If Ψ is convex, then the inputs and outputs sets are also convex, *i.e. EA5* implies *EA6*.

A further characterization of the shape of the frontier relates to returns to scale (RTS). According to a standard definition in economics, RTS express the relation between a proportional change in inputs to a productive process and the resulting proportional change in output. If an n per cent rise in all inputs produces an n per cent increase in output, there are constant returns to scale (CRS). If output rises by a larger percentage than inputs, there are increasing returns to scale (IRS). If output rises by a smaller percentage than inputs, there are decreasing returns to scale (DRS). Returns to scale can be described as properties of the correspondence sets $C(y)$ and/or $P(x)$. We follow here the presentation of Simar and Wilson (2002, 2006b). The frontier exhibits *constant returns to scale* (CRS) everywhere if and only if:

$$\forall (x, y) \text{ s.t. } x \in \partial C(y) \text{ then } \alpha x \in \partial C(\alpha y), \forall \alpha > 0$$

or equivalently[6],

$$\forall \alpha > 0, C(\alpha y) = \alpha C(y).$$

[6] Analogous expressions hold in terms of $P(x)$: $\forall \alpha > 0$, $P(\alpha x) = \alpha P(x)$.

Constant Returns to Scale in the *neighborhood* of a point (x, y) s.t. $x \in \partial C(y)$ are characterized by $C(\alpha y) = \alpha C(y)$ for some $\alpha > 0$.

Increasing Returns to Scale in the *neighborhood* of a point (x, y) s.t. $x \in \partial C(y)$ implies that $(\alpha x, \alpha y) \notin \Psi$ for $\alpha < 1$.

Decreasing Returns to Scale in the *neighborhood* of a point (x, y) s.t. $x \in \partial C(y)$ implies that $(\alpha x, \alpha y) \notin \Psi$ for $\alpha > 1$.

A frontier that exhibits increasing, constant and decreasing returns to scale in different regions is a *Variable Returns to Scale* (VRS) frontier.

The assumptions we have introduced here are intended to provide enough structure to create meaningful and useful technologies. Generally speaking, we will not impose all of these axioms on a particular technology, rather we will select subsets of these assumptions that are suitable for the particular problem under study.

***

Turning back to the production set itself, the above definitions allow us to characterize any point (x, y) in Ψ as:

input efficient if $x \in \partial C(y)$

input inefficient if $x \notin \partial C(y)$

output efficient if $y \in \partial P(x)$

output inefficient if $y \notin \partial P(x)$.

From what stated above, DMUs are efficient, *e.g.* in an input-oriented framework, if they are on the boundary of the input requirement set (or, for the output oriented case, on the boundary of the output correspondence set). In some cases, however, these efficient firms may not be using the fewest possible inputs to produce their outputs. This is the case where we have slacks. This is due to the fact that the Pareto-Koopmans efficient subsets of the boundaries of $C(y)$ and $P(x)$, *i.e.* eff $C(y)$ and eff $P(x)$, may not coincide with the Farrell-Debreu boundaries $\partial C(y)$ and $\partial P(x)$, *i.e.*[7]:

$$\text{eff } C(y) = \Big\{x \mid x \in C(y),\ x' \notin C(y)\ \forall x' \leq x, x' \neq x\Big\} \subseteq \partial C(y), \quad (2.8)$$

$$\text{eff } P(x) = \Big\{y \mid y \in P(x),\ y' \notin P(x)\ \forall y' \geq y, y' \neq y\Big\} \subseteq \partial P(x). \quad (2.9)$$

[7] We give an illustration in Section 2.5 in Figure 2.2 where we describe DEA estimators of efficient frontier.

Once the efficient subsets of Ψ have been defined, we may define the efficiency measure of a firm operating at the level (x_0, y_0) by considering the distance from this point to the frontier. There are several ways to achieve this but a simple way suggested by Farrell (1957), in the lines of Debreu (1951), is to use a *radial* distance from the point to its corresponding frontier. In the following we will concentrate our attention on radial measures of efficiency. Of course, we may look at the efficient frontier in two directions: either in the input direction (where the efficient subset is characterized by $\partial C(y)$) or in the output direction (where the efficient subset is characterized by $\partial P(x)$).

The Farrell input measure of efficiency for a firm operating at level (x_0, y_0) is defined as:

$$\theta(x_0, y_0) = \inf\{\theta | \theta x_0 \in C(y_0)\} = \inf\{\theta | (\theta x_0, y_0) \in \Psi\}, \qquad (2.10)$$

and its Farrell output measure of efficiency is defined as:

$$\lambda(x_0, y_0) = \sup\{\lambda | \lambda y_0 \in P(x_0)\} = \sup\{\lambda | (x_0, \lambda y_0) \in \Psi\}. \qquad (2.11)$$

So, $\theta(x_0, y_0) \leq 1$ is the radial contraction of inputs the firm should achieve to be considered as being input-efficient in the sense that $(\theta(x_0, y_0)x_0, y_0)$ is a frontier point. In the same way $\lambda(x_0, y_0) \geq 1$ is the proportionate increase of output the firm should achieve to be considered as being output efficient in the sense that $(x_0, \lambda(x_0, y_0)y_0)$ is on the frontier.

It is interesting to note that the efficient frontier of Ψ, in the radial sense, can be characterized as the units (x, y) such that $\theta(x, y) = 1$, in the input direction (belonging to $\partial C(y)$) and by the (x, y) such that $\lambda(x, y) = 1$, in the output direction (belonging to $\partial P(x)$). If the frontier is continuous, frontier points are such that $\theta(x, y) = \lambda(x, y) = 1$. The efficient frontier is unique but we have two ways to characterize it.

It is sometimes easier to measure these radial distances by their inverse, known as *Shephard distance functions* (Shephard, 1970). The Shephard input distance function provides a normalized measure of Euclidean distance from a point $(x, y) \in \mathcal{R}_+^{p+q}$ to the boundary of Ψ in a radial direction orthogonal to y and is defined as:

$$\delta^{in}(x, y) = \sup\{\theta > 0 | (\theta^{-1}x, y) \in \Psi\} \equiv (\theta(x, y))^{-1}, \qquad (2.12)$$

with $\delta^{in}(x, y) \geq 1, \forall (x, y) \in \Psi$. Similarly, the Shephard output distance function provides a normalized measure of Euclidean distance from a point $(x, y) \in \mathcal{R}_+^{p+q}$ to the boundary of Ψ in a radial direction orthogonal to x:

$$\delta^{out}(x, y) = \inf\{\lambda > 0 | (x, \lambda^{-1}y) \in \Psi\} \equiv (\lambda(x, y))^{-1}. \qquad (2.13)$$

For all $(x, y) \in \Psi$, $\delta^{out}(x, y) \leq 1$. If either $\delta^{in}(x, y) = 1$ or $\delta^{out}(x, y) = 1$ then (x, y) belongs to the frontier of Ψ and the firm is technically efficient.

As pointed out in Simar and Wilson (2001), no behavioral assumptions are necessary for measuring technical efficiency. From a purely technical viewpoint, either the input or the output distance function can be used to measure technical efficiency - the only difference is in the direction in which distance to the technology is measured. The way of looking at the frontier will typically depend on the context of the application. For instance, if the outputs are exogenous and not under the control of the Decision Makers (*e.g.* as in most of the public services), input efficiency will be of main interest, since the inputs are the only elements under the control of the managers. But even in this case, both measures are available.

2.4 A taxonomy of efficient frontier models

The analysis of the existent literature is a necessary step for the advancement of a discipline. This is particularly true for the field of efficiency and productivity research that in the last decades has known an exponential increasing in the number of methodological and applied works. For a DEA bibliography over 1978-1992, see Seiford (1994, 1996) and for an extension till 2001 see Gattoufi, Oral and Reisman (2004). In Cooper, Seiford and Tone (2000) about 1,500 DEA references are reported. Other bibliographic studies include: Emrouznejad (2001) and Taveres (2002).

As a consequence, a comprehensive review of the overall literature would require another whole work. Therefore, the aim of this section is to propose a general taxonomy of efficient frontier models that gives an overview on the different approaches presented in literature for estimating the efficient frontier of a production possibility set. Here the review could be biased toward the nonparametric approach, due to our commitment and involvement with nonparametric methods most. Anyway, we give several references also on the parametric approach that could be useful for those interested in it.

In the previous section we described the economic model underlying the frontier analysis framework based on the Activity Analysis Model. This model is based on some representations of the production set Ψ on which we can impose different axioms. Nevertheless, the production set Ψ, the boundary of the input requirement set $\partial C(y)$ and of the output correspondence set $\partial P(x)$, together with the efficiency scores in the input and output space, $\theta(x, y)$ and $\lambda(x, y)$, are unknown.

The econometric problem is thus how to estimate Ψ, and then $\partial C(y)$, $\partial P(x)$, $\theta(x, y)$, $\lambda(x, y)$, from a random sample of production units $\mathcal{X} = \{(X_i, Y_i) \mid i = 1, ..., n\}$.

Starting from the first empirical application of Farrell (1957) several different approaches for efficient frontier estimation and efficiency score calculation have been developed.[8]

In Figure 2.1 we propose an outline of what we believe have been the most influential works in productivity and efficiency analysis, starting from the pioneering work by Farrell (1957). Of course, our outline is far from being complete and *all-inclusive*. Figure 2.1 shows some of the articles, books and special issues of journals (*i.e. Journal of Econometrics* JE, *Journal of Productivity Analysis* JPA, *European Journal of Operational Research*, EJOR) that have mainly influenced the writing of this work, trying to balance them according to the adopted approach.

As it is evident from Figure 2.1 we have taken into consideration mainly the nonparametric approach as we believe that thanks to its last developments, it can be considered as being very flexible and very useful for modeling purpose.

We may classify efficient frontier models according to the following *criteria*:[9]

1 The specification of the (functional) form for the *frontier function*;

2 The presence of noise in the sample data;

3 The type of data analyzed.

Based on the first *criterium* (functional form of the frontier) is the classification in:

- *Parametric Models.* In these models, the attainable set Ψ is defined trough a *production frontier function*, $g(x, \beta)$, which is a known mathematical function depending on some k unknown parameters, *i.e.* $\beta \in \mathcal{R}^k$, where generally y is univariate, *i.e.* $y \in \mathcal{R}_+$. The main advantages of this approach are the economic interpretation of parameters and the statistical properties of estimators; more critical are the choice of the function $g(x, \beta)$ and the handling of multiple inputs, multiple outputs cases (for more on this latter aspect see Section 4.7 below where we introduce multivariate parametric approximations of nonparametric and robust frontiers).

- *Nonparametric Models.* These models do not assume any particular functional form for the frontier function $g(x)$. The main pros of this approach are the robustness to model choice and the easy handling of multiple inputs, multiple outputs case; their main limitations are the estimation of unknown functional and the *curse of dimensionality*[10], typical of nonparametric methods.

---

[8]For an introduction see *e.g.*, Coelli, Rao and Battese (1998) and Thanassoulis (2001).

[9]These *criteria* follow Simar and Wilson (2006b), where a comprehensive statistical approach is described.

[10]The curse of dimensionality, shared by many nonparametric methods, means that to avoid large variances and wide confidence interval estimates a large quantity of data is needed.

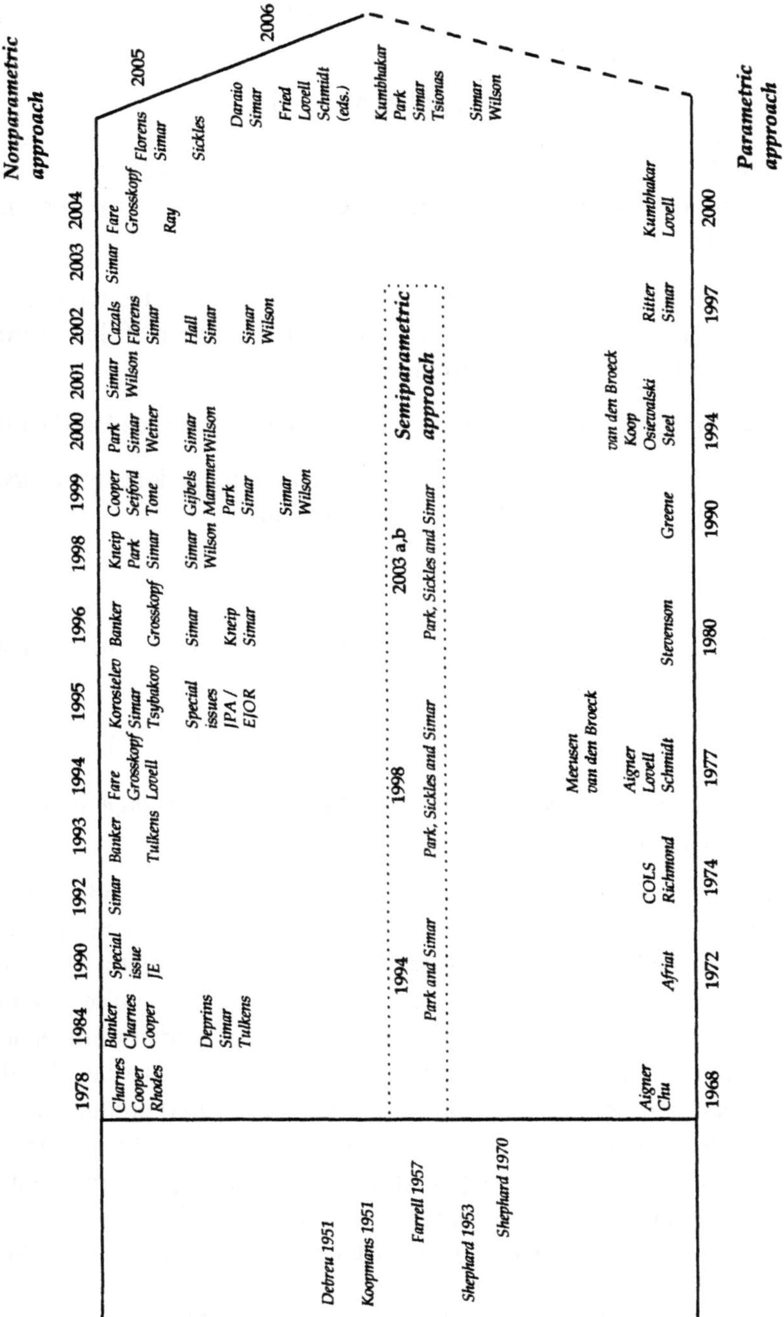

Figure 2.1. An overview of the literature on efficient frontier estimation.

Based on the second *criterium* (presence of noise) is the classification in:

- *Deterministic Models*, which assume that all observations (X_i, Y_i) belong to the production set, *i.e.*

$$Prob\{(X_i, Y_i) \in \Psi\} = 1$$

  for all $i = 1, ..., n$. The main weakness of this approach is the sensitivity to "super-efficient" outliers. Robust estimators are able to overcome this drawback.

- *Stochastic Models*, in which there might be noise in the data, *i.e.* some observations might lie outside Ψ. The main problem of this approach is the identification of noise from inefficiency.

Based on the third *criterium* (type of data analyzed) is the classification in:

- *Cross-sectional Models*, in which the data sample is done by observations on n firms or DMUs (Decision Making Units):

$$\mathcal{X} = \{(X_i, Y_i)|i = 1, ..., n\}$$

- *Panel Data Models*, in which the observations on the n firms are available over T periods of time:

$$\mathcal{X} = \{(X_{it}, Y_{it}) \mid i = 1, ..., n; t = 1, ..., T\}.$$

  Panel data allow the measurement of *productivity change* as well as the estimation of technical progress or regress.

Generally speaking, productivity change occurs when an index of outputs changes at a different rate than an index of inputs does. Productivity change can be calculated using index number techniques to construct a Fisher (1922) or Tornqvist (1936) productivity index. Both these indices require quantity and price information, as well as assumptions concerning the structure of technology and the behavior of producers. Productivity change can also be calculated using nonparametric techniques to construct a Malmquist (1953) productivity index. These latter techniques do not require price information or technological and behavioral assumptions, but they require the estimation of a representation of production technology. Nonparametric techniques are able not only to calculate productivity change, but also to identify the sources of measured productivity change.

A survey of the theoretical and empirical work on Malmquist productivity indices can be found in Färe, Grosskopf and Russell (1998). On the theoretical side the survey includes a number of issues that have arisen since the Malmquist productivity index was proposed by Caves, Christensen and Diewert

(1982). These issues include the definition of the Malmquist productivity index; although all are based on the distance functions that Malmquist employed to formulate his original quantity index, variations include the geometric mean form used by Färe, Grosskopf, Lindgren and Roos (1989) and the quantity index form by Diewert (1992). The survey of the empirical literature presents studies on the public sector, banking, agriculture, countries and international comparisons, electric utilities, transportation, and insurance. See also Lovell (2003), and Grosskopf (2003) for an historical perspective and an outline of the state of the art in this area.

Although productivity change is not the main focus of FDH, it can be inferred from information on efficiency change and technical change that is revealed by FDH. The technique was developed by Tulkens that named it "sequential FDH". For an illustration of the sequential FDH see Lovell (1993, pp. 48-49). On this topic see also Tulkens and Vanden Eeckaut (1995a, 1995b).

By combining the three *criteria* mentioned above, several models have been studied in literature:

- *Parametric Deterministic Models*, see *e.g.* Aigner and Chu (1968), Afriat (1972), Richmond (1974), Schmidt (1976) and Greene (1980) for cross-sectional and panel data;

- *Parametric Stochastic Models*, most of these techniques are based on the maximum likelihood principle, following the pioneering works of Aigner, Lovell and Schmidt (1977) and Meeusen and van den Broeck (1977). For a recent review see Kumbhakar and Lovell (2000). In the context of panel data, stochastic models (see Schmidt and Sickles, 1984, and Cornwell, Schmidt, and Sickles, 1990) have *semiparametric* generalizations, in which a part of the model is parametric and the rest is nonparametric (see Park and Simar, 1994; Park, Sickles and Simar, 1998; and Park, Sickles and Simar, 2003a, b).

- *Nonparametric Deterministic Models* for cross-sectional and panel data. Traditional references on these models include: Färe, Grosskopf and Lovell (1985, 1994), Fried, Lovell and Schmidt (1993), and Charnes, Cooper, Lewin and Seiford, 1994. Recent and updated references are Cooper, Seiford and Tone (2000), Ray (2004) and Färe and Grosskopf (2004).

- *Nonparametric Stochastic Models* for cross-sectional data (see Hall and Simar, 2002; Simar, 2003b; Kumbhakar, Park, Simar and Tsionas, 2004) and panel data (see Kneip and Simar, 1996; and Henderson and Simar, 2005).

The mainly used approaches in empirical works are the nonparametric (deterministic) frontier approach and the (parametric) stochastic frontier approach.

In the following, when we refer to nonparametric frontier approach we indicate the deterministic version of it; when we talk about stochastic frontier approach we refer to its parametric version.

The nonparametric frontier approach, based on envelopment techniques (DEA FDH), has been extensively used for estimating efficiency of firms as it relays only on very few assumptions for Ψ. On the contrary, the stochastic frontier approach (SFA) allows the presence of noise but it demands parametric restrictions on the shape of the frontier and on the Data Generating Process (DGP) in order to permit the identification of noise from inefficiency and the estimation of the frontier. Fried, Lovell and Schmidt (2006) offer an updated presentation of both approaches. A statistical approach which unifies parametric and nonparametric approaches can be found in Simar and Wilson (2006b).

2.5 The nonparametric frontier approach

In this section we introduce the most known nonparametric estimators of efficient frontiers.

As we have seen in Section 2.3 devoted to the presentation of the economic model, we can equivalently look at the efficient boundary of Ψ from the input space or from the output space.

The *input oriented* framework, based on the input requirement set and its efficient boundary, aims at reducing the input amounts by as much as possible while keeping at least the present output levels. This is also called "input-saving" approach to stress the fact that the outputs level remains unchanged and input quantities are reduced proportionately till the frontier is reached. This is a framework generally adopted when the *decision maker* can control the inputs but has not the control of the outputs. For instance, this is the case of public enterprises which are committed to offer some public services and are interested in the management of the inputs, in the sense of their minimization.

Alternatively, we can take into account the output space and look at the output correspondence set and its efficient boundary. The *output oriented* framework looks at maximize output levels under at most the present input consumption. This approach is also known as "output-augmenting" approach, because it holds the input bundle unchanged and expand the output level till the frontier is reached. In practice, whether the input or output-oriented measure is more appropriate would depend on whether input conservation is more important than output augmentation.

For the relation existent among input and output efficiency measures, see Deprins and Simar (1983).

The main nonparametric estimators available are the Data Envelopment Analysis (DEA) and the Free Disposal Hull (FDH) which we describe in the subsections that follow.

2.5.1 Data Envelopment Analysis (DEA)

The DEA estimator of the production set, initiated by Farrell (1957) and operationalized as linear programming estimators by Charnes, Cooper and Rhodes (1978), assumes the free disposability and the convexity of the production set Ψ. It involves measurement of efficiency for a given unit (x, y) relative to the boundary of the convex hull of $\mathcal{X} = \{(X_i, Y_i), i = 1, ..., n\}$:

$$\widehat{\Psi}_{DEA} = \Big\{(x, y) \in \mathcal{R}_+^{p+q} \mid y \leq \sum_{i=1}^{n} \gamma_i Y_i; x \geq \sum_{i=1}^{n} \gamma_i X_i, \text{ for } (\gamma_1, ..., \gamma_n) \text{ s.t. } \sum_{i=1}^{n} \gamma_i = 1; \gamma_i \geq 0, i = 1, ..., n\Big\} \quad (2.14)$$

$\widehat{\Psi}_{DEA}$ is thus the smallest free disposal convex set covering all the data.

The $\widehat{\Psi}_{DEA}$ in (2.14) allows for Variable Returns to Scale (VRS) and is often referred as $\widehat{\Psi}_{DEA-VRS}$ (see Banker, Charnes and Cooper, 1984). It may be adapted to other returns to scale situations. It allows for:

- *Constant Returns to Scale* (CRS) if the equality constrained $\sum_{i=1}^{n} \gamma_i = 1$ in (2.14) is dropped;
- *Non Increasing Returns to Scale* (NIRS) if the equality constrained $\sum_{i=1}^{n} \gamma_i = 1$ in (2.14) is changed in $\sum_{i=1}^{n} \gamma_i \leq 1$;
- *Non Decreasing Returns to Scale* (NDRS) if the equality constrained $\sum_{i=1}^{n} \gamma_i = 1$ in (2.14) is modified in $\sum_{i=1}^{n} \gamma_i \geq 1$.

The estimation of the input requirement set is given for all y by: $\widehat{C}(y) = \{x \in \mathcal{R}_+^p | (x, y) \in \widehat{\Psi}_{DEA}\}$ and $\partial \widehat{C}(y)$ denotes the estimator of the input frontier boundary for y.

For a firm operating at level (x_0, y_0) the estimation of the input efficiency score $\theta(x_0, y_0)$ is obtained by solving the following linear program (here and hereafter we consider the VRS case):

$$\widehat{\theta}_{DEA}(x_0, y_0) = \inf\Big\{\theta \mid (\theta x_0, y_0) \in \widehat{\Psi}_{DEA}\Big\} \quad (2.15)$$

$$\widehat{\theta}_{DEA}(x_0, y_0) = \min\Big\{\theta \mid y_0 \leq \sum_{i=1}^{n} \gamma_i Y_i; \theta x_0 \geq \sum_{i=1}^{n} \gamma_i X_i; \theta > 0; \sum_{i=1}^{n} \gamma_i = 1;\ \gamma_i \geq 0;\ i = 1, ..., n\Big\}. \quad (2.16)$$

$\widehat{\theta}(x_0, y_0)$ measures the radial distance between (x_0, y_0) and $(\widehat{x}^{\partial}(x_0|y_0), y_0)$ where $\widehat{x}^{\partial}(x_0|y_0)$ is the level of the inputs the unit should reach in order to be on the "efficient boundary" of $\widehat{\Psi}_{DEA}$ with the same level of output, y_0, and the same proportion of inputs; *i.e.* moving from x_0 to $\widehat{x}^{\partial}(x_0|y_0)$ along the ray θx_0. The projection of x_0 on the efficient frontier is thus equal to $\widehat{x}^{\partial}(x_0|y_0) = \widehat{\theta}(x_0, y_0)x_0$.

For the output oriented case, the estimation is done, *mutatis mutandis*, following the previous steps. The output correspondence set is estimated by: $\widehat{P}(x) = \{y \in \mathcal{R}^q_+|(x,y) \in \widehat{\Psi}_{DEA}\}$ and $\partial\widehat{P}(x)$ denotes the estimator of the output frontier boundary for x.

The estimator of the output efficiency score for a given (x_0, y_0) is obtained by solving the following linear program:

$$\widehat{\lambda}_{DEA}(x_0, y_0) = \sup\Big\{\lambda \mid (x_0, \lambda y_0) \in \widehat{\Psi}_{DEA}\Big\}, \tag{2.17}$$

$$\widehat{\lambda}_{DEA}(x_0, y_0) = \max\Big\{\lambda \mid \lambda y_0 \leq \sum_{i=1}^{n} \gamma_i Y_i;\ \ x_0 \geq \sum_{i=1}^{n} \gamma_i X_i;\ \ \lambda > 0;$$
$$\sum_{i=1}^{n} \gamma_i = 1;\ \gamma_i \geq 0;\ i = 1, ..., n\Big\}. \tag{2.18}$$

In Figure 2.2 we display the DEA estimator and illustrate the concept of *slacks* through an example. If we look at the left panel assuming that all firms produce the same level of output, we can see that the DMU E could actually produce 1 unit of y with less input x_1, *i.e.*, it could reduce x_1 by one unit (from 4 to 3) moving from E to D. This is referred to as *input slack*: although the DMU is technical efficient, there is a *surplus* of input x_1.[11] In general, we say that there is slack in input j of DMU i, *i.e.*, x_i^j, if:

$$\sum_{i=1}^{n} \gamma_i x_i < x_i^j\, \widehat{\theta}(x_i, y_i) \tag{2.19}$$

is true for some solution value of γ_i, $i = 1, ..., n$ (see Färe, Grosskopf and Lovell, 1994, for more details).

The same kind of reasoning can be done for the output oriented case, *i.e.* the DMU L could increase the production of y_1 moving from L to M. See Figure 2.2, right panel for a graphical illustration.

Slacks may happen for DEA estimates (as shown in Figure 2.2), as well as for FDH estimates (presented in the next section). It is interesting to note that if the true production set Ψ has no slacks, than slacks are only a small sample problem. Nevertheless, it is always useful to report slacks whenever they are

[11] Remember the "possibility of destroying goods without costs" underlying the frontier representation of the economic model.

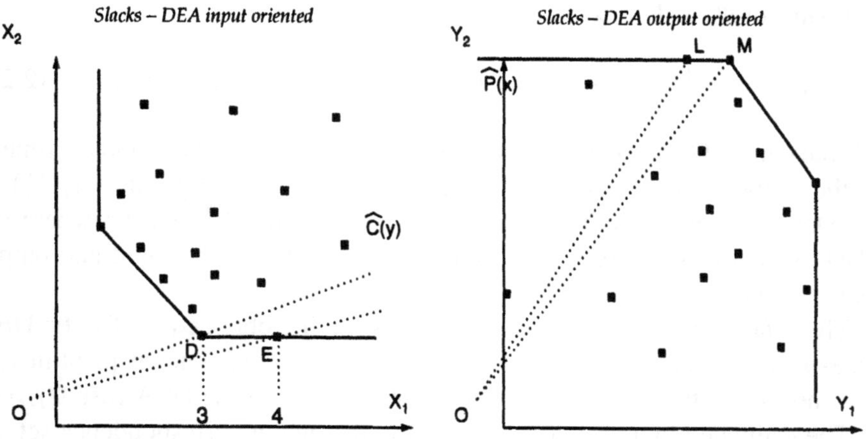

Figure 2.2. Input and Output slacks.

there. It is left to the analyst to decide if it is better to correct for the slacks or just point them.

Once the efficiency measures have been computed, several interesting analysis could be done, such as the inspection of the distribution of efficiency scores and the analysis of the "best performers" or efficient facet of the frontier closer to the analysed DMU, generally called *peer-analysis*, to study the technical efficient units and try to learn from them.

2.5.2 Free Disposal Hull (FDH)

The FDH estimator, proposed by Deprins, Simar and Tulkens (1984), is a more general version of the DEA estimator as it relies only on the free disposability assumption for Ψ, and hence does not restrict itself to convex technologies. This seems an attractive property of FDH since it is frequently difficult to find a good theoretical or empirical justification for postulating convex production sets in efficiency analysis. At this purpose, Farrell (1959) indicates indivisibility of inputs and outputs and economies of scale and specialization as possible violations of convexity. It is important to note also that if the *true* production set is convex then the DEA and FDH are both consistent estimators; however, as pointed later in this section, FDH shows a lower rate of convergence (due to the less assumptions it requires) with respect to DEA. On the contrary, if the *true* production set is not convex, than DEA is not a consistent estimator of the production set, while FDH is consistent.

The FDH estimator measures the efficiency for a given point (x_0, y_0) relative to the boundary of the Free Disposal Hull of the sample $\mathcal{X} = \{(X_i, Y_i), i = 1, ..., n\}$. The Free Disposal Hull of the set of observations (*i.e.* the FDH estimator of Ψ) is defined as:

$$\widehat{\Psi}_{FDH} = \left\{(x,y) \in \mathcal{R}_+^{p+q} \mid y \leq Y_i; x \geq X_i, (X_i, Y_i) \in \mathcal{X}\right\}. \tag{2.20}$$

It is the union of the all positive orthants in the inputs and of the negative orthants in the outputs whose origin coincides with the observed points $(X_i, Y_i) \in \mathcal{X}$ (Deprins, Simar and Tulkens, 1984). See Figures 2.3 and 2.4 where the FDH estimator is compared with the DEA estimator of the input and output requirement sets, respectively.

The efficiency estimators, in this framework, are obtained (as for the DEA case) using a "plug-in principle", *i.e.*, by substituting the unknown quantities (in this case Ψ) by their estimated values (here $\widehat{\Psi}_{FDH}$, for the DEA case $\widehat{\Psi}_{DEA}$).

The estimated input requirement set and the output correspondence set are the following:

$$\widehat{C}(y) = \{x \in \mathcal{R}_+^p | (x,y) \in \widehat{\Psi}_{FDH}\},$$

$$\widehat{P}(x) = \{y \in \mathcal{R}_+^q | (x,y) \in \widehat{\Psi}_{FDH}\}.$$

Their respective efficient boundaries are:

$$\partial\widehat{C}(y) = \{x | x \in \widehat{C}(y), \theta x \notin \widehat{C}(y) \forall 0 < \theta < 1\},$$

$$\partial\widehat{P}(x) = \{y | y \in \widehat{P}(x), \lambda y \notin \widehat{P}(x) \forall \lambda > 1\}.$$

Hence, the estimated input efficiency score for a given point $(x_0, y_0) \in \Psi$ is:

$$\begin{aligned} \widehat{\theta}_{FDH}(x_0, y_0) &= \inf\left\{\theta \mid \theta x_0 \in \widehat{C}(y_0)\right\} \\ &= \inf\left\{\theta \mid (\theta x_0, y_0) \in \widehat{\Psi}_{FDH}\right\}, \end{aligned} \tag{2.21}$$

and the estimated output efficiency score of (x_0, y_0) is given by:

$$\begin{aligned} \widehat{\lambda}_{FDH}(x_0, y_0) &= \sup\left\{\lambda \mid \lambda y_0 \in \widehat{P}(x_0)\right\} \\ &= \sup\left\{\lambda \mid (x_0, \lambda y_0) \in \widehat{\Psi}_{FDH}\right\}. \end{aligned} \tag{2.22}$$

It is clear that for a particular point (x_0, y_0), the estimated distance to the frontiers are evaluated by means of the distance, in the input space ("input oriented") from this point to the estimated frontier of the input requirement set $(\partial\widehat{C}(y))$, and in the output space ("output oriented") by the distance from (x_0, y_0) to the estimated frontier of the output correspondence set $(\partial\widehat{P}(x))$.

It is worthwhile to note that the FDH attainable set in (2.20) can also be characterized as the following set:

$$\widehat{\Psi}_{FDH} = \Big\{(x,y) \in \mathcal{R}_+^{p+q} \mid y \leq \sum_{i=1}^{n} \gamma_i Y_i;\ x \geq \sum_{i=1}^{n} \gamma_i X_i,\ \sum_{i=1}^{n} \gamma_i = 1; \gamma_i \in \{0,1\}, i = 1,...,n\Big\}. \quad (2.23)$$

Therefore the efficiencies can be estimated by solving the following integer linear programs; for the input-oriented case we have:

$$\widehat{\theta}_{FDH}(x_0, y_0) = \min \Big\{\theta \mid y_0 \leq \sum_{i=1}^{n} \gamma_i Y_i; \theta x_0 \geq \sum_{i=1}^{n} \gamma_i X_i, \sum_{i=1}^{n} \gamma_i = 1; \gamma_i \in \{0,1\}, i = 1,...,n\Big\}, \quad (2.24)$$

and for the output-oriented case:

$$\widehat{\lambda}_{FDH}(x_0, y_0) = \max \Big\{\lambda \mid \lambda y_0 \leq \sum_{i=1}^{n} \gamma_i Y_i; x_0 \geq \sum_{i=1}^{n} \gamma_i X_i, \sum_{i=1}^{n} \gamma_i = 1; \gamma_i \in \{0,1\}, i = 1,...,n\Big\}. \quad (2.25)$$

The latter expressions allow to make the comparison easier between the FDH and the DEA estimators (compare for instance (2.23) with (2.14)).

Figure 2.3 illustrates the estimation of the input requirement set $C(y)$ and of its boundary $\partial C(y)$ through FDH and DEA methods. The dashed line represents the FDH estimation of $\partial C(y)$, while the solid line shows the DEA estimation of it. The squares are the observations. The DEA and FDH estimates of efficiency score of production unit B, in Figure 2.3, are respectively: $\widehat{\theta}_{DEA}(x_0, y_0) = |OB''|/|OB| \leq 1$, $\widehat{\theta}_{FDH}(x_0, y_0) = |OB'|/|OB| \leq 1$.

In Figure 2.4 we show the FDH and DEA estimation of the output correspondence set $P(x)$ and its boundary $\partial P(x)$. The dash-dotted line represents the FDH estimator of $\partial P(x)$, while the solid line the DEA estimator of it. The black squares, as before, represent the DMUs. For firm B, the estimates of its efficiency score, in output oriented framework, are: $\widehat{\lambda}_{FDH}(x_0, y_0) = |OB'|/|OB| \geq 1$, $\widehat{\lambda}_{DEA}(x_0, y_0) = |OB''|/|OB| \geq 1$.

Practical computation of the FDH

In practice, the FDH estimator is computed by a simple vector comparison procedure that amounts to a complete enumeration algorithm proposed in Tulkens (1993), which is now explained.

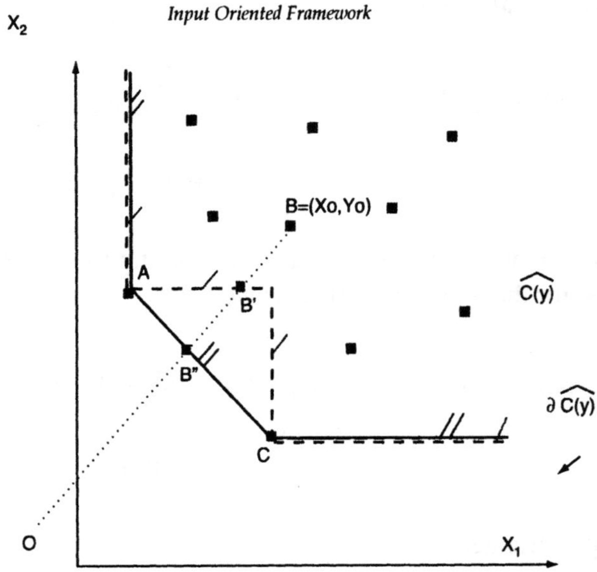

Figure 2.3. FDH and DEA estimation of $C(y)$ and $\partial C(y)$.

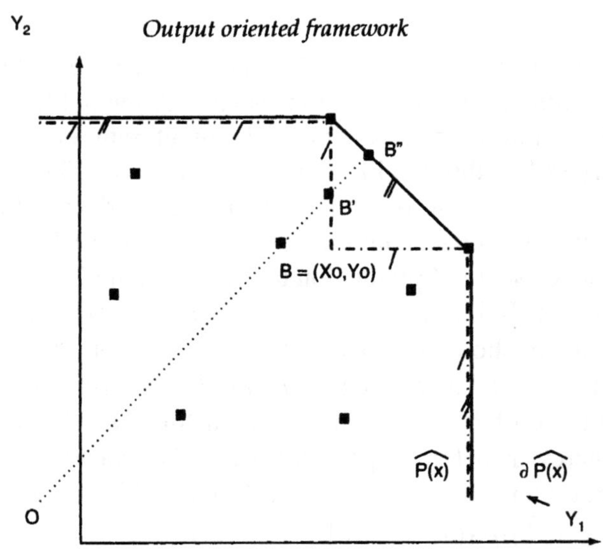

Figure 2.4. FDH and DEA estimation of $P(x)$ and $\partial P(x)$.

For a DMU (x_0, y_0), in a first step, the set of observations which dominates it is determined, and then the estimate of its efficiency score, relative to the dominating facet of $\widehat{\Psi}$ is computed. In the simplest case, with a technology characterized by one input and one output, the set of observations which dominate (x_0, y_0) is defined as:

$$D_0 = \Big\{i|(X_i, Y_i) \in \mathcal{X}, X_i \leq x_0, Y_i \geq y_0\Big\}. \tag{2.26}$$

The "input oriented" efficiency estimate is done through:

$$\widehat{\theta}_{FDH}(x_0, y_0) = \min{}_{i \in D_0} \Big(\frac{X_i}{x_0}\Big), \tag{2.27}$$

and the "output oriented" efficiency is computed via:

$$\widehat{\lambda}_{FDH}(x_0, y_0) = \max{}_{i \in D_0} \Big(\frac{Y_i}{y_0}\Big). \tag{2.28}$$

It has to be noted that as $X_i \leq x_0$ then $\widehat{\theta}_{FDH} \leq 1$. As for the input-oriented case, from the fact that $Y_i \geq y_0$ follows that $\widehat{\lambda}_{FDH} \geq 1$.

In a multivariate setting, the expression (2.21) can be computed through:

$$\widehat{\theta}_{FDH}(x_0, y_0) = \min{}_{i \in D_0} \Big\{\max{}_{j=1,\ldots,p} \Big(\frac{X^{i,j}}{x_0^j}\Big)\Big\}, \tag{2.29}$$

where $X^{i,j}$ is the jth component of $X^i \in \mathcal{R}_+^p$ and x_0^j is the jth component of $x_0 \in \mathcal{R}_+^p$.

It is a *maximin* procedure (for the "input oriented" framework): the "max" part of the algorithm identifies the most dominant DMUs relative to which a given DMU is evaluated. Once the most dominant DMUs are identified, slacks are calculated from the "min" part of the algorithm.

The multivariate computation of expression (2.22) is done by:

$$\widehat{\lambda}_{FDH}(x_0, y_0) = \max{}_{i \in D_0} \Big\{\min{}_{j=1,\ldots,q} \Big(\frac{Y^{i,j}}{y_0^j}\Big)\Big\} \tag{2.30}$$

where $Y^{i,j}$ is the jth component of $Y^i \in \mathcal{R}_+^q$ and y_0^j is the jth component of $y_0 \in \mathcal{R}_+^q$.

The FDH estimator has been applied in several contexts. For a detailed presentation of FDH concepts see Vanden Eeckaut (1997).

Recently, some authors have raised explicit doubts about the economic meaning of FDH, but from the exchange between Thrall (1999) and Cherchye, Kuosmanen and Post (2000), published on the *Journal of Productivity Analysis*, it emerged that FDH can be economically more meaningful than convex monotone hull, also under non-trivial alternative economic conditions.

Hence, FDH technical efficiency measures remain meaningful for theories of the firm that do allow for imperfect competition or uncertainty (see *e.g.* Kuosmanen and Post, 2001, and Cherchye, Kuosmanen and Post, 2001).

One of the main drawbacks of deterministic frontier models (DEA /FDH based) is the influence of "super-efficient" outliers.

This is a consequence of the fact that the efficient frontier is determined by sample observations which are extreme points. Simar (1996) points out the need for identifying and eliminating outliers when using deterministic models. If they cannot be identified, the use of stochastic frontier models is recommended.

See Figure 2.5 for an illustration of the influence of outliers in case of FDH estimation. The same is valid for the DEA case. If point A is an extreme point, outlying the cloud of other points, the estimated efficient frontier is strongly influenced by it. In fact, in Figure 2.5, the solid line is the frontier that envelops point A, while the dash-dotted line does not envelop point A.

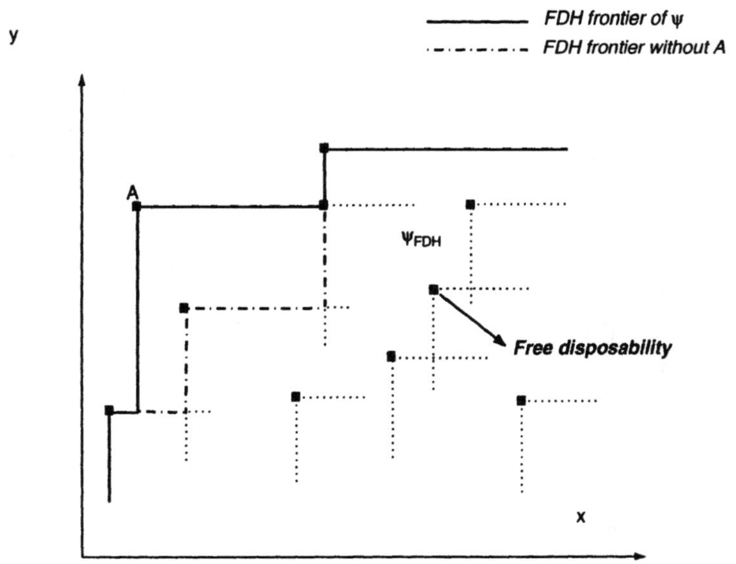

Figure 2.5. Influence of outliers on the FDH estimation of the production set Ψ.

We will come back on this problem in Chapter 4 where we propose robust nonparametric approaches based on various nonparametric measures less influenced by extreme values and outliers, which have also nice statistical properties.

2.6 Recent developments in nonparametric efficiency analysis

In the following, we recall briefly some stream of works that have contributed to the latest advancement of the nonparametric efficiency literature.[12]

Sensitivity of results to data variation and discrimination (in a DEA framework)

The focus of studies on sensitivity and stability is the reliability of classification of DMUs into efficient and inefficient performers. Most analytical methods for studying the sensitivity of results to variations in data have been developed in a DEA framework.

After a first stream of works concentrated on developing solution methods and algorithms for conducting sensitivity analysis in linear programming, a second current of studies analysed data variations in only one input or one output for one unit at a time. A recent stream of works makes it possible to determine ranges within which all data may be varied for any unit before a reclassification from efficient to inefficient status (or *vice versa*) occurs, and for determining ranges of data variation that can be allowed when all data are varied simultaneously for all DMUs. For a review and some references see Cooper, Li, Seiford, Tone, Thrall and Zhu (2001).

As we have seen above, DEA models have a deterministic nature, meaning that they do not account for statistical noise. Some authors (*e.g.*, Land, Lovell and Thore, 1993; Olesen and Petersen, 1995) have proposed the application of the *chance-constrained programming* to the DEA problem in order to overcome its deterministic nature. The basic idea is that of make DEA stochastic by introducing a chance that the constraints on either the envelopment problem or the multiplier problem may be violated with some probability. However, the chance-constrained efficiency measurement requires a large amount of data in addition to inputs and outputs. Moreover, it is based on a strong distributional assumption on the process determining the chance of a constrained to be violated. The analyst in fact has to provide also information on expected values of all variables for all DMUs, and variance-covariance matrices for each variable across all DMUs. An alternative to this approach is given by a fuzzy programming approach to DEA and FDH efficiency measurement.

There is an increasing number of studies that apply the fuzzy set theory in productivity and efficiency contexts. In some production studies, the data that describe the production process cannot be collected accurately due to the fact that measurement systems have not been originally designated for the pur-

[12] See also Lovell (2001) and Fried, Lovell and Schmidt (2006) for a presentation of some recent fruitful research areas introduced in parametric and nonparametric approaches to efficiency analysis.

pose of collecting data and information that are useful for production studies. Sengupta (1992) was the first to introduce a fuzzy mathematical programming approach where the constraints and objective function are not satisfied crisply. Seaver and Triantis (1992) proposed a fuzzy clustering approach for identify unusual or extreme efficient behavior. Girod and Triantis (1999) implemented a fuzzy linear programming approach, whilst Triantis and Girod (1998), and Kao and Liu (1999) used fuzzy set theory, to let the traditional DEA and FDH account for inaccuracies associated with the production plans. A fuzzy pairwise dominance approach can be found in Triantis and Vanden Eeckaut (2000) where, a classification scheme that explicitly accounts for the degree of fuzziness (plausibility) of dominating units is reported.

According to a classification proposed by Angulo-Meza and Pereira Estellita Lins (2002), the methods for increasing discrimination within efficient DMUs in a DEA setting can be classified into two groups:

Methods with a priori information. In these methods, the information provided by a decision-maker or an expert about the importance of the variables can be introduced into the DEA models. There are three main methods devoted to incorporating a priori information or value judgments in DEA:

- *Weight restrictions.* The main objective of the weight restrictions methods is to establish bounds within which the weights can vary, preserving some flexibility/ uncertainty about the real value of the weights.[13]

- *Preference structure models.* These models have been introduced by Zhu (1996) within a framework of non-radial efficiency measures. In this approach, the target for inefficient DMUs is given by a preference structure (represented through some weights) expressed by the decision-maker.

- *Value efficiency analysis.* This method, introduced by Halme, Joro, Korhonen, Salo and Wallenius (2000), aims at incorporate the decision-maker's value judgements and preferences into the analysis, using a two stage procedure. The first stage identifies the decision maker's most preferred solutions through a multiple objective model. The second stage consists in the determination of the frontier based on the most preferred solutions chosen.

Methods that do not require a priori information. These family of models aims at increase discrimination in DEA without the subjectivity, the possibility of biased or wrong judgements, typical of the methods that introduce a priori

[13]See Allen, Athanassopoulos, Dyson and Thanassoulis (1997), and Pedraja-Chaparro, Salinas-Jimenes, Smith and Smith (1997) for a review of some methods within this approach, including direct weight restrictions, cone ratio models, assurance region and virtual inputs and outputs restrictions.

information. The main methods that minimize the intervention of the experts are:

- *Super efficiency*. Andersen and Petersen (1993) proposed this method to rank efficient DMUs.

- *Cross-evaluation*. The main idea of this method is to use DEA in a "peer-evaluation" instead of a classical "self evaluation" evaluated by the classical DEA models.

- *Multiple objective approach*. A Multiple Criteria Data Envelopment Analysis has been proposed by Li and Reeves (1999) to solve the problems of lack of discrimination and inappropriate weighting schemes in traditional DEA.

Extensions to the basic DEA Models

Directional distance functions have been introduced by Chambers, Chung and Färe, (1996) and are based on Luenberger (1992) benefit functions. These functions represent a kind of generalization of the traditional distance functions. Their application leads to measures of technical efficiency from the potential for increasing outputs while reducing inputs at the same time. In order to provide a measure of "directional" efficiency, a *direction*, along which the observed DMU is projected onto the efficient frontier of the production set, has to be chosen. This choice is arbitrary and of course affects the resulting efficiency measures. In addition, those measures are no more scale-invariant. See Färe and Grosskopf (2004) for more details on these "new directions" in efficiency analysis.

Examples of the literature that try to link DEA with a theoretical foundation or that try to overcome and generalize the economic assumptions underlying DEA include: Bogetoft (2000) which links the theoretically oriented agency, incentives and contracts literature with the more practical oriented efficiency measurement literature; and Briec, Kerstens and Vanden Eeckaut (2004a, b) which extend the duality properties to non-convex technologies and propose congestion-based measures in this framework.

Producers face uncertainty about technology reliability and performance. The structure of technology and the existence and magnitude of inefficiency are sensitive to the treatment of risk and uncertainty. On productivity measurement under uncertainty see Chambers and Quiggin (2000) and Chambers (2004).

Statistical inference in efficiency analysis

All what we have seen in the previous description of recent developments does not allow for a *statistical* sensitivity analysis, neither for rigorous statistical testing procedures. This is because the previous literature does not relies on a statistical model; there is not, in fact, a definition of the Data Generating Process (DGP) and there is no room for statistical inference based on the construction of confidence intervals, estimation of the bias, statistical tests of hypothesis and so on.

There is instead a new approach, recently developed, which aims exactly at the analysis of the statistical properties of the nonparametric estimators, trying to overcome most limitations of traditional nonparametric methods and allowing for statistical inference and rigorous testing procedures. This literature is the main focus of this book. To the review of the statistical properties of nonparametric frontier estimators we devote the following Chapter 3. Chapter 4 deals in detail with a family of robust nonparametric measures of efficiency, which are more resistent to the influence of outliers and errors in data while having good statistical properties which let inference feasible in this complex framework. Finally, Chapter 5 illustrates and develop further the topic of conditional and robust measures of efficiency and an alternative way to evaluate the impact of external-environmental variables based on conditional measures of efficiency.

Chapter 3

STATISTICAL INFERENCE IN NONPARAMETRIC FRONTIER ESTIMATION

Since efficiency is measured relative to an estimate of the frontier, estimates of efficiency from nonparametric models are subject to uncertainty due to sampling variation. Bootstrap methods hence, may be used to assess this uncertainty by estimating bias, confidence intervals, testing hypothesis and so on. In the following, we summarize the main results available in literature for statistical inference based on nonparametric estimators of frontiers and efficiency scores (DEA/FDH). In so doing we briefly define the Data Generating Process (DGP) and introduce the statistical foundation of nonparametric frontier models. Then we report the main asymptotic results available and the most important to know properties of these estimators. Finally we briefly describe the bootstrap procedure in this complex case as well as its useful applications in the nonparametric frontier estimation context.

3.1 Statistical foundation

The statistical underpinning of nonparametric frontier models aims at defining a statistical model which allows to analyze the statistical properties of the nonparametric estimators. The knowledge of these properties would, in principle, allow for statistical inference (consistency analysis, bias correction, confidence intervals, test of hypothesis, ...) in this framework[14].

As pointed out in Simar (1996), even in a nonparametric setup, no statistical inference can be conducted without a clear definition of a statistical model that describes the DGP.

[14] For a selective survey on statistical inference in nonparametric frontier estimation see Grosskopf (1996). Recent reviews are Simar and Wilson (2000a and 2006a).

Let us start with a simple case where we only have a univariate output and we want to carry out an output oriented efficiency analysis. By considering this simple case, the reader will more easily understand the analogy with standard regression models, parametric or nonparametric ones. The nonparametric frontier can be defined as some unknown function $\psi(x)$ sharing some properties (monotonicity, possibly concavity, ...) that can be expressed as follows:

$$y_i = \psi(x_i) - u_i, \; u_i \geq 0 \tag{3.1}$$

where $y_i \in \mathcal{R}_+$ is the output and $x_i \in \mathcal{R}^p$ is the vector of inputs. The random term $u_i \geq 0$ represents a combination of random elements which explains why an observed firm is below the frontier and so is (output-)inefficient. The statistical model is complete when we define the conditional probability distribution function (pdf) of u, $f(u|x)$. This pdf can be very general, just satisfying some regularity conditions, the conditioning on x indicates that we may consider heteroscedastic models where the distribution of the inefficiencies may depend on the level of the input x. Combined with the pdf on x, this induces a joint pdf on (x, y), $f(x, y)$.

Under such statistical model, the observation of the sample $\mathcal{X} = \{(x_i, y_i), i = 1, \ldots, n\}$ allows one to make inferences on the unknown functional ψ and the unknown $f(x, y)$ or on any of its component, generally, $f(u|x)$ will have some interest for the researcher. The DGP is, hence, completely characterized by $f(x, y)$ which has as support $\Psi = \{(x, y) \in \mathcal{R}_+^p \times \mathcal{R}_+ \mid y \leq \psi(x)\}$. If restrictive parametric assumptions are done on ψ and/or on $f(x, y)$ (typically through parametric assumptions on $f(u|x)$), there exists a lot of tools for doing inference by using appropriate ordinary least squares (OLS) procedures or even maximum likelihood techniques. We will come back to this kind of parametric models in Sections 4.6 and 4.7 where more advanced techniques of estimation will be proposed. In a nonparametric setup, we have to use other tools for doing inference.

In this section we describe a more general statistical model that is useful to derive asymptotic properties of our nonparametric estimators. As we will see below, it also provides the appropriate bootstrap algorithms for doing inference in practice. In fact very few hypothesis are required to define this DGP. We follow here and summarize the presentation as in Simar and Wilson (2006a). These *Statistical Assumptions (SA)* complement the economic assumptions *EA* described in Section 2.3.

SA1: RANDOM SAMPLE. *The sample observations (x_i, y_i) in $\mathcal{X}$ are realizations of identically and independently distributed random variables (X, Y) with probability density function $f(x, y)$ with support $\Psi \subset \mathcal{R}_+^p \times \mathcal{R}_+^q$:* $\text{Prob}((X, Y) \in \Psi) = 1$.

This assumption is common in most empirical studies and just states that the observations are considered as random draws from a population of firms (this is typically what is done in the simple model described above, even in a parametric approach).

SA2: POSITIVENESS. *The density $f(x, y)$ is strictly positive on the boundary of Ψ and is continuous in any direction toward the interior of Ψ.*
This is a sufficient (but not necessary) condition for proving the consistency of nonparametric estimators. It says that the probability of observing firms in an open neighborhood of the frontier is strictly positive. Note that assumption SA2 could be relaxed but at a cost of losing some performance of the nonparametric estimators (rate of convergence).

The next assumption is not strictly speaking a statistical assumption but is a technical condition which insures that the true boundary is sufficiently smooth.

SA3: SMOOTHNESS. *For all (x, y) in the interior of Ψ, the functions $\theta(x, y)$ and $\lambda(x, y)$ are differentiable in both arguments.*
It is a sufficient condition used by Kneip, Simar and Wilson (2003) to derive the asymptotic distribution of the DEA estimator, for the FDH estimator (where Ψ is not assumed to be convex), only Lipschitz continuity of the functions is required in Park, Simar and Weiner (2000).

Summing up, the DGP $\mathcal{P}$ is completely characterized by the knowledge of $f(x, y)$ and of its support Ψ with the regularity conditions (SA1–SA3) described above. Hence, we can write $\mathcal{P} = \mathcal{P}(\Psi, f(\cdot, \cdot))$.

3.2 Introducing stochastic noise in the model

The statistical model defined above introduces the stochastic elements which allow to describe how a random observation (X_i, Y_i) is generated on the attainable set Ψ. The DGP is characterized by the joint probability density function $f(x, y)$. We will see below that this allows to make inference on the quantities of interest in efficiency analysis, even if the complexity of the problem will force the practitioner to use bootstrap algorithms for practical purposes. We will also see in Chapter 4, that this statistical model can also be reformulated in terms of nonstandard cumulative distribution functions, where the Farrell-Debreu efficiency scores can be shown to be defined from their properties. This will provide a natural way for introducing the robust estimators of the frontier and of the efficiencies based on partial-frontier concepts.

All these approaches contain stochastic elements in a so-called *deterministic frontier* framework, where it is supposed that all the observations $(X_i, Y_i), i = 1 \ldots, n$ belong to the attainable set Ψ. Mathematically we write $\text{Prob}\{(X_i, Y_i) \in \Psi\} = 1$. This seems to be a quite natural assumption in most applications but this implies that no stochastic noise is allowed in the model. In econometrics, stochastic noise is generally introduced in regression models, for instance, for allowing error in measurements, random shocks, chance,... In a frontier setup, we refer then to *stochastic frontier models* where, till now, most of the work in the literature has been done in a complete parametric setup. Pioneering work refer to Aigner, Lovell and Schmidt (1977) and Meeusen and van den Broeck (1977), with other developments in Greene (1990, 1993) and Stevenson (1980). A recent comprehensive reference is Kumbhakar and Lovell (2000).

All these approaches rely on very restrictive parametric assumption about the shape of the frontier and about the distribution of the efficiencies (some non-negative random variable like half-normal, truncated normal, exponential, or gamma densities) and about the distribution of the noise (usually a normal variate). Usually maximum likelihood estimators (MLE) are derived and statistical inference is rather straightforward and valid if the model is correctly specified. Parametric estimators incur the risk of misspecification which generally results in inconsistency. Beside the restrictive parametric assumptions and the risk of misspecification, parametric stochastic frontier models suffers from other problems in finite sample situation (a common situation for the practitioner). We only briefly mention here the identification problems as described in Ritter and Simar (1997) and the MLE computations themselves along with the difficulty of inference on the efficiency scores as described in Simar and Wilson (2005).

Nonparametric estimators avoid the risk of misspecification but at a cost of complexity. As pointed in Simar and Wilson (2006a), introducing noise in DEA/FDH framework is still a challenge and an open issue. The problem is difficult because without some restrictions on the model, a stochastic nonparametric model is not identified. Hall and Simar (2002) discuss this issue in details. However, Hall and Simar show that if the noise is not too large (in terms of noise to signal ratio) a reasonable estimator of the boundary can be found by identifying the point near the deterministic boundary where a nonparametric estimator of the density of the noisy data presents a maximum of the absolute value of its gradient. These ideas have been extended to the multivariate setup in Simar (2003b) where stochastic versions of DEA/FDH estimators have been developed when the noise is of moderate size. In particular the method provides versions of the DEA/FDH very robust to outliers and extreme values.

In a different setup, Kumbhakar, Park, Simar and Tsionas (2004) propose a general approach for nonparametric stochastic frontier model using local maximum likelihood methods. The idea is to start with an anchorage parametric model, in the line of Aigner, Lovell and Schmidt (1977) and then by localizing, generate a very flexible model approximating a much wider class of models than the chosen anchorage model.

In the case of a panel of data, much more information is available and the identification problem can more easily be handled. This was done in Kneip and Simar (1996) where a general nonparametric model is proposed in this particular setup. The drawback is that in practice, a large number of time periods is needed for getting sensible results. New directions in this area have been proposed by Henderson and Simar (2005).

In this book we focus the presentation on deterministic frontier models, so that the popular nonparametric envelopment estimators can be considered. But since we know these estimators are sensible to extreme value and outliers (due to the absence of noise in the model), we pay special attention to develop estimators which are robust to these extreme points: this will be the major topic of Chapter 4. In the next sections we summarize the main known statistical properties of the DEA/FDH estimators and we indicate how the bootstrap can be implemented to solve practical inferential problems.

3.3 Asymptotic results

When estimating a statistical model from a "partial" information coming from a sample of size n, a natural question which should be raised is the following: "Has the estimate I obtain anything to see with the unknown characteristic of the model it is supposed to estimate?".

3.3.1 Consistency

The first minimal property one would like to achieve is *consistency*. Roughly speaking consistency means that if the sample size increases, an estimator $\widehat{\theta}$ will converge to the true but unknown value θ it is supposed to estimate. Mathematically, we will say that $\widehat{\theta} \xrightarrow{p} \theta$ as $n \to \infty$, meaning that as the sample size increases to infinity, the probability of the error $|\widehat{\theta} - \theta|$ being greater than any positive value $\varepsilon > 0$ converges to zero. This is a minimal property that an estimator should have to be reliable. Another important issue is then the rate of convergence of the consistent estimator. It indicates the possibility of getting sensible results with finite samples estimators. In classical parametric statistics (like linear regression models), estimators achieve $\sqrt{n}$-consistency, meaning that the order of the error of estimation is decreasing to zero like $n^{-1/2}$ when $n \to \infty$. We write:

$$\widehat{\theta} - \theta = O_p(n^{-1/2}). \tag{3.2}$$

In nonparametric frontier estimation, for decades nobody worried about these issues, neither for the DEA nor for the FDH estimators. The first result which appeared was due to Banker (1993), who proved the consistency of the DEA efficiency scores in the very particular univariate case (one input for input orientation, or one output in the output orientation). For instance, in the input orientation (one input) the obtained result can be written as:

$$\widehat{\theta}_{DEA}(x, y) \xrightarrow{p} \theta(x, y), \tag{3.3}$$

where no indication was given about the rates of convergence. These rates where obtained for the DEA (where convexity of Ψ is required) and for the FDH case (where convexity of Ψ is not required) in Korostelev, Simar and Tsybakov (1995). For instance in the output oriented case (one output) they obtained:

$$d_\triangle(\widehat{\Psi}_{FDH}, \Psi) = O_p(n^{-\frac{1}{p+1}}),$$
$$d_\triangle(\widehat{\Psi}_{DEA}, \Psi) = O_p(n^{-\frac{2}{p+2}}),$$

where $d_\triangle(\widehat{\Psi}, \Psi)$ is the Lebesgue measure of the difference between the two sets and where p is the number of inputs (similar rates are obtained for the corresponding efficiency measures). The rates of convergence reflect the *curse of dimensionality* typical of many nonparametric statistical techniques; if p is large, the estimators exhibit very low rates of convergence, and much larger quantity of data is needed to get sensible estimates (*i.e.* to avoid large variances and very wide confidence interval estimates) than in the case of small number of inputs p. Note that for $p = 1$ we obtain a better rate $n^{-2/3}$ than the standard parametric rate $n^{-1/2}$.

Much later, Kneip, Park and Simar (1998) for the DEA case and Park, Simar and Weiner (2000) for the FDH case obtained the proof of the consistency of the estimated efficiency scores in the full multivariate setup ($p, q > 1$) along with their rates of convergence. The difficulty here was to handle the radial nature of the difference between the efficiency scores. Formally they obtain:

$$\widehat{\theta}_{DEA}(x, y) - \theta(x, y) = O_p(n^{-\frac{2}{p+q+1}}), \tag{3.4}$$
$$\widehat{\theta}_{FDH}(x, y) - \theta(x, y) = O_p(n^{-\frac{1}{p+q}}). \tag{3.5}$$

These results again reflect the curse of dimensionality which is even worse for the multivariate case since the convergence rates are affected by $p + q$ rather than merely by p (or q), as for the former univariate case.

These results are encouraging: the methods used by researchers since decades where indeed consistent! But these results are of little practical importance for doing inference. To achieve this we need the sampling distributions of the estimators in order to derive the eventual bias, or to compute its standard deviation or even better to build confidence intervals for individual efficiency scores $\theta(x, y)$.

In this complex situation, the only hope is to obtain asymptotic results, *i.e.* a reasonable approximation of the sampling distribution of the estimator when n is large enough (in the same spirit that a Central Limit Theorem gives an approximate normal distribution of a sample mean when n is large enough). We will see below that if today theoretical results are available, they will be of little practical interest but will be useful to prove the consistency of the bootstrap alternative.

3.3.2 Sampling distributions

The first available result is for the bivariate DEA case ($p = q = 1$) and is due to Gijbels, Mammen, Park and Simar (1999). For instance, for the input orientation, they obtain the asymptotic result, when $n \to \infty$,

$$n^{\frac{2}{3}}\left(\widehat{\theta}_{DEA}(x,y) - \theta(x,y)\right) \overset{\text{asy.}}{\sim} F(\cdot,\cdot) \tag{3.6}$$

where $F(\cdot,\cdot)$ is a regular distribution function known up to some unknown constants. These constants depend on the DGP and are related to the curvature of the frontier and the value of the joint density $f(x,y)$ at the corresponding frontier point $(\theta(x,y)x, y)$ in the input orientation). Gijbels, Mammen, Park and Simar (1999) provide also the tabulation of the quantiles of a pivotal correspondent of $F(\cdot,\cdot)$. This allows to build confidence intervals for the efficiency score $\theta(x,y)$.

The multivariate DEA case ($p, q \geq 1$) was much more difficult to handle, due to the difficulty of characterizing the dominating facet of (x,y) in $\widehat{\Psi}_{DEA}$ and due to the radial nature of the Farrell-Debreu measures. Kneip, Simar and Wilson (2003) obtain the following result, when $n \to \infty$,

$$n^{\frac{2}{(p+q+1)}}\left(\frac{\widehat{\theta}_{DEA}(x,y)}{\theta(x,y)} - 1\right) \overset{\text{asy.}}{\sim} Q(.) \tag{3.7}$$

where no closed analytical form for $Q(.)$ is available, but only a mathematical expression showing its existence and its good properties (in particular that it is a non-degenerate distribution function). Of course a similar result could be obtained for the difference $\widehat{\theta}_{DEA}(x,y) - \theta(x,y)$ rather than for the ratio and also for the output oriented case. But this result is of little practical importance because the limiting distribution is difficult to manipulate. However this result is of fundamental theoretical importance to prove the consistency of the appropriate bootstrap approach (see below). Hence, the bootstrap will appear to be the only practical alternative to do inference in this setup.

The multivariate FDH case ($p, q \geq 1$) was easier to handle and Park, Simar and Weiner (2000) derive the following result, when $n \to \infty$,

$$n^{\frac{1}{(p+q)}}\left(\widehat{\theta}_{FDH}(x,y) - \theta(x,y)\right) \overset{\text{asy.}}{\sim} Weibull(\cdot,\cdot) \tag{3.8}$$

here, again, the limiting Weibull depends on some unknown parameters depending on the DGP but which can be estimated. This result allows to obtain bias corrected estimators and confidence intervals for the efficiency scores, however, Park, Simar and Weiner illustrate how imprecise is the asymptotic distribution when $p+q$ is large with moderate sample sizes (for instance, they recommend n to be larger than say 1000 if $p+q=5$). Again, similar results are derived for the output oriented case.

Therefore, as a conclusion, even if these results have a real theoretical importance and even if they are potentially useful to estimate asymptotic bias and variance, as well as asymptotic confidence intervals, they remain asymptotic results which may be misleading when used with small or moderate sample sizes. Moreover, additional noise is introduced when estimates of the unknown parameters of the limiting distributions are used in constructing estimates of confidence intervals. We note also that in the DEA case there are no closed analytical forms for the multivariate case. So the bootstrap seems to be an unavoidable alternative.

3.4 Bootstrap techniques and applications

The bootstrap is indeed an attractive alternative to the theoretical limiting distributions described above. The bootstrap is intended to provide approximations of the sampling distributions of $\widehat{\theta}(x,y) - \theta(x,y)$ or of $\dfrac{\widehat{\theta}(x,y)}{\theta(x,y)}$ where (x,y) is the unit under interest. The nonparametric estimator $\widehat{\theta}(x,y)$ can be the FDH estimator (if we do not assume convexity of Ψ) or the DEA estimator. The presentation below is for the DEA case, we will summarize later the available results for the FDH case. We follow the presentation of Simar and Wilson (2000a, 2006a).

The bootstrap is a data-based simulation method for statistical inference. As reported by Efron and Tibshirani (1993, p.5), the use of the term bootstrap derives from the phrase *to pull oneself up by one's bootstrap*, widely thought to be based on one of the eighteenth century Adventures of Baron Munchausen, by Rudolph Erich Raspe[15]. The essence of the bootstrap idea (Efron 1979, Efron and Tibshirani, 1993) is to approximate the sampling distributions of interest by simulating (or mimicking) the DGP.

The basic idea behind the bootstrap can be summarized as follows. Consider the simple problem where a DGP (a statistical model) $\mathcal{P}$ generates a random sample $\mathcal{X} = \{X_1, \ldots, X_n\}$ of size n. Suppose we want to investigate the sampling distribution of an estimator $\widehat{\theta}$ of some unknown parameter θ. In general, θ is one particular characteristic of the DGP $\mathcal{P}$ and $\widehat{\theta} = \widehat{\theta}(\mathcal{X})$ is a statistics function of the random sample $\mathcal{X}$. The knowledge of $\mathcal{L}(\widehat{\theta}(\mathcal{X}))$, the sampling distribution of $\widehat{\theta}(\mathcal{X})$, is all what we need to evaluate the bias, the standard deviation of $\widehat{\theta}(\mathcal{X})$ and to derive bounds of confidence intervals of any desired level for θ.

[15]The Baron had fallen to the bottom of a deep lake. Just when it looked like all was lost, he thought to pick himself up by his own bootstraps.

Except in very few simple problems (like estimating the mean and the variance of a normal model) the sampling distribution $\mathcal{L}(\widehat{\theta}(\mathcal{X}))$ is unknown or only asymptotic approximations are available. The aim of the bootstrap is to provide an approximation of this distribution which will be easy to obtain by using Monte-Carlo approximations. Under regularity conditions the only thing that will be required to implement the bootstrap is a consistent estimator of the DGP $\mathcal{P}$.

Indeed, if this DGP $\mathcal{P}$ would be known, it would be very easy to approximate the sampling distribution of $\widehat{\theta}(\mathcal{X})$ without any mathematical developments, by a simple Monte-Carlo experiment that the computer could perform for us. We could indeed simulate a large number of times a random sample $\mathcal{X}^\star$ from $\mathcal{P}$ and then compute the corresponding value of $\widehat{\theta}(\mathcal{X}^\star)$ in each Monte-Carlo trial. By repeating this exercise a larger number of time the Monte-Carlo empirical distribution of the observed values $\widehat{\theta}(\mathcal{X}^\star)$ would provide a Monte-Carlo approximation of the true but unknown sampling distribution $\mathcal{L}(\widehat{\theta}(\mathcal{X}))$. This is a direct consequence of the strong law of large number and the quality of the approximation depends only on the number of replications in the Monte-Carlo exercise (that the user can chose as large as she/he wants): no mathematics is needed here, only some computing time on the computer that will perform this simulation.

The bootstrap principle is now easy to explain: since $\mathcal{P}$ is unknown, we will *plug-in* an appropriate consistent estimator $\widehat{\mathcal{P}}$ in the place of $\mathcal{P}$ in the Monte-Carlo experiment above. Here we will call a bootstrap sample a random sample $\mathcal{X}^\star$ generated from $\widehat{\mathcal{P}}$. If some care is taken on how to generate these bootstrap samples, it can be proven, when the bootstrap works, that the empirical (Monte-Carlo) bootstrap distribution of $\widehat{\theta}(\mathcal{X}^\star)$, which is conditional on $\widehat{\mathcal{P}}$, approximates the unknown $\mathcal{L}(\widehat{\theta}(\mathcal{X}))$. In fact as we will see below, to build confidence intervals it is more appropriate to rather approximate the unknown distribution of $\widehat{\theta}(\mathcal{X}) - \theta$ by the bootstrap distribution of $\widehat{\theta}(\mathcal{X}^\star) - \widehat{\theta}(\mathcal{X})$ conditional on the estimate $\widehat{\mathcal{P}}$. The error of estimation $\widehat{\theta}(\mathcal{X}) - \theta$ is sometimes refereed as the estimation error in the *real world* whereas, $\widehat{\theta}(\mathcal{X}^\star) - \widehat{\theta}(\mathcal{X})$ is the error of estimation in the *bootstrap world* where the true unknown $\mathcal{P}$ and θ have been replaced by the known observed $\widehat{\mathcal{P}}$ and $\widehat{\theta}(\mathcal{X})$.

In many simple applications, the easiest way to generate a random sample $\mathcal{X}^\star$ according an estimate $\widehat{\mathcal{P}}$ of $\mathcal{P}$, is to mimic what has been done in the real world. In the real world $\mathcal{X} = \{X_1, \ldots, X_n\}$ is generated from $\mathcal{P}$, so a nonparametric estimator of $\mathcal{P}$ could be chosen as the empirical process which gives a mass $1/n$ at each observed sample point $X_i \in \mathcal{X}$. So a bootstrap sample will be defined as $\mathcal{X}^\star = \{X_1^\star, \ldots, X_n^\star\}$, where each $X_j^\star$ is obtained by drawing with replacement from the n values $\{X_1, \ldots, X_n\}$. This is sometimes refereed as the *naive* bootstrap and is very easy to implement.

When we say that the bootstrap works we mean that the bootstrap approximation is consistent, or in other words that when the sample size n of $\mathcal{X}$ increases, the bootstrap distribution of $\widehat{\theta}(\mathcal{X}^\star)-\widehat{\theta}(\mathcal{X})$ conditional on $\widehat{\mathcal{P}}$ converge to the true distribution of $\widehat{\theta}(\mathcal{X}) - \theta$. This is the crucial point for the bootstrap. It is often true in statistics that the bootstrap (when correctly implemented) is consistent, but it is well known also that there are cases where the bootstrap is inconsistent. This may depend on the model, on the properties of the estimate $\widehat{\mathcal{P}}$ but also *on the way to generate random samples* $\mathcal{X}^\star$ from $\widehat{\mathcal{P}}$. This is particularly true in the case of estimating boundaries or support of random variables, as it is the case in frontier models. This issue is discussed below where consistent solutions are provided.

3.4.1 Bootstrap in frontier models

The first use of the bootstrap in frontier models is attributed to Simar (1992). Its development for nonparametric envelopment estimators was introduced by Simar and Wilson (1998).[16]

The definition of the DGP is a crucial step for the bootstrap procedure. If the DGP is not defined, it is not clear which process the bootstrap is mimicking. We have seen above that the DGP can be denoted by $\mathcal{P} = \mathcal{P}(\Psi, f(\cdot,\cdot))$ to stress the fact that it is fully characterized by the knowledge of Ψ and of the joint density $f(x, y)$ in the input-output space.

We describe the general setting adopting an input oriented framework with VRS (Variable Returns to Scale) DEA. For practical purposes, it is advantageous to express the input-oriented efficiency in terms of the Shephard (1970) input-distance function introduced in Section 2.3 and defined in (2.12) as $\delta(x, y) = (\theta(x, y))^{-1}$. Extensions to the output-oriented framework are straightforward. The objective is thus to investigate the *sampling distribution* of $(\widehat{\delta}(x, y) - \delta(x, y))$ for a given DMU (x, y).

Due to our knowledge of the DGP $\mathcal{P}$, we can produce a consistent estimator $\widehat{\mathcal{P}}$ of $\mathcal{P}$ from the data $\mathcal{X}$: $\widehat{\mathcal{P}} = \mathcal{P}(\widehat{\Psi}, \widehat{f}(\cdot,\cdot))$. So, in the *true world*, $\mathcal{P}$ and $\delta(x, y)$ are unknown ((x, y) is a given fixed point of interest), but in the *bootstrap world*, the consistent estimate $\widehat{\mathcal{P}}$ and $\widehat{\delta}(x, y)$ are known and can take the place of $\mathcal{P}$ and of $\delta(x, y)$.

Therefore, we can generate data sets from $\widehat{\mathcal{P}}$. Denote by $\mathcal{X}^\star = \{(X_i^\star, Y_i^\star), i = 1, ..., n\}$ a data-set generated by $\widehat{\mathcal{P}}$. This pseudo-sample defines the corresponding quantities $\widehat{\Psi}^\star$ and $\widehat{\delta}^\star(x, y)$ which can be viewed as estimators of

[16] Some other bootstrap procedures have been presented in literature, but their inconsistence have been demonstrated, see below.

the corresponding quantities $\widehat{\Psi}$ and $\widehat{\delta}(x, y)$. They are defined by:

$$\widehat{\Psi}^\star = \Big\{(x, y) \in \mathcal{R}^{p+q} \mid y \leq \sum_{i=1}^{n} \gamma_i Y_i^\star; x \geq \gamma_i X_i^\star; \\ \sum_{i=1}^{n} \gamma_i = 1; \gamma_i \geq 0; i = 1, ..., n\Big\} \tag{3.9}$$

$$\widehat{\delta}^\star(x, y) = \sup\Big\{\delta \mid (\frac{x}{\delta}, y) \in \widehat{\Psi}^\star\Big\}.$$

The latter can be calculated through the following linear program:

$$(\widehat{\delta}^\star(x, y))^{-1} = \min\Big\{\theta > 0 \mid y \leq \sum_{i=1}^{n} \gamma_i Y_i^\star;\ \theta x \geq \sum_{i=1}^{n} \gamma_i X_i^\star; \\ \sum_{i=1}^{n} \gamma_i = 1; \gamma_i \geq 0;\ i = 1, ..., n\Big\}. \tag{3.10}$$

Conditionally on $\mathcal{X}$, the sampling distribution of $\widehat{\delta}^\star(x, y))$ is (in principle) *known* since $\widehat{\mathcal{P}}$ is known, although it may be difficult to compute analytically. Monte Carlo methods can be used to easily approximate the sampling distribution of $\widehat{\delta}^\star(x, y)$.

Using $\widehat{\mathcal{P}}$ to generate B samples $\mathcal{X}_b^\star$, for $b = 1, ..., B$, and applying the linear program described above, for the given unit (x, y) we obtain a set of pseudo estimates $\{\widehat{\delta}_b^\star(x, y)\}_{b=1}^B$. The empirical distribution $\{\widehat{\delta}_b^\star(x, y)\}_{b=1}^B$ is the Monte Carlo approximation of the distribution of $\widehat{\delta}^\star(x, y)$ conditional on $\widehat{\mathcal{P}}$.

If the bootstrap method is consistent, the available bootstrap distribution of $\widehat{\delta}^\star(x, y)$ will "mimic" the original unknown sampling distribution of the estimator of interest $\widehat{\delta}(x, y)$. More precisely:

$$(\widehat{\delta}^\star(x, y) - \widehat{\delta}(x, y))|\widehat{\mathcal{P}} \overset{\text{approx.}}{\sim} (\widehat{\delta}(x, y) - \delta(x, y))|\mathcal{P}. \tag{3.11}$$

Since the left hand side of (3.11) is available (though the Monte-Carlo exercise), it can be used to provide properties usually obtained from the right-hand side. In particular we can use the bootstrap approximation to estimate the bias of the DEA estimator or to estimate the quantiles of the sampling distribution of $(\widehat{\delta}(x, y) - \delta(x, y))$ in order to build confidence intervals.

In Table 3.1 below, the analogy between the original inferential problem and the bootstrap is described in terms of an analogy between the *real world*, where we want to make inference about the parameter $\delta(x, y)$ but most of the desired quantities are unknown, and the *bootstrap world*, where we mimic the real world but where everything is *known* and so can be computed or simulated by Monte-Carlo methods. In practice, as described in the next subsections, the available $G_{\widehat{\mathcal{P}}}(t)$ will serve to approximate the unknown $G_{\mathcal{P}}(t)$ (for correcting bias or evaluate standard deviation of estimates) and $H_{\widehat{\mathcal{P}}}(t)$ will be used to estimate the quantiles of the unknown $H_{\mathcal{P}}(t)$ providing bootstrap confidence intervals.

Table 3.1. Summary of the bootstrap principle for inference on $\delta(x, y)$.

REAL WORLD	BOOTSTRAP WORLD
$\mathcal{P} = \mathcal{P}\big(\Psi, f(\cdot,\cdot)\big)$ unknown $\delta(x, y)$ unknown	Given $\mathcal{X}$, $\widehat{\mathcal{P}} = \mathcal{P}\big(\widehat{\Psi}, \widehat{f}(\cdot,\cdot)\big)$ is known $\widehat{\delta}(x, y)$ is known
DGP $\mathcal{P}$ generates $\mathcal{X}$ $\Downarrow$ $\widehat{\delta}(x, y)$ estimator of $\delta(x, y)$	DGP* $\widehat{\mathcal{P}}$ generates $\mathcal{X}^*$ $\Downarrow$ $\widehat{\delta}^*(x, y)$ estimator of $\widehat{\delta}(x, y)$
Sampling distribution $G_{\mathcal{P}}(t) = \text{Prob}_{\mathcal{P}}(\widehat{\delta}(x, y) \leq t)$	Bootstrap distribution $G_{\widehat{\mathcal{P}}}(t) = \text{Prob}_{\widehat{\mathcal{P}}}(\widehat{\delta}^*(x, y) \leq t)$
Moments $E_{\mathcal{P}}(\widehat{\delta}(x, y))$ $Var_{\mathcal{P}}(\widehat{\delta}(x, y))$	Moments $E_{\widehat{\mathcal{P}}}(\widehat{\delta}^*(x, y))$ $Var_{\widehat{\mathcal{P}}}(\widehat{\delta}^*(x, y))$
$W = \widehat{\delta}(x, y) - \delta(x, y)$ $H_{\mathcal{P}}(t) = \text{Prob}_{\mathcal{P}}(W \leq t) \Rightarrow a_\beta = H_{\mathcal{P}}^{-1}(\beta)$ $\Downarrow$ CI for $\delta(x, y)$ $\left[\widehat{\delta}(x, y) - a_{1-\alpha/2}, \widehat{\delta}(x, y) - a_{\alpha/2}\right]$	$W^* = \widehat{\delta}^*(x, y) - \widehat{\delta}(x, y)$ $H_{\widehat{\mathcal{P}}}(t) = \text{Prob}_{\widehat{\mathcal{P}}}(W^* \leq t) \Rightarrow \widehat{a}_\beta = H_{\widehat{\mathcal{P}}}^{-1}(\beta)$ $\Downarrow$ Bootstrap CI for $\delta(x, y)$ $\left[\widehat{\delta}(x, y) - \widehat{a}_{1-\alpha/2}, \widehat{\delta}(x, y) - \widehat{a}_{\alpha/2}\right]$

3.4.2 Correcting the bias of $\widehat{\delta}(x, y)$

An estimator is a random variable since it is computed as a function of a random sample. An unbiased estimator has the desirable property that its mean is equal to the target value of the parameter being estimated. In our case, we know by construction that the DEA estimator $\widehat{\delta}(x, y)$ is a biased estimator of $\delta(x, y)$ (for the input Shephard distance considered here, $\widehat{\delta}(x, y) < \delta(x, y)$

with probability one, so the true $E_{\mathcal{P}}(\widehat{\delta}(x,y)) < \delta(x,y))$. Formally the bias of $\widehat{\delta}(x,y)$ is defined as:

$$\text{bias}(\widehat{\delta}(x,y)) = E_{\mathcal{P}}(\widehat{\delta}(x,y)) - \delta(x,y), \tag{3.12}$$

which of course cannot be computed, because the sampling distribution of $\widehat{\delta}(x,y)$, denoted $G_{\mathcal{P}}(t)$ in Table 3.1, is unavailable (even the asymptotic approximation is too complicated to handle).

However the bootstrap approximation is available and so we will estimate the bias of $\widehat{\delta}(x,y)$ by the following:

$$\widehat{\text{bias}}(\widehat{\delta}(x,y)) = E_{\widehat{\mathcal{P}}}(\widehat{\delta}^{\star}(x,y)) - \widehat{\delta}(x,y). \tag{3.13}$$

In practice, the expectation is given by the mean of the Monte-Carlo realizations of $\{\widehat{\delta}_b^{\star}(x,y)\}_{b=1}^{B}$. So our bootstrap estimate of the bias is obtained through:

$$\widehat{\text{bias}}(\widehat{\delta}(x,y)) \approx \frac{1}{B}\sum_{b=1}^{B} \widehat{\delta}_b^{\star}(x,y) - \widehat{\delta}(x,y). \tag{3.14}$$

In the same way the standard deviation of the DEA estimator $\widehat{\delta}(x,y)$ is obtained as the square-root of the variance of the bootstrap distribution denoted $G_{\widehat{\mathcal{P}}}(t)$ in Table 3.1. Namely:

$$\widehat{\text{std}}^2(\widehat{\delta}(x,y)) \approx \frac{1}{B}\sum_{b=1}^{B} \widehat{\delta}_b^{\star,2}(x,y) - \Big(\frac{1}{B}\sum_{b=1}^{B} \widehat{\delta}_b^{\star}(x,y)\Big)^2. \tag{3.15}$$

A bias corrected estimator is then obtained by defining:

$$\begin{aligned} \widetilde{\delta}(x,y) &= \widehat{\delta}(x,y) - \widehat{\text{bias}}(\widehat{\delta}(x,y)) \\ &= 2\,\widehat{\delta}(x,y) - \frac{1}{B}\sum_{b=1}^{B} \widehat{\delta}_b^{\star}(x,y). \end{aligned} \tag{3.16}$$

However, it is well known that correcting for the bias introduces additional noise (increasing the variance of the estimator). As a rule of thumb, Efron and Tibshirani (1993) recommend not to correct for the bias unless $|\widehat{\text{bias}}(\widehat{\delta}(x,y))| > \widehat{\text{std}}(\widehat{\delta}(x,y))/4$. In practice, due to inherent bias of the DEA estimator, the bias-correction has almost always to be performed. Numerical examples are provided in the second part of this book.

3.4.3 Bootstrap confidence intervals for $\delta(x,y)$

The construction of confidence intervals is obtained by determining the quantile of $H_{\mathcal{P}}(t)$, the sampling distribution of $W = \widehat{\delta}(x,y) - \delta(x,y)$. Indeed, if

$H_{\mathcal{P}}(\cdot)$ were known, it would be easy to find, for instance, the values $a_{0.025}$ and $a_{0.975}$ such that:

$$\text{Prob}_{\mathcal{P}}(a_{0.025} \leq \widehat{\delta}(x,y) - \delta(x,y) \leq a_{0.975}) = 0.95,$$

leading to the confidence interval of level 0.95 for $\delta(x,y)$:

$$\text{Prob}_{\mathcal{P}}(\widehat{\delta}(x,y) - a_{0.975} \leq \delta(x,y) \leq \widehat{\delta}(x,y) - a_{0.025}) = 0.95. \quad (3.17)$$

Since the quantiles a_β are unknown, the quantiles of the bootstrap distribution of $W^\star = \widehat{\delta}^\star(x,y) - \widehat{\delta}(x,y)$, denoted by $H_{\widehat{\mathcal{P}}}(t)$ in Table 3.1, will provide the appropriate approximation. If $\hat{a}_{0.025}$ and $\hat{a}_{0.975}$ are such that

$$\text{Prob}_{\widehat{\mathcal{P}}}(\hat{a}_{0.025} \leq \widehat{\delta}^\star(x,y) - \widehat{\delta}(x,y) \leq \hat{a}_{0.975}) = 0.95,$$

the bootstrap confidence interval for $\delta(x,y)$ is obtained as:

$$\text{Prob}_{\mathcal{P}}(\widehat{\delta}(x,y) - \hat{a}_{0.975} \leq \delta(x,y) \leq \widehat{\delta}(x,y) - \hat{a}_{0.025}) \approx 0.95. \quad (3.18)$$

The quantiles $\hat{a}_\beta$ are directly obtained from the quantiles of the Monte-Carlo distribution of the values $\{\widehat{\delta}_b^\star(x,y)\}_{b=1}^B$ themselves as follows, for all $\beta \in [0,1]$:

$$\hat{a}_\beta = \hat{c}_\beta - \widehat{\delta}(x,y), \quad (3.19)$$

where $\hat{c}_\beta$ is the β-quantile of the empirical distribution of the values $\{\widehat{\delta}_b^\star(x,y)\}_{b=1}^B$. Note that the method just described and known as the *basic bootstrap* method for building confidence intervals, automatically adjusts for the bias of the DEA estimates.

The amplitude (the length) of the obtained interval will reflect the uncertainty we have about the real value of the efficiency score of the unit operating at the level (x,y) and estimated as being $\widehat{\delta}(x,y)$. This uncertainty may vary from place to place, it depends where (x,y) is located: if the DEA frontier above (x,y) is determined by many sample points (X_i, Y_i), the precision can be great but if it is only determined by very few (even only one) sample point, the length of the confidence interval will be much greater, reflecting the uncertainty we have above the real position of the reference frontier for this point (x,y). We know also from the results from Gijbels, Mammen, Park and Simar (1999) that the sampling variation of the estimates also depends on the curvature of the real efficient frontier above (x,y). This will be illustrated in some of the applications described in the second part of this book.

3.4.4 Is the bootstrap consistent?

The bootstrap is consistent if the relation (3.11) holds. This will depend on the way the pseudo-samples are generated. Since $\mathcal{P}$ generates $\mathcal{X} = \{(X_i, Y_i), i =$

$1, ..., n\}$, a *naive* estimator of $\mathcal{P}$ would be $\mathcal{P}(\widehat{\Psi}, \widehat{f}(\cdot,\cdot))$ where $\widehat{f}(\cdot,\cdot)$ would be the empirical distribution function of (X_i, Y_i), defined as the discrete distribution that put a probability $\frac{1}{n}$ on each point (X_i, Y_i). Then a bootstrap sample $\mathcal{X}^\star = \{(X_i^\star, Y_i^\star), i = 1, ..., n\}$ would simply be obtained by randomly sampling with replacement from $\mathcal{X}$.

Unfortunately, it is well known from the bootstrap literature (Bickel and Freedman, 1981, Efron and Tibshirani, 1993) that in a boundary estimation framework, this bootstrap procedure does not provide a consistent approximation of the desired sampling distribution as in (3.11). Simar and Wilson (1999a, b) discuss this issue in the context of multivariate frontier estimation. As illustrated below, the problem comes from the fact that in the naive bootstrap, the efficient facet that determines in the original sample $\mathcal{X}$ the value of $\widehat{\delta}$ appears too often, and with a fixed probability, in the pseudo-samples $\mathcal{X}_b^\star$ and this fixed probability does not vanish even when $n \to \infty$.

Two solutions have been proposed to overcome this problem: either *subsampling*, meaning that we will draw pseudo-samples of size m smaller than n, say $m = [n^\gamma]$, where $\gamma < 1$ and $[a]$ stands for integer part of a number a or *smoothing techniques*, meaning the use of a smooth estimate $\widehat{f}(\cdot,\cdot)$, in place of the discrete empirical one of the naive approach. Kneip, Simar and Wilson (2003) prove the consistency of both approaches in the case of strictly convex attainable sets Ψ.

Subsampling techniques

Subsampling is certainly the easiest procedure to apply: we follow the procedure described above, with the only difference that the pseudo-samples $\mathcal{X}_{m,b}^\star$ for $b = 1, \ldots, B$ are of size m in place of size n and so the reference sets in (3.9) and (3.10) are determined by these pseudo-samples of size m only. The procedure is consistent for any value of $\gamma < 1$, but the drawback is that data-driven procedures for determining an optimal value of γ for a particular data-set have not yet been investigated. In practice, several values of γ in the range $[0.5, 1)$ can be tried and values of γ where the results show some stability indicate reasonable choices for this parameter.

Smoothing techniques

The idea of the smooth bootstrap (see Siverman and Young, 1987) is to draw the pseudo observations $(X_i^\star, Y_i^\star)$ from a *smooth* estimate of the density $f(x, y)$. We know how to produce such smooth estimates (see *e.g.* Silverman, 1986, Scott, 1992 or Simonoff, 1996) by using kernel estimators but the problem is complicated here by the fact that the range of (x, y) is bounded by the boundary of the unknown Ψ. Simar and Wilson (1998, 2000b) propose procedures which are easy to apply. These procedures will exploit the radial nature of the Farrell-Debreu efficiency scores and of the Shephard distance functions.

To take this radial nature into account, it is easier to transform the Cartesian coordinates (x, y) into polar coordinates for the input vector x when input efficiency scores are investigated as it is the case in our presentation (the output oriented case would use polar coordinates for the output vector y).

The polar coordinates for x are defined by its modulus $\omega = \omega(x) \in \mathcal{R}^+$ where $\omega(x) = \sqrt{(x'x)}$, and its angle $\eta = \eta(x) \in [0, \frac{\pi}{2}]^{p-1}$, where for $j = 1, ..., p-1, \eta_j = \arctan(\frac{x^{j+1}}{x^1})$ if $x^1 > 0$ or $\eta_j = \frac{\pi}{2}$ if $x^1 = 0$.

The density $f(x, y)$ can be transformed, or represented by a density $f(\omega, \eta, y)$ on the new coordinates and the latter joint density can be decomposed as:

$$f(\omega, \eta, y) = f(\omega \mid \eta, y) f(\eta \mid y) f(y), \tag{3.20}$$

where we suppose all the conditionals exist. So that for the frontier point $x^\partial(y)$ on the ray defined by the input vector x has modulus for the output level y is given by $\omega(x^\partial(y)) = \inf\{\omega \in \mathcal{R}_+ | f(\omega|y, \eta) > 0\}$, and $\delta(x, y) = \dfrac{\omega(x)}{\omega(x^\partial(y))}$.

We see by the latter expression that the transformation in polar coordinates induces a conditional pdf for $\delta(x, y)$ given (y, η), namely $f(\delta|y, \eta)$, with support over $[1, \infty)$. Hence, in a certain sense we have transformed the density $f(x, y)$ expressed in Cartesian coordinates into a density on "polar-type" coordinates $f(\delta, \eta, y) = f(\delta \mid \eta, y) f(\eta \mid y) f(y)$. Consequently, now, the DGP is characterized by $\mathcal{P} = \mathcal{P}(\Psi, f(\delta, \eta, y))$. The reader can see here the analogy with the simple model (3.1) in Section 3.1, where u was the univariate random inefficiency term; here this term is replaced by δ which has a conditional density $f(\delta \mid \eta, y)$.

The idea of the smooth bootstrap is to use as DGP in the bootstrap world $\widehat{\mathcal{P}} = \mathcal{P}(\widehat{\Psi}, \widehat{f}(\delta, \eta, y))$, where $\widehat{f}(\delta, \eta, y)$ will be a smooth continuous density estimate of the unknown density from the sample of observed values $(\widehat{\delta}_i, \eta_i, Y_i)$ obtained by the polar transformation described above of the original data (X_i, Y_i) and where the unknown δ_i, have been replaced by the estimates $\widehat{\delta}_i = \widehat{\delta}(X_i, Y_i)$ (which are the distance functions in the bootstrap world, *i.e.*, with respect to the attainable set $\widehat{\Psi}$).

Simar and Wilson (2000b) propose an algorithm to simulate pseudo-data $(\delta_i^\star, \eta_i^\star, Y_i^\star)$ and to transform them back in Cartesian coordinates to obtain the bootstrap pseudo-sample $\mathcal{X}^\star = \{(X_i^\star, Y_i^\star),\ i = 1, \ldots, n\}$. The procedure is rather complicated because in the kernel estimation we have to take into account a boundary condition for δ that have to be greater than 1. The procedure implies a reflection method (Schuster, 1985, Silverman, 1986) in the $p+q$ dimensional space: we add to the original points $(\widehat{\delta}_i, \eta_i, Y_i)$ the points $(2 - \widehat{\delta}_i, \eta_i, Y_i)$. By doing so, we achieve consistency of the density estimate even near its boundary points (see Simar and Wilson, 2000b for further details).

The homogeneous smooth bootstrap

The bootstrap procedure is simplified if we are ready to make an additional assumption on the DGP. In particular we assume that the distribution of the inefficiencies is homogeneous over the input-output space. This is the analog to the assumption of homoscedasticity in regression models. Formally we suppose that:

$$f(\delta \mid y, \eta) = f(\delta). \tag{3.21}$$

This may be a reasonable assumptions in many practical situations.

With this homogeneity assumption, the problem of the bootstrap is similar to the bootstrap in homoscedastic regression models where the bootstrap is based on the residuals (see Freedman, 1981). In the present context, the residuals corresponds to the estimated distance from the fitted frontier of $\widehat{\Psi}$ which are the DEA efficiency scores $\widehat{\delta}_i,\ i = 1, \ldots, n$.

So we generate a pseudo observation, $(\delta_i^\star, \eta_i^\star, Y_i^\star)$, conditional to the original observed values for the input mix and for the output level $(\eta_i^\star, Y_i^\star) = (\eta_i, Y_i)$ and we only have to generate inefficiencies by generating a univariate value for the input Shephard distance $\delta_i^\star$. This is done by generating $\delta_i^\star$ from a smooth density estimate of $f(\delta)$ obtained from the n data values $\{\widehat{\delta}_i;\ i = 1, \ldots, n\}$.

Nonparametric smooth density estimation

A standard nonparametric smooth density estimate is obtained by a kernel density estimate (Silverman, 1986):

$$\widehat{f}(\delta) = \frac{1}{nh} \sum_{i=1}^{n} K\Big(\frac{\delta - \widehat{\delta}_i}{h}\Big), \tag{3.22}$$

where $K(\cdot)$ is a kernel function (usually a continuous standardized density with mean 0 and variance 1) and h is the bandwidth controlling the scale of the kernel function. The density estimate is the mean of n densities centered at the observed values $\widehat{\delta}_i$ with standard deviation given by the bandwidth h. The choice of the kernel function is not crucial in defining the density estimate (the results are very stable to this choice and often a standard gaussian density is chosen for $K(\cdot)$) however the smoothing parameter h has to be carefully determined. Too small values of h (*under smoothing*) localize too much the kernels and the average $\widehat{f}(\delta)$ will be quite irregular; at the limit if $h \to 0$, the density estimate converges to the discrete empirical density with mass $1/n$ at each observed points $\widehat{f}(\delta)$. Too large values of h will *over smooth* the estimate; at the limit if $h \to \infty$, the density estimate converges to a flat uniform density.

Silverman (1986) shows that if $f(\cdot)$ is gaussian, an optimal value for h, minimizing the mean integrated squared error between $\widehat{f}(\delta)$ and $f(\delta)$, is given by:

$$h = 1.06 s_n n^{-1/5},$$

where s_n is the empirical standard deviation of the n values $\widehat{\delta}_i$. This is known as the *normal reference rule.* It has been shown by Silverman that the choice

$$h = 1.06 \min(s_n, r_n/1.34) n^{-1/5}, \tag{3.23}$$

where r_n is the interquartile range of the n data points, is more robust to departures form the gaussian assumption for $f(\cdot)$. This latter rule is referred as the *robust normal reference rule.* It is very popular and give generally reasonable values for the bandwidth. Other empirical rules have been proposed in the literature, like the Sheather and Jones (1991) method which tries to be still more robust to departures from the normal assumption, by using higher order empirical moments of the data points.

As a matter of fact the problem is slightly more complicated here for two reasons: (i) there is a spurious mass at one in the sample of values $\widehat{\delta}_i$, $i = 1, \ldots, n$, and (ii) there is a boundary effect since $\delta \geq 1$ by definition and the estimate in (3.22) does not verify this constraint. As suggested in Simar and Wilson (2006a), the first problem is solved by deleting the spurious ones, in this step of bandwidth and density estimation, and the second problem is addressed by using the reflection method (see Silverman, 1986 for details). Formally, we consider only the m values of $\widehat{\delta}_i > 1$, for $i = 1, \ldots, m$ with $m < n$, then we consider the set of the $2m$ values $\{2 - \widehat{\delta}_1, \ldots, 2 - \widehat{\delta}_m, \widehat{\delta}_1, \ldots, \widehat{\delta}_m\}$ which are now symmetrically distributed around 1. Then we compute the kernel density estimate with this series (without any boundary condition). Analog to (3.22), we have:

$$\widehat{g}_h(\delta) = \frac{1}{2mh_m} \sum_{i=1}^{m} K\Big(\frac{\delta - \widehat{\delta}_i}{h_m}\Big) + K\Big(\frac{\delta - 2 + \widehat{\delta}_i}{h_m}\Big), \tag{3.24}$$

The optimal bandwidth by using the empirical rule (3.23) here is obtained by:

$$h_m = 1.06 \min(s_{2m}, r_{2m}/1.34)(2m)^{-1/5},$$

where now s_{2m} and r_{2m} are computed from the $2m$ reflected data. As pointed above, the distribution of these reflected values is by construction symmetric around 1 and we observed in many applications a bell-shape for the distribution of these reflected values. Therefore the robust normal-reference rule giving h_m offers in many applications a reasonable value for the bandwidth not far from the optimal one.

Note that automatic data-driven techniques based on cross-validation exist for selecting the optimal bandwidth in (3.24) (see *e.g.* Silverman, 1986). The most usual one is based on leave one-out least-squares cross-validation function that find the optimal h_m that minimizes the following criterion:

$$CV(h) = \int_{-\infty}^{+\infty} \widehat{g}_h(\delta)\, d\delta - \frac{1}{2m} \sum_{i=1}^{2m} \widehat{g}^2_{h,(i)}(\delta), \tag{3.25}$$

where $\widehat{g}_{h,(i)}(\delta)$ is the leave one-out estimator of $g(\delta)$ based on the $2m$ values except $\widehat{\delta}_i$. Another automatic data-driven technique based on likelihood cross-validation is described in Section 5.3, where a variable bandwidth is obtained in a different context by using a k-Nearest Neighbor approach.

Note that in many applications the solution of (3.25) is not very far from the simple empirical rule (3.24). Note also that, as pointed in Simar and Wilson (1998), the bootstrap results are relatively stable to small changes in the selected bandwidth. Therefore, as a reasonable first guess for h_m, we might suggest the use of the easy rule (3.24).

Finally, as suggested by Simar and Wilson (2006a), the value of h_m (whatever being the rule used to obtain it) has to be adjusted for scale and sample size:

$$h = h_m \Big(\frac{2m}{n}\Big)\Big(\frac{s_n}{s_{2m}}\Big). \tag{3.26}$$

The density estimate is then obtained through:

$$\widehat{f}(\delta) = \begin{cases} 2\widehat{g}_h(\delta) & \text{if} \delta > 1, \\ 0 & \text{otherwise.} \end{cases} \tag{3.27}$$

How to generate the $\delta_i^\star$ from $\widehat{f}(\delta)$ and build a bootstrap sample $\mathcal{X}^\star$?

Simar and Wilson (1998, 2006a) provide an easy to implement algorithm where it is shown that the density estimate $\widehat{f}(\delta)$ is even not needed to generate the $\delta_i^\star$. We only need the selected value of h and the original DEA scores $\{\widehat{\delta}_i;\ i = 1, \ldots, n\}$.

The algorithm is going as follows:

[1] we first draw a random sample of size n with replacement (as in the naive bootstrap) from the set of the $2n$ reflected original DEA scores $\{2 - \widehat{\delta}_1, \ldots, 2 - \widehat{\delta}_n, \widehat{\delta}_1, \ldots, \widehat{\delta}_n\}$, obtaining $\{\widetilde{\delta}_i^\star;\ i = 1, \ldots, n\}$.

[2] Then we smooth the naive bootstrap resampled values by perturbating $\widetilde{\delta}_i^\star$ with a random noise generated from the kernel density with scale given by the bandwidth h. So we obtain:

$$\widetilde{\widetilde{\delta}}_i^\star = \widetilde{\delta}_i^\star + h\,\varepsilon_i,\ i = 1, \ldots, n,$$

where ε_i is a random draw from a standard normal distribution (because we have used gaussian kernel).

[3] Then we have to refine by correcting for the mean and the variance of the smoothed values (see Efron and Tibshirani, 1993, for details):

$$\delta_i^{\star\star} = \overline{\tilde{\delta}}^{\star} + \frac{\tilde{\delta}_i^{\star} - \overline{\tilde{\delta}}^{\star}}{\sqrt{1 + h^2/s^{\star 2}}}, \ i = 1, \ldots, n,$$

where $\overline{\tilde{\delta}}^{\star}$ and $s^{\star 2}$ are the empirical mean and variance of the n values $\tilde{\delta}_i^{\star}$.

[4] Finally we come back to measures greater than one by reflecting the values smaller than one. For $i = 1, \ldots, n$ we define:

$$\delta_i^{\star} = \begin{cases} 2 - \delta_i^{\star\star} & \text{if} \quad \delta_i^{\star\star} < 1, \\ \delta_i^{\star\star} & \text{otherwise.} \end{cases}$$

[5] A bootstrap sample $\mathcal{X}^{\star}$ is now obtained by generating inefficient inputs $X_i^{\star}$, inside the DEA attainable set and conditional on the original input mix η_i and the original output level Y_i. This is achieved by defining:

$$\mathcal{X}^{\star} = \{(X_i^{\star}, Y_i^{\star}) \mid Y_i^{\star} = Y_i \text{ and } X_i^{\star} = \frac{\delta_i^{\star}}{\widehat{\delta}_i} X_i, \ i = 1, \ldots, n\}. \quad (3.28)$$

The denominator of the ratio multiplying the input vector X_i projects the original observed data point X_i on the DEA efficient facet on the ray defined by X_i, then the numerator projects the frontier point inside the DEA attainable set, on the same ray, by the random bootstrap factor $\delta_i^{\star}$. This is done for each data point $i = 1, \ldots, n$.

As already explained above, by redoing the above steps 1–5 B times, we end up with B bootstrap samples $\mathcal{X}_b^{\star}$. Then for any fixed point of interest (x, y), we can build the Monte-Carlo sequence of pseudo estimates $\{\widehat{\delta}_b^{\star}(x, y)\}_{b=1}^{B}$ by solving (3.10) with reference set $\mathcal{X}_b^{\star}$. The empirical distribution $\{\widehat{\delta}_b^{\star}(x, y)\}_{b=1}^{B}$ is the bootstrap approximation of the sampling distribution of $\widehat{\delta}(x, y)$.

Note that the computation burden can be important: to derive this series of B values (where in practice B should be at least equal to 2000, to get reasonable Monte-Carlo approximations even in the tails of the distribution), we have to solve B DEA linear programs (3.10) (plus n DEA programs to get the original DEA efficiency scores $\widehat{\delta}_i$). In many applications the point of interest (x, y) will be each of the original data points (x_i, y_i), $i = 1, \ldots, n$. If confidence intervals of the efficiency scores for each data point are desired, then we will have to solve $n(B+1)$ linear programs. However, there exist software packages which have already implemented the bootstrap algorithm described above. We refer in particular to FEAR by P. Wilson (Wilson, 2005a, b, c) and to DEAsoft developed and marketed by Performance Improvement Management Ltd.

In the Applications Part of the book we will illustrate this algorithm.

The debate on how correctly implement the bootstrap

In this simplified homogeneous version of the bootstrap it is easy to understand why the naive bootstrap is not consistent (the same argument applies in the more general bootstrap algorithms mentioned above). This issue opened a debate on the consistency of the bootstrap in frontier models, reported in the *Journal of Productivity Analysis*[17]. Things are now very clear and can be summarized as follows.

Suppose in the homogeneous case we use a naive bootstrap yielding the values $\{\tilde{\delta}_i^\star,\ i = 1\ldots, n\}$ drawn randomly with replacement from the original set $\{\widehat{\delta}_i;\ i = 1, \ldots, n\}$. As observed in Simar and Wilson (1999a), it is easy to verify that:

$$\text{Prob}\Big(\widehat{\delta}^\star(x,y) = \widehat{\delta}(x,y)|\widehat{\mathcal{P}}\Big) = 1 - \Big(1 - \frac{1}{n}\Big)^n > 0,$$

i.e. a fixed number depending only on the sample size n whatever the real DGP $\mathcal{P}$ is. This problem does not vanish when n is increasing since:

$$\lim_{n\to\infty} \text{Prob}\Big(\widehat{\delta}^\star(x,y) = \widehat{\delta}(x,y)|\widehat{\mathcal{P}}\Big) = 1 - e^{-1} \approx 0.632. \qquad (3.29)$$

The naive bootstrap is inconsistent because there is no reason why this probability should be equal to this fixed number, independently of any feature of the real DGP $\mathcal{P}$. In fact, if $f(\delta)$ is continuous on $[1, \infty)$, the probability should be zero since in this case:

$$\text{Prob}\Big(\widehat{\delta}(x,y) - \delta(x,y)|\mathcal{P}\Big) = 0.$$

3.4.5 Applications of the bootstrap

The bootstrap has been introduced in several applications related to non-parametric frontiers estimation. These useful applications include the correction for the bias and confidence intervals for efficiency scores; applications to Malmquist indices and its various decomposition (Simar and Wilson, 1999c); tests procedure to assess returns to scale (Simar and Wilson, 2002); statistical procedures to compare the means of several groups of producers can be found in Simar and Zelenyuk (2003) and test for the equality of the densities

[17]See Ferrier and Hirschberg, 1997; Simar and Wilson 1999a; Ferrier and Hirschberg, 1999; Simar and Wilson 1999b.

of inefficiencies of two groups of firms is implemented in Simar and Zelenyuk (2004).

In addition, there may be uncertainty about the structure of the underlying statistical model in terms of whether certain variables are relevant or whether subsets of variables may be aggregated. Tests of hypotheses about the model structure have been introduced in Simar and Wilson (2001).

We apply most of these bootstrap-based procedures in the applications of the Part II of this work. In particular we will explain how to use the bootstrap algorithm to test returns to scale in Section 6.3 and to test the equality of the mean of efficiency scores of two groups of units in Section 6.5.

3.4.6 Bootstrapping FDH estimators

For the FDH case, only very recently Jeong and Simar (2005) have proven that the subsampling procedures provide consistent approximations of the sampling distribution of $\widehat{\delta}(x,y) - \delta(x,y)$. As described above sub-samples are random samples of size $m = [n^{\gamma}]$ where $\gamma < 1$, with replacement from the original data $\{(X_i, Y_i),\, i = 1, \ldots, n\}$. The procedure is very easy and very fast to implement. Some Monte-Carlo experiments have shown that the procedure is rather robust to the choice of the size of the sub-samples (choice of $\gamma < 1$) as far as bias and variance of the estimators are concerned. However, for building confidence intervals, the choice of this tuning parameter γ seems crucial for obtaining sensible coverage probabilities. The problem comes from the fact that an FDH efficiency score is characterized by only one data point, and this data point will reappear too often in the bootstrap sample. This comes from the discontinuous nature of the FDH boundary. Hence, Jeong and Simar (2005) advocate the use of a smoothed FDH frontier for making inference. The discontinuity of the FDH frontier (in the $p = q = 1$ case, the "stair-case" aspect of the frontier) may be a drawback of this estimator, because in most applications we may expect the true frontier being continuous. They propose a linearized version of the FDH (the Linearized FDH, called LFDH) by linear interpolating adjacent FDH efficient vertices. When $p = q = 1$ the procedure is trivial and can be done by hand; in multivariate setup they propose an algorithm to identify the FDH vertices to be interpolated by using the Delannay triangulation (or tessellation). See Simar and Wilson (2006a) for a non mathematical presentation of the LFDH.

Chapter 4

NONPARAMETRIC ROBUST ESTIMATORS: PARTIAL FRONTIERS

The main objective of this chapter is the presentation of robust frontiers as a way for overcoming some of the drawbacks of traditional nonparametric techniques (DEA/FDH based estimators). In particular, we deal with order-m and order$-\alpha$ frontiers, and related efficiency measures. Known for being more robust to extremes or outliers in the data, these "partial" or "robust" frontiers have several interesting properties that make them a very useful tool for empirical applications. Among these properties we recall the same rate of convergence of parametric estimators, that for practical works means that the "curse of dimensionality" (the request of thousands of observations for avoiding a great statistical imprecision) can be avoided. In the first section, following Daraio and Simar (2005a) which generalise previous results of Cazals, Florens and Simar (2002), we reformulate the activity analysis framework under a probabilistic perspective. Section two outlines the basic concepts and properties of order-m frontiers. Besides, the following section presents another probabilistic concept of frontier, the frontiers of order-α, and illustrates a new probabilistic measure of efficiency. Then we summarize the main properties of order-m and order-α frontiers. Afterwards, the presentation of the output oriented framework is outlined. Finally, we illustrate a method recently introduced by Florens and Simar (2005) to parametrically approximate robust and nonparametric frontiers. The main advantage of this approach, in an applied perspective, is the obtainment of robust estimators of coefficients of parametric models that can easily be interpreted by the analyst. In the last section of the chapter we propose a procedure to extend the parametric approximation in a full multivariate set-up (multi-output and multi-input).

4.1 A re-formulation based on the probability of being dominated

Daraio and Simar (2005a), extending the ideas of Cazals, Florens and Simar (2002), propose an alternative probabilistic formulation of the production process.

The production process, presented in Section 2.3 within an activity analysis framework, can be described by the joint probability measure of (X, Y) on $\mathcal{R}_+^p \times \mathcal{R}_+^q$. This joint probability measure is completely characterized by the knowledge of the probability function $H_{XY}(\cdot,\cdot)$ defined as:

$$H_{XY}(x, y) = \text{Prob}(X \leq x, Y \geq y). \tag{4.1}$$

The support of the probability $H_{XY}(\cdot,\cdot)$ is the production set Ψ and $H_{XY}(x, y)$ can be interpreted as the probability for a unit operating at the level (x, y) to be dominated. Daraio and Simar (2005a) point out that this function is a non-standard distribution function, having a cumulative distribution form for X and a survival form for Y. In the input oriented framework, this joint probability can be decomposed as follows:

$$\begin{aligned} H_{XY}(x, y) &= \text{Prob}(X \leq x \mid Y \geq y)\,\text{Prob}(Y \geq y) \\ &= F_{X|Y}(x|y)\,S_Y(y), \end{aligned} \tag{4.2}$$

where $F_{X|Y}(x|y)$ is the conditional distribution function of X and $S_Y(y)$ is the survivor function of Y; we suppose the conditional distribution and survival functions exist (*i.e.*, $S_Y(y) > 0$ and $F_X(x) > 0$). The conditional distribution $F_{X|Y}$ is non-standard due to the event describing the condition (*i.e.*,$Y \geq y$ instead of $Y = y$, the latter is assumed in a standard regression framework). We can now define the efficiency scores (in a radial sense) in terms of the support of these probabilities. The input oriented efficiency score $\theta(x, y)$ for $(x, y) \in \Psi$ is defined for all y with $S_Y(y) > 0$ as:

$$\theta(x, y) = \inf\{\theta \mid F_{X|Y}(\theta x|y) > 0\} = \inf\{\theta \mid H_{XY}(\theta x, y) > 0\}. \tag{4.3}$$

The idea here is that the support of the conditional distribution $F_{X|Y}(\cdot \mid y)$ can be viewed as the attainable set of input values X for a unit working at the output level y. It can be shown that under the free disposability assumption, the lower boundary of this support (in a radial sense) provides the Farrell-efficient frontier, or the input benchmarked value.

A nonparametric estimator is then easily obtained replacing the unknown $F_{X|Y}(x \mid y)$ by its empirical version:

$$\widehat{F}_{X|Y,n}(x \mid y) = \frac{\sum_{i=1}^{n} \boldsymbol{I}(X_i \leq x, Y_i \geq y)}{\sum_{=1}^{n} \boldsymbol{I}(Y_i \geq y)}, \tag{4.4}$$

where $\boldsymbol{I}(\cdot)$ is the indicator function that has to be read as follows: $\boldsymbol{I}(k) = 1$ if k is true, $\boldsymbol{I}(k) = 0$ otherwise.

The resulting estimator of the input efficiency score for a given point (x, y) coincides with the FDH estimator of $\theta(x, y)$:

$$\widehat{\theta}_{FDH}(x, y) = \inf\{\theta \mid (\theta x, y) \in \widehat{\Psi}_{FDH}\} \tag{4.5}$$
$$= \inf\{\theta \mid \widehat{F}_{X|Y,n}(\theta x \mid y) > 0\}. \tag{4.6}$$

In the output oriented framework, the probability function $H_{XY}(\cdot, \cdot)$ may be decomposed as follows:

$$\begin{aligned} H_{XY}(x, y) &= \text{Prob}(Y \geq y \,|\, X \leq x)\, \text{Prob}(X \leq x) \\ &= S_{Y|X}(y|x)\, F_X(x), \end{aligned} \tag{4.7}$$

where $S_{Y|X}(y|x) = \text{Prob}(Y \geq y \,|\, X \leq x)$ denotes the conditional survivor function of Y and $F_X(x) = \text{Prob}(X \leq x)$ denotes the distribution function of X that we assume exists, *i.e.* $F_X(x) > 0$.

The output efficiency score may be defined accordingly:

$$\lambda(x, y) = \sup\{\lambda \,|\, S_{Y|X}(\lambda y|x) > 0\} = \sup\{\lambda \,|\, H_{XY}(x, \lambda y) > 0\}. \tag{4.8}$$

As for the input oriented case, a nonparametric estimator of $\lambda(x, y)$ is obtained by plugging in Equation (4.8) the empirical conditional survival function $\widehat{S}_{Y|X,n}(y|x)$ given by:

$$\widehat{S}_{Y|X,n}(y|x) = \frac{\widehat{H}_{XY,n}(x, y)}{\widehat{H}_{XY,n}(x, 0)}, \tag{4.9}$$

where,

$$\widehat{H}_{XY,n}(x, y) = \frac{1}{n} \sum_{i=1}^{n} \boldsymbol{I}(x_i \leq x, y_i \geq y). \tag{4.10}$$

Again, this estimator coincides with the FDH estimator of $\lambda(x, y)$.

The FDH estimator $\widehat{\Psi}_{FDH}$, as well as its convex version $\widehat{\Psi}_{DEA}$, are very sensitive to extremes and outliers, since, as estimators of the "full" set Ψ, they envelop all the data points of the observed set $\mathcal{X}$ (this is seen by looking to the inf and sup operator in (4.6) and (4.8)). The corresponding frontiers of $\widehat{\Psi}_{FDH}$ and $\widehat{\Psi}_{DEA}$, can be viewed as estimators of the "full" frontier of Ψ. As an alternative, partial frontiers can be investigated. They do not correspond to the boundary of Ψ and are such that the full frontier can be viewed as a limiting case of the partial frontiers. These frontiers correspond to another benchmark frontier against which DMU will be compared. The advantage is that their nonparametric estimators will not envelop all the data points and so will be more robust to extreme and outlying data points. Two partial frontiers have been investigated in the literature: the order-m frontiers and the order-α quantile frontiers. They are introduced in the two next sections.

4.2 Order-m frontiers and efficiency scores

The order-m frontiers, and their derived efficiency scores, have been proposed by Cazals, Florens and Simar (2002). As pointed above, the support of $F_{X|Y}(\cdot \mid y)$ defines the attainable set of input values X for a unit working at the output level y. Instead of looking at the lower boundary of this support, we may define as a benchmark value, the average of the minimal value of inputs for m units randomly drawn according $F_{X|Y}(\cdot \mid y)$, *i.e.*, units producing at least the output level y. This defines the input order-m frontier.

In the simplest univariate case (all firms produce one unit of output), order-m frontiers (input oriented framework) can be introduced as follows. Consider a fixed integer $m \geq 1$. The *order-m* lower boundary of X is defined as *the expected value of the minimum of m random variables $X^1, ..., X^m$ drawn from the distribution function of X*. The formal definition is the following:

$$\phi_m = E[\min(X^1, ..., X^m)] = \int_0^\infty [1 - F_X(x)]^m dx. \tag{4.11}$$

The value ϕ_m is the expected minimum achievable input-level among m DMUs drawn from the population of firms that, in this simplest case, produce one unit of output. It can be proven that $\lim_{(m \to \infty)} \phi_m = \phi$ and that, for all finite value of m, $\phi_m \geq \phi$.

The nonparametric estimator of ϕ_m is given by plugging the empirical distribution function of X in equation (4.11):

$$\widehat{\phi}_{m,n} = \widehat{E}[\min(X^1, ..., X^m)] = \int_0^\infty [1 - \widehat{F}_{X,n}(x)]^m dx. \tag{4.12}$$

The relations between ϕ and ϕ_m remain valid between their empirical counterparts: $\widehat{\phi}_n$ and $\widehat{\phi}_{m,n}$. For all finite values of m we have: $\widehat{\phi}_{m,n} \geq \widehat{\phi}_n$.

We remark that in the standard case, $\widehat{\phi}_n \leq X_i, \; i = 1, ..., n$ but this is no more the case in the order-m frontier estimator, $\widehat{\phi}_{m,n}$, even for large values of m. The reasons for this different behavior of $\widehat{\phi}_{m,n}$ with respect to $\widehat{\phi}_n$ are mainly due to the expected operator in the definition of ϕ_m (see equation (4.11)) and to the finiteness of m.

The extension at the bivariate case is straightforward: we consider the process generating the input levels X by the conditional distribution of X given that $Y \geq y$. The full frontier function $\phi(y)$ is defined as the minimal achievable input level for producing at least the output y. It may be written as:

$$\phi(y) = \theta(x, y)\, x = \inf\{x \mid F_{X|Y}(x \mid y) > 0\}. \tag{4.13}$$

Now, given a fixed integer value of $m \geq 1$, we can define the (expected) *order-m* lower boundary of X for DMUs producing at least y, as *the expected value of the minimum of m random variables $X^1, ..., X^m$ drawn from the distribution* *function of X given that* $Y \geq y$. The formal definition is the following:

$$\phi_m(y) = E[\min(X^1, ..., X^m)|Y \geq y] = \int_0^\infty [1 - F_{X|Y}(x|y)]^m dx \quad (4.14)$$

Again, for all values of y and for all finite values of m, $\phi_m(y) \geq \phi(y)$ and for all y, $\lim_{(m \to \infty)} \phi_m(y) = \phi(y)$.

See Figure 4.1 for an illustration.

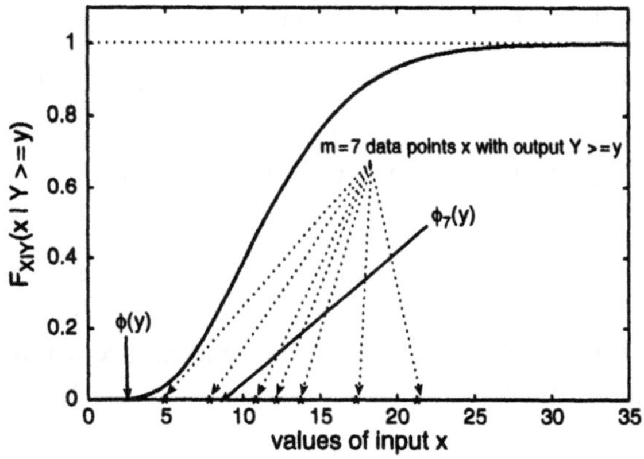

Figure 4.1. Input order-m frontier in the bivariate case. For any value of y, $\phi_m(y) = \mathrm{E}\left[\min(X^1, \ldots, X^m) \mid Y \geq y\right]$. Here the stars $X^1, \ldots, X^7$ are $m = 7$ draws from $F_{X|Y}(x|Y \geq y)$.

The expected frontier of order-m, $\phi_m(y)$, has an economic meaning: it is the expected minimum value of input achievable among a fixed number of m firms drawn from the population of firms producing at least a level of output y; it represents another reasonable benchmark value for a firm producing a level of output y.

The nonparametric estimation of $\phi_m(y)$ can be done by plugging in the empirical distribution function in equation (4.14):

$$\widehat{\phi}_{m,n}(y) = \widehat{E}[\min(X^1, ..., X^m)|Y \geq y] = \int_0^\infty [1 - \widehat{F}_{X|Y}(x|y)]^m dx \quad (4.15)$$

where $X^1, ..., X^m$ are m i.i.d. (independent and identically distributed) R.V. (Random Variables) generated by the empirical distribution function of X given that $Y \geq y$ whose distribution function is $\widehat{F}_{X|Y}(x|y)$.

The relations between the order-m frontier and the full frontier remain valid with their estimators $\widehat{\phi}_{m,n}(y)$ and $\widehat{\phi}_n(y)$, the FDH estimator of the frontier.

The extension to the multivariate inputs case, is done by defining order-m efficiency measures.

For a given level of outputs y in the interior of the support of Y, consider now m i.i.d. random variables $X_i, i = 1, \ldots, m$ generated by the conditional p-variate distribution function $F_{X|Y}(x \mid y)$ and define the set:

$$\Psi_m(y) = \{(x, y') \in \mathcal{R}_+^{p+q} \mid x \geq X_i, y' \geq y, i = 1, \ldots, m\}. \quad (4.16)$$

Then, for any x, we may define:

$$\tilde{\theta}_m(x, y) = \inf\{\theta \mid (\theta x, y) \in \Psi_m(y)\}. \quad (4.17)$$

Note that $\tilde{\theta}_m(x, y)$ may be computed by the following formula:

$$\tilde{\theta}_m(x, y) = \min_{i=1,\ldots,m} \left\{ \max_{j=1,\ldots,p} \left(\frac{X_i^j}{x^j} \right) \right\}. \quad (4.18)$$

$\tilde{\theta}_m(x, y)$ is a random variable since the X_i are random variables generated by $F_{X|Y}(x \mid y)$.

The order-m input efficiency measure is defined, according to Daraio and Simar (2005a), as follows:

$$\begin{aligned} \theta_m(x, y) &= E(\tilde{\theta}_m(x, y) \mid Y \geq y), & (4.19)\\ &= \int_0^\infty (1 - F_{X|Y}(ux \mid y))^m du & (4.20)\\ &= \theta(x, y) + \int_{\theta(x,y)}^\infty (1 - F_{X|Y}(ux \mid y))^m du, & (4.21) \end{aligned}$$

A nonparametric estimator of $\theta_m(x, y)$ is straightforward: we replace the true $F_{X|Y}(\cdot \mid y)$ by its empirical version, $\widehat{F}_{X|Y,n}(\cdot \mid y)$. We have:

$$\begin{aligned} \hat{\theta}_{m,n}(x, y) &= \widehat{E}(\tilde{\theta}_m(x, y) \mid Y \geq y) & \\ &= \int_0^\infty (1 - \widehat{F}_{X|Y,n}(ux \mid y))^m du, & (4.22)\\ &= \hat{\theta}_n(x, y) + \int_{\hat{\theta}_n(x,y)}^\infty (1 - \widehat{F}_{X|Y,n}(ux \mid y))^m du & (4.23) \end{aligned}$$

Hence, in place of looking for the lower boundary of the support of $F_{X|Y}(x \mid y)$, as was typically the case for the full-frontier and for the efficiency score $\theta(x, y)$, the order-m efficiency score can be viewed as the expectation of the minimal input efficiency score of the unit (x, y), when compared to m units randomly drawn from the population of units producing more outputs than the level y. This is certainly a less extreme benchmark for the unit (x, y) than the "absolute" minimal achievable level of inputs: it is compared to a set of m peers producing more than its level y and we take as benchmark, the expectation of the minimal achievable input in place of the absolute minimal achievable input.

Note that the order-m efficiency score is not bounded by 1: a value of $\theta_m(x, y)$ greater than one indicates that the unit operating at the level (x, y) is more efficient than the average of m peers randomly drawn from the population of units producing more output than y. Then for any $x \in \mathcal{R}_+^p$, the expected minimum level of inputs of order-m is defined as $x_m^\partial(y) = \theta_m(x, y)\, x$ which can be compared with the full-frontier $x^\partial(y) = \theta(x, y)\, x$.

Order-m frontiers are estimators of the frontier, that for finite m, do not envelop all the observed data points and therefore, are less sensitive to extreme points and/or to outliers. As m increases and for fixed n, $\hat{\theta}_{m,n}(x, y) \to \hat{\theta}_n(x, y)$.

Daraio and Simar (2005b) define convex and local convex order-m frontiers as well as a practical method to compute them.

Economic meaning of order-m input efficiency measures

Consider the firm (x, y); it produces a level of output y using a quantity x of inputs. We recall that $\phi_m(y)$ is not the efficient frontier of the production set, but it gives the *expected minimum input among a fixed number of m potential competing firms producing more than* y. The comparison of x with $\phi_m(y)$ is important, from an economic point of view, as it gives a clear indication of how efficient the firm is, compared with these m potential firms. The value m represents the number of potential firms (drawing from the population of firms) producing at least the output level of y, against which we want to benchmark the analyzed firm.

Let us give some examples of the economic meaning of the order-m input efficiency measures. If a firm (x, y) has an efficiency score $\widehat{\theta}_{m,n}(x, y) = 0.9$ (1.4), means that it uses 10% more inputs -radial extension- (uses 40% less inputs - proportionate reduction) than the expected value of the minimum input level of m other firms drawn from the population of firms producing a level of output $\geq y$. On the contrary, if $\widehat{\theta}_{m,n}(x, y) = 1$, the firm (x, y) uses the same level of inputs than the expected value of the minimum input level of m other firms drawn from the population of firms producing at least y of output, *i.e.* the firm is on the efficient boundary of the order-m frontier in the input space direction.

Computational aspects

For the computation of order-m efficiency $\hat{\theta}_{m,n}(x,y)$ the univariate integral (4.23) could be evaluated by numerical methods[18], even when the number of inputs $p \geq 1$.

However, numerical integration can be avoided by an easy Monte-Carlo algorithm, proposed by Cazals, Florens and Simar (2002), that we describe below, as fast for small values of m such as $m = 10$, but much slower when m increases:

[1] For a given y, draw a sample of size m with replacement among those X_i such that $Y_i \geq y$ and denote this sample by $(X_{1,b} \ldots, X_{m,b})$.

[2] Compute $\tilde{\theta}^b_m(x,y) = \min_{i=1,\ldots,m}\left\{\max_{j=1,\ldots,p}\left(\frac{X^j_{i,b}}{x^j}\right)\right\}$.

[3] Redo [1]-[2] for $b = 1, \ldots, B$, where B is large.

[4] Finally, $\hat{\theta}_{m,n}(x,y) \approx \frac{1}{B}\sum_{b=1}^{B}\tilde{\theta}^b_m(x,y)$.

The quality of the approximation can be tuned by increasing B, but in most applications, say $B = 200$, seems to be a reasonable choice.

4.3 Order-α quantile-type frontiers

The partial order-m frontiers have the advantage of sharing very nice properties and since m is an integer, the mathematics behind this object is not too complicated. Even if the order m of the frontier has some economic interpretation (benchmarking against m competitors), in practice and as discussed above, m serves as a trimming parameter which allows to tune the percentage of points that will lie above the order-m frontier. The idea behind order-α quantile-type frontier is to go the other way around: determine the frontier by fixing first the probability $(1-\alpha)$ of observing points above this order-α frontier.

Using the probabilistic formulation developed above in Section 4.1, it is easy to adapt the order-m ideas to order-α quantile type-frontiers. These estimators were introduced for the univariate case by Aragon, Daouia and Thomas-Agnan (2003) and extended to the multivariate setting by Daouia and Simar (2004).

As for order-m frontiers, we develop the presentation for the input oriented case. A summary for the output oriented case is provided in Section 4.5. Consider first the case where we only have one input and several outputs $y \in \mathcal{R}^q_+$. In the preceding section, for a firm operating at the level (x,y), the benchmark is the order-m partial frontier determined by the expected minimal input among m peers randomly drawn in the population of firms producing at least a level y

[18] For the numerical integration we use the build-in Matlab "quad" procedure (based on adaptive Simpson quadrature).

of outputs. Here, for the same unit, the benchmark will be the order-α quantile frontier defined as the input level not exceeded by $(1-\alpha) \times 100$-percent of firms among the population of units producing at least a level y of outputs. Formally:

$$\phi_\alpha(y) = \inf\{x \mid F_{X|Y}(x \mid y) > 1-\alpha\}. \tag{4.24}$$

This frontier can be viewed as a nonstandard conditional quantile frontier, where the word "nonstandard" means that we focus on the unusual conditioning $Y \geq y$ in the cdf $F_{X|Y}(\cdot \mid y)$ considered here.

In Figure 4.2 we illustrate the concept for $\alpha = 0.90$. In this picture, $\phi(y)$ is the full frontier level, it is given by the left boundary of the support of $F_{X|Y}(\cdot \mid y)$, $\phi_\alpha(y)$ corresponds to the $(1-\alpha)$ quantile of $F_{X|Y}(\cdot \mid y)$.

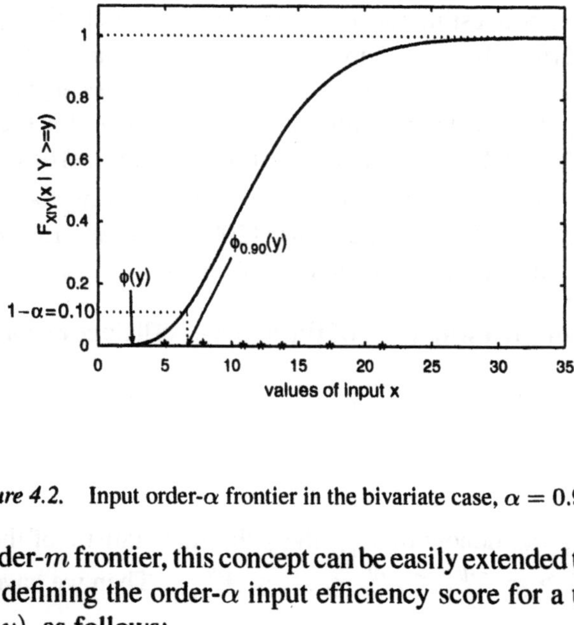

Figure 4.2. Input order-α frontier in the bivariate case, $\alpha = 0.90$.

As for the order-m frontier, this concept can be easily extended to the multiple inputs case by defining the order-α input efficiency score for a unit operating at the level (x, y), as follows:

$$\theta_\alpha(x, y) = \inf\{\theta \mid F_{X|Y}(\theta x \mid y) > 1-\alpha\}. \tag{4.25}$$

It is a radial version of quantile type function $\phi_\alpha(y)$ of the univariate input case: in this latter case we have $\phi_\alpha(y) = \theta_\alpha(x, y)x$. From the expression (4.25), it appears clearly that $\theta_\alpha(x, y)$ converges to the usual Farrell-Debreu input efficiency score $\theta(x, y)$ when $\alpha \to 1$. The order-α efficiency score has a nice interpretation: for instance if $\theta_\alpha(x, y) = 1$, then the unit is said to be efficient at the level $\alpha \times 100\%$ since it is dominated by firms producing more output than y with a probability $1-\alpha$. If $\theta_\alpha(x, y) < 1$, then the unit (x, y)

has to reduce its input to the level $\theta_\alpha(x,y)x$ to reach the input efficient frontier of level $\alpha \times 100\%$. Note that here $\theta_\alpha(x,y)$ can be greater than one indicating that a firm (x,y) can increase its input by a factor $\theta_\alpha(x,y)$ to reach the same frontier. Therefore, this latter firm is considered as super-efficient with respect to the order-α frontier level.

Nonparametric estimators are easily obtained by plugging, as for the order-m frontiers, the empirical cdf in the expression above, we have:

$$\widehat{\phi}_{\alpha,n}(y) = \inf\{x \mid \widehat{F}_{X|Y,n}(x \mid y) > 1-\alpha\}, \tag{4.26}$$

and for the multivariate input case, we obtain:

$$\widehat{\theta}_{\alpha,n}(x,y) = \inf\{\theta \mid \widehat{F}_{X|Y,n}(\theta x \mid y) > 1-\alpha\}. \tag{4.27}$$

Here again it appears clearly that when $\alpha \to 1$, $\widehat{\theta}_{\alpha,n}(x,y)$ converges to the FDH input efficiency score $\widehat{\theta}_{FDH}(x,y)$.

The nonparametric estimators of order-α frontier or efficiency scores shares the same properties than their order-m analogs. In summary, they are $\sqrt{n}$-consistent estimator of their population analogs, they are asymptotically unbiased and normally distributed with a known expression for the variance (see Aragon, Daouia and Thomas-Agnan (2005) for the properties of $\widehat{\phi}_{\alpha,n}(y)$ and Daouia and Simar, 2004 for those of $\widehat{\theta}_{\alpha,n}(x,y)$). Using tools of robustness theory, it is shown in Daouia and Simar (2004) that the order-α frontiers are more robust to extremes than the order-m frontiers.

Computation of the estimators of the order-α efficiency scores

Let $M_y = n\widehat{S}_{Y,n}(y) > 0 = \sum_{i=1}^n \boldsymbol{I}(Y_i \geq y)$, and define:

$$\mathcal{X}_i = \max_{k=1,\cdots,p} \frac{X_i^k}{x^k}, \quad i=1,\cdots,n.$$

For $j = 1,\cdots,M_y$, denote by $\mathcal{X}^y_{(j)}$ the j-th order statistic of the observations $\mathcal{X}_i$ such that $Y_i \geq y$: $\mathcal{X}^y_{(1)} \leq \mathcal{X}^y_{(2)} \leq \ldots \leq \mathcal{X}^y_{(M_y)}$. Then we have,

$$\begin{aligned}
\widehat{F}_{X|Y,n}(\theta x|y) &= \frac{\sum_{i|Y_i\geq y} \boldsymbol{I}(\mathcal{X}_i \leq \theta)}{M_y} = \frac{\sum_{j=1}^{M_y} \boldsymbol{I}(\mathcal{X}^y_{(j)} \leq \theta)}{M_y} \\
&= \begin{cases} 0 \ \text{ if } \ \theta < \mathcal{X}^y_{(1)} \\ \frac{j}{M_y} \ \text{ if } \ \mathcal{X}^y_{(j)} \leq \theta < \mathcal{X}^y_{(j+1)}, \ j=1,\cdots,M_y-1 \\ 1 \ \text{ if } \ \theta \geq \mathcal{X}^y_{(M_y)}. \end{cases}
\end{aligned}$$

It follows,

$$\widehat{\theta}_{\alpha,n}(x,y) = \begin{cases} \mathcal{X}^y_{((1-\alpha)M_y)} & \text{if } \ (1-\alpha)M_y \in \mathcal{N} \\ \mathcal{X}^y_{([(1-\alpha)M\ ]+1)} & \text{otherwise,} \end{cases}$$

where $\mathcal{N}$ denotes the set of all nonnegative integers. If x is univariate, $\widehat{\phi}_{\alpha,n}(y) = \widehat{\theta}_{\alpha,n}(x, y)x$. Therefore, the computation of $\widehat{\theta}_{\alpha,n}(x, y)$ is very fast and very easy since it only implies sorting routines.

Monotone estimators of the partial frontiers

As discussed in Cazals, Florens and Simar (2002) and Aragon, Daouia and Thomas-Agnan (2005), for the univariate input case, the partial frontiers $\phi_m(y)$ and $\phi_\alpha(y)$ are monotone function of y. However, the nonparametric estimators $\widehat{\phi}_{m,n}(y)$ and $\widehat{\phi}_{\alpha,n}(y)$ can be not monotone in y in finite samples. Daouia and Simar (2005) propose an easy way to isotonize these estimators to achieve the appropriate monotonicity. It is shown that these isotonized versions are even more robust to extreme and outliers than the original nonparametric estimators.

A new measure of efficiency

As pointed by Daouia and Simar (2004), for every attainable point $(x, y) \in \Psi$, there exists an α such that $\theta_\alpha(x, y) = 1$. This α could serve as an alternative measure of input efficiency score. If $F_{X|Y}(x \mid y)$ is continuous in x, this quantity is given (input orientation) by:

$$\alpha^{input}(x, y) = 1 - F_{X|Y}(x \mid y). \tag{4.28}$$

In other words, one may set the estimated performance measure for a unit operating at the level (x, y) to be the order α of the estimated quantile frontier which passes through this unit. This new concept of efficiency, the α efficiency, is illustrated in Figure 4.3. Suppose that we want to measure the efficiency score of a unit located at the point A (this is a unit which produces a level of output y using a level of input indicated by the point A on the x-axis). Its input efficiency score is equal to $\alpha^{input}(A) = 0.30$ since 70% of the units producing at least the level y of output are using less input than unit A.

This idea has been first proposed by Aragon, Daouia and Thomas-Agnan (2003) in the univariate case: they analyze the properties of these measures and the properties of their nonparametric estimators. The multivariate extension comes from Daouia and Simar (2004). These nonparametric estimators are obtained by using the empirical counterparts of the distribution function. We have to take into account the discreteness of empirical distributions. It can be shown that the correct expression for the nonparametric estimator of $\alpha^{input}(x_i, y_i)$, in the input orientation, is given by:

$$\widehat{\alpha}^{input}(x_i, y_i) = 1 - \widehat{F}_{X|Y,n}(x_i|y_i) + \frac{1}{M_{y_i}}. \tag{4.29}$$

In Figure 4.4 we illustrate all the nonparametric and robust measures introduced in the previous sections (input oriented framework). The illustration is presented

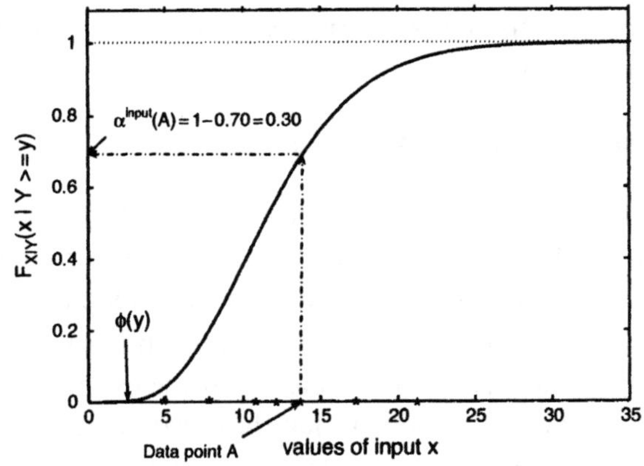

Figure 4.3. An illustration of α^{input} measure of efficiency in the bivariate case.

for $\alpha = 0.90$ and $m = 7$. In this figure, $\phi(y)$ is the full frontier level, it is given by the left boundary of the support of $F_{X|Y}(\cdot \mid y)$, $\phi_\alpha(y)$ corresponds to the $(1-\alpha)$ quantile of $F_{X|Y}(\cdot \mid y)$ and $\phi_m(y)$ is the expectation of the minimum of m virtual data points (here 7) generated by $F_{X|Y}(\cdot \mid y)$. We represent by the stars on the x-axis, 7 potential values of these random data points and we show where $\phi_7(y)$ could be around. The measure α^{input} is the new probabilistic efficiency measure defined above.

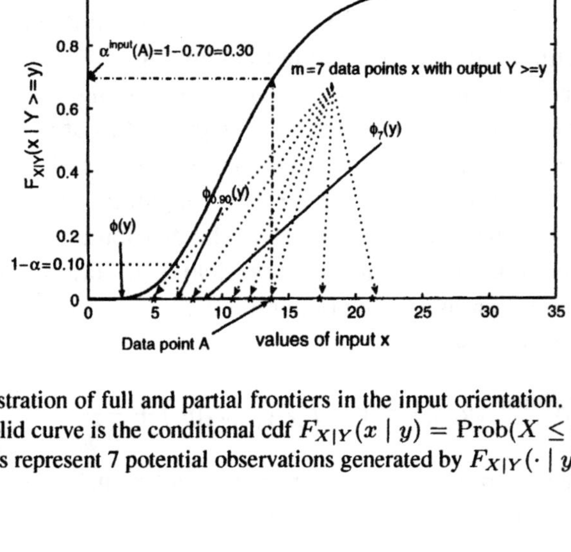

Figure 4.4. Illustration of full and partial frontiers in the input orientation. Here $m = 7$ and $\alpha = 0.90$: the solid curve is the conditional cdf $F_{X|Y}(x \mid y) = \text{Prob}(X \leq x \mid Y \geq y)$. The stars on the x-axis represent 7 potential observations generated by $F_{X|Y}(\cdot \mid y)$.

4.4 Properties of partial frontier estimators

In this section we summarize the most important properties of partial frontiers.

4.4.1 Statistical properties

The asymptotic properties of order-m and order-α frontiers and related efficiency scores have been analyzed by Cazals, Florens and Simar (2002) and Daouia and Simar (2004). In particular, they show the $\sqrt{n}$-consistency of $\hat{\theta}_{m,n}(x, y)$ to $\theta_m(x, y)$ for m fixed, as $n \to \infty$, and the $\sqrt{n}$-consistency of $\hat{\theta}_{\alpha,n}(x, y)$ to $\theta_\alpha(x, y)$ for α fixed, as $n \to \infty$ respectively. In addition, they prove that the related nonparametric estimators are asymptotically unbiased and asymptotically normally distributed.

4.4.2 Robust estimators of the full frontier

Another interesting feature of the partial frontiers is that when $m \to \infty$ (or when $\alpha \to 1$), the partial frontiers $\phi_m(y)$ ($\phi_\alpha(y)$, respectively) converge to the full frontier $\phi(y)$. For multivariate inputs we have the same properties for the efficiency scores: $\theta_m(x, y)$ ($\theta_\alpha(x, y)$, respectively) converges to $\theta(x, y)$, the Farrell-Debreu efficiency score computed with respect to the full frontier.

We have also similar properties for the nonparametric estimators $\widehat{\phi}_{m,n}(y)$ ($\widehat{\phi}_{\alpha,n}(y)$, respectively) and $\widehat{\theta}_{m,n}(x, y)$ ($\widehat{\theta}_{\alpha,n}(x, y)$) which converge to their FDH correspondent $\widehat{\phi}_n(y)$ or $\widehat{\theta}_{FDH}(x, y)$ as $m \to \infty$ ($\alpha \to 1$, respectively).

These properties allow the use of partial frontiers as robust estimators of the full frontier itself. The idea is to consider the order of the frontier (either m or α) as a function of n such that $m = m(n) \to \infty$ and $\alpha = \alpha(n) \to 1$ as $n \to \infty$ at appropriate rates, so that the partial frontiers converge to the full frontier and we can hope that their nonparametric estimators will also converge to the full frontier. For finite n however, the partial order frontiers do not envelop all the data points and hence are more robust to extreme and outlying points.

All the theory behind this idea has been provided in Cazals, Florens and Simar (2002) and in Daouia and Simar (2004): the resulting nonparametric estimators of the partial frontiers converge indeed to the full frontier itself as $n \to \infty$, sharing the same limiting Weibull distribution than the FDH estimator. For instance for the input oriented order-α efficiency score we have:

$$n^{1/(p+q)}\left(\widehat{\theta}_{\alpha(n),n}(x, y) - \theta(x, y)\right) \overset{\text{approx.}}{\sim} Weibull(\mu_{NW,0}^{p+q}, p + q) \text{ as } n \to \infty,$$

where $\mu_{NW,0}$ is a constant described in Park, Simar and Weiner (2000). Order-m estimators share the same properties and the same is true for the output oriented measures.

See Daraio and Simar (2005a), Daouia and Simar (2004, 2005) and Daouia, Florens and Simar (2005) for illustrations of these robustness properties in simulated samples. These robustness properties can also be exploited in the detection of outliers as explained below.

4.4.3 Advantages of using partial frontiers

Partial frontiers and related measures of efficiency show some nice statistical properties together with several "appealing" economic features that deserve some comments.

First of all, for their ability of not enveloping all data points, these robust measures of frontiers and the related efficiency scores are less influenced and hence more robust to extreme values and outliers. For empirical applications, this property means that we can avoid one of the more important limitation of the traditional nonparametric estimators, related to their deterministic nature.

Second, as a consequence of their statistical properties, robust measures of efficiency do not suffer of the *curse of dimensionality* shared by most nonparametric estimators and by the DEA/FDH efficiency estimators. Again this is a very important property for empirical works since it states that we can work with samples of moderate size and we do not require large samples to avoid imprecise estimation (*e.g.* large confidence intervals). In a lot of real data applications, in fact, there is not the availability of such a huge amount of data.

Third, and even more important is the economic interpretation of order-m measures of efficiency, and the appealing notion of order-α and in particular of α measures of efficiency. In particular, the parameter m has a *dual* nature. It is defined as a "trimming" parameter for the robust nonparametric estimation. It defines also the level of *benchmark* one wants to carry out over the population of firms. We propose to use m in its dual meaning to provide both robust estimations and a *potential competitors* analysis. The first task can be accomplished by plotting the percentage of points outside order-m frontier in function of m. By consulting this graph we may choose the value of m which corresponds to the target (or desired) *degree of robustness*, *i.e.* the percentage of high performers of the population we want to exclude in our *more realistic* benchmarking comparison (comparative analysis or performance evaluation).

The second application of m concerns the evaluation of a *potential competitors scenario*, in which for each firm we choose the potential competitors (m) against which we want to benchmark its performance and in this choice we take into account the turbulence of the competitive environment faced by the firm. The choice of m, hence, is related to the dynamics, the structure and characteristics of the considered market. We might also build several *simulated* competitive scenarios, by setting several values of m. In setting the values of m, however, there are neither fixed rules nor automatic procedure, as m can be any positive integer number. Nevertheless, for the choice of the "most reasonable" values of m, the statistical properties of estimators have to be considered together with the economic meaning of parameters. Even if m is independent from n (the number of analyzed firms, the sample size), the values of m might be fixed by considering the possible number of *potential* competitors we want "more realistically" benchmark our firm against. Furthermore, in most empirical applications of order-m efficiency measures, we noted that for $m \geq 200$ the order-m efficiency score is almost equal to the FDH efficiency score, *i.e.* the asymptotic result $\lim_{m\to\infty} \widehat{\theta}_{m,n}(x,y) = \widehat{\theta}_{FDH,n}(x,y)$ in practice, happens already for values such that $m \geq 200$. Leading by these considerations, we can define a grid of values for m to use in the sensitivity analysis, to build simulated competitive scenarios, that can be particularly useful for the analysis of industries and markets with an intensive and dynamic competition.

The economic meaning of order-α and α measures of efficiency is very interesting and useful. If order-α measures of efficiency could be roughly considered as a kind of "continuous version" of their order-m brothers, α measures have also an immediate economic meaning. They are based on the idea that there exists for each firm in the comparison set a quantile frontier which passes through it, on which the firm is efficient (either along the input dimension or along the output dimension). If the quantile on which the firm is efficient (in the input orientation) is 0.2, this means that there are 80% ($1 - 0.2 = 0.8$) of the firms in the comparison set (firms producing at least the same level of outputs) which outperform the considered firm by using less inputs. So that we can interpret $1 - \alpha$ as a firm's probability of being dominated on the input dimensions by the other firms producing at least the same level of output. Accordingly, is the interpretation for the output oriented case.

4.4.4 Detection of outliers

Partial frontiers (order-m and order-α) have been shown to be also very useful to detect outliers or extreme data. Indeed, the problem of extremes and outliers is a relevant question that has been addressed by several authors (among others by Wilson, 1995).

Simar (2003a), proposes the use of order-m frontiers to accomplish this difficult task. Of course the same procedure may apply order-α measures. Here, in the presentation, we follow Simar (2003a) and detail the procedure for the input orientation. The adaptation to the output orientation is straightforward. The main idea is that if some data points remain outside the partial order frontier even when m increases (or when α increases), this may warn these data points as potential outliers. Being outside the partial frontier is warned by values of $\widehat{\theta}_{m,n}(X_i, Y_i)$ (or $\widehat{\theta}_{\alpha,n}(X_i, Y_i)$) larger than 1.

The first issue to address is the choice of the values of m (or α). In choosing these values, it has also to be decided from what *threshold level* of the order-m (order-α) efficiency score we decide to flag a potential outlier. Some reasonable threshold values distant from one could be chosen on a grid of values $1 + \tau$, where $\tau = 0.20, 0.30, 0.40, 0.50$ (for the output oriented case, a point outside the partial frontier being detected by efficiency scores less than one, the grid would be defined by $1 - \tau$).

Thus for the order-m scores, the main steps of the computations are:

[1] Compute for each data point (X_i, Y_i), for $i = 1, ..., n$, its *leave-one-out* input efficiency score *i.e.* its order-m input efficiency score leaving out the observation (X_i, Y_i) from the reference set. Denote by $\widehat{\theta}^{(i)}_{m,n}(X_i, Y_i)$ the "leave-one-out" efficiency score and the corresponding reference set by $\mathcal{X}^{(i)}$.

[2] Compute $\widehat{\theta}^{(i)}_{m,n}(X_i, Y_i)$, for $i = 1, ..., n$, for several reasonable value of m, *e.g.* $m = 10, 25, 50, 75, 100, 150$.

[3] Compute also the number of points used to estimate the conditional distribution function $F_{X|Y}(x \mid y \geq Y_i)$, *i.e.* the number of points in $\mathcal{X}^{(i)}$ with $y \geq Y_i$. Denote this number as $N_{input}(X_i, Y_i)$. It is the number of points used to estimate the p-variate distribution function. If $N_{input}(X_i, Y_i)$ is small or even equal to zero, the correspondent point (X_i, Y_i) lies at the border of the sample values $\mathcal{X}$. $N_{input}(X_i, Y_i)$ thus indicates how the point (X_i, Y_i) is near to the border of the support of data points.

[4] For each values in τ, plot the percentage of points in the sample $\mathcal{X}$ with

$$\widehat{\theta}^{(i)}_{m,n}(X_i, Y_i) \geq 1 + \tau \tag{4.30}$$

as a function of m. This curve represents the percentage of points outside the order-m frontier as function of m for all the threshold values defined by the grid τ.

The computations for the output-oriented case are *mutatis mutandis* the same as above.

The interpretation of the results is based on the following statement: any point is outlying the cloud of points of data set $\mathcal{X}$ in the input direction (output direction) when its order-m input (output) efficiency score is greater (smaller) than one. The data points with input order-m efficiency measure greater than one, even if m increases, or with small values of N_{input} should be flagged as being extremes. In the output oriented case, the points with order-m efficiency score smaller than one, even if m increases, or with small values of N_{output} should also be flagged as extremes. When data points are detected as extremes in both directions (input and output), they are warned as potential outliers.

For doing this, we need to choose at which level we consider that m is "large". This may be achieved by looking at the plots obtained above, showing the percentage of points outside order-m frontiers for the different threshold values τ. By construction, these curves should decrease when m increases, and if there are no outliers, they should converge approximately linearly to the percentage of points having a leave-one-out FDH score greater than one (smaller than one for the output-oriented case). As a consequence, any strong deviation from linearity should indicate the potential existence of outliers: if the curves show an *elbow effect* (sharp negative slope, followed by a smooth decreasing slope) they indicate that the points remaining outside the order-m frontier for this value of m have to be further analyzed by the procedure described above and eventually warned as potential outliers.

Beside this, we have also to select m such that a reasonable percentage of points remains outside the frontier. It has been suggested (Barnett and Lewis, 1995) to use the rule of thumb $\frac{\sqrt{n}}{n}$ as a reasonable upper bound for the percentage of outliers in a sample of size n.

Of course, once the potential outliers have been identified, they have to be carefully analyzed to understand "why" they are outliers. Very often outliers (when not due to errors) contains useful information on the process under analysis (missing variables in the model, etc...).

4.5 Summary of the results for the output oriented case

We briefly summarize here the corresponding concepts for the output oriented case.

Order-m frontiers and related efficiency scores

Note that when y is univariate, the frontiers can be defined in terms of production functions. For instance, the full frontier (the production function) for an input level x is defined as:

$$\psi(x) = \lambda(x, y)\, y = \sup\{y \mid S_{Y|X}(y \mid x) > 0\}. \tag{4.31}$$

Then, the expected *order-m* frontier is defined, for a fixed integer value of $m \geq 1$ as *the expected value of the maximum of m random variables* $Y^1, ..., Y^m$ *drawn from the conditional distribution function of* Y *given that* $X \leq x$.

Its formal definition is:

$$\psi_m(x) = E[\max(Y^1, ..., Y^m)|X \leq x] = \int_0^\infty (1 - [F_{Y|X}(y \mid x)]^m)\, dy. \tag{4.32}$$

Its nonparametric estimator can be defined and computed by:

$$\widehat{\psi}_{m,n}(x) = \widehat{E}[\max(Y^1, ..., Y^m)|X \leq x] = \int_0^\infty (1 - [\widehat{F}_{Y|X,n}(y|x)]^m)\, dy. \tag{4.33}$$

The asymptotic properties of this estimator are the same, *mutatis mutandis*, than the estimator in the input-oriented framework.

The multivariate extension $y \in \mathcal{R}_+^q$ can be presented as follows. For a given level of inputs x in the interior of the support of X, consider m i.i.d. random variables $Y_i, i = 1, \ldots, m$ generated by the conditional q-variate distribution function $F_{Y|X}(y \mid x) = \text{Prob}(Y \le y \mid X \le x)$ and define the set:

$$\Psi_m(x) = \{(x', y) \in \mathcal{R}_+^{p+q} \mid x' \le x, Y_i \le y, i = 1, \ldots, m\}. \tag{4.34}$$

Then, for any y, we may define:

$$\begin{aligned}\tilde{\lambda}_m(x, y) &= \sup\{\lambda \mid (x, \lambda y) \in \Psi_m(x)\} \\ &= \max_{i=1,\ldots,m} \left\{ \min_{j=1,\ldots,q} \left(\frac{Y_i^j}{y^j} \right) \right\}.\end{aligned} \tag{4.35}$$

The order-m output efficiency measure is defined as follows. For any $y \in \mathcal{R}_+^q$, the (expected) order-m output efficiency measure denoted by $\lambda_m(x, y)$ is defined for all x in the interior of the support of X as:

$$\lambda_m(x, y) = E(\tilde{\lambda}_m(x, y) \mid X \le x), \tag{4.36}$$

where we assume the existence of the expectation.

As above, for any $y \in \mathcal{R}_+^q$ and for all x in the interior of the support of X, if $\lambda_m(x, y)$ exists, we have:

$$\begin{aligned}\lambda_m(x, y) &= \int_0^\infty \left[1 - (1 - S_{Y|X}(uy \mid x))^m\right] du \\ &= \lambda(x, y) - \int_0^{\lambda(x,y)} (1 - S_{Y|X}(uy \mid x))^m du.\end{aligned} \tag{4.37}$$

From this, it is easily seen that $\lim_{m\to\infty} \lambda_m(x, y) = \lambda(x, y)$. A nonparametric estimator of $\lambda_m(x, y)$ is given by:

$$\begin{aligned}\widehat{\lambda}_{m,n}(x, y) &= \int_0^\infty \left[1 - (1 - \widehat{S}_{Y|X,n}(uy \mid x))^m\right] du \\ &= \widehat{\lambda}_n(x, y) - \int_0^{\widehat{\lambda}_n(x,y)} (1 - \widehat{S}_{Y|X,n}(uy \mid x))^m du.\end{aligned} \tag{4.38}$$

Let us give an example of the economic meaning of the order-m output efficiency measure $\widehat{\lambda}_{m,n}(x, y)$ by looking at a firm operating at the level (x, y) and such that $\lambda_{m,n}(x, y) = 1.8$. This firm produces a level of output -in radial extension- that is equal to 0.56, *i.e.* $1/1.8$, times the expected value of the maximum level of output of m other firms drawn from the population of firms using a level of inputs $\le x$. A value of $\lambda_{m,n}(x, y) = 0.5$ would indicate that the firm produces $2 = 1/0.5$ times more output than the expected value of the maximum level of output of m other firms drawn from the same population.

As for the input oriented case, the computation of the order-m efficiency $\widehat{\lambda}_{m,n}(x, y)$ may be done either by numerical integration, calculating the univariate integral in (4.38), or adapting the Monte Carlo algorithm presented in Section 4.2 (for the input oriented case) as follows:

[1] For a given x, draw a sample of size m with replacement among those Y_i such that $X_i \leq x$ and denote this sample by $(Y_{1,b}, \ldots, Y_{m,b})$.

[2] Compute $\tilde{\lambda}_m^b(x,y) = \max_{i=1,\ldots,m}\left\{\min_{j=1,\ldots,q}\left(\frac{Y_{i,b}^j}{y^j}\right)\right\}$.

[3] Redo [1]-[2] for $b = 1, \ldots, B$, where B is large.

[4] Finally, $\hat{\lambda}_{m,n}(x,y) \approx \frac{1}{B}\sum_{b=1}^{B} \tilde{\lambda}_m^b(x,y)$.

Again, the approximation can be tuned by increasing B.

Order-α frontiers and related efficiency scores

Let $x \in \mathcal{R}_+^p$ and y be univariate, then the order-α production function can be defined as:

$$\psi_\alpha(x) = \sup\{y \mid S_{Y|X}(y \mid x) > 1 - \alpha\}. \tag{4.39}$$

It is the level of output not exceeded by $(1-\alpha) \times 100$-percent of firms among the population of units using less input than x. For the multivariate output case, we define the output oriented order-α efficiency score of a unit operating at the level (x, y) as:

$$\lambda_\alpha(x,y) = \sup\{\lambda \mid S_{Y|X}(\lambda y \mid x) > 1 - \alpha\}. \tag{4.40}$$

Again $\lambda_\alpha(x,y)$ converges to $\lambda(x,y)$, the usual Farrell-Debreu output efficiency score, when $\alpha \to 1$. In the univariate output case we have $\psi_\alpha(x) = \lambda_\alpha(x,y)y$ and in general, $\lambda_\alpha(x,y)$ gives the proportionate reduction (if < 1) or increase (if > 1) in outputs needed to move the unit (x,y) to the order-α output frontier, so that it is dominated by firms using less input than x with a probability $1-\alpha$.

The nonparametric estimators are obtained by plugging the empirical version of the survival function $S_{Y|X}(y \mid x)$ in the expression above. For the univariate output case we have:

$$\widehat{\psi}_{\alpha,n}(x) = \sup\{y \mid \widehat{S}_{Y|X,n}(y \mid x) > 1 - \alpha\}. \tag{4.41}$$

In the multivariate setup we have:

$$\widehat{\lambda}_{\alpha,n}(x,y) = \sup\{\lambda \mid \widehat{S}_{Y|X,n}(\lambda y \mid x) > 1 - \alpha\}. \tag{4.42}$$

Mutatis mutandis, the estimators shares the same properties as for the input oriented case ($\sqrt{n}$-consistency and asymptotic normality). We have also $\widehat{\lambda}_{\alpha,n}(x,y)$ converges to the FDH estimator $\widehat{\lambda}_{FDH}(x,y)$, if $\alpha \to 1$.

The computations of $\widehat{\lambda}_{\alpha,n}(x,y)$ is obtained through the following simple sorting algorithm. Indeed, define:

$$\mathcal{Y}_i = \min_{k=1,\cdots,q} \frac{Y_i^k}{y^k}, \quad i = 1, \cdots, n,$$

and let $N_x = n\widehat{F}_{X,n}(x) = \sum_{i=1}^{n} \mathbf{I}(X_i \leq x)$ be non null. For $j = 1, \cdots, N_x$, denote by $\mathcal{Y}_{(j)}^x$ the j-th order statistic of the observations $\mathcal{Y}_i$ such that $X_i \leq x$: $\mathcal{Y}_{(1)}^x \leq \mathcal{Y}_{(2)}^x \leq \ldots \leq \mathcal{Y}_{(N_x)}^x$. We have:

$$
\begin{aligned}
\widehat{S}_{Y|X,n}(\lambda y|x) &= \frac{\sum_{i|X_i \leq x} \mathbf{I}(Y_i \geq \lambda y)}{N_x} = \frac{\sum_{i|X_i \leq x} \mathbf{I}(\lambda \leq \mathcal{Y}_i)}{N_x} \\
&= \frac{\sum_{j=1}^{N_x} \mathbf{I}(\lambda \leq \mathcal{Y}_{(j)}^x)}{N_x} \\
&= \begin{cases} 1 & \text{if} \quad \lambda \leq \mathcal{Y}_{(1)}^x \\ \frac{N_x - j}{N_x} & \text{if} \quad \mathcal{Y}_{(j)}^x < \lambda \leq \mathcal{Y}_{(j+1)}^x, \; j = 1, \cdots, N_x - 1 \\ 0 & \text{if} \quad \lambda > \mathcal{Y}_{(N_x)}^x. \end{cases}
\end{aligned}
$$

It follows,

$$
\widehat{\lambda}_{\alpha,n}(x,y) = \begin{cases} \mathcal{Y}_{(\alpha N_x)}^x & \text{if} \quad \alpha N_x \in \mathcal{N}^* \\ \mathcal{Y}_{([\alpha N_x]+1)}^x & \text{otherwise,} \end{cases} \tag{4.43}
$$

where $\mathcal{N}^*$ denotes the set of positive integers and $[\alpha N_x]$ denotes the integral part of αN_x.

A new probabilistic measure of efficiency

As we have seen for the input oriented case, for every attainable point $(x, y) \in \Psi$, there exists an α such that $\lambda_\alpha(x, y) = 1$, and the value of this α could become an alternative measure of output efficiency score. Under the continuity of the survival function $S_{Y|X}(y \mid x)$, this new probabilistic measure can be defined as $\alpha^{output}(x, y) = 1 - S_{Y|X}(y \mid x)$. Put it in another way, we may set the estimated performance measure for a unit operating at the level (x, y) to be the order α of the estimated quantile frontier which passes through this unit. This new measure of efficiency is illustrated in Figure 4.5 which summarizes also all the other robust and nonparametric efficiency measures in the output oriented framework. Suppose that we want to measure the efficiency score of a unit located at the point A (this unit uses a level of input x for producing a level of output y indicated by the point A on the x-axis). Its output efficiency score is equal to $\alpha^{output}(A) = 0.75$ since 25% of the units using a level of input less or equal to x are producing a level of output higher than those of unit A.

A nonparametric estimator of this new efficiency measure (which takes into account the discreteness of the empirical survival function) for the output oriented case is given by:

$$
\widehat{\alpha}^{output}(x_i, y_i) = 1 - \widehat{S}_{Y|X,n}(y_i|x_i) + \frac{1}{N_x}. \tag{4.44}
$$

Figure 4.5 also illustrates the main efficiency measures introduced in this section for the output oriented framework. Here $\alpha = 0.90$, $m = 7$, and $\psi(x)$ is the full frontier level, it is given by the right boundary of the support of $S_{Y|X}(\cdot \mid x)$. $\psi_\alpha(x)$ corresponds to the $(1-\alpha)$ quantile of $S_{Y|X}(\cdot \mid x)$ and $\psi_m(y)$ is the expectation of the maximum of m virtual data points generated by $S_{Y|X}(\cdot \mid x)$. The stars on the x-axis are 7 potential values of these random data points and $\psi_7(y)$ shows where $\psi_m(y)$ could be around.

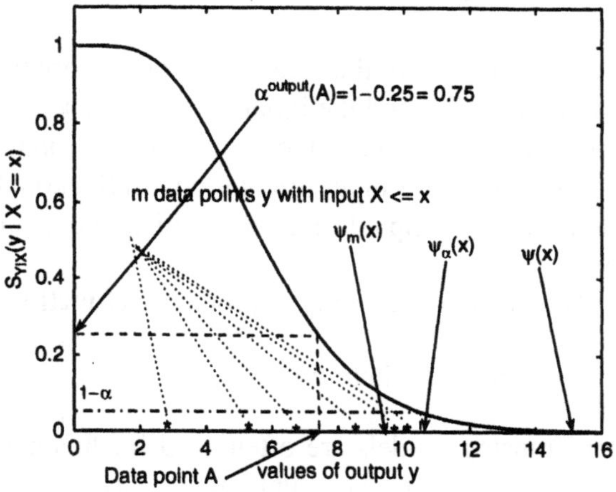

Figure 4.5. Illustration of full and partial frontiers in the output orientation. Here $m = 7$ and $\alpha = 0.90$: the solid curve is the conditional survival function $S_{Y|X}(\cdot \mid x) = \text{Prob}(Y \geq y \mid X \leq x)$. The stars on the x-axis represent 7 potential observations generated by $S_{Y|X}(\cdot \mid x)$.

4.6 Parametric approximations of robust and nonparametric frontiers

Nonparametric estimators are very appealing because they rely on very few assumptions on the shape of the frontier (like free disposability and eventually concavity) and on the stochastic process which generates the data on Ψ (except some general regularity conditions). However, this flexibility and generality has some drawbacks. For instance it is not easy in these nonparametric models to make a sensitivity analysis of the production of outputs to some particular inputs or to infer about elasticities, and other coefficients. On the contrary, parametric models for the production frontier (or for a cost or an input function) allow easier and richer economic interpretation. But of course, we have the risk of misspecification resulting in a risk of inconsistent estimates.

The parametric approaches to model a production frontier are straightforward and estimates are obtained trough least-squares methods or maximum likelihood techniques. However, as pointed by Florens and Simar (2005) these standard parametric approaches for frontier estimation suffer from additional drawbacks that will be briefly described below. Florens and Simar (2005) propose a new method which overcomes most of these drawbacks by providing the best parametric approximation of a frontier which is non parametrically estimated in a first stage. Using the robust version of the nonparametric estimators in this first step (order-m as in Florens and Simar, 2005, or order-α as in Daouia, Florens and Simar, 2005), we obtain at the end estimators of the parameters of the models sharing nice statistical properties ($\sqrt{n}$-consistency and asymptotic normality). So the inference on the parameters, or functions of the parameters is very easy.

In this section, we will present the ideas in the output orientation where the output y is univariate $y \in \mathcal{R}_+$ and the input $x \in \mathcal{R}_+^p$, hence we are interested in a production function. The same could be done for an input function where $x \in \mathcal{R}_+$ and $y \in \mathcal{R}_+^q$, by using input orientation. In Section 4.7, we will see how these concepts can be adapted to a full multivariate setup with multiple inputs and outputs.

Consider a suitable parametric family of production function defined on $\mathcal{R}_+^p$:

$$\{\varphi(\cdot \mid \theta) \text{ where } \theta \in \Theta \subseteq \mathcal{R}^k\}. \tag{4.45}$$

Cobb-Douglas or Translog models are often used for this parametric family. The parametric model for the frontier can be written as:

$$y = \varphi(x;\theta) - u,$$

where $u \geq 0$. The classical estimation of this model depends on the assumptions we want to impose on the error term u. If no particular assumption is made on u (except independence between u and x), shifted least-squares can be used (also called Modified OLS, MOLS). In this framework, a standard OLS is used to estimate the shape of the frontier and then all the residuals are shifted to satisfy $u \geq 0$ and so to identify the intercept. If some parametric density is chosen for u, we can improve the estimation of the intercept by estimating the parameters of this density and identifying the intercept by some moment conditions on the residuals (this is the Corrected OLS, COLS). In addition, with this full parametric model, maximum likelihood estimators (MLE) can be computed. For details see Greene (1980), Deprins and Simar (1985) or Kumbhakar and Lovell (2000).

The advantages of these methods are that they are easy to implement and that they achieve $\sqrt{n}$-consistency, even for the intercept if COLS or MLE is used. Nevertheless, the main drawback of these regression-type estimators is that they require strong assumptions on the stochastic part of the model. Since u is independent of x, we have $E(y|x) = \varphi(x;\theta) - E(u)$, where $E(u) = \mu$ is a constant. At a shift μ, $\varphi(x;\theta)$ is the regression of y on x. As a consequence, whatever the method used, $\varphi(x;\hat{\theta})$ will capture the shape of the "middle" of the cloud of points, whereas the frontier (and its characteristics) are properties of the boundary of the observed cloud of points. Besides, in addition to the independence assumption between u and x, these methods require specific distributional parametric assumption for the efficiency term u (at least for COLS and MLE), where in general, very few is known *a priori* on the shape of this distribution. Finally, as most of the deterministic models, the procedure is very sensitive to extremes or outliers.

4.6.1 Two stage methods

Coming back to ideas suggested in a descriptive way by Simar (1992), Florens and Simar (2005) propose a two stage method for estimating the parametric model, which overcomes most of the drawbacks just mentioned above. It is based on the following steps. In a first stage we project the cloud of data points on a nonparametric frontier, to capture in a flexible way the shape of the boundary of the cloud of points. After that, in a second stage, we fit the appropriate parametric model on these projected points. Of course a nonparametric full frontier estimator could be used in the first step but then it would suffer of the same drawback (of traditional methods) of being sensitive to outliers. Florens and Simar (2005) suggest as an alternative the use of the robust partial order-m frontiers in the first stage. Daouia, Florens and Simar (2005) extend this approach to order-α quantile type frontiers as first stage estimators. All the statistical theory of these two stage methods has been provided in these two papers. We briefly summarize the results after defining some useful notation.

Let us denote with $\varphi(x)$ the true but unknown production frontier, we want to estimate θ providing the best parametric approximation of the frontier function $\varphi(\cdot)$. The pseudo-true value of θ can be defined as:

$$\theta_0 = \arg\min_{\theta} \left[\sum_{i=1}^{n} (\varphi(x_i) - \varphi(x_i; \theta))^2 \right]. \tag{4.46}$$

Of course if the parametric model is true, then θ_0 is the true value of the parameter.

We can similarly define the pseudo-true values for the partial frontiers $\varphi_m(\cdot)$ or $\varphi_\alpha(\cdot)$, as follows:

$$\theta_0^m = \arg\min_{\theta} \left[\sum_{i=1}^{n} (\varphi_m(x_i) - \varphi(x_i; \theta))^2 \right], \tag{4.47}$$

$$\theta_0^\alpha = \arg\min_{\theta} \left[\sum_{i=1}^{n} (\varphi_\alpha(x_i) - \varphi(x_i; \theta))^2 \right]. \tag{4.48}$$

The estimation procedure is then straightforward. We plug-in the nonparametric estimator in place of the unknown $\varphi, \varphi_m, \varphi_\alpha$ in the above expressions. This leads to:

$$\hat{\theta}_n = \arg\min_{\theta} \left[\sum_{i=1}^{n} (\widehat{\varphi}_{FDH,n}(x_i) - \varphi(x_i;\theta))^2 \right], \tag{4.49}$$

$$\hat{\theta}_n^m = \arg\min_{\theta} \left[\sum_{i=1}^{n} (\widehat{\varphi}_{m,n}(x_i) - \varphi(x_i;\theta))^2 \right], \tag{4.50}$$

$$\hat{\theta}_n^\alpha = \arg\min_{\theta} \left[\sum_{i=1}^{n} (\widehat{\varphi}_{\alpha,n}(x_i) - \varphi(x_i;\theta))^2 \right]. \tag{4.51}$$

The statistical properties of these estimators are derived in Florens and Simar (2005) and in Daouia, Florens and Simar (2005). They can be summarized as follows:

$$\hat{\theta}_n - \theta_0 = o_p(1)$$
$$\sqrt{n}(\hat{\theta}_n^m - \theta_0^m) \overset{\text{approx.}}{\sim} \mathcal{N}_k(0, V_m)$$
$$\sqrt{n}(\hat{\theta}_n^\alpha - \theta_0^\alpha) \overset{\text{approx.}}{\sim} \mathcal{N}_k(0, V_\alpha)$$

where an explicit expression is obtained for V_m and V_α. In practice however, it is simpler to use a bootstrap algorithm, that we describe below[19], to provide consistent estimators of these variances. Note that for the full frontier parameters we only have consistency and not the asymptotic normality. This is another argument to favor the use of partial frontiers in the first step calculations. In addition, as explained below, by choosing m or α large enough, we estimate also the full frontier itself.

Note also that here no particular assumption is made on the error term when fitting the parametric model: we do not need a particular parametric distribution, we do not require homoscedasticity, the error term can be related to the level of the inputs x. Hence, clearly, most of the drawbacks of the regression-type estimators are overcome with this two-stage approach.

We have seen above that $\widehat{\varphi}_{m(n),n}$ and $\widehat{\varphi}_{\alpha(n),n}$ are robust estimator of φ, the full frontier itself, if $m(n) \to \infty$ and $\alpha(n) \to 1$ when $n \to \infty$. Daouia, Florens and Simar (2005) prove that if $m(n)$ and $\alpha(n)$ are such that:

$$\lim_{n\to\infty} m(n) = \infty, \quad \lim_{n\to\infty} m(n)(\log n/n)^{1/2} = 0, \quad \lim_{n\to\infty} n(1-\alpha(n)) = 0.$$

Then, as $n \to \infty$ the partial frontier estimates converge to the parameters of the full frontier model:

$$\hat{\theta}_n^{m(n)} - \theta_0 = o_p(1),$$
$$\hat{\theta}_n^{\alpha(n)} - \theta_0 = o_p(1).$$

[19]See also the appendix of Florens and Simar (2005) for additional details.

For finite n, partial frontier estimators provide more robust estimators of θ_0 because the nonparametric estimator of the frontiers will not envelop all the data points, as is the case, instead, for the FDH estimator.

In practice, we select m, or α by tuning the number of points staying out of the frontier, then we estimate the corresponding $\hat{\theta}_n^m$ or $\hat{\theta}_n^\alpha$ and use the asymptotic normal distribution for inference, with a bootstrap estimate of the variance. Below we describe the bootstrap algorithm while in the next section we show how these ideas can be extended to a full multivariate setup.

4.6.2 The bootstrap algorithms

The evaluation of the covariance matrices V_m and V_α is rather complicated. For practical purposes of inference on the value of θ_0^m and θ_0^α, it will be easier to approximate these matrices by a bootstrap method. As pointed in Florens and Simar (2005), the naive bootstrap is consistent here because in the estimation of θ_0^m or θ_0^α, we do not estimate the boundary of the support of the distribution of (x, y).

We present the algorithm for the order-α parametric approximation, the same could be done for the order-m approximation case. The aim is to approximate the asymptotic distribution of $\sqrt{n}(\widehat{\theta}_n^\alpha - \theta_0^\alpha)$ by its bootstrap analog, *i.e.*, the bootstrap distribution of $\sqrt{n}(\widehat{\theta}_n^{\alpha,*} - \theta_0^{\alpha,*})$, where $\widehat{\theta}_n^{\alpha,*}$ and $\theta_0^{\alpha,*}$ are the bootstrap analogs of $\widehat{\theta}_n^\alpha$ and of θ_0^α, respectively.

We have to be careful when defining these bootstrap analogs. They depend on how the pseudo-true values are defined. Florens and Simar give in their appendix three versions of the algorithm but here due to our definition of the pseudo-true value given in equation (4.48), the algorithm can be written as follows:

[1] Draw a random sample of size n with replacement from $\mathcal{X} = \{(x_i, y_i)|i = 1, \ldots, n\}$ to obtain the bootstrap sample $\mathcal{X}_b^* = \{(x_{i,b}^*, y_{i,b}^*)|i = 1, \ldots, n\}$.

[2] With this sample $\mathcal{X}_b^*$, compute $\sqrt{n}(\widehat{\theta}_{b,n}^{\alpha,*} - \theta_{0,b}^{\alpha,*})$ where:

$$\theta_{0,b}^{\alpha,*} = \arg\min_\theta \frac{1}{n}\sum_{i=1}^n \left(\widehat{\varphi}_{\alpha,n}(x_{i,b}^*) - \varphi(x_{i,b}^*;\theta)\right)^2, \quad (4.52)$$

$$\widehat{\theta}_{b,n}^{\alpha,*} = \arg\min_\theta \frac{1}{n}\sum_{i=1}^n \left(\widehat{\varphi}_{\alpha,n}^*(x_{i,b}^*) - \varphi(x_{i,b}^*;\theta)\right)^2, \quad (4.53)$$

where for any $x \in \mathcal{R}^p$, $\widehat{\varphi}_{\alpha,n}(x)$ is the nonparametric estimation of $\varphi_\alpha(x)$ obtained from the original sample $\mathcal{X}$ and $\widehat{\varphi}_{\alpha,n}^*(x)$ is the nonparametric estimation of $\varphi_\alpha(x)$ obtained from the bootstrap sample $\mathcal{X}^*$. These estimators[20] are evaluated in (4.52) and (4.53) at the bootstrap values $x^*_{i,b}$, $i = 1, \ldots, n$.

[3] Redo steps [1] and [2], a large number of times, $b = 1, \ldots, B$.

The empirical distribution of $\sqrt{n}(\widehat{\theta}^{\alpha,*}_{b,n} - \theta^{\alpha,*}_{0,b})$, $b = 1, \ldots, B$ approximates the distribution of $\sqrt{n}(\widehat{\theta}^{\alpha}_{n} - \theta^{\alpha}_{0})$ and can be used for doing inference (bootstrap confidence intervals, percentiles methods, ...). In particular, its variance matrix approximates V_α. Illustrative examples will be given in Part II of this book (see Section 7.5).

4.7 Multivariate parametric approximations

The two stage approach presented above can indeed be extended to the multivariate setup by using parametric approximations of distance functions. A modelization of Shephard distance function by flexible parametric models has been proposed by Grosskopf, Hayes, Taylor and Weber (1997) and its statistical properties have been investigated by Coelli (2000). However, what they proposed is based on regression-type techniques of estimation, and shares all the drawbacks described in the preceding section. On the contrary, we suggest, following Florens and Simar (2005), to use a two-stage approach: first estimate in a nonparametric way the distance functions, and then, fit the estimated values by an appropriate parametric model. We will see below how to apply this approach to translog distance functions, extensively used in the literature. The translog function can indeed be seen as a quadratic approximation of the real function in the log scale. The Cobb-Douglas function, besides, is just a particular case of the translog, where only the linear approximation is considered.

We make the presentation in the output oriented case, that is easy to translate for the input orientation. Now we analyse a full multivariate setup, *i.e.* $x \in \mathcal{R}^p_+$ and $y \in \mathcal{R}^q_+$. Let $\delta(x, y)$ be the Shephard output distance function (introduced as the inverse of Farrell efficiency score in Section 2.3, see (2.13)):

$$\delta(x, y) = \inf\{\delta | (x, y/\delta) \in \Psi\} \equiv (\lambda(x, y))^{-1}.$$

From its definition and the discussion in Section 2.3, it is easily seen that the distance function shares the following properties: (i) for all $(x, y) \in \Psi$, $\delta(x, y) \leq 1$; (ii) $\delta(x, y) = 1$, if and only if (x, y) is on the efficient boundary of Ψ; (iii) $\delta(x, y)$ is homogeneous of degree one in y: $\delta(x, \eta y) = \eta\delta(x, y)$ for all $\eta > 0$. Of course, the parametric models proposed for approximating these distances should be constrained to satisfy their properties.

[20] In the common case where $\varphi_\alpha(x; \theta)$ is linear in θ, the solutions of (4.52) and (4.53) are obtained by simple OLS techniques. Otherwise nonlinear least squares methods have to be used.

Also order-m output distance function , $\delta_m(x, y)$, and order-α output distance function $\delta_\alpha(x, y)$ can be considered by taking the inverse of the corresponding λ measures defined in the preceding sections. These partial frontiers have to be preferred if we want to be more robust to extreme data points.

Consider now a parametric family of functions defined on $\mathcal{R}_+^p \times \mathcal{R}_+^q$, denoted by $\{\varphi(\cdot, \cdot; \theta) \mid \theta \in \Theta \subset \mathcal{R}^k\}$, such that:

$$\forall (x, y) \text{ and } \forall \eta > 0, \quad \varphi(x, \eta y; \theta) = \eta \varphi(x, y; \theta).$$

Our aim is to estimate θ providing the best parametric approximation of the distance function $\delta(\cdot, \cdot)$.

As in Florens and Simar (2005) we can define the pseudo-true value of θ as:

$$\theta_0 = \arg\min_\theta \left[\sum_{i=1}^{n} (\delta(x_i, y_i) - \varphi(x_i, y_i; \theta))^2 \right]. \tag{4.54}$$

Finally the estimation is obtained by solving the following equation:

$$\hat{\theta}_n = \arg\min_\theta \left[\sum_{i=1}^{n} (\hat{\delta}_{FDH}(x_i, y_i) - \varphi(x_i, y_i; \theta))^2 \right]. \tag{4.55}$$

The same procedure can be followed with partial frontiers to get more robust estimators of θ_0. This is achieved by using $\hat{\delta}_m$ or $\hat{\delta}_\alpha$ in place of $\hat{\delta}_{FDH}$ in Equation (4.55).

By Florens-Simar (2005) and Daouia-Florens-Simar (2005) the resulting estimators share the same statistical properties as in the preceding section, namely consistency for the full frontier approximation, $\sqrt{n}$-consistency and asymptotic normality for the partial frontiers parameters.

In the following subsections we present two examples of parametric models for $\ln \delta(x, y)$ based on the Generalized Cobb-Douglas and the Translog functions.

4.7.1 Generalized Cobb-Douglas parametric model for $\ln \delta(x, y)$

In this case, the candidate parametric model is linear in the logs of the arguments:

$$\ln \delta(x, y) \approx \ln \varphi(x, y; \theta) = \alpha_0 + \alpha' \ln x + \beta' \ln y. \tag{4.56}$$

The homogeneity of order one in y implies that for all $\eta > 0$,

$$\ln \varphi(x, \eta y; \theta) = \ln \eta + \ln \varphi(x, y; \theta) \quad \text{so that} \quad \beta' i_q = 1,$$

where i_q is a vector of ones of length q.

The pseudo-true values $\theta_0 = (\alpha_0, \alpha, \beta)$ are defined as the solution of the following problem:

$$\theta_0 = \arg \min_{\alpha_0,\alpha,\beta_2} \left[\sum_{i=1}^{n} \left(\ln \delta(x_i, y_i) - [\alpha_0 + \alpha' \ln x_i + \beta_2' \ln y_i^2 + (1 - \beta_2' i_{q-1}) \ln y_i^1] \right)^2 \right],$$

where y^1 is the first component of y and y^2 and β_2 are the($(q-1) \times 1)$ vectors of the last $q-1$ components of y and β. Then the last parameter is identified by the homogeneity condition $\beta_1 = 1 - \beta_2' i_{q-1}$. Equivalently the pseudo-true values can be defined as:

$$\theta_0 = \arg \min_{\alpha_0,\alpha,\beta_2} \left[\sum_{i=1}^{n} \left(\ln(1/y_i^1)\delta(x_i, y_i) - [\alpha_0 + \alpha' \ln x_i + \beta_2' \ln \tilde{y}_i^2] \right)^2 \right],$$

where $\tilde{y}_i^2 = y_i^2 / y_i^1$ and $\beta_1 = 1 - \beta_2' i_{q-1}$. Finally the problem for defining the pseudo-true value can be written as:

$$\theta_0 = \arg \min_{\alpha_0,\alpha,\beta_2} \left[\sum_{i=1}^{n} \left(- \ln y_i^{*,1} - [\alpha_0 + \alpha' \ln x_i + \beta_2' \ln \tilde{y}_i^2] \right)^2 \right], \quad (4.57)$$

where y^* is the value of y projected on the output efficient frontier: $y^* = y/\delta(x, y)$. Note that $\tilde{y}^2 \equiv \tilde{y}^{*,2} = y^{*,2}/y^{*,1}$. Again $\beta_1 = 1 - \beta_2' i_{q-1}$.

Of course, in the last expression $\delta(x_i, y_i)$ are unknown, so are the $y_i^{*,1}$. Following the ideas of Florens and Simar (2005) we replace them by their nonparametric estimates (full frontier, or preferably robust partial frontier estimates):

$$\hat{y}^* = y/\hat{\delta}_{FDH,n}(x, y) \text{ or } \hat{y}^* = y/\hat{\delta}_{m,n}(x, y) \text{ or } \hat{y}^* = y/\hat{\delta}_{\alpha,n}(x, y).$$

For example, for the full-frontier approach, the estimators is defined by the following estimation equation:

$$\hat{\theta}_n = \arg \min_{\alpha_0,\alpha,\beta_2} \left[\sum_{i=1}^{n} \left(- \ln \hat{y}_i^{*,1} - [\alpha_0 + \alpha' \ln x_i + \beta_2' \ln \tilde{y}_i^2] \right)^2 \right],$$

and then $\hat{\beta}_{1,n} = 1 - \hat{\beta}_{2,n}' i_{q-1}$. The same could be done for $\hat{\theta}_n^m$ and for $\hat{\theta}_n^\alpha$.

Let's now compare this approach with the classical approach by Grosskopf, Hayes, Taylor and Weber (1997) and Coelli (2000), where the following model is estimated by COLS, MOLS or MLE:

$$- \ln y_i^1 = \alpha_0 + \alpha' \ln x_i + \beta_2' \ln \tilde{y}_i^2 + u_i,$$

where $u_i > 0$ is considered as the inefficiency term. The difference comes from the left-hand side term of the equation and from the stochastics on the efficiency distribution: in our approach we use the projected values on the nonparametric frontier and we do not make any assumption on the error term.

The drawbacks of this classical regression-based approach are well known: restrictive and non realistic assumptions on u (*e.g*, homoscedasticity), and problems of consistency (u is not independent from $\tilde{y}^2$), see Coelli (2000). With our approach we overcome all these difficulties and get more sensible results because the real (non-parametric estimated) values of the distance functions are directly fitted by the appropriate model.

4.7.2 Translog parametric model for $\ln \delta(x, y)$

Here the parametric model can be written as:

$$\ln \delta(x, y) \approx \varphi(x, y; \theta) = \alpha_0 + \alpha' \ln x + \beta' \ln y + \frac{1}{2}[\ln x' \ln y'] \, \Gamma \begin{bmatrix} \ln x \\ \ln y \end{bmatrix},$$

where $\Gamma = \Gamma'$ is symmetric. The homogeneity of degree one in y imposes $p + q + 1$ constraints:

$$\begin{array}{ll} \beta' i_q = 1, & \text{1 constraint} \\ \Gamma_{12}\, i_q = 0, & p \text{ constraints} \\ \Gamma_{22}\, i_q = 0, & q \text{ constraints} \end{array}$$

$$\text{where } \Gamma = \begin{pmatrix} \Gamma_{11} & \Gamma_{12} \\ \Gamma_{21} & \Gamma_{22} \end{pmatrix}.$$

Here the pseudo true values of θ are defined through the equation:

$$\begin{aligned} \theta_0 = \arg \min_{\alpha_0, \alpha, \beta_2, \Gamma_{11}, \tilde{\Gamma}_{12}, \tilde{\Gamma}_{22}} & \left[\sum_{i=1}^{n} \Big(-\ln y_i^{*,1} - [\alpha_0 + \alpha' \ln x_i + \tilde{\beta}_2' \ln \tilde{y}_i^2 \right. \\ & \left. + \frac{1}{2} \ln x_i' \Gamma_{11} \ln x_i + \ln x_i' \tilde{\Gamma}_{12} \ln \tilde{y}_i^2 + \frac{1}{2} \ln \tilde{y}_i^{\prime,2} \tilde{\Gamma}_{22} \ln \tilde{y}_i^{\prime,2}] \Big)^2 \right]. \end{aligned}$$

where: $\quad \beta = (\beta_1 \quad \tilde{\beta}_2')', \quad \Gamma_{12} = \begin{pmatrix} a & \tilde{\Gamma}_{12} \end{pmatrix}$ and $\Gamma_{22} = \begin{pmatrix} c_{11} & c_2' \\ c_2 & \tilde{\Gamma}_{22} \end{pmatrix}$

with $a \in \mathcal{R}^p$, $\tilde{\Gamma}_{12}$ is $(p \times (q-1))$, $c = (c_{11} \quad c_2')' \in \mathcal{R}^q$ and $\tilde{\Gamma}_{22}$ is $((q-1) \times (q-1))$. Here the missing parameters are identified through the homogeneity conditions (see below).

The estimation of $\alpha_0, \alpha, \beta_2, \Gamma_{11}, \tilde{\Gamma}_{12}, \tilde{\Gamma}_{22}$ is straightforward: we replace the unknown $y_i^{*,1} = y_i^1 / \delta(x_i, y_i)$ by the nonparametric estimates

$$\hat{y}_i^{*,1} = y_i^1 / \hat{\delta}_{FDH,n}(x_i, y_i)$$

or by $y_i^1/\hat{\delta}_{m,n}(x_i, y_i)$ or by $y_i^1/\hat{\delta}_{\alpha,n}(x_i, y_i)$ if more robust estimators are desired.

The estimator for (β_1, a, c) will be recovered from the homogeneity constraints:

$$\beta' i_q = 1 \Longrightarrow \hat{\beta}_1 = 1 - \hat{\beta}_2' i_{q-1}$$
$$\Gamma_{12}\, i_q = 0 \Longrightarrow \hat{a} = -\hat{\hat{\Gamma}}_{12}\, i_{q-1}$$
$$\Gamma_{22}\, i_q = 0 \Longrightarrow \begin{cases} \hat{c}_2 = -\hat{\hat{\Gamma}}_{22}\, i_{q-1} \\ \hat{c}_{11} = -\hat{c}_2\, i_{q-1} \end{cases} .$$

Finally, at the end of the procedure we have now the full parameter estimates: $\left(\hat{\alpha}_0, \hat{\alpha}, \hat{\beta}, \widehat{\Gamma}\right)$. By applying the results of Florens and Simar (2005) and of Daouia, Florens and Simar (2005), we have all the desired statistical inference based on the appropriate normal asymptotic distribution. Here too, the bootstrap is used in practice to make inference on the parameters θ for the partial frontiers approximations (order-α or order-m). All the details of the algorithm have been presented in Section 4.6.2 above. They are easily adaptable to this multivariate setup. Again the bootstrap can be used either to estimate the variance V_m or V_α of the estimators in the asymptotic normal approximation, or to provide directly percentile confidence intervals. The method is illustrated on real data in Section 7.5.

Chapter 5

CONDITIONAL MEASURES OF EFFICIENCY

This chapter deals with the important topic of the introduction of external-environmental variables in frontier models. It is useful to explain why these factors are important for comparative efficiency analysis and it shows the potential of some recently introduced diagnostic tools for capturing their impact on the performance of the analysed firms.

The evaluation of the influence of external-environmental factors on the efficiency of producers is a relevant issue related to the explanations of efficiency, the identification of economic conditions that create inefficiency, and finally to the improvement of managerial performance.

The meaning and the economic role played by external-environmental variables are strictly linked to the economic field firms are operating in. The choice of the environmental variables has to be done on a case-by-case basis, having a good knowledge of the production process characteristics and by taking into account the economic field of application.

From an economic point of view, we are interested in the evaluation of the influence of Z variables on the performance of the firms. To be able to evaluate this influence we have, firstly, to introduce the variables in the frontier estimation problem and then we have to address some questions, like the following: "Is the production process (and then the efficiency scores of firms) affected by the Z variables?"; if the answer to this question is yes, "How we can evaluate their influence?".

The aim of this chapter is therefore to present "how" *environmental variables* can be introduced in the probabilistic formulation of efficient frontier estimation (described in the previous chapter) and to propose "a way" to *operationalize* their introduction. The first purpose (introduction of Z variables) is addressed in a following section which presents a full set of conditional (to Z) measures of efficiency in a full frontiers (DEA/FDH) setting and in a robust (or partial) frontiers (order-m and order-α) setting. The second purpose (measuring the influence of Z) is handled through the introduction of an *econometric methodology* to follow in practical applications, based on the evaluation of the global influence of Z on the production process, and on a decomposition of the *conditional* (full or partial) efficiency of firm into some indicators with an interesting economic meaning. In particular, we propose to decompose the *conditional* efficiency of a firm into the *unconditional* (full or robust) efficiency score, an *externality* index - that measures the environmental conditions in which the firm operates in, *i.e.* favorable vs. unfavorable- and a *producer intensity* index, that measures the individual level of exploitation of the "environmental conditions", *i.e.* opportunities vs. threats of the "environment". This decomposition is particularly useful to facilitate comparative economic analysis of DMU' performance as it is shown in the applications reported in Part II of this book.

Here we complete the approach proposed by Daraio and Simar (2005a, 2005b) for full and order-m frontiers (extending previous results by Cazals, Florens and Simar, 2002), applied to order-α frontiers by Daouia and Simar (2004). In particular we discuss at length and explain in details how to evaluate the impact of multivariate Z on full and robust productive efficiency of DMU. Furthermore, a new conditional probabilistic efficiency measure is introduced in Section 5.2.3.

After a brief overview on the relevant literature on the introduction of external-environmental variables in nonparametric frontier models reported in the next section, Section 5.2.3 introduces a complete set of "conditional" measures of efficiency, *i.e.* efficiency measures which take into account these external-environmental variables, and presents their computational aspects. This presentation will let the applied economist to catch the basic functioning mechanism of the techniques. After that, Section 5.3 describes how to select the bandwidth to compute the conditional estimators for both univariate and multivariate Z. Afterwards, Section 5.4 explains in details and with simple illustrations the econometric methodology useful to interpret the plots and decompose the conditional efficiency measures. Finally, a series of simulation exercises illustrates the usefulness of the methodology and how to practically implement the proposed approach.

5.1 Explaining efficiency in the literature

The measurement of productive efficiency is only a first step of an efficiency study. A natural complement is the investigation on explanatory variables of the distribution of efficiency scores. Put it in another way, it is important to know and measure in what extent external- environmental variables affect the performance of the DMUs we are comparatively gauging.

Hence, the basic idea underlying the introduction of *external- environmental* variables is that of enriching the analysis of efficiency comparison by taking into account *extra information*, related to the production process, but that are neither inputs nor outputs under the control of the producer.

The nature of this extra information is such that it cannot be considered neither as an input nor as an output of the production process but it is able to affect the performance of the firms, in this sense we said above that these variables are "related" to the production process.

For instance, as *external/environmental variables* we can consider some *additional* information provided by the variables $Z \in \mathcal{R}^r$ which are "exogenous" to the production process itself, but may explain part of it; some environmental variables can not be under the control of the manager of the firm, at least in the short run and so on.

Lovell (1993, p. 53) distinguishes the inputs/outputs of the production process as "variables under the control of the decision maker during the time period under consideration", from *explanatory* variables that are "variables over which the decision maker has no control during the time period under consideration".

Bartelsman and Doms (2000), in their empirical review, find that some of the external/environmental *factors behind the patterns* (source of asymmetries) that are thought to be important include form of ownership, quality of the workforce, labor relations, technology international exposure, and the regulatory environment.

Other exogenous variables that can influence the production process are: input and output quality indicators, regulatory constraints, competitive environment (competitive vs monopolistic), service network characteristics; structure of property rights; type of ownership (private-public or domestic-foreign); environmental factors (conditions of the environment), location characteristics, age and other characteristics of plants, and so on.

In a broader perspective, Morroni (2006) indicates as environmental conditions the characteristics of information and knowledge, the techniques and equipment available, the individual aims, the individual capabilities, the degree of uncertainty, the structural change and the institutional and market conditions[21].

Traditionally, the main focus of the literature on efficiency estimation has been the evaluation of the performance of producers with a similar input/output structure. In the nonparametric approach, with the exception of some pioneering works by Seitz (1966, 1971) and Timmer (1971), the explanation of the distribution of efficiency scores through some explaining factors or "factors

[21]For a detailed discussion on the interplay between environmental conditions and internal conditions see Morroni (2006), p. 31 ff.

behind patterns" (as Bartelsman and Doms, 2000 call them) has started to be studied in literature only during the last decades[22].

An explicit reference to the importance of environmental variables can be found in Lewin and Minton (1986) which define a research agenda for determining organizational *effectiveness*, whose main points are: 1) to be capable of analytically identifying relatively most effective organizations in comparison to relatively least effective organizations; 2) to be capable of deriving a single summary measure of relative effectiveness of organizations in terms of their utilization of resources and their environmental factors to produce desired outcomes; 3) to be able to handle noncommensurate, conflicting multiple outcome measures, multiple resource factors and multiple environmental factors outside the control of the organization being evaluated; and not be dependent on a set of a priori weights or prices for the resources utilized, environmental factors or outcome measures; 4) to be able to handle qualitative factors such as participant satisfaction, extent of information processing available, degree of competition, etc.; 5) to be able to provide insight as to factors which contribute to relative effectiveness ratings; 6) to be able to maintain equity in the evaluation.

As we have seen above, the exploration of the reasons for productivity/efficiency differentials across production units is a relevant issue. When these external factors $Z \in \mathcal{R}^r$ are continuous mainly two approaches have been proposed in literature but both are flawed by restrictive prior assumptions on the DGP and/or on the role of these external factors on the production process.

The first family of models is based on a *one-stage* approach (see *e.g.* Banker and Morey, 1986a; Banker and Morey, 1986b for categorical external factors; Färe, Grosskopf, Lovell and Pasurka, 1989; Färe, Grosskopf and Lovell, 1994, p. 223-226), where these factors Z are considered as free disposal inputs and/or outputs which contribute to define the attainable set $\Psi \subset \mathcal{R}_+^p \times \mathcal{R}_+^q \times \mathcal{R}^r$, but which are not active in the optimization process defining the efficiency scores. In this case, the efficiency scores conditional to the Z are:

$$\theta(x, y|z) = \inf\{\theta \mid (\theta x, y, z) \in \Psi\}, \tag{5.1}$$

and the estimator of Ψ is defined as above by adding the variables Z in defining the FDH and /or the DEA enveloping set. Here the variable Z is considered as an input if it is conducive (favorable, advantageous, beneficial) to efficiency and as an output if it is detrimental (damaging, unfavorable) to efficiency. The drawback of this approach is twofold: first we have to know *a priori* what is the role of Z on the production process, and second, we have to assume the free disposability (and eventually convexity, if DEA is used) of the corresponding extended attainable set Ψ.

[22]For the introduction of external-environmental variables in parametric frontier models, see Kumbhakar and Lovell (2000).

The second family of models is based on a *two-stage* approach. Here the estimated efficiency scores are regressed, in an appropriated limited dependent variable parametric regression model (like truncated normal regression models) on the environmental factors Z. Recently, some models in this family propose also three-stage and four-stage analysis as extension of the two-stage approach.

In particular, Fried, Schmidt, and Yaisawarng (1999) propose a *four-stage* procedure that is based on a traditional DEA without external factors from which radial Farrell technical efficiency scores are computed as well as inputs slacks or outputs surpluses. In the second stage, a system of equations is specified in which the dependent variable for each equation is the sum of slacks (or surpluses in the output oriented case). To estimate the set of equations OLS (Ordinary Least Squares), SUR (Seemingly Unrelated Regression) or tobit regression are suggested to be used, according to the type of data. The third stage uses the parameters estimated in the second stage to predict the total input slacks (or output surpluses). These predicted values represent the "allowable" slack (surplus) due to the operating environment, and are used to calculate adjusted values for the primary inputs or outputs. Finally, the fourth stage consists in re-run the DEA model under the initial input-output specification, using the adjusted data set.

Fried, Lovell, Schmidt, and Yaisawarng (2002) propose as alternative a *three-stage* approach. In the first stage a DEA is applied to obtain an initial evaluation of the performance of producers. In the second stage a stochastic (parametric) frontier is used to account for environmental effects and statistical noise. In the third stage, DEA is applied on the adjusted data, taking into account environmental effects and statistical noise.

As pointed out by Simar and Wilson (2003), also these models - as the others in the two-stage family - are flawed by the fact that the usual inference on the obtained estimates of the regression coefficients is not available. They state: "none of the studies that employ two-stage approaches have described the underlying data-generating process. Since the DGP has not been described, there is some doubt about what is being estimated in the two-stage approaches". In addition, DEA estimates are by construction biased estimators of the unbiased efficiency scores. Finally, a more serious problem arises from the fact that DEA efficiency estimates are serially correlated and that the error term in the second stage is correlated with the regressors. As stated by Simar and Wilson (2003) "consequently, standard approaches to inference [...] are invalid".

Simar and Wilson (2003) give a list of references where the two-stage approach has been used and propose two bootstrap-based algorithms to obtain more accurate inference. However, even when corrected by the bootstrap, this two-stage approach has two inconveniences.

First, it relies on a *separability* condition between the input $\times$ output space and the space of Z values: the extended attainable set is the cartesian product

$\Psi \times \mathcal{R}^r$ and hence, the value of Z does not influence neither the attainable set Ψ nor the position of the frontier of the attainable set: Z acts only on the stochastic process pushing firms far from the frontier.

Second, the regression in the second stage relies on some *parametric* assumptions (like linear model and truncated normal error term in most studies. Recently, Park, Simar and Zelenyuk, 2006, have proposed a nonparametric approach using maximum likelihood techniques). In the next section we see how to avoid these limitations.

5.2 Introducing external-environmental variables

The probabilistic formulation of the production process described in Section 4.1 allows to overcome the limitations of previous approaches since external-environmental factors can easily be introduced in the DGP.

The basic idea developed in Daraio and Simar (2005a) is that the joint distribution of (X, Y) conditional on $Z = z$ defines the production process if $Z = z$. By analogy with (4.1), the support of $H_{X,Y|Z}(x, y|z) = \text{Prob}(X \leq x, Y \geq y \mid Z = z)$ defines Ψ^z, the attainable production set when $Z = z$. For an input conditional measure of efficiency, this joint distribution can be decomposed as follows:

$$H_{X,Y|Z}(x, y|z) = F_{X|Y,Z}(x \mid y, z) S_{Y|Z}(y|z), \tag{5.2}$$

for all y such that $S_{Y|Z}(y|z) = \text{Prob}(Y \geq y \mid Z = z) > 0$ and where $F_{X|Y,Z}(x \mid y, z) = \text{Prob}(X \leq x \mid Y \geq y, Z = z)$. Hence, for all y such that $S_{Y|Z}(y|z) > 0$, Ψ^z can also be defined by the support of $F_{X|Y,Z}(\cdot \mid y, z)$. Then, as above in (4.3), the lower boundary of the latter will define the lower boundary achievable for a unit producing an output level y with an environment described by the value z. Formally we have:

$$\theta(x, y \mid z) = \inf\{\theta \mid F_{X|Y,Z}(\theta x \mid y, z) > 0\}. \tag{5.3}$$

Note again that the conditioning on Y is the event $Y \geq y$ (because Y represents the outputs) and the conditioning on Z is defined, as in a regression framework, by $Z = z$. Hence Ψ^z can be described as:

$$\Psi^z = \{(x', y) \in \mathcal{R}_+^{p+q} \mid x' \geq x^{\partial,z}(y) \text{ for } (x, y) \in \Psi\}, \tag{5.4}$$

where $x^{\partial,z}(y)$ is the efficient level of input, conditional on $Z = z$, for an output level y: $x^{\partial,z}(y) = \theta(x, y \mid z)\, x$, where $(x, y) \in \Psi$. Clearly, $\Psi^z \subseteq \Psi$.

5.2.1 Conditional full frontier measures

Daraio and Simar (2005a) propose a plug-in nonparametric estimator of $F_{X|Y,Z}(\cdot \mid y, z)$ in the expression (5.3) defining $\theta(x, y \mid z)$. Due to the equality in the conditioning on Z this requires some smoothing techniques. At this purpose they suggest a kernel estimator defined as follows:

$$\widehat{F}_{X|Y,Z,n}(x \mid y, z) = \frac{\sum_{i=1}^{n} \boldsymbol{I}(x_i \leq x, y_i \geq y) K((z - z_i)/h)}{\sum_{i=1}^{n} \boldsymbol{I}(y_i \geq y) K((z - z_i)/h)}, \tag{5.5}$$

where $K(\cdot)$ is the kernel and h is the bandwidth of appropriate size[23]. Hence, we obtain the "conditional FDH efficiency measure" as follows:

$$\widehat{\theta}_{FDH}(x, y \mid z) = \inf\{\theta \mid \widehat{F}_{X|Y,Z,n}(\theta x \mid y, z) > 0\}. \tag{5.6}$$

Daraio and Simar (2005a) pointed out that for kernels with unbounded support, like the gaussian kernel, it is easy to show that $\widehat{\theta}_{FDH}(x, y|z) \equiv \widehat{\theta}_{FDH}(x, y)$: the estimate of the full-frontier efficiency is unable to detect any influence of the environmental factors. Therefore, in this framework of conditional boundary estimation, kernels with compact support have to be used.

For any (symmetric) kernel with compact support (*i.e.*, $K(u) = 0$ if $|u| > 1$, as for the uniform, triangle, Epanechnikov or quartic kernels, see *e.g.* Silverman, 1986), the conditional FDH efficiency estimator is given by:

$$\widehat{\theta}_{FDH}(x, y|z) = \inf\{\theta \mid \widehat{F}_{X|Y,Z,n}(\theta x \mid y, z) > 0\} \tag{5.7}$$

$$= \min_{\{i | Y_i \geq y, |Z_i - z| \leq h\}} \left\{ \max_{j=1,\ldots,p} \left(\frac{X_i^j}{x^j} \right) \right\}. \tag{5.8}$$

In this framework, the estimation of conditional full frontiers does not depend on the chosen kernel but only on the selected bandwidth. This will be different for the conditional order-m and order-α measures defined below.

The conditional attainable set Ψ^z is estimated by:

$$\widehat{\Psi}^z_{FDH} = \{(x', y) \in \mathcal{R}_+^{p+q} \mid x' \geq \hat{x}^{\partial, FDH, z}(y) \text{ for } (x, y) \in \widehat{\Psi}_{FDH}\}, \tag{5.9}$$

where $\hat{x}^{\partial, FDH, z}(y)$ is the estimated conditional efficient level of inputs:

$$\hat{x}^{\partial, FDH, z}(y) = \widehat{\theta}_{FDH}(x, y|z)\, x \text{ for } (x, y) \in \widehat{\Psi}_{FDH}.$$

Daraio and Simar (2005b) define also a conditional DEA estimator and address its computational issue. Consistency and asymptotic properties of these conditional estimators are investigated in Jeong, Park and Simar (2006).

5.2.2 Conditional order-m measures

The conditional order-m input efficiency measure is defined in Daraio and Simar (2005a), where only free disposability is assumed. For a given level of

---

[23] Issues about the practical choice of the bandwidth are discussed in Section 5.3.

outputs y in the interior of the support of Y, we consider the m i.i.d. random variables $X_i, i = 1, \ldots, m$ generated by the conditional p-variate distribution function $F_{X|Y,Z}(x \mid y, z)$ and we define the conditional random set:

$$\widetilde{\Psi}_m^z(y) = \{(x, y') \in \mathcal{R}_+^{p+q} \mid x \geq X_i, y' \geq y, \; i = 1, \ldots, m\}. \tag{5.10}$$

Note that this set depends on the value of z since the X_i are generated through the conditional distribution function. For any $x \in \mathcal{R}_+^p$, the conditional order-m input efficiency measure given that $Z = z$, denoted by $\theta_m(x, y|z)$ is then defined as:

$$\theta_m(x, y|z) = E_{X|Y,Z}(\tilde{\theta}_m^z(x, y) \mid Y \geq y, Z = z), \tag{5.11}$$

where $\tilde{\theta}_m^z(x, y) = \inf\{\theta \mid (\theta x, y) \in \widetilde{\Psi}_m^z(y)\}$ and the expectation is relative to the distribution $F_{X|Y,Z}(\cdot \mid y, z)$. It is shown by Daraio and Simar (2005a) (Theorem 3.1) that $\theta_m(x, y|z)$ converges to $\theta(x, y|z)$ when $m \to \infty$.

A nonparametric estimator of $\theta_m(x, y|z)$ is provided by plugging the nonparametric estimator of $F_{X|Y,Z}(x|y, z)$ proposed in (5.5), which depends on the kernel and on the chosen bandwidth. Formally, the estimator can be obtained by:

$$\begin{aligned} \widehat{\theta}_m(x, y|z) &= \widehat{E}_{X|Y,Z}(\tilde{\theta}_m^z(x, y) \mid y, z) && (5.12) \\ &= \int_0^\infty (1 - \widehat{F}_{X|Y,Z,n}(ux \mid y, z))^m du. && (5.13) \end{aligned}$$

This involve the computation of a one-dimensional numerical integral.

Since $\widehat{\theta}_m(x, y|z) \to \widehat{\theta}_{FDH}(x, y|z)$ when $m \to \infty$, the order-m conditional efficiency score can again be viewed as a robust estimator of the conditional efficiency score $\theta(x, y|z)$ when choosing $m = m(n) \to \infty$ with $n \to \infty$. For finite m, the corresponding attainable set will not envelop all the data points and so is more robust to extremes or outlying data points.

Cazals, Florens and Simar (2002) prove the consistency of this estimator and derive its asymptotic law. Daraio and Simar (2005b) propose also a conditional convex order$-m$ estimator.

Computational aspects

As we described in Section 4.2 the computation of order-m efficiency $\hat{\theta}_{m,n}$ (x, y) could be done either by evaluating the univariate integral (4.23) via numerical methods, or by an easy Monte-Carlo algorithm.

Similarly, the conditional order-m efficiency $\hat{\theta}_{m,n}(x, y \mid z)$ can be computed either evaluating the integral (5.13) by numerical methods or using an adapted version of the Monte-Carlo algorithm recalled above. This Monte-Carlo algorithm for the conditional input order-m efficiency works as follows. Suppose that h is the chosen bandwidth for a particular kernel $K(\cdot)$:

[1] For a given y, draw a sample of size m with replacement, and with a probability $K((z-z_i)/h)/\sum_{j=1}^{n} K((z-z_j)/h)$, among those X_i such that $Y_i \geq y$. Denote this sample by $(X_{1,b},\ldots,X_{m,b})$;

[2] compute $\tilde{\theta}_m^{b,z}(x,y) = \min_{i=1,\ldots,m}\left\{\max_{j=1,\ldots,p}\left(\frac{X_{i,b}^j}{x^j}\right)\right\}$.

[3] Redo [1]-[2] for $b = 1,\ldots,B$, where B is large.

[4] Finally, $\hat{\theta}_{m,n}(x,y \mid z) \approx \frac{1}{B}\sum_{b=1}^{B} \tilde{\theta}_m^{b,z}(x,y)$.

However, for large m, the numerical univariate integral in (5.13) is much faster to compute.

5.2.3 Conditional order-α measures

An alternative to the order-m partial frontier to obtain robust conditional measure, robust to extreme data points and outliers, is the order-α quantile-type frontier described in Section 4.3. The extension of these conditional measures to order-α has been proposed by Daouia and Simar (2004). We continue the presentation with the input orientation.

In place of looking for the conditional input efficiency score with respect to the full conditional frontier, as above, $\theta(x,y \mid z) = \inf\{\theta \mid F_{X|Y,Z}(\theta x \mid y,z) > 0\}$, we rather consider the $(1-\alpha)$ quantile of the same conditional cumulative distribution function (cdf). Formally, the conditional order-α input efficiency measure given that $Z = z$, denoted by $\theta_\alpha(x,y|z)$ is defined for all y in the interior of the support of Y as:

$$\theta_\alpha(x,y|z) = \inf\{\theta \mid F_{X|Y,Z}(\theta x|y,z) > 1-\alpha\}. \tag{5.14}$$

We have the same interpretation we had for the order-α efficiency scores except that here we condition additionally on the environmental variables $Z = z$. In other words, $\theta_\alpha(x,y|z)$ is the proportionate reduction (if < 1) or increase (if > 1) of inputs, the unit operating at the level (x,y) and confronted to environmental conditions z, should achieve to reach the conditional to z input efficient frontier of level $\alpha \times 100\%$. Being on this frontier ($\theta_\alpha(x,y|z) = 1$) means the unit is dominated by firms producing more output than y and confronted with the same environmental conditions z, with a probability $1-\alpha$. Daouia and Simar (2004) analyse the properties of this measure and as expected, it is easy to prove that $\theta_\alpha(x,y|z)$ converges to $\theta(x,y|z)$ when $\alpha \to 1$.

A nonparametric estimator is given by plugging, in (5.14), the nonparametric estimator of $F_{X|Y,Z}(\cdot)$ introduced above. It can be shown, with the notations introduced in Section 4.3, that:

$$\widehat{F}_{X|Y,Z,n}(\theta x|y,z) \quad = \quad \frac{1}{Q_{y,z}}\sum_{j=1}^{M_y} \mathbf{I}(\mathcal{X}_{(j)}^y \leq \theta) K\left((z - Z_{[j]}^y)/h_n\right)$$

$$= \begin{cases} 0 & \text{if} \quad \theta < \mathcal{X}^y_{(1)} \\ \ell_k & \text{if} \quad \mathcal{X}^y_{(k)} \le \theta < \mathcal{X}^y_{(k+1)}, \ k = 1, \cdots, M_y - 1 \\ 1 & \text{if} \quad \theta \ge \mathcal{X}^y_{(M_y)}, \end{cases}$$

where, for $j = 1, \cdots, M_y$, $Z^y_{[j]}$ denotes the observation Z_i corresponding to the order statistic $\mathcal{X}^y_{(j)}$, $Q_{y,z} = \sum_{i=1}^n \boldsymbol{I}(Y_i \ge y) K(\frac{z - Z_i}{h_n})$, and finally $\ell_k = (1/Q_{y,z}) \sum_{j=1}^k K\left((z - Z^y_{[j]})/h_n\right)$.

Thus the nonparametric estimator of the conditional order-α input efficiency measure given that $Z = z$ is given by:

$$\widehat{\theta}_{\alpha,n}(x, y|z) = \begin{cases} \mathcal{X}^y_{(1)} & \text{if} \quad 0 \le 1 - \alpha < \ell_1 \\ \mathcal{X}^y_{(k+1)} & \text{if} \quad \ell_k \le 1 - \alpha < \ell_{k+1}, \\ & k = 1, \cdots, M_y - 1. \end{cases} \tag{5.15}$$

Again this is easy and very fast to compute since it is only based on enumerative algorithms. Daouia and Simar (2004) have proven the consistency of these conditional estimators.

A new measure of conditional input efficiency

Extending the ideas presented in Section 4.3, for every attainable point $(x, y) \in \Psi$, there exists an α_z such that $\theta_{\alpha_z}(x, y|z) = 1$. This α_z could serve as an alternative measure of conditional input efficiency score. If $F_{X|Y,Z}(x \mid y, z)$ is continuous in x, this quantity is given, for the input orientation, by:

$$\alpha_z^{input}(x, y) = 1 - F_{X|Y,Z}(x \mid y, z). \tag{5.16}$$

In other words, one may set the estimated conditional performance measure for a unit operating at the level (x, y) facing the environmental conditions z, to be the order α_z of the estimated conditional quantile frontier which passes through this unit. This new measure of conditional efficiency, the conditional α efficiency, may be estimated by the following quantity:

$$\widehat{\alpha}_{z,n}^{input} = 1 - \ell_{k-1}, \tag{5.17}$$

where k is the index such that $\mathcal{X}^y_{(k)} = 1$, ℓ_k was defined above and we set $\ell_0 = 0$.

This new measure has an appealing economic interpretation. The quantity $(1 - \alpha_z^{input}(x, y))$ is the firm (x, y)'s probability of being dominated in the inputs space, given its level of outputs, taking into account its external-environmental conditions $Z = z$.

Hence, a simple indicator of the impact of external factors on firms performance may be $\alpha_{Q^z} = \frac{\alpha_z^{input}(x,y)}{\alpha^{input}(x,y)}$, where $\alpha^{input}(x, y)$, defined in (4.28), is the unconditional corresponding measure. Let us give some examples on how to interpret this indicator.

- If $\alpha_{Q^z} > 1$, then $(1 - \alpha_z^{input}(x,y)) < (1 - \alpha^{input}(x,y))$ In this case, for the firm operating at the level (x, y) the probability of being dominated given the condition $Z = z$ is lower than that of being dominated without taking into account the external conditions.

- If $\alpha_{Q^z} = 1$, then $(1 - \alpha_z^{input}(x,y)) = (1 - \alpha^{input}(x,y))$ Here, the probabilities are equal, hence it seems that the external conditions do not play any role.

- If $\alpha_{Q^z} < 1$, then $(1 - \alpha_z^{input}(x,y)) > (1 - \alpha^{input}(x,y))$ In this situation, the probability of being dominated given the condition $Z = z$ is higher than that of being dominated without taking into account the external conditions.

An application of this new measure and related indicators on real data is reported in Chapter 8, where their usefulness is also shown.

In Table 5.1 we report all the nonparametric and robust measures of efficiency introduced in this book as well as the main related references. The presentation in the table is done for the input oriented framework. However, most of the cited references report or just outline the output oriented correspondent measures that will be described in the following section.

5.2.4 Summary for the output oriented case

In this section we briefly show how to adapt the conditional measures developed above for the input orientation to the output orientation. We have seen in Section 4.1 that the Farrell-Debreu output efficiency score can be characterized as $\lambda(x, y) = \sup\{\lambda \mid S_{Y|X}(\lambda y \mid x) > 0\}$, where $S_{Y|X}(y \mid x) = \text{Prob}(Y \geq y \mid X \leq x)$. The FDH nonparametric estimator of $\lambda(x, y)$ is then provided by the empirical version of $S_{Y|X}(y \mid x)$:

$$\widehat{S}_{Y|X,n}(y \mid x) = \frac{\sum_{i=1}^{n} \boldsymbol{I}(X_i \leq x, Y_i \geq y)}{\sum_{i=1}^{n} \boldsymbol{I}(X_i \leq x)}.$$

Then, the FDH estimator of the output efficiency score for a given point (x, y) can be written as $\hat{\lambda}_n(x, y) = \sup\{\lambda \mid \widehat{S}_{Y|X,n}(\lambda y \mid x) > 0\}$. *Mutatis mutandis*, all the output oriented measures share the same properties as their input oriented correspondent.

Table 5.1. A summary of nonparametric and robust efficiency measures presented in this book with the most important references. Input orientation.

	Unconditional Measures	Conditional Measures
Full Frontiers	$\widehat{\theta}_{DEA}(x,y)$ *Farrell (1957)* *Charnes, Cooper and Rodhes (1978)*	$\widehat{\theta}_{DEA}(x,y \mid z)$ *Daraio and Simar (2005b)*
	$\widehat{\theta}_{FDH}(x,y)$ *Deprins, Simar and Tulkens (1984)*	$\widehat{\theta}_{FDH}(x,y \mid z)$ *Daraio and Simar (2005a)*
Robust Frontiers	$\widehat{\theta}_m(x,y)$ *Cazals, Florens and Simar (2002)* *and Daraio and Simar (2005a,b)*	$\widehat{\theta}_m(x,y \mid z)$ *Cazals, Florens and Simar (2002)* *and Daraio and Simar (2005a,b)*
	$\widehat{\theta}_\alpha(x,y)$ *Aragon et. al. (2002)* *and Daouia and Simar (2004)*	$\widehat{\theta}_\alpha(x,y \mid z)$ *Daouia and Simar (2004)*
	$\widehat{\alpha}_n^{input}$ *Aragon et. al. (2003)* *Daouia and Simar (2004)* *and this book*	$\widehat{\alpha}_{z,n}^{input}$ *this book*

Conditional full-frontier

When conditioning on environmental factors we have to replace $S_{Y|X}(y \mid x)$ by $S_{Y|X,Z}(y \mid x, z) = \text{Prob}(Y \geq y \mid X \leq x, Z = z)$ so we obtain the definition of the output conditional full-frontier efficiency measure:

$$\lambda(x, y|z) = \sup\{\lambda \mid S_{Y|X,Z}(\lambda y|x, z) > 0\}. \tag{5.18}$$

A nonparametric estimator of the conditional full-frontier efficiency $\lambda(x, y|z)$ is given by plugging in its formula a nonparametric estimator of $S_{Y|X,Z}(y|x, z)$. We can use the following smoothed estimator:

$$\widehat{S}_{Y|X,Z,n}(y|x,z) = \frac{\sum_{i=1}^{n} \boldsymbol{I}(X_i \leq x, Y_i \geq y) K\left((z - Z_i)/h_n\right)}{\sum_{i=1}^{n} \boldsymbol{I}(X_i \leq x) K\left((z - Z_i)/h_n\right)}, \tag{5.19}$$

where K is the kernel and h_n is the bandwidth of appropriate size. Again, kernels with compact support have to be used. The computation of this estimator is very easy. We obtain:

$$\begin{aligned}\widehat{\lambda}_n(x,y|z) &= \sup\{\lambda \mid \widehat{S}_{Y|X,Z,n}(\lambda y|x,z) > 0\} \\ &= \max_{\{i|X_i \geq x, |Z_i - z| \leq h\}} \left\{ \min_{j=1,\ldots,q} \left(\frac{Y_i^j}{y^j} \right) \right\}.\end{aligned}$$

Conditional order-m frontier

The conditional order-m output efficiency measure is introduced as follows. For a given level of inputs x, consider the m i.i.d. random variables Y_i, $i = 1, \ldots, m$ generated by the conditional q-variate survival function $S_{Y|X,Z}(y \mid x, z)$ and define the set:

$$\Psi_m^z(x) = \{(u,v) \in \mathcal{R}_+^{p+q} \mid u \leq x, Y_i \leq v,\ i = 1, \ldots, n\}. \qquad (5.20)$$

Note that this random set depends on the value of z since the Y_i are generated through $S_{Y|X,Z}(y \mid x, z)$. Then, for any y, we may define $\tilde{\lambda}_m^z(x,y) = \sup\{\lambda \mid (x, \lambda y) \in \Psi_m^z(x)\}$. The conditional order-$m$ output efficiency measure is defined as:

$$\lambda_m(x,y|z) = E_{Y|X,Z}(\tilde{\lambda}_m^z(x,y) \mid X \leq x, Z = z).$$

It can be computed as:

$$\lambda_m(x,y|z) = \int_0^\infty [1 - (1 - S_{Y|X,Z}(uy \mid x,z))^m]du, \qquad (5.21)$$

where again it can be shown that $\lim_{m\to\infty} \lambda_m(x,y|z) = \lambda(x,y|z)$. A non-parametric estimator of $\lambda_m(x,y|z)$ is given by:

$$\begin{aligned}\widehat{\lambda}_m(x,y|z) &= \int_0^\infty \left[1 - (1 - \widehat{S}_{Y|X,Z,n}(uy \mid x,z))^m\right] du \\ &= \widehat{\lambda}_n(x,y|z) - \int_0^{\widehat{\lambda}_n(x,y|z)} (1 - \widehat{S}_{Y|X,Z,n}(uy \mid x,z))^m du. \qquad (5.22)\end{aligned}$$

The Monte Carlo algorithm presented in Section 5.2.2 can be easily adapted to the output orientation.

Conditional order-α frontier

Similarly, we can define the conditional order-α output efficiency measure given that $Z = z$ as:

$$\lambda_\alpha(x,y|z) = \sup\{\lambda \mid S_{Y|X,Z}(\lambda y|x,z) > 1 - \alpha\}. \qquad (5.23)$$

A nonparametric estimator of $\lambda_\alpha(x, y|z)$ is provided by plugging in its formula the nonparametric estimator of $S_{Y|X,Z}(y|x, z)$. Formally, it is defined as:

$$\widehat{\lambda}_{\alpha,n}(x, y|z) = \sup\{\lambda \,|\, \widehat{S}_{Y|X,Z,n}(\lambda y|x, z) > 1 - \alpha\}.$$

Here also we have $\lim_{\alpha\to 1} \widehat{\lambda}_{\alpha,n}(x, y|z) = \widehat{\lambda}_n(x, y|z)$. The computation of the estimator can be described as follows, by using the notations introduced in Chapter 4. For $j = 1, \cdots, N_x$, denote by $Z^x_{[j]}$ the observation Z_i corresponding to the order statistic $\mathcal{Y}^x_{(j)}$, and let $R_{x,z} = \sum_{i=1}^n \boldsymbol{I}(X_i \le x) K(\frac{z - Z_i}{h_n}) > 0$. Then it can be shown that:

$$\begin{aligned} \widehat{S}_{Y|X,Z,n}(\lambda y|x, z) &= \frac{1}{R_{x,z}} \sum_{j=1}^{N_x} \boldsymbol{I}(\lambda \le \mathcal{Y}^x_{(j)}) K\left((z - Z^x_{[j]})/h_n\right) \\ &= \begin{cases} 1 \ \text{ if } \ \lambda \le \mathcal{Y}^x_{(1)} \\ L_{k+1} \ \text{ if } \ \mathcal{Y}^x_{(k)} < \lambda \le \mathcal{Y}^x_{(k+1)}, \ k = 1, \cdots, N_x - 1 \\ 0 \ \text{ if } \ \lambda > \mathcal{Y}^x_{(N_x)}, \end{cases} \end{aligned}$$

where $L_{k+1} = (1/R_{x,z}) \sum_{j=k+1}^{N_x} K\left((z - Z^x_{[j]})/h_n\right)$. The estimator is then computed as follows:

$$\widehat{\lambda}_{\alpha,n}(x, y|z) = \begin{cases} \mathcal{Y}^x_{(k)} \ \text{ if } \ L_{k+1} \le 1 - \alpha < L_k, \ k = 1, \cdots, N_x - 1 \\ \mathcal{Y}^x_{(N_x)} \ \text{ if } \ 0 \le 1 - \alpha < L_{N_x}. \end{cases} \tag{5.24}$$

A new measure of conditional output efficiency

Here, for every attainable point $(x, y) \in \Psi$, there exists an α_z such that $\lambda_{\alpha_z}(x, y|z) = 1$, this α_z could serve as an alternative measure of conditional output efficiency score. If $S_{Y|X,Z}(y \mid x, z)$ is continuous in y, this quantity is given, as for the input orientation, by:

$$\alpha_z^{output}(x, y) = 1 - S_{Y|X,Z}(y \mid x, z). \tag{5.25}$$

It may be estimated by the following quantity:

$$\widehat{\alpha}_{z,n}^{output} = 1 - L_{k+1}, \tag{5.26}$$

where k is the index such that $\mathcal{Y}^x_{(k)} = 1$, L_{k+1} was defined above and we set $L_{N_x+1} = 0$.

5.3 Bandwidth selection

It is well known in nonparametric smoothing that the choice of the kernel is not so important (in the sense that the results are very robust to this choice) but that the choice of the bandwidth may be crucial. We have already discussed in Section 3.4 the bandwidth selection issue for bootstrapping DEA efficiency scores, where we reported also some simple rules of thumb which can be easily put in place and seem work pretty well. Here, for the computation of conditional measures of efficiency we propose a very simple and easy to compute rule based on a k-Nearest Neighbor (k-NN) method to select the bandwidth. We will present the ideas in the simplest case where Z is univariate and where a family of continuous kernels with compact support is available (like, triangular, quartic or Epanechnikov kernels) and then we will adapt the presentation for multivariate Z with an easy to implement kernel with compact support based on truncated multivariate normal kernels.

5.3.1 Univariate case

The idea is that the smoothing in computing our Z-conditional efficiency estimators, *e.g.*, (5.6) for the input oriented case, comes from the smoothing in the estimation of the conditional distribution function $\widehat{F}_{X|Y,Z,n}(x \mid y, z)$, see equation (5.5). This is due to the continuity of the variable Z. Hence, we suggest in a first step to select a bandwidth h which optimizes in a certain sense the estimation of the density of Z. We propose to use the likelihood cross validation criterion for the choice of h.

The method of likelihood cross-validation is a natural development of the idea of using likelihood to judge the adequacy of fit of a statistical model. The rationale behind the method, as applied to density estimation, is as follows. Suppose that, in addition to the original data set, an independent observation Y from f were available. Then the log likelihood of f as the density underlying the observation Y would be $\log f(Y)$; regarding $\hat{f}$ as a parametric family of densities depending on the window width h, but with the data $X_1, ..., X_n$ fixed, would give $\log \hat{f}(Y)$, regarded as a function of h, as the log likelihood of the smoothing parameter h. Now, since an independent observation Y is not available, we could omit one of the original observations X_i from the sample used to construct the density estimate, and then use X_i as the observation Y. This would give log likelihood $\log \hat{f}_h^{(-i)}(X_i)$, where $\hat{f}_h^{(-i)}$ is defined as:

$$\hat{f}_h^{(-i)}(x) = \frac{1}{(n-1)h} \sum_{j=1, j \neq i}^{n} K\left(\frac{x - X_j}{h}\right),$$

Since there are no reasons to motivate the choice of which observation to leave out, the log likelihood is averaged over each choice of omitted X_i, to give the following score function:

$$CV(h) = n^{-1} \sum_{i=1}^{n} \log\left(\hat{f}_h^{(-i)}(X_i)\right).$$

The likelihood cross-validation choice of h is then the value of h which maximizes the function $CV(h)$ for the given data[24].

The likelihood cross validation criterion we apply in our methodology is based on a k-NN method: this allows to obtain bandwidths which are localized, insuring we have always the same number k of observations Z_i in the local neighbor of the point of interest z when estimating the density of Z.

Therefore, we define a grid of values of k to evaluate the leave-one-out kernel density estimate of Z. We set the range of possible values of k in order to have as lower bound a k equal to 5% of observations, and as upper bound a reasonable value of k which corresponds to the 25% of the n observations. For this grid of values of k, we evaluate the leave-one-out kernel density estimate of Z, $\hat{f}_k^{(-i)}(Z_i)$ for $i = 1, \ldots, n$ and find the value of k which maximizes the score function:

$$CV(k) = n^{-1} \sum_{i=1}^{n} \log\left(\hat{f}_k^{(-i)}(Z_i)\right),$$

where

$$\hat{f}_k^{(-i)}(Z_i) = \frac{1}{(n-1)h_{Z_i}} \sum_{j=1, j\neq i}^{n} K\left(\frac{Z_j - Z_i}{h_{Z_i}}\right),$$

and h_{Z_i} is the local bandwidth chosen such that there exist k points Z_j verifying $|Z_j - Z_i| \leq h_{Z_i}$.

Afterwards, in a second step, in order to compute $\widehat{F}_{X|Y,Z,n}(x \mid y, z)$ (and $\widehat{S}_{Y|X,Z,n}(y \mid x, z)$ for the output-oriented case), we have to take into account for the dimensionality of x and y, and the sparsity of points in larger dimensional spaces. Consequently, we expand the local bandwidth h_{Z_i} by a factor $1 + n^{-1/(p+q)}$, increasing with $(p+q)$ but decreasing with n.

The issue of choosing an optimal bandwidth in this setup is still an open research question but the empirical method that we propose here turns out to provide very sensible results, as shown by our simulated examples (see below) and in most of our applications with real data (see Part II of this book). See also the comments at the end of the next section devoted to the multivariate case.

5.3.2 Multivariate case

Silverman (1986), Scott (1992) and Simonoff (1996) have investigated the problem of multivariate density estimation with multivariate gaussian kernels and they have proposed reasonable empirical rules for the choice of the optimal bandwidths which can be shown to approximate, in some favorable cases, the optimal choice of the bandwidth.

[24] For more details see *e.g.* Silverman (1986).

The problem is that each component of Z has its own dispersion and so the bandwidths should be scaled accordingly for each component. More generally, if one wants to estimate a r-dimensional density by kernel smoothing we must choose a kernel function $K(u)$ where $u \in \mathcal{R}^r$, such that $K(u) \geq 0$ and $\int_{\mathcal{R}^r} K(u)\, du = 1$. Then we have to select a bandwidth matrix H which has to be a $(r \times r)$ positive definite matrix. The scaled kernel function can then be written as $K_H(u) = |H|^{-1}K(H^{-1}u)$ where $|H|$ stands for the determinant of the matrix H. Then a density estimate for Z could be written as:

$$\widehat{f}(z) = \frac{1}{n}\sum_{i=1}^{n} K_H(Z_i - z) = \frac{1}{n|H|}\sum_{i=1}^{n} K(H^{-1}(Z_i - z)).$$

A popular and simple choice of the kernel is the product kernel with a diagonal matrix for the bandwidths: $K(u) = \prod_{j=1}^{r} K_j(u_j)$ and $H = \text{diag}(h_1, \ldots, h_r)$, where the $K_j(u_j)$ are standard univariate kernels and where generally the univariate bandwidths are scaled to the standard deviation of each components of Z, $h_j = s_j h$ with s_j being the standard deviation of Z^j. In this case an estimator of the multivariate density can be written as:

$$\widehat{f}(z) = \frac{1}{nh^r \prod_{j=1}^{r} s_j} \sum_{i=1}^{n} \prod_{j=1}^{r} K(\frac{Z_i^j - z^j}{hs_j}),$$

where only a univariate h has to be selected. More generally, if we want to take into account for some dependence among the components of Z, we could use a multivariate kernel as follows. The basic kernel function in this case is the standard r-variate normal density $K(u) = 1/(2\pi)^{r/2}\exp\{-u'u/2\}$, and we may choose as bandwidth matrix the following scaled matrix $H = hS^{1/2}$, where S is the empirical covariance matrix of the r components of Z. The density estimate appears then to be:

$$\widehat{f}(z) = \frac{1}{n(2\pi)^{r/2}h^r|S|^{1/2}} \sum_{i=1}^{n} \exp\{-\frac{1}{2h^2}(Z_i - z)'S^{-1}(Z_i - z)\}.$$

Empirical rules of the literature suggest to choose either

$$h = \{4/(d+2)\}^{1/(d+4)} n^{-1/(d+4)}$$

which is optimal for independent multivariate normal if independent normal kernels are used, or even simpler $h = n^{-1/(d+4)}$. Of course h could also be chosen by some k-nearest neighbor techniques.

The above approach is simple but is not very convenient in our setup because we need kernels with compact support and we prefer to take benefit for the possible dependence between the components of Z and so avoid product kernels with compact support. This is the reason why we develop a truncated multivariate normal kernel approach. The idea is very simple, we truncate the basic gaussian kernel $K(u)$ on a sphere of radius one and in order to obtain a continuous kernel at the boundary (which is preferable when estimating continuous densities), we rescale it so that the truncated kernel is equal to zero on the boundary sphere defined by $u'u = 1$. After some analytical manipulations, this leads to a new basic kernel bounded on the sphere of radius one defined as:

$$K^*(u) = \frac{\exp\{-u'u/2\} - \exp\{-1/2\}}{C - \exp\{-1/2\}\frac{\pi^{r/2}}{\Gamma(1+r/2)}} \boldsymbol{I}(u'u \leq 1),$$

where $C = (2\pi)^{r/2}\text{Prob}(\chi_r^2 \leq 1)$ is a constant and χ_r^2 is a chi-square random variable with r degrees of freedom. $K^*(u)$ is a regular continuous density centered in zero and bounded on the unit sphere. Then, as before, we choose the bandwidth matrix scaled by the covariance structure $H = hS^{1/2}$. By doing so we end up with the following kernel function:

$$K_H^*(u) = \frac{1}{h^r|S|^{1/2}(C - \exp\{-1/2\}\frac{\pi^{r/2}}{\Gamma(1+r/2)})}$$
$$\times\left(\exp\{-\frac{1}{2h^2}u'S^{-1}u\} - \exp\{-1/2\}\right)\boldsymbol{I}(u'S^{-1}u \leq h^2). \tag{5.27}$$

This is a truncated normal distribution, truncated at the ellipsoid $u'S^{-1}u \leq h^2$ of "radius" h, the density being scaled so that it is continuous (equal to zero) on its boundary. Finally, the expression for the density estimate of Z may be written as above as:

$$\widehat{f}(z) = \frac{1}{n}\sum_{i=1}^{n} K_H^*(Z_i - z). \tag{5.28}$$

Here again only one bandwidth has to be selected, we will use the k-nearest neighbor principle: we select a local bandwidth h_z such that the ellipsoid centered in z with shape matrix S^{-1} and "radius" h_z contains exactly k data points Z_i. An optimal value for k is then obtained as explained above by likelihood cross-validation. Of course, as for the univariate case, once h_i is determined, we correct it in a second step to expand the local bandwidth h_i by a factor $1 + n^{-1/(p+q)}$.

In all our applications below, it is the method we have used even for the particular case of $r = 1$. The method provided very sensible results and nice estimators of the density of Z (uni- and multivariate) and the conditional efficiency scores that derive from this kernel and bandwidth choice showed a great stability to small changes in the change of k. We compared also with some of the empirical rules proposed above and the results were often similar although in some cases (dependence among the Z's) the latter could be a wrong choice.

The same remark about the stability of the results with respect to the bandwidth choice in this setup was already made by Simar and Wilson (1999c) for Malmquist indices, and by Daraio and Simar (2005a,b) for the conditional and convex efficiency measures, compared-for the univariate bandwidth case-with the Sheather and Jones (1991) method.

5.4 An econometric methodology

Once we have handled the introduction of Z variables in the frontier estimation framework, both in the full frontier and in the robust partial frontiers (order-m or order-α), we propose a method to evaluate their influence on the production process.

After that, we propose a decomposition of the *conditional efficiency* (again, full and robust) very useful to evaluate the effect of Z on the efficiency of the firm, disentangling the following aspects of the firm's performance: *Internal* or *managerial* efficiency (unconditional efficiency); *Externality* effects of the environment (level of Z): positive vs. negative externality; *Individual Intensity* on environmental conditions (level of *exploitation* of the environment).

5.4.1 Global effect of *Z* on the production process

For analyzing the global influence of Z on the production process, the comparison of $\hat{\theta}_n(x, y \mid z)$ with $\hat{\theta}_n(x, y)$ (and of $\hat{\lambda}_n(x, y \mid z)$ with $\hat{\lambda}_n(x, y)$ for the output oriented case) is certainly of interest. When Z is univariate, a scatter plot of the ratios[25] $Q^z = \hat{\theta}_n(x, y \mid z)/\hat{\theta}_n(x, y)$ (or of $Q^z = \hat{\lambda}_n(x, y \mid z)/\hat{\lambda}_n(x, y)$) against Z and its smoothed nonparametric regression line would be helpful to describe the influence of Z on efficiency. As will be shown below, what we propose here is an exploratory tool for highlighting the influence of Z on the efficiency structures. At this stage of our research, we do not provide inferential tools for this analysis but show the usefulness of the approach in practical problems.

The framework of our nonparametric regression smoothing is the following. For the input oriented case, we have:

$$Q_i^z = g(Z_i) + \epsilon_i, i = 1, ..., n, \tag{5.29}$$

where $Q_i^z = \dfrac{\hat{\theta}_n(X_i, Y_i \mid Z_i)}{\hat{\theta}_n(X_i, Y_i)}$, ϵ_i is the usual error term with $E(\epsilon_i|Z_i) = 0$, and g is the *mean regression function*, since $E(Q_i^z \mid Z_i) = g(Z_i)$.

In this exploratory phase we choose the simple smoothed nonparametric regression estimator introduced by Nadaraya (1964) and Watson (1964). The

[25] We can do the same with the differences $\hat{\theta}_n(x, y \mid z) - \hat{\theta}_n(x, y)$, but since efficiency scores are proportions, ratios seem very natural.

Nadaraya-Watson estimator of the regression function g is the following:

$$\widehat{g}(z) = \frac{\sum_{i=1}^{n} K(\frac{z-Z_i}{h}) Q_i^z}{\sum_{i=1}^{n} K(\frac{z-Z_i}{h})}. \tag{5.30}$$

Note that this estimator can be written in the following form:

$$\widehat{g}(z) = \sum_{i=1}^{n} (\frac{w_i}{\sum_{j=1}^{n} w_j}) Q_i^z, \tag{5.31}$$

where $w_i = K(\frac{z-Z_i}{h})$, and hence, it is a linear combination of the Q_i^z. Therefore, the mean smoothed regression function is a *weighted average* of the Q_i^z, where the weights are represented by the kernels.

Accordingly, for the output oriented case, we have the same Nadaraya-Watson estimator of the regression function g, where:

$$Q_i^z = \frac{\widehat{\lambda}_n(X_i, Y_i \mid Z_i)}{\widehat{\lambda}_n(X_i, Y_i)}.$$

The choice of the bandwidth h, for the smoothed nonparametric regression, has been done applying a least-squares cross-validation automatic procedure[26]. In the following applications we use a Gaussian kernel K.

Interpreting the effect of Z

In an input-oriented framework, if the smoothed nonparametric regression is *increasing*, it indicates that Z is detrimental (unfavorable) to efficiency and when this regression is *decreasing*, it specifies a Z factor conducive (favorable) to efficiency.

In the first case (*unfavorable* Z) the environmental variable acts like an "extra" *undesired* output to be produced asking for the use of more inputs in production activity, hence Z has a "negative" effect on the production process. In this case $\hat{\theta}_n(x, y \mid z)$, the efficiency computed taking Z into account, will be much larger than the unconditional efficiency $\hat{\theta}_n(x, y)$ for large values of Z then for small value of Z. This is due to the fact that for firms with an high level of Z, the efficiency score without taking into account Z is much smaller than

[26]For more details, see *e.g.* Härdle (1990).

that–one computed taking into account Z; in this last case, the effect of Z let the efficiency score going up. Consequently, the ratios $Q^z = \hat{\theta}_n(x, y \mid z)/\hat{\theta}_n(x, y)$ will increase, on average, with Z.

In the second case (*favorable* Z), the environmental variable plays a role of a "substitutive" input in the production process, giving the opportunity to "save" inputs in the activity of production; in this case, Z has a "positive" effect on the production process. It follows that the conditional efficiency $\hat{\theta}_n(x, y \mid z)$ will be much larger than $\hat{\theta}_n(x, y)$ for small values of Z (less substitutive inputs) than for large values of Z. Here again, this is due to the fact that firms with a small value of Z do not exploit the positive effect of Z, and then, when we take into account Z, their efficiency score goes up. Therefore, the ratios $Q^z = \hat{\theta}_n(x, y \mid z)/\hat{\theta}_n(x, y)$ will, on average, decrease when Z increases.

Since we know that full-frontier estimates, and the derived estimated efficiency scores, are very sensitive to outliers and extreme values, we do also the same analysis for the more robust order-m and order-α efficiency scores. Thus, in the empirical illustrations reported in the following section, we present also the nonparametric smoothed regression of the ratios $Q^z_m = \hat{\theta}_{m,n}(x, y \mid z)/\hat{\theta}_{m,n}(x, y)$ on Z and of $Q^z_\alpha = \hat{\theta}_{\alpha,n}(x, y \mid z)/\hat{\theta}_{\alpha,n}(x, y)$ respectively.

Mutatis mutandis, the same could be done in the output oriented case, with similar conclusions to detect the influence of Z on efficiency. In this case, the influence of Z goes in the opposite direction: an *increasing* regression corresponds to favorable environmental factor and a *decreasing* regression indicates an unfavorable factor. In an output oriented framework, a favorable Z means that the environmental variable operates as a sort of "extra" input *freely available*: for this reason the environment is "favorable" to the production process. Consequently, the value of $\hat{\lambda}_n(x, y \mid z)$ will be much smaller (greater efficiency) than $\hat{\lambda}_n(x, y)$ for small values of Z than for large values of Z. Here again, as for the input oriented case, this is due to the fact that firms with small values of Z do not take advantage from the favorable environment, and then, when Z is taking into account their efficiency scores improves, *i.e.* the value of $\hat{\lambda}_n(x, y \mid z)$ is smaller, indicating a greater efficiency. The ratios $Q^z_i = \hat{\lambda}_n(X_i, Y_i \mid Z_i)/\hat{\lambda}_n(X_i, Y_i)$ will increase with Z, on average.

In the case of unfavorable Z, the environmental variable works as a "compulsory" or *unavoidable* output to be produced to face the negative environmental condition. Z in a certain sense penalizes the production of the outputs of interest. In this situation, $\hat{\lambda}_n(x, y|z)$ will be much smaller than $\hat{\lambda}_n(x, y)$ for large values of Z. Here, firms with an high level of Z are "more" negatively influenced by the environment with respect to firms with a low level of Z: for that reason their efficiency score taking Z into account is much higher with respect to their unconditional efficiency. As a result, the regression line of $Q^z_i = \hat{\lambda}_n(X_i, Y_i \mid Z_i)/\hat{\lambda}_n(X_i, Y_i)$ over Z will be decreasing.

Two simple illustrations to fix the ideas

In this paragraph we describe two simple production processes in which the environmental variable Z is favorable (boiler case) and unfavorable (fridge case). We show also the usefulness of robust measures to reveal conditional local effects when there are extreme observations in the comparison set.

The Boiler case

The production process consists in an electric kettle which has to heat some waters at 100 grades centigrade. We observe the performance of n firms, using electric energy in kWh as input, to produce a certain amount of heated water. Suppose that the output (heated water) is equal for all firms and is equal to one liter, *i.e.* $Y = 1$. The input X is the energy in kWh, and the environmental variable Z is the "external temperature".

This is a simple production process in which the variable Z has a positive influence on the production process, as if the external temperature (Z) is high, the firm will need less energy (X) to heat the water (Y), and hence Z acts like a "substitutive input".

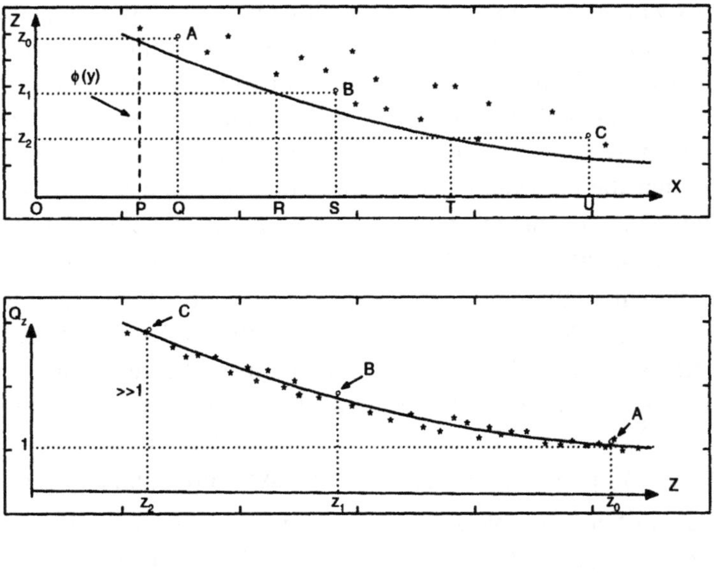

Figure 5.1. The Boiler case. Z favorable.

In Figure 5.1 we show a simple example to explain why the smoothed regression line of the ratios $Q_i^z = \hat{\theta}_n(X_i, Y_i \mid Z_i)/\hat{\theta}_n(X_i, Y_i)$ on Z is *decreasing* when Z is favorable. Hence, Figure 5.1 (bottom panel) explains the decreasing trend of the smoothed regression of the ratios Q^z on Z whereas the top panel shows the "isoquant" of the production process which shows a "substitutive effect" existing between Z and X. To illustrate, Figure 5.1 represents also the following firms:

$$\begin{aligned} A &= (x_0, Y, z_0) \text{ that uses a level of input } x_0 = OQ, \\ B &= (x_1, Y, z_1) \text{ that uses a level of input } x_1 = OS, \\ C &= (x_2, Y, z_2) \text{ that uses a level of input } x_2 = OU. \end{aligned}$$

The efficient frontier FDH ($\phi(y)$) is given by the minimum value of input X used among the analyzed firms (here y is equal for all firms); it corresponds to the value OP.

For the firms A, B and C, the *conditional* and *unconditional* FDH efficiency scores, together with their ratios Q_z, are the following:

$$\begin{aligned} \widehat{\theta}_A(x_0, Y|z_0) &= \frac{OP}{OQ} \; ; \widehat{\theta}_A(x_0, Y) = \frac{OP}{OQ} \Rightarrow Q_A^z = 1; \\ \widehat{\theta}_B(x_1, Y|z_1) &= \frac{OR}{OS} \; ; \widehat{\theta}_B(x_1, Y) = \frac{OP}{OS} \Rightarrow Q_B^z > 1; \\ \widehat{\theta}_C(x_2, Y|z_2) &= \frac{OT}{OU} \; ; \widehat{\theta}_C(x_2, Y) = \frac{OP}{OU} \Rightarrow Q_C^z >> 1. \end{aligned}$$

Note that firm A has the highest value of Z (compared with firm B and firm C). Due to the "substitution effect" between Z and X, in correspondence to this value of $Z = z_0$, we have the lowest value of the minimum of X (in this case OP). Firm B has a level of $Z = z_1$ lower than z_0 but higher than z_2. As a result, for firm B the minimum value of X taking Z into account is OR, that is higher than OP but lower than OT (the minimum value of X for the firm C taking Z into account). As a consequence, we have the corresponding order of the ratios $Q_C^z > Q_B^z > Q_A^z$.

The Fridge case

In this case the production process consists in a refrigerator that has to produce several liters of glaced water (the output Y); the input X is the energy measured in kWh and the environmental factor (Z) is the external temperature.

This is a typical case of unfavorable Z. The bottom panel of Figure 5.2 illustrates the explanation of the *increasing* trend of the smoothed regression of $Q_i^z = \hat{\theta}_n(X_i, Y_i \mid Z_i)/\hat{\theta}_n(X_i, Y_i)$ on Z (bottom panel) through an "isoquant" of a production process (in the top panel) which shows a Z as an undesired output to be produced requiring the use of more input X.

Following the same arguments as in the Boiler case, the reader will indeed understand that in this case of unfavorable Z, the nonparametric regression line of Q_i^z over Z will be increasing as shown in Figure 5.2.

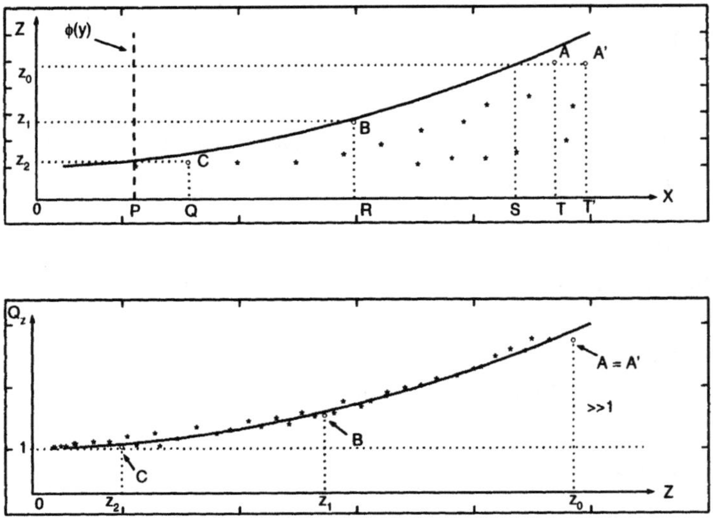

Figure 5.2. The Fridge case. Z unfavorable.

All what has been said for the input-oriented case applies *mutatis mutandis* also for the interpretation of the output-oriented case, where an increasing nonparametric regression line points to a positive effect of Z on the production efficiency whilst a decreasing nonparametric regression line points to a negative impact of Z. By construction, $\widehat{\lambda}(x, y)$ ($\widehat{\theta}(x, y)$) scores are ≥ 1 (≤ 1), $\widehat{\lambda}(x, y|z) \leq \widehat{\lambda}(x, y)$ ($\widehat{\theta}(x, y|z) \geq \widehat{\theta}(x, y)$), and therefore $Q_i^z \leq 1$ ($Q_i^z \geq 1$).

The same kind of reasoning applies again for the order-m and order-α conditional and unconditional efficiency scores. Note that here the ratios $Q_{m,i}^z$ and $Q_{\alpha,i}^z$ are not bounded by 1 and $\widehat{\lambda}_m(x, y|z)$ ($\widehat{\theta}_m(x, y|z)$) is not necessarily $\leq \widehat{\lambda}_m(x, y)$ ($\geq \widehat{\theta}_m(x, y)$), as well as for $Q_{\alpha,i}^z$ ratios.

Moreover, robust ratios have the advantage of being able to show the impact of external factors even if some extreme observations may mask it when using full frontier ratios. This case is illustrated in Figures 5.3 and 5.4 which show in the top panel the case of a production process consisting in a fridge as we have seen above, in which there are 3 units (marked in the picture as bigger stars with dotted square around) consisting in fridges of a new generation, that are perfectly isolated and then are not influenced by the external temperature. In this case, we see from Figure 5.3 (bottom panel) that full frontier ratios are not able to capture the effect of the external factor: the smoothing nonparametric regression line is straight due to the influence of these extremes. On the contrary,

Figure 5.4 (bottom panel) shows what the impact of external factor is, because partial frontiers are not influenced by these fridges of new generation. We will see in Section 6.4 an illustration of this case on real data.

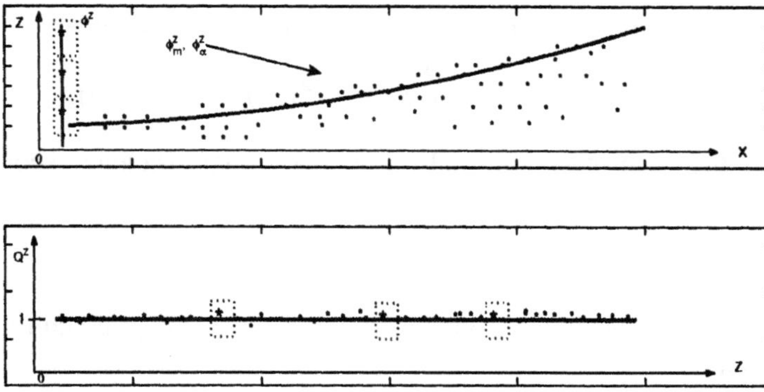

Figure 5.3. The Fridge case with outliers. Full frontier case

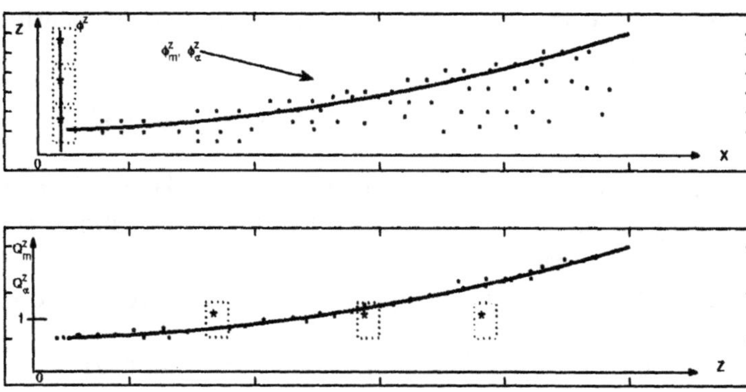

Figure 5.4. The Fridge case with outliers. Partial frontiers case

5.4.2 A decomposition of conditional efficiency

Using the methodology described above on the introduction of Z and the evaluation of its influence, we can also provide a decomposition of the performance of the firm, as represented by its conditional efficiency scores.

We propose to disentangle the performance of the firm (x, y), as measured by the *Conditional Efficiency* index, named $CE^z(x, y)$, in three main indicators:

an indicator of the *internal* or managerial efficiency, *i.e.* the *Unconditional Efficiency* score named $UE(x, y)$; an indicator of the level of Z owned by the firm, the *Externality Index*, named $EI^z(x, y)$; and finally, an *Individual Index* which measures the firm *intensity* in catching the opportunities or threats by the environment, named $II^z(x, y)$.

Expressing the proposed decomposition in formulae we have:

$$CE^z(x,y) = UE(x,y) * EI^z(x,y) * II^z(x,y). \tag{5.32}$$

We define the ratio of conditional on unconditional efficiency score, Q^z, as follows:

$$Q^z = \frac{CE^z(x,y)}{UE(x,y)}. \tag{5.33}$$

The *Externality Index* is the expected value of the ratio Q^z given that $Z = z$, and is given by:

$$EI^z(x,y) = \widehat{E}(Q^z|Z = z); \tag{5.34}$$

whilst the *Individual Index* is given as follows:

$$II^z(x,y) = \frac{Q^z}{EI(x,y)}. \tag{5.35}$$

In the input orientation, the conditional and unconditional measures of efficiency are given by:

$$CE^z(x,y) \equiv \widehat{\theta}(x,y|z); \;\; UE(x,y) \equiv \widehat{\theta}(x,y). \tag{5.36}$$

Note that the *externality index* defined in equation (5.34), may be estimated using the Nadaraya-Watson nonparametric estimator defined above (see equation (5.30)) or another nonparametric estimator.

For the output oriented case, in equation (5.32) we have only to substitute:

$$CE^z(x,y) \equiv \widehat{\lambda}(x,y|z); \;\; UE(x,y) \equiv \widehat{\lambda}(x,y). \tag{5.37}$$

The same is for robust (order-m and order-α) measures, where we have to substitute in equation (5.32) the relative conditional and unconditional efficiency scores in the selected orientation.

For the interpretation of the proposed indicators, and the evaluation of the influence of Z at the firm level, a major role is played by the ratio Q^z, the ratio of conditional on unconditional measure of efficiency. If we are in an input or output orientation, and $Q^z = 1$, this means that conditional and unconditional efficiency scores are equal (this applies both to full and robust efficiency scores). This value of the ratio points to a situation in which the external factors do not affect the performance of the analysed firm. On the contrary, if we are in an input oriented framework and $Q^z > 1$ this means that taking Z into account lead to an higher efficiency score of the firm.

The externality index $EI^z(x, y) = \widehat{E}(Q^z|Z)$ represents the *expected* influence of Z on the performance of the firm: it depends on the own level of Z. It should be interpreted taking into account the global effect of Z on the production process and what said above for the ratio Q^z. If $EI^z = 1$ this means that the firm considered operates in a situation in which we expect that given the level of the environment, Q^z should be equal to one. When $EI^z > 1$ this means that the firm works at a level of environment with an expected $Q^z > 1$.

Finally, the Individual Index tells us how the firm performed with respect to the expected value of its performance; *i.e.* an $II^z = 1$ means that the firm's Q^z is exactly equal to $\widehat{E}(Q^z|Z)$. If the $II^z > 1$ this means that the effect of the environment on the efficiency score of the firm under consideration is higher with respect to its expected value. On the contrary, if the $II^z < 1$ we are considering a firm for which the environmental externality is lower then what expected for its level of Z.

Summing up, considering the above indications, consulting the smoothed nonparametric regression plot of Q^z over Z, and taking into account the minimum and maximum level of Z, we are able to interpret the effect of Z at firm level, on the efficiency score of firm, by decomposing the conditional efficiency score in its main components: unconditional efficiency, externality index and individual index.

The same interpretation, given for the input-oriented case, *mutatis mutandis*, can be done in the output-oriented framework, recalling that $\widehat{\lambda}(x, y) \geq 1$, and hence $Q^z \leq 1$.

Accordingly is also the interpretation for the decomposition of the Robust Conditional Efficiency index (of order-m and order-α). In the robust case, note that the ratio of conditional and unconditional efficiency can be higher, equal or lower than one (both in the input and in the output orientation). In Chapter 8 we illustrate how these indicators may be useful in an application on Aggressive Growth mutual funds data.

5.5 Simulated illustrations

In this section we illustrate the econometric methodology presented above using simulated examples which describe multiple input-output production processes conditioned by univariate and multivariate external-environmental factors. These illustrations show to the reader how to implement in practice our method. See also Chapters 6 to 8 for applications done on real data sets.

5.5.1 Univariate Z

In this example, we simulate a multi-input ($p = 2$) and multi-output ($q = 2$) production process in which the function describing the efficient frontier is (as in Park , Simar and Weiner, 2000) the following:

$$y^{(2)} = 1.0845(x^{(1)})^{0.3}(x^{(2)})^{0.4} - y^{(1)} \tag{5.38}$$

where $y^{(j)}$ ($x^{(j)}$) denotes the jth component of y (of x) for $j = 1, 2$. We draw $X_i^{(j)}$ independent uniforms on $(1, 2)$ and $\tilde{Y}_i^{(j)}$ independent uniforms on $(0.2, 5)$. Then the generated random rays in the output space are characterized by the slopes $S_i = \tilde{Y}_i^{(2)}/\tilde{Y}_i^{(1)}$. Finally, the generated random points on the frontier are defined by:

$$Y_{i,eff}^{(1)} = \frac{1.0845(X_i^{(1)})^{0.3}(X_i^{(2)})^{0.4}}{S_i + 1} \tag{5.39}$$

$$Y_{i,eff}^{(2)} = 1.0845(X_i^{(1)})^{0.3}(X_i^{(2)})^{0.4} - Y_{i,eff}^{(1)}. \tag{5.40}$$

The efficiencies are generated by $\exp(-U_i)$ where U_i are drawn from an exponential with mean $\mu = 1/3$. Finally, in a standard setup (without environmental factors), we define $Y_i = Y_{i,eff} * \exp(-U_i)$.

On this data set, we introduce the dependency on an environmental factor Z, adapting Case 1 of Daraio and Simar (2005a). Z is uniform on $(1, 4)$ and such that it has a quadratic negative impact on the production process till a Z value of 2.5 and then a quadratic positive impact (here we consider an output oriented framework):

$$Y_i^{(1)} = [1 + (Z - 2.5)^2] * Y_{i,eff}^{(1)} * \exp(-U_i) \tag{5.41}$$

$$Y_i^{(2)} = (1 + |Z - 2.5|) * Y_{i,eff}^{(2)} * \exp(-U_i). \tag{5.42}$$

We simulate $n = 100$ observations according to this scenario.

In the nonparametric estimation, we have chosen a truncated gaussian kernel for the smoothing; we remark that the results are very stable if other kernels with compact support are used. Figure 5.5 illustrates the likelihood cross validation plot for the choice of the number of the Nearest Neighbourhood (NN), that in this case is 18.

For the choice of the values of m and α, the inspection of Figure 5.6 is particularly useful as it shows a sensitivity analysis on the percentage of points outside the partial frontiers in a sensitive way, *i.e.* after a threshold value of 0.15 (we applied the procedure described in Section 4.4.4, in particular in Equation (4.30) we use a $\tau = 0.15$). We have chosen, then, $m = 50$ and $\alpha = 0.985$ such that the percentages of points outside the partial frontiers be close to zero. These values are such that both order-α and order-m efficiency scores

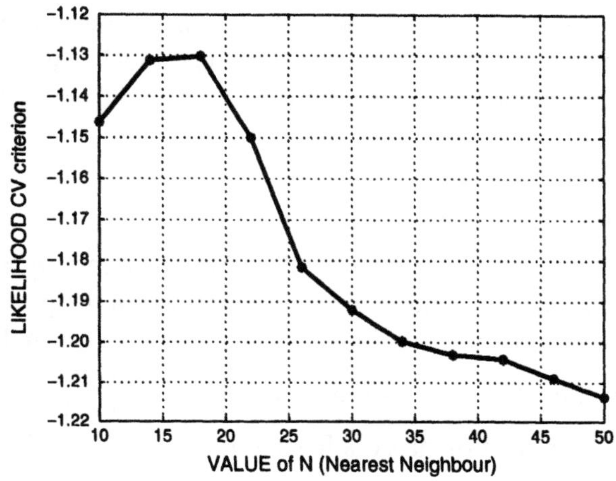

Figure 5.5. Simulated example with univariate Z. Likelihood cross validation plot for the choice of the number of the Nearest Neighbourhood (NN). Here the number of k – NN which maximizes the likelihood cross validation criterion is 18.

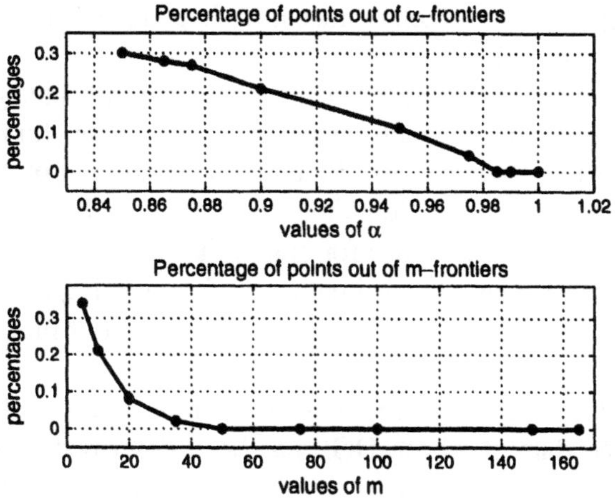

Figure 5.6. Simulated example with univariate Z. Plots of the percentage of points outside order-m and order-α frontiers.

are very close to FDH efficiency scores because in this scenario we do not have outliers. In practice, the choice of these two "tuning" parameters (m and α) may also be governed by their economic interpretation.

The results are displayed in Figure 5.7. In all panels (top for the FDH case, middle for the α frontier case and bottom for the m frontier) as expected, we see that the ratios (of conditional and unconditional FDH, α and m efficiency scores) allow to detect the "$U-$ shaped" effect of Z on the production process.

5.5.2 Multivariate *Z*

Two independent components

In this exercise the multi-input ($p = 2$) and multi-output ($q = 2$) data set is simulated according to the same scenario described in the previous Section 5.5.1, but the Z variable now is drawn from a bivariate normal distribution with mean $\mu = [2.5 \;\; 2.5]$ and covariance matrix $\Sigma = \begin{pmatrix} 0.25 & 0 \\ 0 & 0.25 \end{pmatrix}$. The dependence of the production process from Z is introduced as follows:

$$Y_i^{(1)} = (1 + |Z_1 - 2.5|^3) * Y_{i,eff}^{(1)} * (1 + Z_2) * \exp(-U_i)$$
$$Y_i^{(2)} = (1 + |Z_1 - 2.5|^3) * Y_{i,eff}^{(2)} * (1 + Z_2) \exp(-U_i),$$

where $Y_{i,eff}^{(.)}$ are generated as in Section 5.5.1, and the U_i are drawn from an exponential with mean $\mu = 1/2$. Again, we simulate $n = 100$ observations according to this scenario which defines a U-shaped pattern around 2.5 for Z_1 and a linear pattern for Z_2.

In the nonparametric estimation, we have chosen a truncated gaussian kernel for the smoothing as before, which can be easily generalised for the multivariate case. Figure 5.8 illustrates the likelihood cross validation plot for the choice of the number of the Nearest Neighbourhood ($NN = 30$) for the estimation of the density of Z, which we use for computing the conditional measures of efficiency. Figure 5.9 shows the estimation of Z done using our k-NN approach as well as its contour plot. As it appears from the contour plot, Z_1 and Z_2 are independent.

To set the value of m and α to compute the robust partial efficiency scores for the simulated dataset whose DGP has been described above, we plot in Figure 5.10 the percentage of points which are outside the partial frontiers after a threshold value of 0.15. By inspecting Figure 5.10 we choose the value of $m = 35$ and the value of $\alpha = 0.965$ so that we leave outside a percentage of points close to zero.

Some results are displayed in Figures 5.11 and 5.12. In particular, Figure 5.11 shows the global impact of the external variables Z on the simulated production process providing, the surface of Q^z on Z_1 and Z_2.

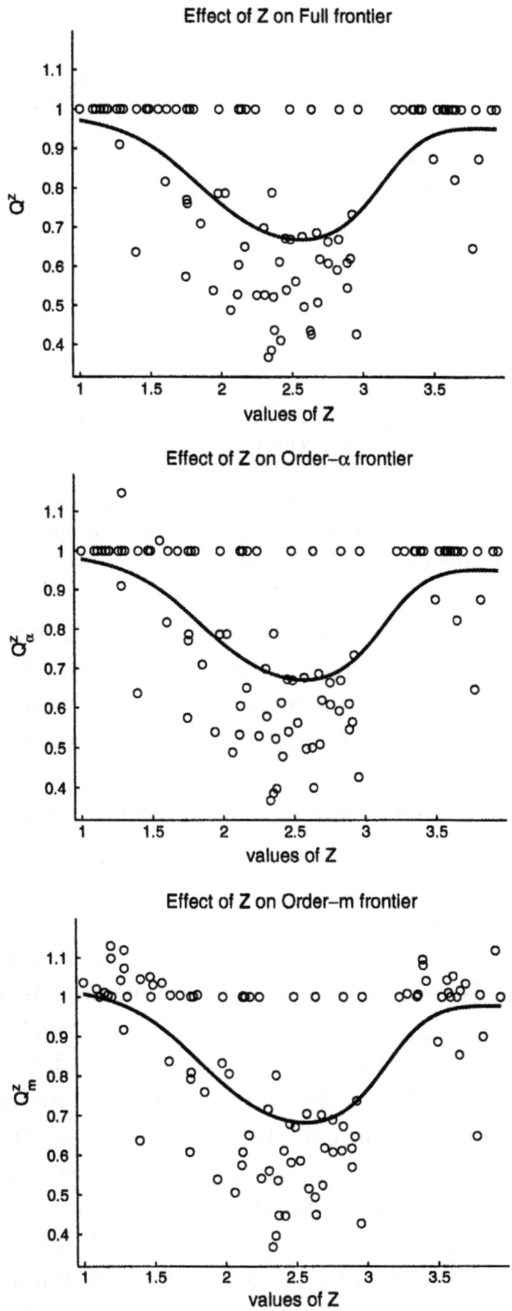

Figure 5.7. Simulated example with univariate Z. Smoothed nonparametric regression of Q^z on Z (top panel), of Q^z_α on Z (middle panel) and of Q^z_m on Z (bottom panel).

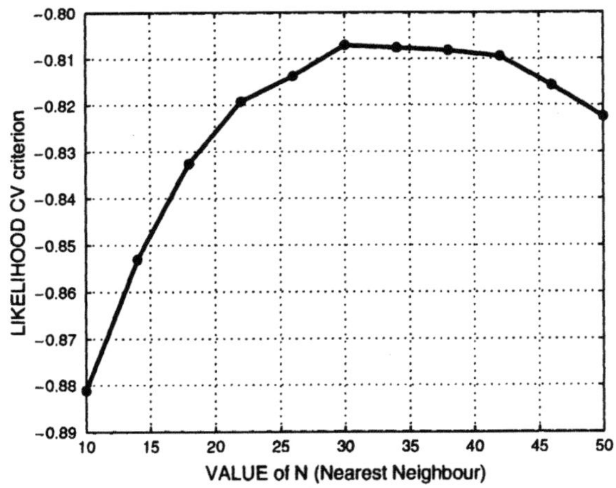

Figure 5.8. Simulated example with multivariate Z. Likelihood cross validation plot for the choice of the number of the Nearest Neighbourhood (NN). Here the number of k − NN which maximizes the likelihood cross validation criterion is 30.

Figure 5.12 provides a more detailed information on the impact of Z on the simulated production process. It plots the ratios Q^z against Z_1 (top panel) and Z_2 (bottom panel) at the three quartiles of the other component of Z. As we expected, we recover a positive U-shaped effect of Q^z on Z_1 and a positive linear effect on Z_2.

The same effects were obtained also for Q^z_α and Q^z_m (here we do not have outliers).

Two correlated components

Figure 5.13 shows another simulated bivariate Z variable in which Z_1 and Z_2 are correlated (0.75). We introduced this new Z in the same scenario described above (U-shaped effect of Z_1, linear effect of Z_2) and compute the conditional and unconditional nonparametric and robust efficiency indices as well as their ratios. Figure 5.14 shows the results. Since Z_1 and Z_2 are highly correlated (0.75), in a normal bivariate setup, the two effects are confounded: the linear effect is added to the quadratic one giving the result we can see; a sort of "mixture" of the two effects with a slightly more pronounced curvature for Z_1. This example shows that if we have independent Z variables, we can finely recover their marginal impact on the production process, but if the Z variables are correlated (as they are in Figure 5.14) then their marginal impact has to be more carefully examined.

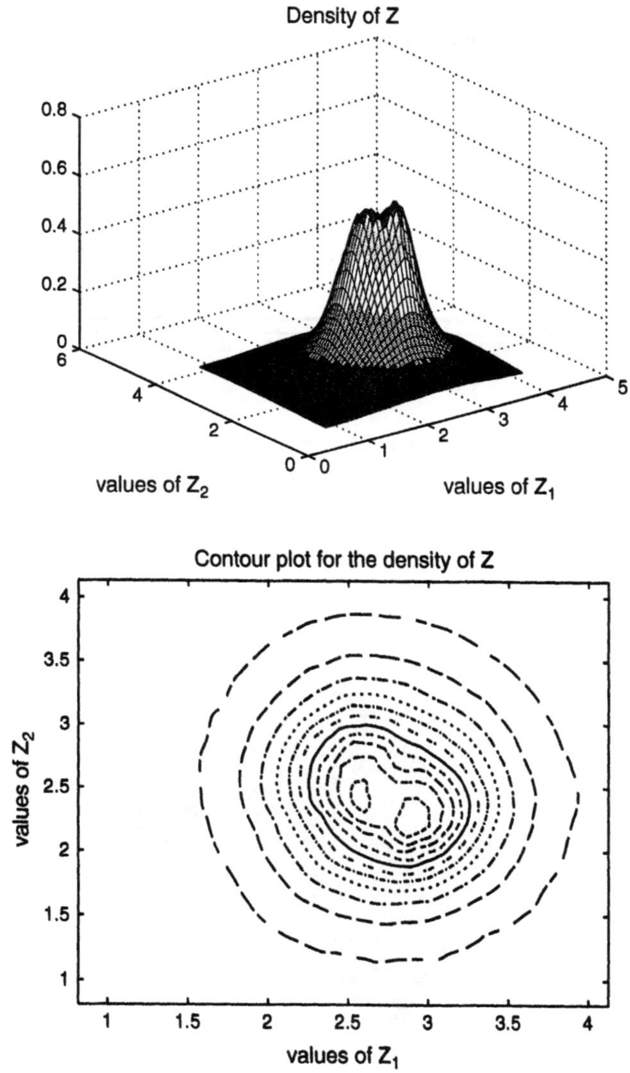

Figure 5.9. Density of Z and Contour plot of the density of Z.

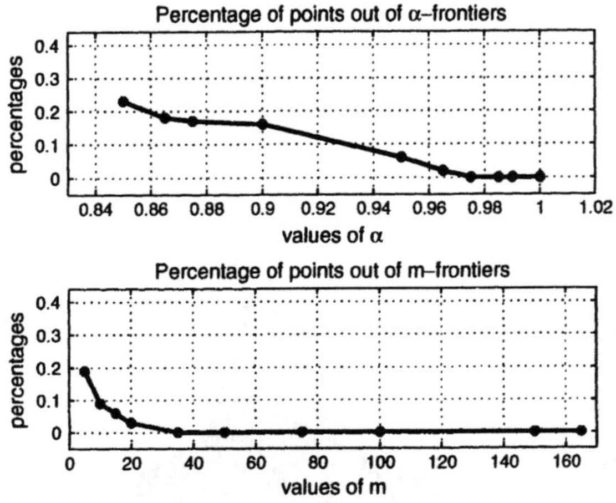

Figure 5.10. Simulated example with multivariate Z. Plots of the percentage of points outside order-m and order-α frontiers.

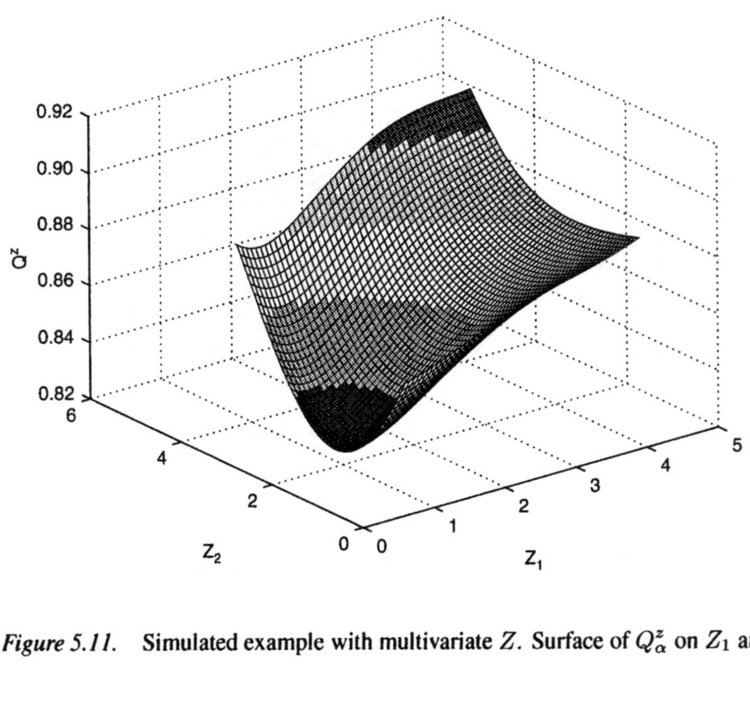

Figure 5.11. Simulated example with multivariate Z. Surface of Q_{α}^{z} on Z_1 and Z_2.

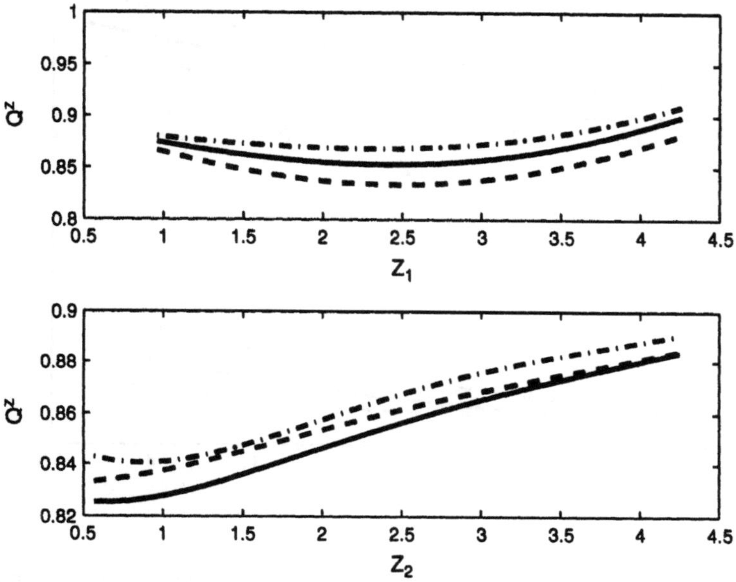

Figure 5.12. Simulated example with multivariate Z. Top panel smoothed nonparametric regression of Q^z on Z_1 for Z_2's quartiles. Bottom panel smoothed nonparametric regression of Q^z on Z_2 for Z_1's quartiles. The dashed line corresponds to the first quartile, the solid line to the median and the dashdot line to the third quartile.

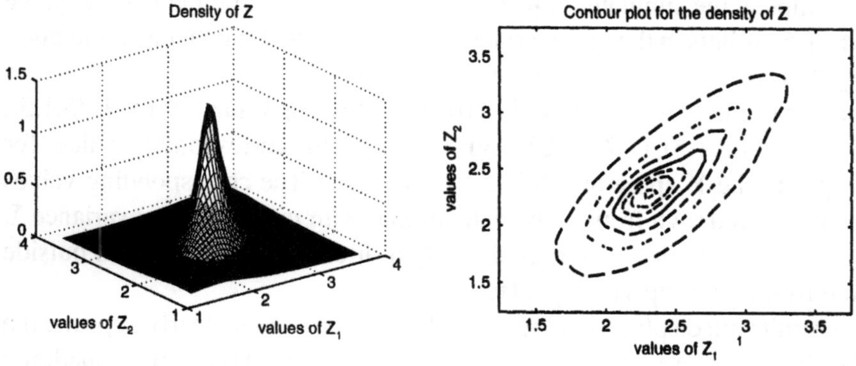

Figure 5.13. Density of Z and Contour plot of the density of Z. Z_1 and Z_2 are correlated.

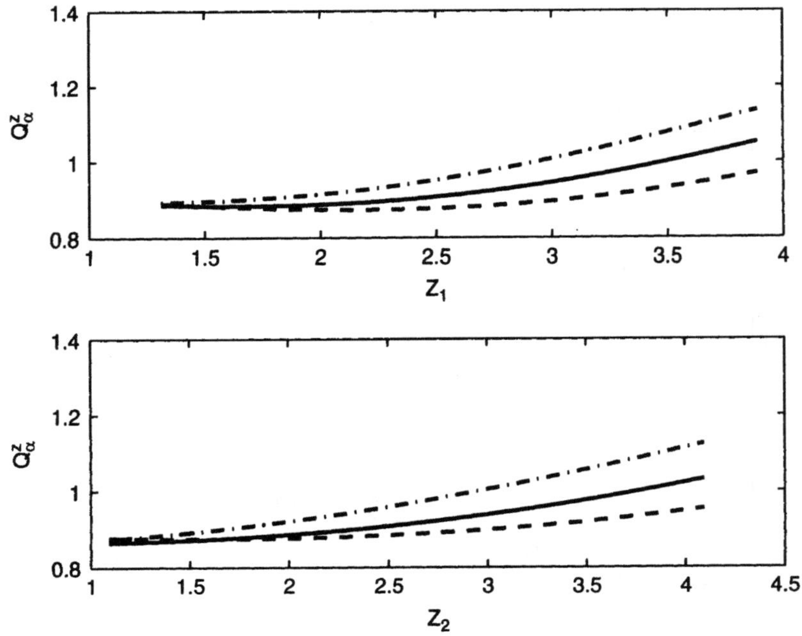

Figure 5.14. Simulated example with multivariate Z. Z_1 and Z_2 are correlated. Top panel smoothed nonparametric regression of Q^z_α on Z_1 for Z_2's quartiles. Bottom panel smoothed nonparametric regression of Q^z_α on Z_2 for Z_1's quartiles. Dashed line = first quartile, solid line = median, and dashdot line = third quartile.

Sensitivity to outliers

To complete the simulated illustration of our econometric methodology, we introduce 5 outliers in the multivariate Z (independent components) simulation setting described at the beginning of this section.

These extremes points are introduced at the following values of X: (1.25,1.5), (1.25, 1.75), (1.5,1.5), (1.75, 1.25) and (1.5, 1.25), the corresponding values for the slopes in the Y space are (0.25, 0.75, 1, 3, 5). The corresponding values of Z have been drawn from a bivariate normal with mean μ and covariance Σ (as above). Finally the outliers in the output direction were projected outside the true frontier multiplying by a factor of 2.5.

The results are displayed in Figures 5.15 and 5.16. As it clearly appears, the FDH estimator, in presence of the 5 outliers, fails to detect the correct quadratic effect of Z_1 on the production process (the curvature is missed, see Figure 5.15), but the order$-\alpha$ estimator is able to reproduce the simulated effect of Z_1 (see Figure 5.16). We obtain a similar result for the order$-m$ case.

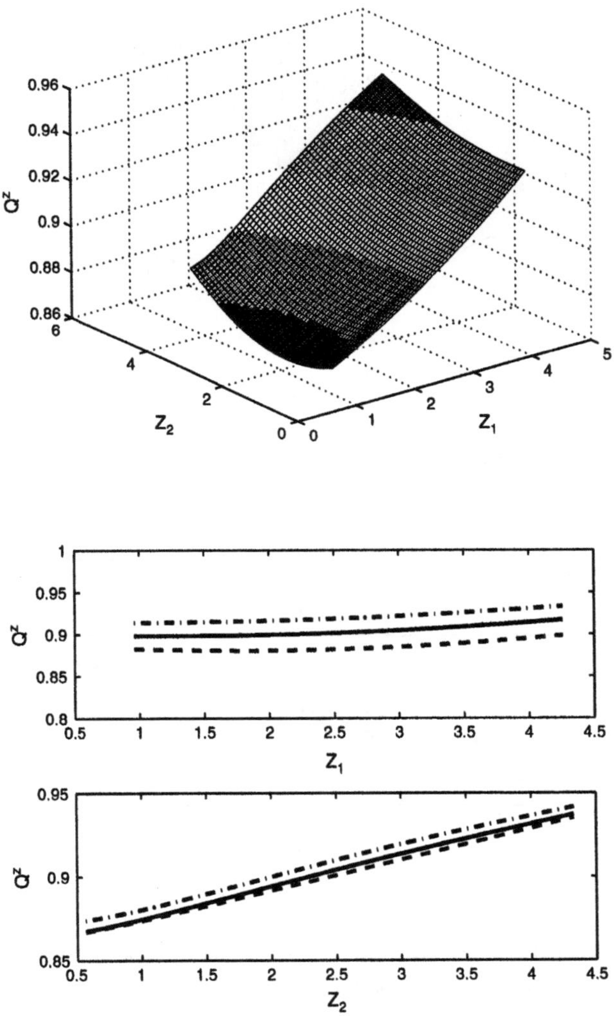

Figure 5.15. Simulated example with multivariate Z and 5 outliers. Surface of Q^z on Z_1 and Z_2 (top graph). Bottom graph: smoothed nonparametric regression of Q^z on Z_1 for Z_2's quartiles (top panel) and on Z_2 for Z_1's quartiles (bottom panel); dashed line = first quartile, solid line = median and dashdot line = third quartile.

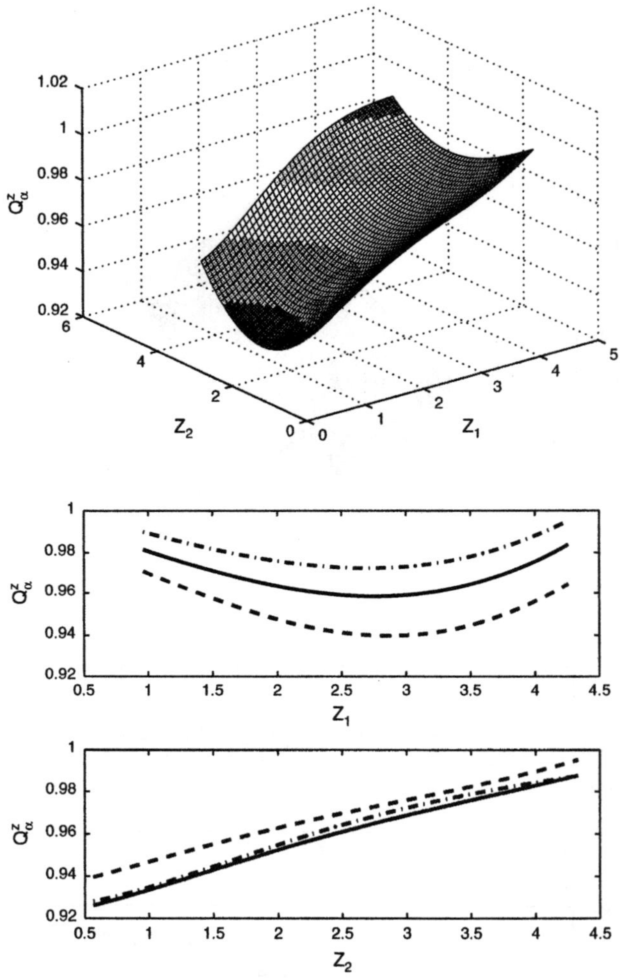

Figure 5.16. Simulated example with multivariate Z and 5 outliers. Surface of Q_α^z on Z_1 and Z_2 (top graph). Bottom graph: smoothed nonparametric regression of Q_α^z on Z_1 for Z_2's quartiles (top panel) and on Z_2 for Z_1's quartiles (bottom panel); dashed line = first quartile, solid line = median and dashdot line = third quartile.

This illustration confirms that it is always useful to compare the results obtained using full frontier efficiency estimators with those obtained applying robust partial frontiers measures.

PART II

APPLICATIONS

Chapter 6

INSURANCE INDUSTRY: IN SEARCH FOR ECONOMIES OF SCALE, SCOPE AND EXPERIENCE IN THE ITALIAN MOTOR-VEHICLE SECTOR

6.1 Introduction

The analysis of the Italian insurance market is interesting because of the dramatic changes that have occurred in the business during the past two decades.

With more than 43 millions of circulating vehicles, 754 vehicles per thousand of inhabitants and 103 vehicles per km of road, 13,842 million of Euro of direct premiums and 416 million of Euro of losses in 2001 (ANIA -Italian Association of Insurance companies- data), the automobile liability business is the most important insurance line in Italy, accounting for about 60.7% of Non-life insurance business and for almost 24% of total insurance premiums (2001). Its nature of compulsory insurance, the increasing of its tariffs and their influence on the inflation rate, together with the growing role played by biological damage reimbursements and by frauds, have opened a deep and sometimes harsh debate both in the political and technical environments, on the measures to be adopted in order to take under control premium levels, to increase efficiency and to promote competition.

The insurance industry in Italy, as well as in other European countries, has been traditionally subject to stringent regulation affecting pricing, contractual provisions, establishment of branches, solvency standards, and numerous additional operational details. Competitive intensity was very low, with minimal price and product competition and stable profit margins (Swiss Re 1996, 2000b).

The implementation of the EU's Third Generation Directives, beginning on July 1st, 1994, represented a major step in creating conditions in the EU resembling those in a single deregulated national market. In the last years, numerous events have taken place that have reduced existing barriers among financial institutions and countries and increased the competitive pressures in the market. The following are some of the most relevant factors: a) changes in the national and the EU law systems reducing the barriers among financial institutions and increasing information transparency between the insurer/distributor and the customer; b) development of new communication and information technologies and of new management methods (with the consequent increase of information transmission between the insurer and the distributors); c) increased financial sophistication of customers, who are more interested in financial problems, better educated, and more demanding; d) internationalization of markets; e) increased importance of insurance products in families saving portfolios; f) growing inadequacy of social security pension systems and the consequent increase in the demand for life insurance products; and g) birth of new financial intermediaries.

Despite of these changes, an analysis by Swiss Re (2000b) finds that personal lines insurance markets have remained *localised.* One reason explaining the slowness of the emergence of cross-border competition is that the European Directives did not completely eliminate the ability of host countries to influence insurance markets. For example, EU member countries can still utilize taxation to discriminate between domestic companies and those based in other EU countries (Hess and Trauth 1998). In addition, there are significant differences in contract law across European nations (Swiss Re 1996), impeding contract standardisation. Domestic insurers also are likely to have an advantage in their home markets because of cultural affinities, established brand names and distribution networks, and buyer perceptions that such firms have higher quality or financial stability than foreign firms. Finally, foreign insurers may be at a disadvantage in comparison with domestic insurers in terms of their knowledge of the underwriting characteristics of buyers, exposing foreign firms to higher informational asymmetry and adverse selection problems in comparison to domestic firms. It is interesting to see in more details how these recent changes have affected the Italian insurance market.

The Italian discipline of the insurance sector has seen its fundamental year in 1912 (Law 04/04/1912, no. 305) when the Istituto Nazionale delle Assicurazioni (INA) has been created and the affirmation of the principles of "authorisation of admission" and of "control on tariffs" has been ratified (this law regulated only the life business). With the transfer, in 1923, of the control of the insurance sector to the Ministry of Industry, begins a long period in which insurance companies experiment a kind of subjection in respect to the public administration. Only from the Seventies we observe a deep process of legislation, mainly due to the European Community regulations. We had three basic directives.

First directives regulate and harmonise the discipline of the "freedom of establishment": a company with its head office in a country member of the EU can open branches in other EU countries, to which is given the control on the activity of the branch, according to the principle of the "host country control".

Second directives, as well as partially modify the first ones, deal with the "freedom of services", in particular with reference to industrial and commercial risks, and to automobile insurance. The disposition of these directives is the possibility for insurers to operate in other EU countries without trade barriers and without the obligation to open a head office in loco.

Third directives, as well as partially modify the first and the second ones, ratify: a) the application of the principle of the "home country control"; b) the "single EU licence" allowing to operate in whole EU; c) the deregulation in the control of tariffs.

The Legislator's intervention incentives the passage from a strong protectionist context to a wider and free market for insurance. In particular, the July, 1st 1994 has been a milestone for the insurance sector. With the coming into force of the third directives on life and non-life business, in fact, a common European market for insurance services has been created. The aim of this discipline is to promote competition among insurers and benefit customers in terms of a widening supply, reduction of tariffs and increase of quality of services. The motor-vehicle insurance business, in particular, has known the strongest deregulation process. Starting from July, 1st 1994 the public Authorities could not control tariffs and insurance policy conditions anymore. The companies started to be free to fix prices according to customers' risk attitudes, and introduced the new tariffs system based on the bonus/malus mechanism. In Italy, seven direct selling companies for telephone and on-line selling were set up and services started to be improved with the opening of call centres working 24 hours a day.

Today, in Italy the insurance sector is under the control of three Authorities: a) the Consob (National Commission for the stock exchange market), on the subject of *transparency* on the company's information (Law 58/98); b) the ISVAP (Italian Control and Vigilance Authority of the insurance sector), on the subject of *stability* and of *transparency* on premiums and tariffs (Law 576/82); c) the Antitrust Authority, on the subject of *competition* (Law 287/90).

In the last years the debate between insurers and Customers Associations has been very harsh.

On the one side, companies maintain that the Automobile market is very competitive, as the high differentiation in the tariffs demonstrates. Moreover, the newly-born companies dealing with telephone and on-line selling - having lower operating costs - have played a vital role in improving market efficiency by limiting tariffs increase.

On the other side, Customers Associations have strongly argued that after 1994 tariffs have grown, according to the estimation measures, between the 50% and 100%.

Some main events occurred:

1) the Government, due to the impact of insurance Automobile prices on inflation, in 2000 froze tariffs (Law 26/05/2000, n. 137), decision censured because of its incompatibility with European laws;

2) the Italian Antitrust Authority sanctioned (measure no. 8546 - I377 Bulletin no. 30, 14 August 2000) a quite large number of companies - 41 insurers - for violation of the competition discipline (fined, as reported, 361,5 million Euro);

3) the exhaustive enquiry no. 11891 of the Italian Antitrust Authority on the motor vehicle insurance, dated 17 April 2003 (Bulletin no. 16-17 2003), showed that besides the information exchange as collusive behaviour (already assessed by the measure no. 8546 of 2000), the Italian motor vehicle insurance market presents anomalies which certainly do not incentivate companies to compete.[27] In Italy, the *liberalisation* process did not push insurance companies to increase the competition among them, as happened in other European countries. The conclusions reached by the Antitrust Authority asked for a radical innovation of the distribution channels, a renewal of the remuneration-incentive system of agents and of the refunding system.

4) Recently (measure no. 14926 of the 30 November 2005), the Antitrust Authority sanctioned the Italian National Association of Insurers (ANIA, Associazione Nazionale delle Imprese Assicurative, fined as reported 2 million Euro) for violation of the competition discipline and collusive behaviour of its members with the Italian Associations of professionals in charge of insurance damage liquidation (Associazioni dei periti).

From a theoretical perspective, a principal objective of financial services deregulation[28] is to improve market efficiency and enhance consumer choice through increased competition. Efficiency gains can occur as the result of the market *consolidation*. Consolidation, in fact, has the potential to improve efficiency in an industry if it forces poorly performing firms exiting the market or if it allows firms to take advantage of *scale economies* reducing unit costs of

[27] For an analysis of the information exchange and of the Italian Antitrust intervention in the insurance market under a law and economic perspective see Porrini (2004).

[28] Useful references on the deregulation of the U.S. banking industry are Berger, Kashayap and Scalise (1995), and Barth, Dan Brumbaugh and Wilcox (2000). The deregulation of European banking is discussed in Barth, Nolle and Rice (1997); and the deregulation in the Japanese financial system is analysed by Deckle (1988) and Goto (1999). The deregulation of the European insurance industry is illustrated in Hogan (1995), Swiss Re (1996), and Hess and Trauth (1998); and the deregulation of the Japanese insurance industry is presented in Swiss Re (2000a).

production. Moreover, firms offering different product lines also may realize *economies of scope*. Nevertheless, the empirical evidence on economies of scale and scope is contradictory: while some studies found efficiency gains others show no efficiency gains or efficiency losses.[29]

It is also interesting to analyse the impact of the age of companies on their performance, as proxy for their ability in survivor in a growingly competitive market, and as a proxy for the experience acquired along time.

The main aim of this chapter is to provide new empirical evidence on classic industrial organisation topics such as economies of scale, scope and of experience, analysing the Italian motor-vehicle insurance business. Besides we provide also a bootstrap-based test on returns to scale and a bias-corrected estimation of the efficiency scores of Italian insurers (along with 95% confidence intervals). Analysing data of 2000, we provide also a test on the comparison of structural efficiency of 'fined' vs. 'non fined' companies. Fined companies are insurers hit in 2000 by the Antitrust measure no. 8546 (recalled above) for anti-competitive behavior, while the non fined ones are companies not sanctioned by the Antitrust measure.

The chapter is organised as follows. The next section presents the data analysed, the inputs and outputs chosen as well as a normalized principal components analysis to explore the dataset. After that, a procedure allowing the aggregation of inputs and outputs is illustrated. The section that follows shows the results of the bootstrapping exercise for a sensitivity analysis of the efficiency scores and for a test on returns to scale. Then, economies of scale, scope and experience are analysed and, finally, the main results are summarised in the concluding section.

6.2 Data description

To give an outline on the dynamics of the Italian insurance market from 1982 to 2001 we show in Figure 6.1 and in Figure 6.2 the trend of nominal and real rate of growth of gross premiums (direct business).

Table 6.1 defines the Nominal and Real rate of growth of premiums illustrated in Figures 6.1 to 6.2.

A definition of the lines of business plotted can be found in Table 6.2.

Regarding the nominal and real rates of growth of gross premiums (direct business) in the period 1992-2001, it is interesting to note that the automobile business (Motor vehicles line - MV) has experimented a series of ups and downs until the first half of Nineties, with a downward convergence in the

[29] Useful surveys are Berger and Humphrey (1997); Cummins and Weiss (2001), and Amel, Barnes, Panetta and Salleo (2002). See also Harker and Zenios (2000) for an overview on the performance of financial institutions and its linkages with efficiency, innovation and regulation.

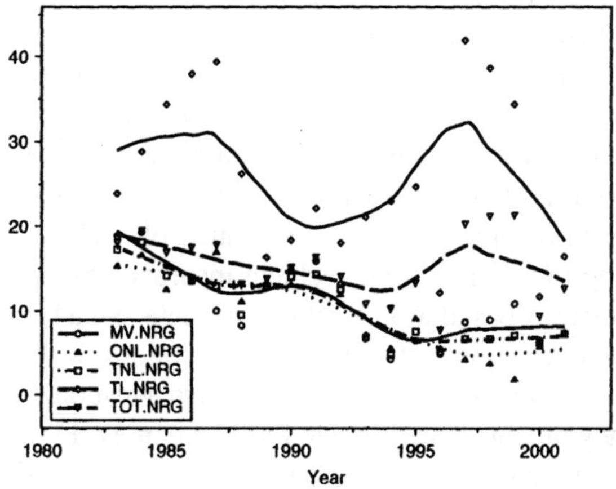

Figure 6.1. Nominal rate of growth - gross premiums (direct business) by line of business, years 1982-2001.

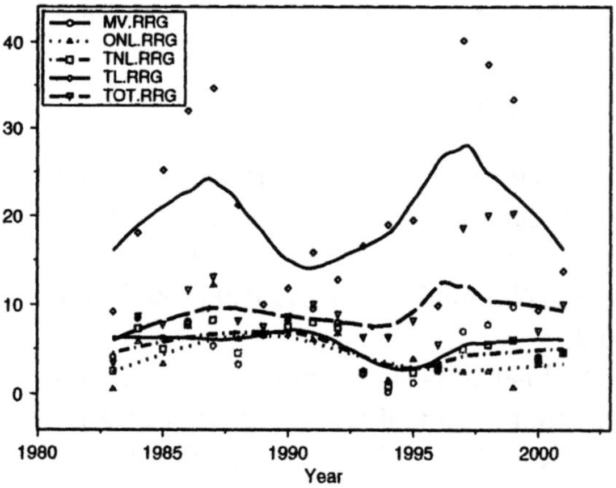

Figure 6.2. Real rate of growth - gross premiums (direct business) by line of business, years 1982-2001.

Table 6.1. Definition of Nominal and Real rate of growth.

Variable	Definition
NRG	Nominal Rate of growth year t [(premium year t/premium year t-1) *100-100]. It is the increase of nominal premium in the business considered.
RRG	Real Rate of growth=NRG-CPI
CPI	Consumer Price Index (percentage variation on previous year: up to 1995 of Italy, from 1996 of Europe, the harmonised Consumer Price. Source: Bank of Italy)

Table 6.2. Definition of rate of growth by line of business.

Variable	Definition
MV_NRG	Motor vehicles premiums Nominal Rate of growth
MV_RRG	Motor vehicles premiums Real Rate of growth
ONL_NRG	Other Non life premiums Nominal Rate of Growth
ONL_RRG	Other Non life premiums Real Rate of Growth
TNL_NRG	Total Non Life premiums Nominal Rate of Growth
TNL_RRG	Total Non Life premiums Real Rate of Growth
TL_NRG	Total Life premiums Nominal Rate of Growth
TL_RRG	Total Life premiums Real Rate of Growth
TOT_NRG	Total premiums Nominal Rate of Growth
TOT_RRG	Total premiums Real Rate of Growth

1992-1994 period, and that after the deregulation period, both the nominal and the real rate of growth of premiums have started to increase again (with a stop in 2000 and 2001, when the Government imposed a price freeze on motor-third party liability). This is particularly significant because the rate of growth of premiums of other non-life lines continued to decline also after 1994.

It is interesting to note the difference in the evolution of the real rate of growth of automobile business in comparison with the real rate of growth of the other non-life lines (see Figure 6.2). In fact, as most of them are mature lines, we would expected that they experienced a similar dynamics.

In the analysis which follows we use ANIA (Italian Association of Insurance Companies) official data. We had access to the balance sheet and income statements data as well as several features of the companies: date of foundation, information on the activity of the firm, i.e. if it is a generalist insurer operating both in life and non-life business, if it is specialist of a business (life or non-life), if it works in the auto liability business and so on.

In our empirical analysis we selected insurers operating in Italy, active and working in the motor-vehicle business in the year 2000, and operating in the market also in 1999 in order to compute the changes in reserves necessary in the construction of the outputs (see the discussion in the next paragraph). We selected a recent dataset available, in order to show the power of advanced robust and nonparametric methods for the evaluation of the performance of insurers. The number of retained companies is of 78. The 71.79% of our sample (*i.e.* 56 firms) are active only in the non-life business, *i.e.* are *specialist* insurers (SPEC); the remaining 28.21% (*i.e.* 22 insurers) is made by *generalist* insurers (GEN), active both in the life and nonlife business. Furthermore, 37 firms of our sample (the 47.44%) were hit by the Italian Antitrust intervention (measure no. 8546 of 2000) for collusive behavior based on exchange of information. Hereafter we call these fined companies as FIN, in opposition to non fined companies, called NFIN. We notice also that most generalist insurers have been fined by the Antitrust intervention.[30]

6.2.1 Definition of outputs and inputs

The definition of the inputs and outputs of insurers is a critical step in an efficiency analysis. This is due to the fact that insurers offer services to customers and most of their outputs are intangible (as it is the case for financial services).

The main approaches used to measure the outputs and inputs of insurers have been reviewed in Cummins and Weiss (2001), where also a review of studies applying frontier methodologies to the insurance industry is provided.

The main services provided by insurers are (the presentation below follows Cummins and Weiss, 2001, p.790):

1. ***Risk-pooling and risk-bearing.*** Insurance provides a mechanism through which consumers and businesses exposed to losses can engage in risk reduction through pooling. The actuarial, underwriting, and related expenses incurred in risk pooling are important components of value added in the industry. Insurers also add value by holding equity capital to bear the residual risk of the pool.

2. ***"Real" financial services*** relating to insured losses. Insurers provide a variety of real services for policyholders including financial planning, risk management, and the supply of legal defence in liability disputes. By contracting with insurers to provide these services, policyholders take ad-

[30]The total number of companies hit by the Italian Antitrust Authority is 41, hence in our sample we have more than 90% of the overall fined companies.

vantage of insurers' specialised expertise to reduce the costs associated with managing risks.

3. ***Intermediation.*** For life insurers, financial intermediation is a principal function, accomplished through the sale of asset accumulation products such as annuities. For non-life insurers, intermediation is an important but incidental function, resulting from the collection of premiums in advance of claim payments.

Transactions flow data, such as the number of applications processed, the number of policies issued, the number of claims settled, etc., are not easily available. However, a satisfactory proxy for the amount of risk-pooling and real insurance services provided is the value of real losses incurred (Cummins, Turchetti, Weiss, 1996; Berger, Cummins, and Weiss, 1997; Cummins, Weiss, and Zi, 1999). Losses incurred are defined as the losses that are expected to be paid as the result of providing insurance coverage during a particular period of time. Because the objective of risk-pooling is to collect funds from the policyholder pool and redistribute them to those who incur losses, proxying output by the amount of losses incurred seems quite appropriate.

Losses are also a good proxy for the amount of real services provided, since the amount of claims settlement and risk management services also are highly correlated with loss aggregates.

Insurers perform also services in connection with claims occurring in prior years that have not yet been settled or claims resulting from contingent events. As a proxy for these services, in the definition of the output we consider, for each year, the sum of the paid claims and the claims reserves of the year, minus the claims reserves of previous year. By doing so, in the definition of the output, we consider as proxy of financial services the sum of paid claims and changes in reserves.

Finally, we identify 3 inputs and 2 outputs as well as some external factors described in Table 6.3.

A descriptive statistics on inputs, outputs and external factors is offered in Table 6.4. Inputs and outputs are expressed in thousands of Euros, Market shares are percentages. The management index is given by the ratio of management expenses on the total volume of premiums. It is an indicator of the intensity of the company's managerial activity.

In the efficiency analysis which follows we adopt an input oriented framework. This choice is mainly due to our interest in understanding how efficiently insurers were in using their resources (inputs) given that, at least in the short run, the quantity and quality of outputs cannot be affected in a substantial way. Moreover, this choice is also consistent with all the international literature of the field (see *e.g.* Cummins and Weiss, 2001) as well as with previous studies on

Table 6.3. Definition of Inputs, Outputs and External Factors.

Variable code	*Type of variable*	*Description*
in1	*Input 1*	Labour
in2	*Input 2*	Physical Capital
in3	*Input 3*	Financial capital
ou1	*Output 1*	Incurred losses and changes in reserves
ou2	*Output 2*	Invested assets
zx1	*Ext. factor 1*	Age at 2000 (number of years active on the market till 2000)
zx2	*Ext. factor 2*	Market share
zx3	*Ext. factor 3*	Management index (manag. exp/tot premium)

Table 6.4. Descriptive statistics on inputs, outputs and external factor considered in the analysis. Italian motor vehicle insurers (78 obs).

Variable	*mean*	*stand. dev.*	*min value*	*max value*
in1	128341.846	293996.564	301.000	2266839.000
in2	101892.795	211575.880	4.000	1078654.000
in3	1656299.051	4631613.110	6056.000	36607503.000
ou1	343555.308	581724.310	52.000	3229235.000
ou2	1351788.590	3621866.838	6046.000	27495409.000
zx1	56.128	49.605	1.000	179.000
zx2	0.663	1.167	0.001	6.760
zx3	0.348	0.580	0.083	4.698

the Italian insurance market (Turchetti and Daraio, 2004; Cummins, Turchetti and Weiss, 1996).

In order to avoid the *curse of dimensionality* of nonparametric estimation (here we have only 78 observations in a space at 3+2 dimensions) we tried to reduce the dimensional space of the analysis. After an exploratory analysis, in Section 6.2.3, we provide an illustration of a statistical methodology which might be useful for the dimension reduction in productivity analysis.

6.2.2 An exploratory investigation

Before starting the efficiency analysis, it is always useful to have an idea about the data we are going to deal with. At this purpose there are several multivariate statistical tools which may be of interest to see multivariate dataset (for a clear presentation of these tools in an applied perspective, see Härdle and Simar, 2003). One of the most known tool is the normalized principal component analysis (PCA). This kind of analysis, which aims at reducing the information contained in a multivariate space providing illustrations in two dimensions, was used as a preliminary investigation to an efficiency analysis exercise in Deprins and Simar (1988). A first picture shows the correlation structure existing among the variables; in a second picture, all the individuals are projected on a reduced two dimensional space. The inspection of the correlation matrix reported in Table 6.5 tells us, as it is often the case in productivity analysis, that a strong correlation exists (higher than 0.80 in all the cases) among all inputs and outputs. See also Table 6.7 where the correlations of the first two principal components with the original variables are reported. It appears that the two first principal components summarize 87% of the information. This is the information provided by the cumulated percentage of variance explained by the first two eigenvalues reported in Table 6.6. Hence, we can provide sensible two dimensional pictures, without loosing too much information. Figure 6.3 displays the projections of the original variables: the coordinates are the factor loadings, which are also the correlations of the principal components with the original variables. We see that the first axis characterizes a "size" effect (level) of the activity done by the insurers (it has, in fact, negative correlation with all the activity variables, inputs and ouputs), so it could be interpreted as a "dimensional factor"; the second axis characterizes the "management index" of units. The two axis are orthogonal (no correlation) which indicates very

Table 6.5. Correlations matrix. Italian motor vehicle insurers (78 obs).

	in1	in2	in3	ou1	ou2	zx1	zx2	zx3
in1	1.00	0.85	0.98	0.92	0.98	0.50	0.93	-0.10
in2	0.85	1.00	0.83	0.91	0.86	0.55	0.91	-0.12
in3	0.98	0.83	1.00	0.88	1.00	0.49	0.91	-0.10
ou1	0.92	0.91	0.88	1.00	0.90	0.55	0.98	-0.15
ou2	0.98	0.86	1.00	0.90	1.00	0.50	0.92	-0.10
zx1	0.50	0.55	0.49	0.55	0.50	1.00	0.56	-0.19
zx2	0.93	0.91	0.91	0.98	0.92	0.56	1.00	-0.15
zx3	-0.10	-0.12	-0.10	-0.15	-0.10	-0.19	-0.15	1.00

Table 6.6. Eigenvalues and percentages of variances explained. Italian motor vehicle insurers (78 obs).

eigenvalues	*% of variance*	*cumulated %*
5.9479	0.7435	0.7435
1.0201	0.1275	0.8710
0.6388	0.0799	0.9508
0.2461	0.0308	0.9816
0.1089	0.0136	0.9952
0.0275	0.0034	0.9987
0.0102	0.0013	0.9999
0.0004	0.0001	1.0000

Table 6.7. Correlations of the first two pc's with the original variables (Factors loadings). Italian motor vehicle insurers (78 obs).

Original variable	*% First pc*	*Second pc*
in1	-0.9699	0.0907
in2	-0.9256	0.0204
in3	-0.9573	0.1045
ou1	-0.9651	0.0164
ou2	-0.9688	0.0975
zx1	-0.6198	-0.2918
zx2	-0.9763	0.0191
zx3	0.1629	0.9514

few linear relationship between the dimension and the management index of the units. The age of the companies (number of years they are active on the market) is mainly related to the level of activity and interestingly seems not related to the management index.

Figure 6.4, left panel, provides a two dimensional picture of the insurance companies mapped on the two principal components. The interpretation of this picture is facilitated (highlighted) by looking simultaneously at Figure 6.3 which give the weights of the original variables in the principal components. Hence, on the left of Figure 6.4, we have the big insurance companies (in terms of their level of activity), as an example, company n. 3 is Assicurazioni Generali, company number 1 is RAS, n. 10 is SAI, n.8 is Fondiaria and so on (these companies are among the biggest and most known insurance companies

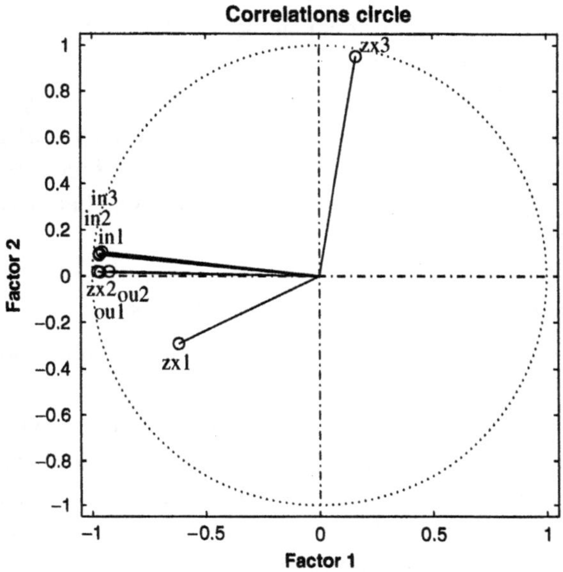

Figure 6.3. Projection of the variables for the Italian Motor-vehicle insurers dataset, year 200C

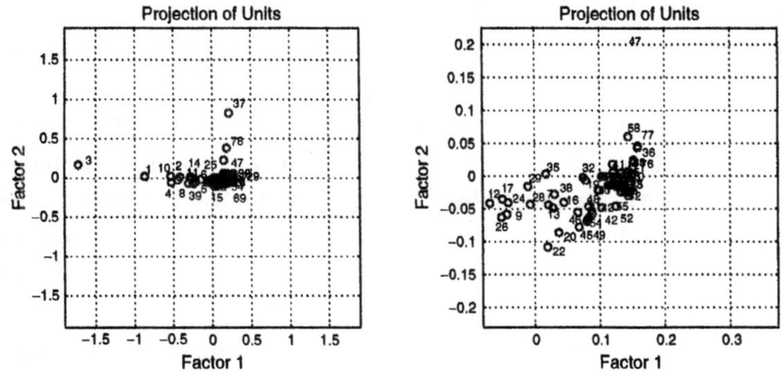

Figure 6.4. Projection of the individual insurers for the Italian Motor-vehicle dataset, year 2000. Right panel a zoom.

in Italy). On the right, small units are present (the origin is the average point). On the north of the picture we find companies with an high management index, on the south, on the contrary, low management index companies. It appears that the company n. 37 is particularly active along the management dimension as well as company n. 78 and company n. 47. These companies are, respectively, Direct Line, DB Assicura and Dialogo Assicurazioni, three relatively new companies working through call center, which do not have a big activity dimension but put in place innovative management policies. According to human capital theories, in fact, companies with an higher management index should outperform those with a lower associated management index.

The right panel of Figure 6.4 is a zoom on the preceding picture which displays the companies near the origin (which is the center of gravity of the cloud of points). Generally speaking, observations which are far from the origin deserve special attention, as they show an atypical behavior. Sometimes extreme points flag potential outliers.

6.2.3 Aggregation of inputs and outputs

The high correlation levels we found among the outputs and among the inputs suggest that a suitable aggregation of inputs and outputs for the efficiency analysis is possible and in this case also recommended, because the *curse of dimensionality* is always present in nonparametric estimation. Indeed the curse of dimensionality implies that working in smaller dimensions tends to provide better estimates of the frontier. Moreover, if we are able to reduce the frontier estimation at the simplest situation (one input one output) it is also possible provide graphical bi-dimensional illustrations of the estimated efficient frontier.

The basic principle (suggested by Mouchart and Simar, 2002) is to find an "input factor", a linear combination of the inputs, which best summarizes the information provided by all the inputs (in this case $p = 3$).

Since this factor has to be interpreted as a proxy for all inputs, it should be positively correlated with all inputs.

In addition, since inputs might be expressed in different units of measure, we must correct for the scale of the inputs (by dividing each input by its standard deviation or its mean). We recall that Farrell-Debreu efficiency scores are radial measures and their DEA estimates have the property of being *scale-invariant*, hence this means that the normalization of the data we perform here does not affect the results of the following efficiency analysis.

Then, we are looking for a vector $a \in \mathcal{R}^3_+$ such that the projection of the (scaled) input data matrix X on the vector a, "best" represents the data matrix X (in terms of minimizing the sum of squares of the residuals). Mathematically, the vector of the n projections is determined by the resulting input factor F_{in}:

$$F_{in} = X\,a = a_1 X_1 + a_2 X_2 + a_3 X_3 \tag{6.1}$$

where $X : (n \times 3)$ is the (scaled) inputs data matrix. It can be shown that the optimal direction vector a is the first eigenvector of the matrix $X'X$ corresponding to its largest eigenvalue λ_1 (see Table 6.9, first column). Note that here, we are in a different situation than in the PCA's case: in this case, the data have not been centered, so that the eigenvalues do not represent the factors' variances. Eigenvalues are rather the "inertia" (or moment of the second order) of the factor. So that the ratio $\lambda_1/(\lambda_1 + \lambda_2 + \lambda_3)$ indicates the percentage

Table 6.8. Input Factor inertia. Italian motor vehicle insurers (78 obs).

%inertia	*%cumul*
0.9429	0.9429
0.0509	0.9937
0.0063	1.0000

Table 6.9. Eigenvectors of the matrix $X'X$. Italian motor vehicle insurers (78 obs).

0.5643	0.2178	0.7963
0.4857	-0.8676	-0.1068
0.6676	0.4471	-0.5954

Table 6.10. Correlations between the input factor (F_{in}) and inputs. Italian motor vehicle insurers (78 obs).

	F_{in}	in1	in2	in3
F_{in}	1.0000	0.9876	0.9089	0.9854
in1	0.9876	1.0000	0.8528	0.9803
in2	0.9089	0.8528	1.0000	0.8326
in3	0.9854	0.9803	0.8326	1.0000

of inertia which is explained by this first factor (see Table 6.8, first column). When this ratio is high (close to 1), it indicates that most of the information contained in the original 3-dimensional data matrix X, is well summarized by the first factor F_{in}. Correlations between F_{in} and $X_1, ..., X_3$ indicate also how well this new one-dimensional variable represents the original ones (see Table 6.10).

In the output space, the same can be done with the 2 (scaled) output variables, providing one output factor:

$$F_{out} = Y\,b = b_1 Y_1 + b_2 Y_2 \tag{6.2}$$

where $Y : (n \times 2)$ is the data matrix of the (scaled) outputs. Here the vector $b \in \mathcal{R}^2_+$ is the first eigenvector of the matrix $Y'Y$, corresponding to its largest eigenvalue (see Table 6.12, first column).

Table 6.11. Output Factor inertia. Italian motor vehicle insurers (78 obs).

%inertia	*%cumul*
0.9591	0.9591
0.0409	1.0000

Table 6.12. Eigenvectors of the matrix $Y'Y$. Italian motor vehicle insurers (78 obs).

0.5527	-0.8334
0.8334	0.5527

Table 6.13. Correlations between the output factor (F_{out}) and outputs. Italian motor vehicle insurers (78 obs).

	F_{out}	ou1	ou2
F_{out}	1.0000	0.9505	0.9915
ou1	0.9505	1.0000	0.9020
ou2	0.9915	0.9020	1.0000

The results of this factor analysis are shown below. We obtain:

$$a = (0.5643 \quad 0.4857 \quad 0.6676)' \tag{6.3}$$

$$b = (0.5527 \quad 0.8334)' \tag{6.4}$$

Therefore, in both cases, the factors are a sort of 'average' of the (scaled) original variables. The percentage of inertia explained by the first factor is very high in both cases (0.9429 for the input factor; 0.9591 for the output case, see Table 6.11): it is certainly appropriate to summarize the information of the full data matrix by these two one-dimensional factors, without loosing too much information. The correlation between the factors and the original variables is also high (above 0.83 for the input case; above 0.90 in the output case, see Table 6.13). This analysis shows that we may describe the production activity of all these units by only one input factor and one output factor. Nevertheless, to reach this conclusion in a *rigorous way*, it may be useful to apply the Simar and Wilson (2001)'s bootstrap based procedures to test for aggregation possibilities (restrictions) on inputs and outputs in efficient frontier models. In our case here we did not perform this test due to the high correlations found between the original variables and their aggregate factors.

6.3 Testing returns to scale and bootstrapping efficiency scores

We applied the bootstrap algorithm described above in Section 3.4 to test the model of returns to scale (RTS) in this application, following the method proposed by Simar and Wilson (2002).

We have seen in Section 2.3 that returns to scale are properties of the boundary Ψ^∂ of the production set. The less restrictive model for RTS is the varying return to scale (VRS) situation where the returns are allowed to be eventually locally increasing, then constant and finally non-increasing.

The first procedure proposed by Simar and Wilson (2002) is to test the more restrictive model of constant returns to scale (CRS) against the VRS: $H_0 : \Psi^\partial$ is globally CRS against $H_1 : \Psi^\partial$ is VRS.

Under VRS, the attainable set is estimated by the free-disposal convex hull of the cloud of points. So we can compute the DEA efficiency scores $\widehat{\theta}_{VRS,n}(X_i, Y_i)$ under this model by solving Equation (2.16). Under the more restrictive CRS model, the DEA estimator is calculated according to Equation (2.16), where the constraint $\sum_{i=1}^{n} \gamma_i = 1$ on the multipliers is dropped, and the resulting DEA scores are denoted by $\widehat{\theta}_{CRS,n}(X_i, Y_i)$.

The VRS estimators are consistent whatever being the hypothesis on RTS, the CRS are only consistent if the CRS hypothesis is true. So, if the CRS hypothesis is true, the two sets of estimators would be very similar. We will use below as test statistics the mean of the ratios of the efficiency scores:

$$T(\mathcal{X}_n) = \frac{1}{n} \sum_{i=1}^{n} \frac{\widehat{\theta}_{CRS,n}(X_i, Y_i)}{\widehat{\theta}_{VRS,n}(X_i, Y_i)}. \tag{6.5}$$

By construction $\widehat{\theta}_{CRS,n}(X_i, Y_i) \leq \widehat{\theta}_{VRS,n}(X_i, Y_i)$ and we will reject the null hypothesis if the test statistics T is too small. The p-value of the null-hypothesis is then obtained by computing:

$$p - \text{value } = \text{Prob}(T(\mathcal{X}_n) \leq T_{obs} | H_0 \text{ is true}), \tag{6.6}$$

where T_{obs} is the value of T computed on the original observed sample $\mathcal{X}_n$.

Of course, we cannot compute this probability analytically but we can approximate this value by using the bootstrap algorithm described in Section 3.4. We simulate B pseudo-samples $\mathcal{X}_n^{*,b}$ of size n under the null (*i.e.* using the CRS estimate of the frontier for generating the pseudo-samples), and for each bootstrap sample we compute the value of $T^{*,b} = T(\mathcal{X}_n^{*,b})$. The p-value is then approximated by the proportion of bootstrap samples with values of $T^{*,b}$ less than the original observed value T_{obs}:

$$p - \text{value } \approx \sum_{b=1}^{B} \frac{\mathbf{1}(T^{*,b} \leq T_{obs})}{B}. \tag{6.7}$$

In the application here, with one input-factor and one output-factor as defined above, we obtain for this test (with $B = 2000$) a p-value of $0.0055 < 0.05$, hence we reject the null hypothesis of CRS.

Before accepting the VRS hypothesis, Simar and Wilson (2002) suggest to perform the following test where the null-hypothesis is less restrictive than the CRS: we test the non-increasing returns to scale (NIRS) model against the VRS: $H_0' : \Psi^\partial$ is globally $NIRS$ against $H_1 : \Psi^\partial$ is VRS.

The procedure is similar to the preceding one where CRS has to be replaced by NIRS and $\widehat{\theta}_{NIRS,n}(X_i, Y_i)$ is computed as in Equation (2.16) where the equality constraint on the multipliers is replaced by the inequality $\sum_{i=1}^{n} \gamma_i \leq 1$. The computations for this second test lead to a p-value of $0.0405 < 0.05$. Hence, we reject H_0' (even if we are close to a border line case) and choose to accept H_1, *i.e.* the hypothesis of VRS.

We can visualize the efficient DEA-VRS frontier in Figure 6.5 with a zoom on the core of the cloud of points in Figure 6.6. Several interesting information can be obtained by inspecting these figures. For instance, we see that companies n. 3 and n. 1 are estimated as efficient; they are also isolated with no other companies to be benchmarked against.

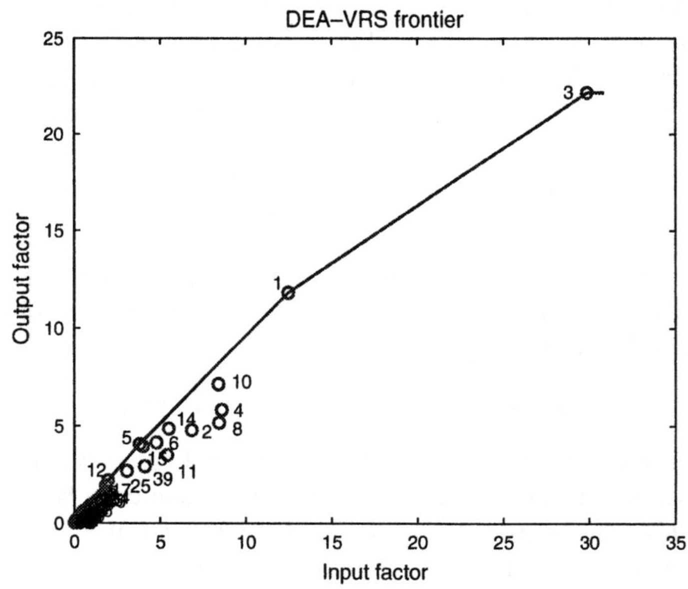

Figure 6.5. Output factor versus Input factor and DEA frontier for the Italian Motor-vehicle dataset, year 2000.

In Table 6.14 (second column) we show the FDH (input oriented) efficiency score computed using the input factor and the output factor (we notice that the computation of the FDH efficiency scores with 3 inputs and 2 outputs led

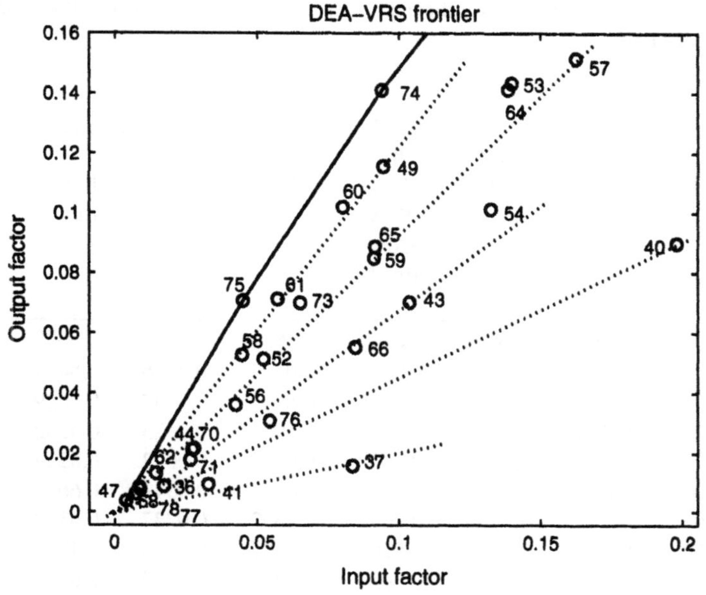

Figure 6.6. Output factor versus Input factor and DEA frontier for the Italian Motor-vehicle dataset, year 2000: a zoom.

to an average efficiency of 0.9956 with 73 efficient observations on a total of 78 observations); the DEA VRS (input oriented) computed with 3 inputs and 2 outputs (third column); the DEA VRS (input oriented) efficiency estimates computed on the input and output factor (fourth column). In the fifth column we report the Bias-corrected DEA VRS efficiency scores computed on the input and output factors; column sixth reports the bias of the DEA efficiency scores, while the seventh column reports the standard deviation of the estimates. When the Bias is larger than the standard deviation (std), the Bias-corrected estimates have to be preferred to the original estimates. Finally, columns eight and nine of Table 6.14 display the Basic Bootstrap (Simar and Wilson, 2000b) 95-percent Confidence Intervals: Lower and Upper Bound. We use the algorithm described in Section 3.4, with $B = 2000$ bootstrap replications.

As noticed above for the FDH case, the DEA estimation in the third column using 3 inputs and 2 outputs is not very reliable. Indeed the rate of convergence, being $n^{2/(p+q+1)}$ (here $78^{2/6} = 4.26$) in this high dimensional space, corresponds roughly as if we had 18 observations in a full parametric model, where the rate of convergence is $n^{1/2}$. This remind us that it is not reasonable to use FDH and DEA estimates with 78 observations in a five dimensional space.

Table 6.14. Bootstrap results: input efficiency scores with VRS model (B=2000) for Italian motor- vehicle insurers.

No. Obs.	FDH Eff IF OF	DEA Eff. Score (VRS) $p=3$ $q=2$	DEA Eff. Score (VRS) IF OF	DEA Eff. Bias Corr. IF OF	Bias	Std	Lower Bound	Upper Bound
1	1.0000	1.0000	1.0000	0.6149	0.3851	0.2927	0.6675	0.9838
2	0.8048	1.0000	0.6725	0.6022	0.0703	0.0516	0.5473	0.6672
3	1.0000	1.0000	1.0000	0.3445	0.6555	0.9137	0.5629	0.9817
4	0.9780	0.9711	0.6709	0.5733	0.0976	0.0675	0.5242	0.6630
5	1.0000	1.0000	1.0000	0.9028	0.0972	0.0672	0.8229	0.9882
6	1.0000	1.0000	0.8127	0.7336	0.0791	0.0549	0.6685	0.8017
7	0.9992	0.9455	0.7009	0.6657	0.0352	0.0227	0.6302	0.6967
8	0.9959	0.9639	0.5964	0.5262	0.0702	0.0498	0.4774	0.5887
9	1.0000	0.8669	0.7897	0.7424	0.0473	0.0299	0.6985	0.7850
10	1.0000	1.0000	0.8605	0.6833	0.1772	0.1204	0.6411	0.8485
11	0.7003	0.8172	0.5989	0.5469	0.0520	0.0360	0.5001	0.5930
12	1.0000	1.0000	1.0000	0.9198	0.0802	0.0469	0.8578	0.9833
13	1.0000	0.8956	0.8334	0.7915	0.0419	0.0269	0.7493	0.8287
14	1.0000	1.0000	0.8503	0.7599	0.0904	0.0662	0.6906	0.8421
15	0.9507	1.0000	0.9244	0.8371	0.0873	0.0610	0.7637	0.9164
16	0.7835	0.9408	0.5246	0.4954	0.0292	0.0166	0.4708	0.5206
17	1.0000	1.0000	0.9362	0.8678	0.0684	0.0410	0.8119	0.9291
18	0.9958	0.8831	0.7829	0.7483	0.0346	0.0232	0.7084	0.7795
19	1.0000	0.9331	0.6818	0.6432	0.0386	0.0216	0.6114	0.6768
20	0.6772	0.9357	0.6227	0.5912	0.0315	0.0188	0.5627	0.6194
21	0.8122	0.8727	0.5568	0.5314	0.0254	0.0159	0.5049	0.5536
22	0.6753	0.8246	0.5219	0.4971	0.0248	0.0151	0.4729	0.5187
23	0.8136	0.7629	0.6594	0.6304	0.0290	0.0194	0.5969	0.6564
24	0.9619	1.0000	0.6887	0.6470	0.0417	0.0262	0.6088	0.6846
25	1.0000	1.0000	0.7987	0.7356	0.0631	0.0415	0.6790	0.7894
26	1.0000	0.9763	0.7376	0.6959	0.0417	0.0266	0.6572	0.7333
27	1.0000	1.0000	0.8595	0.8214	0.0381	0.0248	0.7783	0.8550
28	1.0000	1.0000	0.7721	0.7314	0.0407	0.0266	0.6905	0.7676
29	0.7258	1.0000	0.5381	0.5101	0.0280	0.0182	0.4819	0.5347
30	0.8664	0.9381	0.6980	0.6673	0.0307	0.0206	0.6317	0.6949
31	1.0000	1.0000	1.0000	0.9409	0.0591	0.0314	0.8953	0.9910
32	1.0000	1.0000	0.8145	0.7722	0.0423	0.0257	0.7316	0.8077
33	1.0000	1.0000	1.0000	0.9467	0.0533	0.0303	0.9011	0.9921
34	0.7335	0.9400	0.5576	0.5327	0.0249	0.0166	0.5043	0.5551
35	0.9650	0.9557	0.6347	0.6009	0.0338	0.0219	0.5673	0.6307
36	0.8304	0.8654	0.3978	0.3562	0.0416	0.0340	0.3195	0.3951
37	0.3164	1.0000	0.1333	0.1248	0.0085	0.0060	0.1157	0.1325
38	1.0000	0.9093	0.7699	0.7308	0.0391	0.0253	0.6913	0.7645
39	0.9270	1.0000	0.6543	0.6017	0.0526	0.0354	0.5538	0.6462

Table 6.14 (continued)
Bootstrap results: input efficiency scores with VRS model (B=2000) for Italian motor-vehicle insurers.

No. Obs.	FDH Eff IF OF	DEA Eff. Score (VRS) $p=3$ $q=2$	DEA Eff. Score (VRS) IF OF	DEA Eff. Bias Corr. IF OF	Bias	Std	Lower Bound	Upper Bound
41	0.4386	0.8005	0.2214	0.2001	0.0213	0.0174	0.1795	0.2200
42	1.0000	0.6656	0.6113	0.5801	0.0312	0.0203	0.5490	0.6082
43	0.4324	0.8238	0.4298	0.4000	0.0298	0.0173	0.3778	0.4275
44	1.0000	0.9418	0.5347	0.5044	0.0303	0.0200	0.4730	0.5318
45	0.9107	0.8545	0.5460	0.5185	0.0275	0.0180	0.4906	0.5434
46	1.0000	1.0000	0.7709	0.7294	0.0415	0.0231	0.6945	0.7636
47	1.0000	1.0000	1.0000	0.5434	0.4566	0.2952	0.6623	0.9829
48	0.9960	1.0000	0.7091	0.6766	0.0325	0.0214	0.6404	0.7053
49	0.9945	1.0000	0.8066	0.7544	0.0522	0.0297	0.7141	0.7991
50	1.0000	1.0000	0.7544	0.7141	0.0403	0.0228	0.6796	0.7481
51	0.4368	0.8265	0.4334	0.4024	0.0310	0.0175	0.3817	0.4312
52	0.8549	1.0000	0.6321	0.5945	0.0376	0.0241	0.5603	0.6297
53	0.8908	1.0000	0.6860	0.6382	0.0478	0.0275	0.6050	0.6826
54	0.6055	0.8666	0.4999	0.4693	0.0306	0.0182	0.4432	0.4958
55	1.0000	1.0000	0.8891	0.8378	0.0513	0.0321	0.7928	0.8835
56	1.0000	0.6736	0.5558	0.5246	0.0312	0.0197	0.4954	0.5527
57	0.7657	0.9732	0.6324	0.5924	0.0400	0.0241	0.5610	0.6285
58	1.0000	1.0000	0.7580	0.7124	0.0456	0.0290	0.6715	0.7548
59	0.8796	0.8330	0.6009	0.5636	0.0373	0.0223	0.5324	0.5954
60	1.0000	1.0000	0.8322	0.7812	0.0510	0.0304	0.7378	0.8254
61	1.0000	0.9327	0.7927	0.7378	0.0549	0.0316	0.6970	0.7873
62	1.0000	0.9068	0.6665	0.6187	0.0478	0.0354	0.5680	0.6617
63	0.9749	1.0000	0.8978	0.8523	0.0455	0.0271	0.8112	0.8929
64	0.8991	0.9479	0.6794	0.6307	0.0487	0.0275	0.5983	0.6757
65	0.8763	0.7432	0.6278	0.5894	0.0384	0.0231	0.5567	0.6227
66	0.5308	0.9085	0.4184	0.3927	0.0257	0.0161	0.3701	0.4159
67	0.7492	0.9009	0.5731	0.5415	0.0316	0.0172	0.5157	0.5671
68	1.0000	1.0000	0.7950	0.7083	0.0867	0.0704	0.6359	0.7891
69	0.5065	0.6566	0.4914	0.4657	0.0257	0.0149	0.4433	0.4882
70	1.0000	0.6527	0.5300	0.5000	0.0300	0.0197	0.4690	0.5270
71	1.0000	0.9485	0.4667	0.4386	0.0281	0.0193	0.4081	0.4636
72	0.9062	1.0000	0.5130	0.4850	0.0280	0.0179	0.4588	0.5097
73	0.6892	0.9238	0.6833	0.6359	0.0474	0.0275	0.6005	0.6795
74	1.0000	1.0000	1.0000	0.9280	0.0720	0.0405	0.8804	0.9941
75	1.0000	1.0000	1.0000	0.9303	0.0697	0.0401	0.8787	0.9937
76	0.7796	0.9257	0.3733	0.3525	0.0208	0.0131	0.3329	0.3712
77	0.9491	1.0000	0.7029	0.6113	0.0916	0.0705	0.5496	0.6960
78	1.0000	1.0000	0.7336	0.5876	0.1460	0.1044	0.5457	0.7238

It is interesting to note that the widest intervals correspond to observations no. 3 and no. 1 which are the most remote observations in Figure 6.5. As we have seen before, Figure 6.5 tells us that there are simply no other observations near no. 3 and no. 1 that would help estimate the frontier in their region. Interestingly, the bootstrap is able to automatically take into account the information available for the estimation of each efficiency score: if there are a lot of firms in the same region of a certain unit, then the confidence interval of the efficiency score of this unit will be very thin; on the contrary, if the unit is isolated then its efficiency score will have a wide confidence interval.

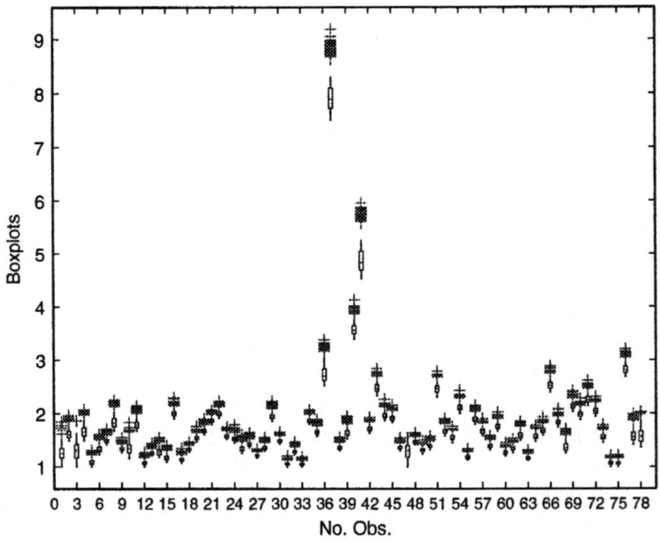

Figure 6.7. Boxplots of the input Shephard efficiency scores (VRS). B=2000. Italian motor-vehicle insurance business (78 obs).

Figure 6.7 illustrates the boxplots of the input Shephard efficiency scores (the inverse of the Farrell efficiency measures) coming out from our bootstrap exercise: it clearly appears that firms no. 37, 41 and 40 are the most inefficient. Figure 6.6 shows, in fact, that unit no. 37 uses a productive mix (as represented by the ray coming from the origin which passes through the unit) that is dominated by the productive mix used by the other firms in the sample. Close to the mix of this unit is firm no. 41, which is on a ray between firm no. 37 and firm no. 40. Slightly better is the situation of firms no. 54 (efficiency score 0.4999), 43 (eff. score 0.4298), 66 (0.4184), 76 (0.3733), 71 (0.4667), which use a technology that combines inputs and outputs more efficiently than the previous firms. Then, we observe firms no. 57, 59, 65, 52 and 70 whose mix dominates the previous firms and which in turns is dominated by the technology of firms no. 49, 60, 61, 58, 62 and finally by the most efficient technology of units 47, 74 and 75.

The inspection of the last two columns of Table 6.14 reveals that the original efficiency estimates lie outside the estimated confidence intervals. This is due to the fact that the original estimates are biased and that the confidence intervals estimates correct for the bias. Finally we note also that for unit no. 3 and no. 1 the relative estimated confidence intervals do not contain the corresponding bias-corrected efficiency scores. This is related to the fact that the bias corrections are made in terms of the original efficiency estimates, while reciprocals are used to construct the confidence interval estimates, and because the sample information in this region is very poor.

6.4 Economies of scale

Government policies encouraging consolidation make sense economically if larger firms tend to be more efficient, if there are unrealised scale economies, and/or if consolidation leads to more vigorous competition that increases market efficiency.

Scale economies might be present in the insurance industry not only because fixed costs are spread over a wider base as firm size increases but also because insurance involves the diversification of risk, which is more effective in larger risk pools. On the other hand, if insurance is primarily a variable cost industry and insurers can use reinsurance to reduce income volatility, significant scale economies may not be present.

For insurance markets where there is the presence of large numbers of very small firms, there is a common belief that those small firms are scale inefficient and not sufficiently robust to compete effectively as the EU moved towards deregulation. It is often argued that larger insurers would provide better value and service to insurance customers and would be more competitive with other EU insurers. Thus, changes in the government policy are often based on the implicit (and untested) assumption that there are significant unrealised scale economies in the industry and that favouring the creation of larger firms would lead to more viable insurers and a more competitive market.

Economies of scale are present if average costs per unit of output decline as the volume of output increases. The usual source of scale economies is the spreading of the firm's fixed costs over a larger volume of output. Fixed costs are present for insurers due to the need of relatively fixed factors of production such as computer systems, managerial expertise, and financial capital. Economies of scale also can arise if operating at larger scale allows managers to become more specialised and therefore more proficient in carrying out specific tasks. Operating at larger scale can reduce the firm's cost of capital if income volatility is inversely related to size. This source of scale economies may be particularly applicable to insurers, because the essence of insurance is risk diversification through pooling. These arguments lead to the prediction that insurance operations are likely to encounter ranges of production characterised by increasing returns to scale, permitting some insurers to reduce unit costs by increasing production, at least within certain limits.

In this section we provide information on whether these critical assumptions are correct and whether consolidation is likely to be beneficial in Italy, by applying the econometric methodology described in Chapter 5. In particular we use the conditional robust efficiency scores, where the external factor is represented by a proxy of the size of the insurer, *i.e.* Z is the market share, to shed lights on the impact of size on the performance of the Italian insurers. This choice seems to be reasonable as market shares gives an approximation of the volume of the activity carried out by the insurers and hence of their dimension. We do not use total costs or incurred losses to proxy size as we use these variables in the construction of inputs and outputs.

Note that the analysis we carry out in this section is quite different than the analysis of Returns to Scale (RTS) done in the previous section. In general, RTS are properties of the frontier of the production set, and are calculated assuming the convexity of the production set and using a deterministic estimator (DEA) which suffers from the curse of dimensionality and of the influence of extremes/outliers. Here we propose to use robust estimators (such as order-m) which do not assume any convexity for the production set, and are less influenced by extreme points. Moreover, the econometric methodology developed in Chapter 5 gives us the possibility of measuring the impact of size at the level of the individual firm as well as globally, offering the opportunity of capturing also local effects if they are at place.

Interestingly, Figure 6.8 shows the scatterplot and a straight smoothed nonparametric regression line of the ratios $Q^z = \hat{\theta}_n(x, y \mid z)/\hat{\theta}_n(x, y)$ on Z. On the contrary, Figure 6.9 - top panel - illustrates an increasing nonparametric regression line of the $Q^z_m = \hat{\theta}_{n,m}(x, y \mid z)/\hat{\theta}_{n,m}(x, y)$ on Z, till around a market share of 1. This trend is confirmed by the ratios Q^z_α reported at the bottom panel of Figure 6.9. Here we chose a level of $m = 35$ and $\alpha = 0.97$ robust at around 10%, and our data driven nearest neighborhood approach selected a $k - NN = 29$.

As extensively explained in Chapter 5, an increasing (decreasing) nonparametric regression line denotes a negative (positive) effect of the external factor (Z) on the performance of benchmarked firms, in an input oriented framework.

This case corresponds exactly to the situation described in Section 5.4 where Figure 5.3 showed no effect, while Figure 5.4 showed a negative impact (here the impact is till $Z = 1$). In this situation, even if in a inputs-outputs space there are not heterogeneous (extreme) units, these extremes may appear in a more complete space in which external factors have a role. This confirms the

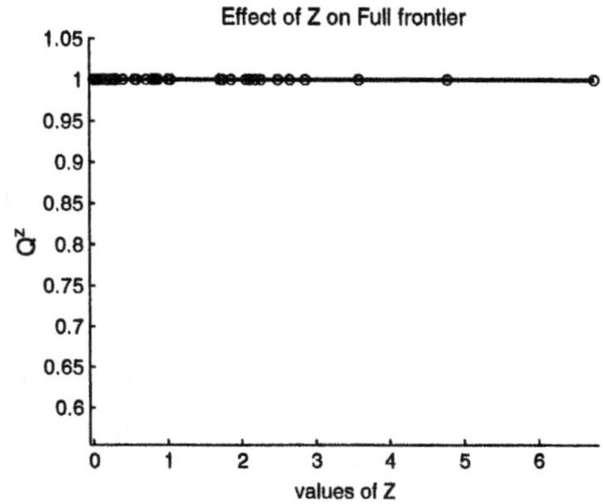

Figure 6.8. Economies of scale in the Italian motor-vehicle insurance business. Full frontier case (78 obs). Z = market share.

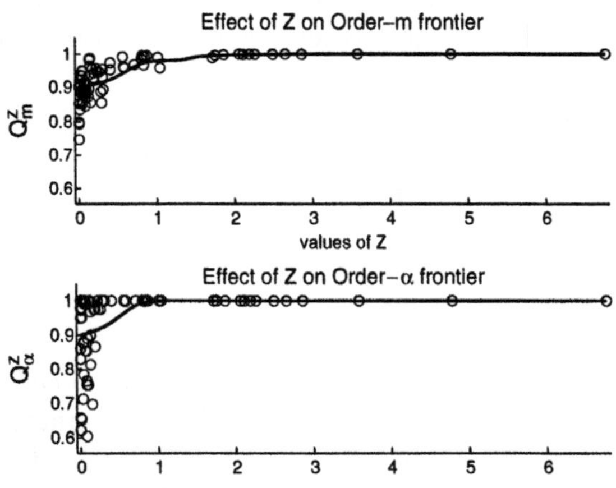

Figure 6.9. Economies of scale in the Italian motor-vehicle insurance business. Partial Frontiers case (78 obs) Z = market share.

usefulness of partial frontiers in revealing the impact of external factors masked in the full frontier case by "different" or extreme points.

By inspecting Figure 6.9 it appears that there are two groups of insurers: a smaller group with big insurance companies (market share greater than 1.5) that is not affected by its dimension, and a larger group with the majority of Italian motor-vehicle companies in it, which is on the increasing part of the nonparametric regression line companies. For this latter group there is a negative influence of size on their performances. As most of Italian insurers are agglomerated on this side of the scatter plot, at this exploratory level, it seems that there is a prevalence of *diseconomies of scale* in the Italian motor-vehicle insurance industry.

6.5 Economies of scope

Economies of scope may arise from a reduction in the search, information, monitoring, and/or transaction costs borne by the company. Costs may be significantly reduced when several financial products are sold by the same firm. In order to investigate on the presence of economies of scope, we compared the performance of generalist versus specialist insurers. Generalist insurers are companies active in both life and non life business; while specialist insurers are active only in the non life business. We tested if the difference on the average efficiency scores of the two groups of insurers was statistically significant by applying the bootstrap-based procedure described in Section 3.4.

Here we use the bootstrap to estimate the $p-$value of a null hypothesis H_0, *i.e.* that generalist (group 1) and specialist (group 2) insurers have the same average efficiency score. The null hypothesis is rejected at the desired level (here $\alpha = 0.05$) when the $p-$value is too small, *i.e.* lower than the desired level.

For group 1 and 2 we can postulate that:

$$H_0 : E(\theta_1) = E(\theta_2)$$

against

$$H_1 : E(\theta_1) > E(\theta_2),$$

where $E(\theta_1)$ is the mean efficiency of generalist insurers and $E(\theta_2)$ is the mean efficiency of specialist insurers. The mean of DEA input efficiency estimates for the $n_1 = 22$ generalist insurers is of 0.7497 (with a std. dev. of 0.2138), while the mean of specialist insurers $n_2 = 56$ is of 0.6658 (with a std. dev. of 0.1786). The full sample size is $n = n_1 + n_2 = 78$ and the full sample is denoted by $\mathcal{X}_n = \mathcal{X}_{n1} \cup \mathcal{X}_{n2}$. The overall mean efficiency is 0.6894 (with a std. dev of 0.1915).

The test statistic we use is the following:

$$T(\mathcal{X}_n) = \frac{n_1^{-1} \sum_{i|(x_i,y_i)\in\mathcal{X}_{n1}} \widehat{\theta}(x_i, y_i)}{n_2^{-1} \sum_{i|(x_i,y_i)\in\mathcal{X}_{n2}} \widehat{\theta}(x_i, y_i)},$$

where $\widehat{\theta}(x_i, y_i)$ is the input oriented DEA VRS efficiency estimator of the unit (x_i, y_i) computed using the full sample as the reference set. When the null is true, then by construction $T(\mathcal{X}_n)$ will be "close" to 1. On the contrary, when the alternative is true, $T(\mathcal{X}_n)$ will be "far" from 1 (*i.e.* larger than one). The p-value for this test has the following form:

$$p - \text{value} = \text{Prob}(T(\mathcal{X}_n) \geq T_{\text{obs}} \mid H_0).$$

The value of the test statistic obtained from our sample is the following: $T_{\text{obs}} = 1.1261$. The p-value cannot be computed analytically but again the bootstrap algorithm of Chapter 3 allows to approximate this value. We generate B pseudo-values $\mathcal{X}_n^{\star,b}$, $b = 1, ..., B$ under the null hypothesis (*i.e.*, considering that the 2 subsamples come from the same DGP, so we resample from the full sample $\mathcal{X}_n$). We compute the test statistics $T^{\star,b} = T(\mathcal{X}_n^{\star,b})$ for each bootstrap sample, then the p-value is computed as:

$$p - \text{value} \approx \sum_{b=1}^{B} \frac{\mathbb{1}(T^{*,b} \geq T_{obs})}{B}. \tag{6.8}$$

In our application here, with $B = 2000$ replications, we obtained a p-value of 0.8780. As a result, the null hypothesis of equality of structural (mean) efficiency between generalist and specialist insurers cannot be rejected.

We found that the average of generalist insurers (working both in the life and in the nonlife business) has an efficiency score (DEA, VRS input oriented) of 0.7497 which seems higher with respect to that one of specialist companies working in the nonlife business (0.6658), nevertheless, this observed difference is not statistically meaningful.

Table 6.15 shows some descriptive statistics on the insurers operating in the Italian motor-vehicle business. It appears that Generalist insurers are bigger and older than the Specialist ones, with an average market share of 1.84 % and an average Age of 94 years against an average market share of 0.20 % and an average Age of 41 for the Specialist ones.

We know also that almost all the Generalist insurers have been fined by the Italian Antitrust Authority. To better understand if there is a substantial difference in the efficiency of fined (FIN) versus not fined (NFIN) insurers, we compare the profile of fined specialist (FIN SPEC) against not fined specialist (NFIN SPEC) insurers. Table 6.15 also displays some descriptive statistics on these two groups: it shows that fined specialist insurers (19 obs.) are bigger and older than not fined companies (37 obs.); they present an average market share of 0.43 % and an average age of 52 years against, respectively 0.08 % and 36 years, for not fined specialist insurers.

By applying the same bootstrap-based procedure described above we tested if there is a significantly difference between the average performance of specialist insurers hit by the Antitrust measure (FIN SPEC) and not fined insurers (NFIN SPEC). The whole mean (VRS input oriented) efficiency estimate is of 0.6820 (with a standard deviation of 0.1890), 56 specialist companies. The average efficiency of fined specialist - 19 units- is 0.7146 (with a st. dev. of 0.2260),

Table 6.15. Some descriptive statistics on Age and size (Mktshare) of Italian motor-vehicle insurers.

Sample	Descr. Stat.	Age	Mktshare
All (78)	*Mean*	56.1	0.6633
	St Dev.	49.6	1.1666
	Min	1.0	0.0001
	Max	179.0	6.7600
	Median	38.0	0.1400
GEN (22)	*Mean*	94.1	1.8373
	St Dev.	47.4	1.6540
	Min	19.0	0.0100
	Max	175.0	6.7600
	Median	78.0	1.8050
SPEC (56)	*Mean*	41.2	0.2022
	St Dev.	42.3	0.3051
	Min	1.0	0.0001
	Max	179.0	1.7100
	Median	25.5	0.0950
FIN SPEC (19)	*Mean*	51.7	0.4321
	St Dev.	51.3	0.4304
	Min	1.0	0.0001
	Max	179.0	1.71
	Median	27	0.2600
NFIN SPEC (37)	*Mean*	35.8	0.0841
	St. Dev	36.4	0.0855
	Min	1.0	0.0001
	Max	121.0	0.3100
	Median	24.0	0.0600

while not fined specialist insurers -37 units- have an average efficiency of 0.6652 (with a st. dev. of 0.1679). $T_{\text{obs}} = \dfrac{0.7146}{0.6652} = 1.0743.$

The estimated p-value of the null hypothesis (equality of means), with $B = 2000$ bootstrap replications, is 0.7755.

Hence, the H_0 of equality of the mean efficiency of fined and not fined specialist insurers cannot be rejected; even if fined insurers seem to be more efficient than the not fined ones, this difference is not significant at any statistically meaningful level.

Therefore, we didn't find any statistically significant difference in the performance of generalist insurers and insurers specialized in the non-life business, and any meaningful difference between "fined" and "not fined" specialist insurers. From our analysis, it seems that in 2000, motor-vehicle insurers working also in the life business do not have exploited economies of scope arising by the selling of several different financial products. It emerged also that in 2000 fined specialist companies -working only in the nonlife business- did not show a different structural (average) efficiency with respect to not fined specialist insurers.

It seems that in 2000, fined companies (who did not respect the competition discipline, as assessed by the Italian Antitrust Authority[31]) did not increase their technical efficiency notwithstanding their anti-competitive behavior: to improve the performance more structural innovations are required.

6.6 Economies of experience

In an industry where the principal good sold is the promise of the compensation of a future possible loss, the trust in the seller is one of the most important factors guiding the customers in their choice. The insured, in fact, has to rely on the ability of the insurer to be alive and to be able to refund him in case of a loss in the future. The reputation and the age of the company or, better, its reputation during the time, are good indicators to look at before granting trust to an insurer. Moreover, the age could be considered as an indicator of consolidated knowledge of the market, as older companies, being in the business for a longer period, should benefit from experience economies or, in other words, should know better than younger companies how the business works and how to manage it.

We explore this issue by using the conditional robust nonparametric efficiency measures (presented in Chapter 5) where the conditioning factor (Z) is represented by the age of insurers.

Figure 6.10 is highly emblematic: there are no maturity in the business effects for the Italian insurance industry. We have in fact a straight nonparametric regression line indicating that the external factor Z -the companies' age- does not affect the efficiency of Italian companies. Hence, the performance of insurers is not influenced by their age, as computed with respect to their date of foundation.

In this application the tuning parameters have been set to $m = 35$ and $\alpha = 0.97$ to reach a level of robustness around 10%. The number of $k - NN$ provided by our data driven procedure is 15.

[31]The whole documentation is available on line, in Italian, on the website of the Italian Antitrust Authority at: `http://www.agcm.it/`.

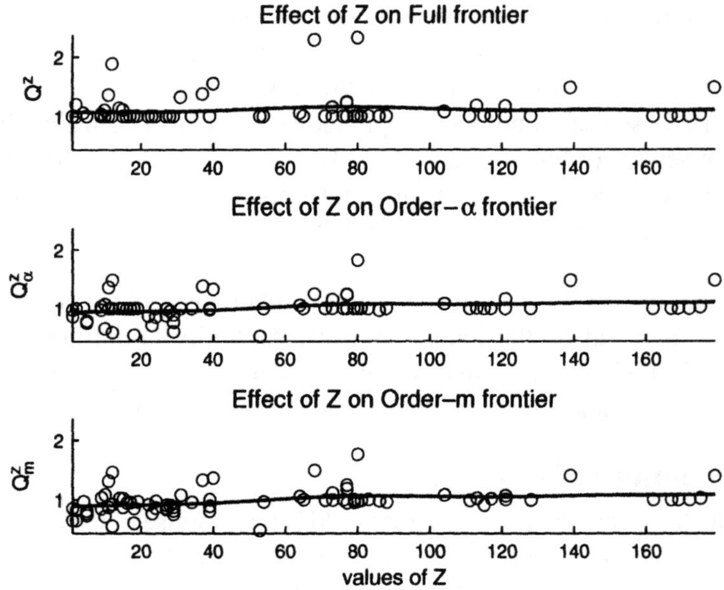

Figure 6.10. Economies of experience in the Italian motor-vehicle insurance business, year 2000 (78 obs.). $Z = Age$ in years from foundation.

6.7 Conclusions

In this chapter we explored some classical issues in the industrial organization literature, adding empirical evidence on the presence of *economies of scale*, *economies of scope* and experience on a sample of Italian insurers, active in the motor-vehicle business, for the year 2000.

The methodology presented in part I of this work offers a rigorous and easy-to-interpret tool for evaluating the performance of insurers. It may be applied to monitor the dynamics of the performance of insurers at a regional, national, European and international level.

We analysed the sensitivity of efficiency scores through bootstrapping and find out also that the Returns to Scale of the frontier of the production set of Italian insurers are variable.

We showed that the application of the probabilistic approach to introduce external-environmental variables is useful to monitor the influence of these factors on the performance of insurers.

Using our approach we tested, with a certain rigor, if some commonly assumed economic principles on the insurance industry are *empirically* well-grounded.

We found that there is a prevalence of *diseconomies of scale* in the Italian motor-vehicle insurance industry. This finding if far from sustain government policies encouraging consolidation. In fact, policies encouraging growth in firm size make sense on scale efficiency ground only if there are many insurers operating with increasing returns to scale. The evidence showed in this chapter (for the year 2000) goes in the opposite direction.

We did not find a statistically significant difference in the performance of generalist insurers and insurers specialized in the non-life business, neither a meaningful difference between "fined" and "not fined" specialist insurers. From our analysis, it seems that in 2000, nonlife insurers working also in the life business have not exploited economies of scope arising by the selling of several different financial products. It emerged also that in 2000 fined companies do not show a structural higher efficiency than not fined specialist insurers. It appears that the anti-competitive behaviour of fined companies did not led to an increase of their technical efficiency: to improve the efficiency and the performance more structural innovations are required, in line with an increase of competition and transparency to offer customers cheaper and better services.

With the evidence presented in this chapter, we showed the importance of having better measures of the *extent* and *dispersion* of efficiency and productivity of insurers. Such information may be helpful to regulators in evaluating the impact of changing market structure, to insurers and other firms seeking to acquire subsidiaries or establish alliances, and to securities markets and buyers evaluating the prospects of particular insurers and national markets.

Chapter 7

THE ECONOMICS OF SCIENCE. AGE, SCALE AND CONCENTRATION EFFECTS IN A PUBLIC RESEARCH SYSTEM

7.1 Introduction

The notion of efficiency is highly problematic in the economics of science. While policy makers and scientists are ready to accept that research activity should be organised in such a way to avoid inefficiencies and waste of resources, the exact definition of what accounts for efficiency is far from being accepted. Several theoretical and methodological problems are still unsolved.

Any notion of efficiency relates a vector of inputs to a vector of outputs. Unfortunately, in scientific research all the elements of efficiency- inputs, outputs and the functional relation between the two- are affected by different kind of issues:

- *definitional problems* concern the definition of inputs and outputs and the identification of the unit of analysis;
- *measurement problems* pertain to the methodologies for collecting inputs and outputs data as well as comparative issues;
- *specification problems* involve endogeneity, assumptions made and dynamic relations.

In the evaluation of productivity, the definition of what accounts for inputs or outputs of scientific research is one of the most crucial point. From a substantive perspective all factors can be considered both as input and as output. There are no definitive answers to this problem. They have to be defined case by case, so that any factor can be considered as input or as output, taking into account the purpose of the analysis. The methodology we apply in this chapter takes the definition of inputs and outputs as given.

A related problem is the identification of the unit of analysis of the scientific research. While it is true that all researchers are members of an institute or department defined by discipline or thematic field, it has been convincingly argued that the appropriate unit of analysis is the laboratory or team (Laredo and Mustar, 2001). Researchers may be members of several projects, that cut across administrative boundaries of institutes. In empirical works, due to the difficulty in analysing laboratories, most studies focus on the institute or department or the university (Ramsden, 1994; Johnston, 1994; Adams and Griliches, 2000). In fact, data at the level of individual researchers are not available, unless case studies on limited scale were put in place. Therefore, the research center or institute as unit of analysis is a good compromise.

In addition to definitional problems, there are also measurement problems. Although standardised international procedures exist for the definition and measurement of research inputs (*e.g.* full time equivalent), very often scientific institutions do not strictly follow these procedures and differ in the meaning they attach to the various input activities. Consequently, much care should be placed in making comparisons. Furthermore, the methodologies for collecting inputs and outputs data have been developed largely independently from each other.[32]

As far as the functional relation between inputs and outputs is concerned, specification problems arise. One of the most fundamental problem is *endogeneity*: the level of inputs in terms of funds and number of researchers is a function of past level of output, so that any specification that does not take these effects into consideration is likely to produce misleading results. Another important problem is that scientific production does not follow the assumptions needed to adopt the production function approach. As a matter of fact, a lot of published studies adopt a production function approach even though its conceptual foundation in science is extremely weak (see Bonaccorsi and Daraio, 2004 for a discussion). In order to overcome these limits, a large literature has applied the nonparametric efficiency analysis approach (mainly using DEA) to assess the technical efficiency of academic research.[33]

Another problem connected to the specification is the dynamic relation between inputs and outputs. While in most production processes the time sequence that relates the use of productive resources to the outcome is fixed and predictable, in science the outcome of research follows from inputs with a time lag structure that is both unknown and variable over time.

---

[32] See Luwel (2004) for a discussion and suggestions for a more integrated approach to construct input and output data.

[33] See among others Coelli (1996), Korhonen, Tainio and Wallenius (2001), Thursby and Kemp (2002). Studies applying DEA to education include Bessent and Bessent (1980); Bessent, Bessent, Kennington and Reagan (1982); Charnes, Cooper and Rhodes (1978); Färe, Grosskopf and Weber (1989), Grosskopf, Hayes, Taylor and Weber (1999), Grosskopf and Moutray (2001). Rousseau and Rousseau (1997, 1998) apply DEA to construct scientometrics indicators and assess research productivity across countries. See also Bonaccorsi and Daraio (2004) for a selective review.

Scientific production is a multi-input, multi-output relation, in which, differently from standard production activity, both inputs and outputs are qualitatively heterogeneous and sometimes incommensurable, the relation is dynamic and not deterministic and the output is lagged but with a non fixed structure.[34]

Ideally, at the level of inputs, one should include:

- human resources (*e.g.* the number of researchers differentiated by age, level of qualification or seniority; technical staff, administrative staff and so on);
- financial resources (*e.g.* governmental research funds, funds raised from the market, and so on);
- physical resources (*e.g.* physical capital, equipment, laboratories, libraries and so on);
- cumulated stock of knowledge (*e.g.* the number and quality of publications in the past).

In practice, it is extremely difficult to collect data on all types of inputs. In most cases very crude data on the number of researchers and on research funds are the only available information.

At the level of outputs, most analyses work with count data (*e.g.* number of publications), although it is clear that the quantity of papers does not have a necessary relation with their quality (for instance measured by normalised received citations) or importance.[35] Moreover, it should be recognised that the outputs of a scientific institute are not limited to publications but include also teaching, training, patents, applied research for industry and other parties, services for the public administration, consulting and the like (see Schmoch, 2004). For this reason, efficiency analyses limited to publication data are still considered with scepticism. Even though bibliometrics methods are widely accepted in the evaluation of research productivity (Daniel and Fisch, 1990; Narin and Hamilton, 1996; van Raan, 1993, 1997), they are viewed with suspicion by some of those being evaluated (Collins, 1991). It is desirable not only that these methods cover many different aspects of research outputs (Martin 1996) but also that the evaluees have a place in helping to create appropriate methodology by identifying the relevant categories of output (Lewison, 1998). Again, in

[34]For a review of the econometric approaches to Science and Technology (S&T) systems see Bonaccorsi and Daraio (2004).

[35]On general bibliometric theory and methodology see Narin (1987), Narin, Olivastro and Stevens (1994), Okubo (1997), Mullins, Snizek and Oehler (1988) and Moed, Glanzel and Schmoch (2004). The bibliometric literature has discussed at length the characteristics of count data; see *e.g.* Garfield and Dorof (1992), Holbrook (1992a, b), Kostoff (1994). Citation data are examined among others in Schubert, Glanzel and Braun (1988), and in Schubert and Braun (1993, 1996). The contributions by Rosenberg (1991), May (1993), Taubes (1993) and King (2004), among others, examine the quality of national scientific production.

practice the collection of data on all these outputs is extremely difficult, unless with field surveys on a limited scale. As a result, for large scale investigations, data on the number of international publications are considered as acceptable.

Any meaningful measure of productivity therefore should be generated by a model of multi-input multi-output production without a fixed functional specification. Despite the problems recalled above, the idea that scientific production must exhibit some relation between the resources employed and the output produced is generally accepted. For practical and policy objectives simple measures of the ratio of output to input are considered an indicator of scientific productivity. As an example, the crude number of paper per researcher, within relatively homogeneous fields, is considered as an acceptable indicator of productivity.

Some related and relevant issues in the economics of science, from a policy making perspective, empirically controversial are:

(a) the existence of *economies of scale* in scientific production, *i.e.* the positive effect of the concentration of resources over large (institutions or) institutes on scientific productivity;

(b) the effects of the territorial agglomeration (concentration) of scientists on scientific productivity. In some countries a policy of locating laboratories and research institutes in the same territorial area has been actively pursued, in search for *economies of agglomeration*;

(c) the exploration of the relation existing between age structure of researchers and scientific productivity. If the effect of age on individual productivity has been largely treated in literature (see for all Levin and Stephan, 1991), there is few evidence on the effect of age structure at the level of research institute.

Hence, this chapter aims at discussing theoretically size, age and concentration effects in science. It also provides empirical evidence analysing the case of the Italian National Research Council (CNR). Founded in 1923, the CNR (Consiglio Nazionale delle Ricerche) is the most important national research institution in Italy, spanning many scientific and technological areas.[36]

The chapter is structured as follows. In the following of this section we discuss size, agglomeration and age effects in science. In Section 7.2 we illustrate the data used in the application. The following sections report the results of the applications of the econometric methodology described in Chapter 5 to the

[36]Studies on the Italian CNR include Bonaccorsi and Daraio (2003a, b, 2005). On the efficiency of the Italian university system see Bonaccorsi, Daraio and Simar (2006).

institutes of the CNR, and provide empirical evidence on these controversial issues. The chapter ends by deriving some policy implications from the described empirical evidence.

Economies of scale, critical mass and concentration

In Chapter 6 we have already discussed on the existence of economies of scale in the Italian insurance market. Here we discuss this topic as applied to the scientific productivity of public research institutes. We recall that in manufacturing production, economies of scale refer to the fact that an increase of ℓ percent in all factors of production determines an increase in output of more than ℓ percent. This notion, applied to science means that, as far as increasing returns to scale are in place, research units should be of large size, in order to optimise the use of their resources and increase productivity. The higher the size of units, the higher scientific productivity. This notion is often invoked to support policies of concentration of resources in larger institutes, forcing small institutes to merge or disappear, or policies of merger and consolidation of scientific institutions. The keyword for these policies is *critical mass*. Public policies based on critical mass and large institutes induce levels of concentration of resources that go beyond the usual level. Concentration is a structural property of institutional systems that allocate research funds in proportion to publishing output. Since publication activity follows a strongly asymmetric distribution, it is not surprising that research funds are not allocated on a uniform basis. As a consequence, a small number of institutions that follow a consistent policy of hiring scientists with a strong publication record absorb a large share of funds. Policies aimed at concentration do not simply follow the structural asymmetry of distribution of publication activity, but aim to actively improve productivity. In Italy, for example, the legislative reform of the National Research Council (Reorganization Decree no. 19 of 1999) has induced a profound change in the administrative structure. The number of institutes has been reduced from 314 in 1999 to 108 in 2001. Many of the smallest institutes were, in effect, the result of fragmentation processes, created around a few researchers and crystallised over time. Given that the administrative burden is, at least to a certain extent, a fixed cost associated to service indivisibility, the existence of a minimum efficient scale for administrative costs is plausible. It should be noted, however, that policy decision makers are often driven by a more general notion that research activity itself, and not merely its administrative side, is subject to increasing returns to scale. This belief is based on the idea that research, like manufacturing, is subject to (a) division of labour; (b) indivisibility in the use of a minimum number of diverse competencies; (c) utilisation of large physical infrastructure. These reasons are sufficient conditions for the emergence of increasing returns to scale in several industries in the manufacturing sector (Scherer 1980; Milgrom and Roberts 1992; Martin 2002). However, the feasibility of these conditions for scientific research is not guaranteed for several reasons.

In science, the knowledge stored in publications allows division of cognitive labour to take place in different places and periods of time. Publication is one of the most important mechanism for promoting division of cognitive labour. This means that placing scientists within the same organisational boundaries is neither a necessary nor a sufficient condition for benefiting from improved division of labour. There may be a form of division of labour that requires the establishment of formal collaboration and coordination of tasks between scientists. Moreover, it is useful to distinguish among division of labour among peers, and of scientists at various stages of careers, and of scientists and technicians or assistants. The former type takes the form of personal links, based on mutual recognition and professional esteem. Only occasionally one can find the entire web of personal peer relationships included within the boundaries of a single organisation. A different type of division of labour takes place when the pattern of personal relations is based on apprenticeship and scientific leadership and requires long periods of joint work and supervision, normally (but not necessarily) within the same institution. Because both types of division of labour require personal in-depth supervision, the size of resulting units is limited by the ability of research directors to monitor closely the work of their research students and collaborators and to contribute to their training. In most scientific fields this amounts to say that the maximum size is quite small, in the order of units or one or two dozens. Summing up, it is unlikely that division of labour per se is a source of increasing returns to scale at the level of institutes.

Indivisibility is another condition invoked for sustaining critical mass policy. In many fields the scientific production requires the combination and coordination of many scientists from different areas, bringing competencies from complementary fields. However indivisibility is more important at the level of team or laboratory than at the level of institute or department. This is because the minimum size of a team or laboratory may be extremely variable across specific areas within the same fields. In general, this means that economies of scale may be important up to a threshold level, then become irrelevant. If the threshold level is quite small, the practical implication is that even small institutes may be highly efficient, provided that their teams or labs meet the minimum requirement.

Access to physical infrastructure is another argument commonly associated to the call for critical mass and concentration of resources in large institutions. However, it cannot be invoked as a general argument in favour of large institutes as the research instrumentation required varies according to the field of research.

On this important issue the evidence is ambiguous and contradictory.

Agglomeration economies

The notion of scientific districts, clusters, poles of excellence or science areas has been prominent in national and regional science policy in the last twenty years. The examples of Silicon Valley and Route 128 (Saxenian, 1996) and the emergence of technopoles and regional clusters (Castells and Hall, 1994; Cooke and Morgan, 1998) have catalysed the attention of analysts and policy makers in all advanced countries. At a regional level the notion of cluster identifies the co-presence and interaction of diverse subjects such as research and educational institutions, firms, innovative public administrations, financial services, technology transfer and other intermediary organisations (Acs, 2000; Scott, 2001). At this level the emphasis is not on clustering of research activities per se, but on clustering of complementary innovative activities in the same area. This general notion, however, has also inspired policies of location of research activities by some large public research institutions. In several countries large public research institutions have pursued a policy of creating geographical concentrations of institutes in the same area. For example in Italy CNR promoted the creation of Research Areas, large agglomerations of institutes in different fields within the same physical infrastructure. In France most research institutes at CNRS and INSERM are located in close areas. Behind these policies there is the idea that proximity favours scientific productivity, insofar as it maximises personal interaction, face-to-face communication, on-site demonstrations and transmission of tacit knowledge, as well as it facilitates identification of complementary competencies, unintentional exchange of ideas, café phenomena, and other serendipitous effects. The focus of our discussion is therefore the notion that concentrating research activities in the same area may bring benefits to scientific productivity. Here we do not enter into a discussion on more general policies for clustering and agglomeration of innovative activities.[37]

Underlying these policies there are some well grounded economic ideas. As it sometimes happens, the original idea is an old one, but it was rediscovered and enlarged more recently. The implicit economic analogy is with the concept of external economies, or Marshallian agglomeration economies (Pyke, Becattini and Sengenberger, 1986). Alfred Marshall observed that the concentration of a large number of manufacturing firms in the same area (industrial district) is not due to chance, but reflects the presence of local externalities in the form of availability of specialised suppliers, highly trained workforce, sources of innovative ideas. Costs of production are therefore lower in an agglomerated area than outside it. More importantly, firms in a district enjoy a particular industrial atmosphere and benefit from processes of collective invention. The large literature on geography and trade (Krugman, 1991) and the geographical

---

[37]For more on this point and on the recent developments of the Economic Geography, see Clark, Feldman and Gertler (2000).

dimension of knowledge spillover effects (Jaffe, Trajtenberg and Henderson, 1993; Audretsch and Feldman, 1996; Zucker, Darby and Armstrong, 1998) gave new emphasis to this idea and spurred this line of policy. Here the main emphasis is on the fact that the diffusion of knowledge may take place via codification and distance transmission, but in most cases requires also personal acquaintance and face to face interaction. This is made easier and cheaper by physical proximity.

However, in concluding her review on innovation, spillovers and agglomeration, Feldman (2000, p.389) states: "Most importantly, we still have a limited understanding of the way in which knowledge spillovers occur and benefit innovative activity. Marshall (1949: 152-153) tells us that knowledge 'is in the air', and although we may cite Marshall, this answer is simply not very satisfying. To date, the mechanisms of externalities and knowledge spillovers have not yet been made explicit. Many researchers have tried to estimate the geographic boundaries of knowledge spillovers. The consensus is that knowledge spillovers are geographically bounded within a limited space over which interaction and communication is facilitated, search intensity is increased, and task coordination is enhanced. [...] In addition, there is also a literature that documents the importance of social interaction, local networks and personal communication in Knowledge transmission, but we do not know how social interaction is initiated, how it evolves into a working relationships and how economically useful knowledge is created".

Hence, there are many reasons for a policy of agglomeration of research activities in the same geographic area. At the same time the importance of agglomeration is an inherently empirical matter and should be evaluated case by case. This chapter gives a contribution to this debate by exploring the existence of economies of agglomeration in conjunction with economies of scale, analysing the research institutes of a public research system: the Italian National Research Council (CNR).

Age effects

The existence of age effects in scientific production is one of the few consolidated stylised facts in the economics and sociology of science. The decline of scientific productivity with age may depend on a variety of factors. On the one hand, as time goes by the initial differences among scientists in individual productivity get larger. Most theories of scientific productivity postulate a stochastic and cumulative mechanism (Simon, 1957) or a Matthew effect (Merton, 1968), whereby those that gain recognition initially in their careers receive reward and resources, which will be used to carry out further research. If this is true, initial differences in individual productivity will tend to be larger over time. Allison and Stewart (1974) found that the Gini index for publications and citations of scientists monotonically increases over time in a series of cohorts from the date of the PhD, with the exception of biologists. This evidence is interpreted as strongly supporting the notion of reinforcement or positive feedbacks[38]. Another way of looking at the problem of age is to model productivity as the outcome of a number of features that interact multiplicatively, rather than additively. For example a model may assume that several elements or mental factors play a role (*e.g.* technical ability, finding important problems, and persistence). As it happens in any multiplicative model, the distribution of productivity is more skewed than the distribution of any of its determinants. As a result, a cohort of scientists starting with a given distribution will end up with a more dispersed distribution and the variance will increase over time. On the other hand, it is plausible that scientists work on research not only for the sake of intrinsic pleasure of scientific puzzle solving, but also in the expectation of receiving future income. If this investment motivation is correct, it will inevitably happen, as in any theory of human capital accumulation with finite horizon, that the level of investment will decrease when scientist approach the date of retirement. Models of human capital are central in the theory of life cycle of scientists. This life cycle effect was found by Levin and Stephan (1991) for most scientific areas with the exception of particle physics. The impact of age at the level of research organisations is less clear, however. Within an institute, for example, experienced scientists might compensate their individual decline with a well organised activity of training of junior researchers, so that productivity at the level of institute is not depressed. Being less creative at the individual level, they might be still prolific in supporting young researchers and identifying promising research avenues that they do not pursue personally. Furthermore, aged scientists may have acquired capabilities in managing and coordinating research teams and laboratories. More generally, little is known on the pattern with which people of different age are mixed within research institutes and the resulting impact on scientific productivity.

These problems are becoming critical in science policy given the alarming evidence on the increasing average age of researchers in most European countries. For example, in Italy the proportion of professors and researchers in the age class 24-44 was 60% in 1984 and only 29% in 2001. Those that entered the academic system in the age class 24-34 were 19% of the total in 1984 and only 5% in 2001 (Avveduto, 2002). To face the problem of ageing of researchers, there are suggestions that a massive effort should be made by hiring waves of new researchers in a concentrated period of time, in order to reduce drastically the average age. While by definition the problem of ageing worsens over time in the absence of recruitment of many young researchers, it is not at all clear what should be the time path of recruitment. This chapter analyses thoroughly the effects of the age structure of researchers on scientific productivity.

[38] For more details on positive feedbacks and research productivity in science, see David (1995).

7.2 Data description

We use data reported in the official Report of 1998, which includes both input data and output data and unofficially data integrated and used in previous studies (Bonaccorsi and Daraio, 2003a,b; 2005) to which we refer for a discussion of the relevance and limitations of these data. Input data include, for example, research funds, funds from external sources or total costs while output data include total number of publications and number of international publications. The research areas considered in the analysis are listed in Table 7.1.

Table 7.1: *Research areas.*

CODE	*RESEARCH AREA*	*N. OBS.*
A10	*Mathematics*	8
A12	*Law and Politics*	5
A13	*History, philosophy and philology*	5
A5	*Economics, sociology and statistics*	7
MA1	*Agriculture*	24
MA2	*Environment and Geology and mining*	26
MA3	*Biotechnologies and Medicine and biology*	27
MA4	*Chemistry*	26
MA5	*Physics*	28
MA6	*Engineering and Innovation and technology*	31

Table 7.2 shows the variables in the dataset (all variables refer to CNR institutes). We follow the definition of variables described in the CNR Report. Monetary variables are left in million of Italian lira (1 euro= 1936,27 lira).

In order to assess the existence of economies of scale related to agglomeration effects in the scientific production of CNR institutes, we apply the econometric methodology described in Chapter 5 of this work, considering the impact of a bivariate external factor (Z) composed by a proxy of size of the institute and a proxy of the concentration of the institutes in the same geographic area.

To account for the influence of proximity between research institutes we constructed the Geographical Agglomeration Index (GAI) as follows. To each institute we assigned one point for each other CNR institute located in the same city that is not of the same research aggregation; and two points for each other CNR institute located in the same city that is also of the same research aggregation of the institute considered. Then we obtained a GAI that goes from 39 to 1, varying between 39 and 33 for the institutes located in Rome, from 23 to 20 for the institute located in Naples, from 16 to 14 for the institutes located in Pisa and so on. An institute has a GAI of 1 if it is the only CNR institute in its own town.

Table 7.2: *Definition of variables.*

VARIABLE	*DEFINITION*
T_PERS	*Total number of personnel*
$RESFUN$	*Total research funds*
N_RESFUN	*Research funds obtained from the state*
M_RESFUN	*Research funds obtained from the market*
T_COS	*Total costs*
$LABCOS$	*Labour costs*
T_RES	*Total number of Researchers*
$TECH$	*Number of Technicians*
ADM	*Number of Administrative Staff*
$ADTECH$	*Number of Adm. Staff and Technicians*
T_PUB	*Total number of publications*
P_INTPUB	*Percent international publications*
$INTPUB$	*Number of International Publications*
PUB_PERS	*Publications per capita*
$IPUPERS$	*International Publications per capita*
PUB_RES	*Publications per researcher*
$IPURES$	*International Publications per researcher*
P_MARFUN	*Percent of funds raised from the market*
P_INV	*Percent of Total costs allocated to investment*
$COPUB$	*Cost per publication*
$COPUBINT$	*Cost per international publication*
$AVIM$	*Average Impact factor*
$INST\_AG$	*Institute age*
	(based on an estimate of the date of foundation)
GAI	*Geographical Agglomeration Index*
$TRES\_AG$	*Average age of Researchers (all types)*

In order to use this measure in our analysis which requires the use of continuous variables, we let the GAI become continuous by simply adding a small number randomly chosen from the continuous uniform distribution on the interval [-0.499,+0.499]. This transformation does not affect the GAI indicator and is suitable for our procedure.

Ideally, the dimension of a research institute is measured by the space it has, by the physical infrastructure (*e.g.* no. of computers), and mostly by the people that work in it. However, we do not have data on the area and physical infrastructure of institutes, and we use the number of researchers and the number of technicians and administrative staff as inputs in our analysis. We have obtained very similar results using as proxy of size the total number of people working in the institutes (T_PERS), using also other proxies such as total costs (T_COS) and labour costs ($LABCOS$) of institutes.

7.3 Scale and concentration effects

In our analysis we use an input oriented framework as our interest lies on the allocation of resources given the level of output obtained by the research institutes. The inputs and outputs used are presented in Table 7.3.

Table 7.3: *Definition of Inputs and Outputs.*

Variable	*Description*
Input 1	No. of Researchers (T_RES)
Input 2	No. of technicians and administrative staff (ADTECH)
Input 3	Normalised Research Funds (N_RESFUN)
Output	Normalised no. of international publications (N_INTPUB)
Ex. factor1	Geographical Agglomeration Index (GAI)
Ex. factor2	Total no. of Personnel (T_PERS)

As output we use the number of international publications of each institutes divided by the mean number of publications of the research area the institute is in. As pointed out in Schubert and Braun (1996), the comparative assessment of scientometric indicators has to be based on normalized scientometric indicators that first gauge them against a properly chosen reference standard, then compare their relative standing. There are basically two types of approaches in setting reference standards for cross-field normalization of scientometric indicators. The first type is based on a prior classification of units into science field categories of the required depth. In the second type for each unit to be assessed, a specific standard is set on the basis of automatic algorithms or human expertise. In this work we choose the first approach that is easier to comprehend and accept, even if we loose in flexibility.[39]

Table 7.4 shows the differences of the average values of labour costs, total costs, research funds and number of international publications by research area.

Hence, we analyse the stability of results using the variables $RESFUN$, T_COS and $LABCOS$ normalized, *i.e.*, dividing by the mean of the research area to which the institutes belong. We notice that we obtained very similar results. In the following we report the results obtained using as inputs T_RES, $ADTECH$, N_RESFUN, and as output N_INTPUB. Z_1 is GAI and Z_2 is T_PERS.

[39]For more details on normalization methods see Schubert and Braun (1996).

Table 7.4: *Average values of Inputs and Outputs by research area.*

RES. AREA	*LABCOS*	*T_COS*	*RESFUN*	*INTPUB*
A10	763.25	1268.50	505.25	31.71
A12	1391.60	1954.20	562.60	8.83
A13	1161.00	1540.11	379.11	13.21
A5	900.71	1380.57	479.86	11.54
MA1	1318.25	1885.00	566.75	21.15
MA2	2036.08	3176.35	1140.27	25.27
MA3	2323.78	3926.26	1602.48	53.00
MA4	2044.88	2855.08	810.19	44.29
MA5	3015.18	4274.64	1259.46	73.77
MA6	2232.00	7053.75	1302.16	33.04

A descriptive statistics on inputs, outputs and external factors is offered in Table 7.5 where mean, standard deviation, minimum, maximum and interquartile range are reported. Very often the impact factor has been used as an output. However, we prefer do not use the average impact factor as further output for a twofold reason. Firstly, we do not have the possibility to check if the self reported average are correct and we do not have its value for all the institutes in the sample. Secondly, journal impact factors as a measure of quality have many general limitations (see Moed and van Leeuwen 1996, Seglen 1997).

Table 7.5: CNR institutes - Descriptive statistics on inputs, outputs and external factors considered in the analysis (169 obs).

VARIABLE	Mean	Std	Min	Max	Iqr
T_RES	13.077	9.057	1.000	45.000	11.300
ADTECH	13.751	12.726	1.000	69.000	11.000
INTPUB_N	1.000	0.601	0.031	3.099	0.800
P_MARFUN	13.862	10.315	1.000	53.000	12.300
TRES_AG	44.363	5.149	33.333	53.455	8.600
INST_AG	28.107	9.123	3.000	43.000	9.000
GAI	14.880	11.090	1.000	39.000	14.000
LABCOS_N	1.053	0.752	0.059	4.090	0.900
T_COS_N	0.939	0.632	0.050	3.555	1.000
RESFUN_N	0.983	0.710	0.028	5.628	0.900
RESFUN	984.083	864.974	45.000	7329.000	718.000
LABCOS	2127.367	1740.406	96.000	9128.000	1849.800
T_COS	3111.450	2483.750	197.000	16457.000	2529.700

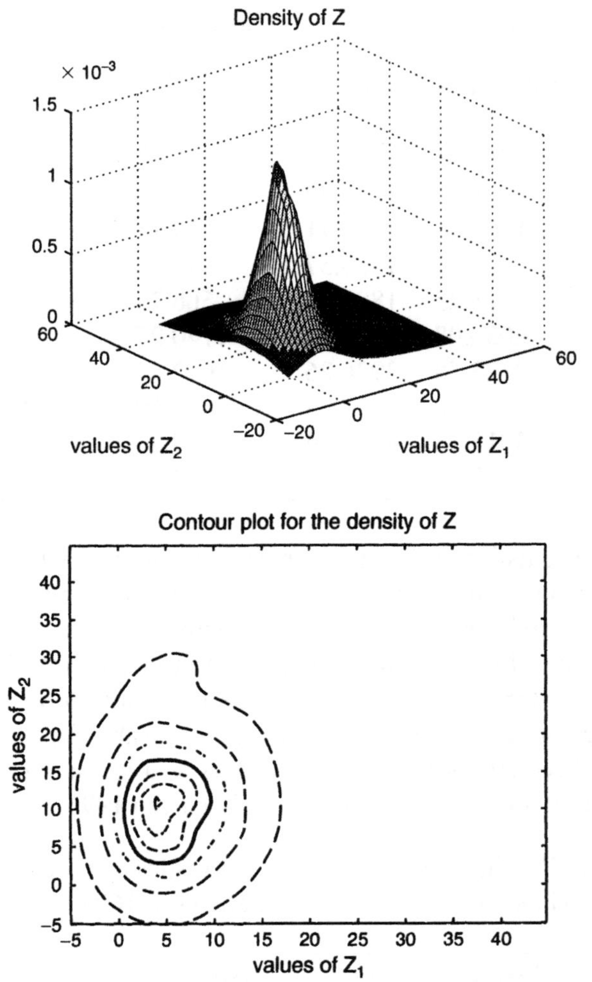

Figure 7.1. Estimation of the density of Z ($Z_1 = GAI$,$Z_2 = T\_PERS$) (top panel) and its contour-plot (bottom panel) CNR institutes (169 obs).

In order to have a robust measure of the global impact of dimension and geographical concentration on the performance of CNR institutes we choose a level of robustness at 10% and we obtain a level of $\alpha = 0.985$ and a level of $m = 50$. The number of nearest neighbors chosen by our datadriven approach is $k - NN = 33$. Figure 7.1 illustrates the quality of the estimation of the density of Z carried out by our bandwidth selection procedure, as well as Z's contour plot. The contour plot shows that the two external factors, size ($Z_2 = T\_PERS$) and geographical concentration ($Z_1 = GAI$) are not correlated.

The main results of our investigation are reported in Figures 7.2 to 7.5. As we can see (Figure 7.2), the ratio of full frontier efficiency estimates Q^z, is influenced by some outliers rather than the robust partial efficiency ratios Q^z_α and Q^z_m. In the full frontier case, in fact, it appears an inverse U-shape pattern determined by the influence of extreme values, that is not confirmed by the robust partial efficiency estimates. This illustration shows the usefulness of robust measures of efficiency.

As we have at length explained in Chapter 5 by means of the simulated examples, in order to detect the global effect of the external factors on the performance of the analysed units, it is of interest the analysis of the behavior of the surface of the ratios of conditional and unconditional efficiency measures: Q^z, Q^z_α and Q^z_m, on Z, as well as the nonparametric smoothed regression of the ratios Q^z (Q^z_α and Q^z_m) on Z_1 at the Z_2's quartiles, and *viceversa*, on Z_2 at the Z_1's quartiles. In particular, these plots are also able to shed lights on the interactions between external factors.

We recall that in an input oriented framework, as is the case here, an *increasing* nonparametric regression line indicates an *unfavorable* external factor, a *decreasing* nonparametric regression line points to a *favorable* external factor, while a *straight* nonparametric regression line denotes *no effect* of the external factor.

Figure 7.2 has shown the usefulness of applying robust (partial) estimators of efficiency to check if the impact of external factors on full frontier estimators is influenced by the presence of outliers, as it is the case here. Therefore, the results reported in Figure 7.3 are not very reliable. Another striking result is evident from Figures 7.4 and 7.5, top panels. We see that there is no influence of the geographical concentration on the performance of CNR institutes till a GAI (Z_1) of 25. In this region of the plots there is the 82.84% of CNR institutes. Only 29 institutes out of 169 have a GAI greater than 26, and are in the region of GAI in which there is a slightly decreasing nonparametric regression line, meaning that there could be a positive influence of geographical concentration on their performance. Even more interesting is the inspection of the bottom panels of Figures 7.4 and 7.5. It appears that there is an increasing trend of the smoothed nonparametric regression line for each number of personnel (T_PERS). Interestingly enough, size *negatively* affects the performance of all CNR institutes.

In this chapter we confirm the results found in a previous work on Italian and French research institutes (see Bonaccorsi and Daraio, 2005). As it comes out from our analysis, scientific productivity seems not favoured by the concentration of resources into larger institutes geographically agglomerated.

7.4 Age effects on CNR scientific productivity

With respect to age, our interest is in evaluating the impact of age distribution on productivity. This effect is different from the one assumed in the life

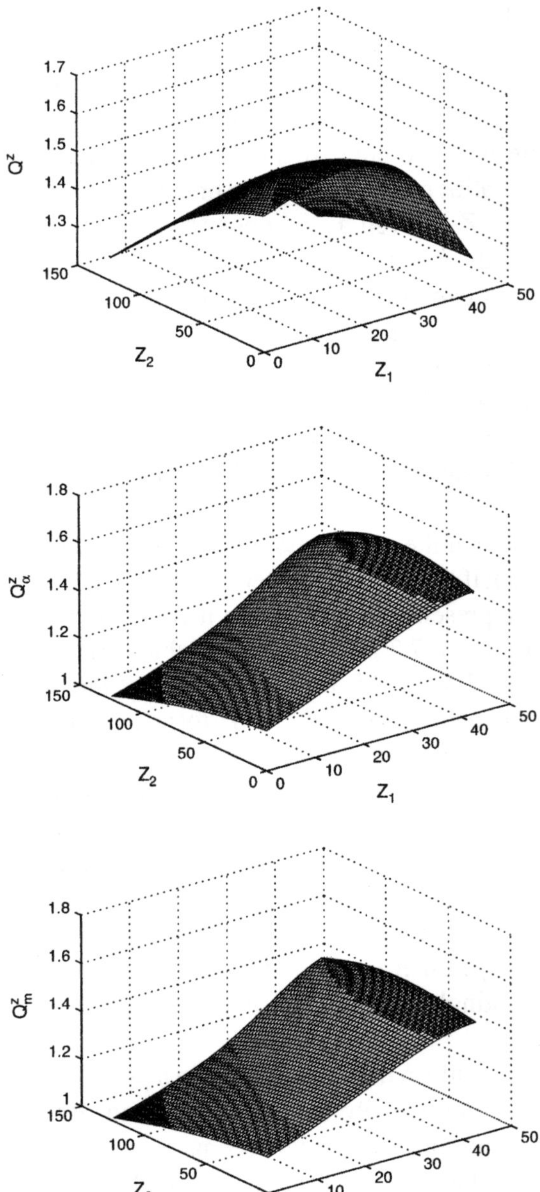

Figure 7.2. Scale and concentration effects on CNR institutes (169 obs).Surface of Q^z on Z_1 and Z_2 (top panel), surface of Q^z_α on Z_1 and Z_2 (middle panel), and surface of Q^z_m on Z_1 and Z_2 (bottom panel). $Z_1 = GAI$, $Z_2 = T\_PERS$. $\alpha = 0.985$ and $m = 50$.

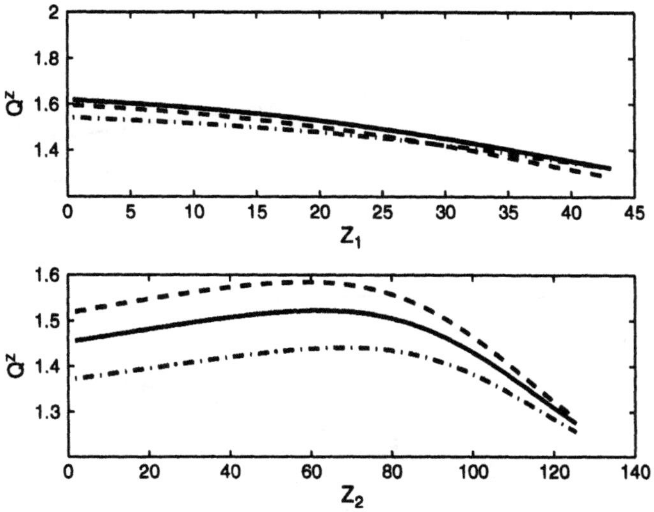

Figure 7.3. Scale and concentration effects on CNR institutes (169 obs). Smoothed nonparametric regression of Q^z on $Z_1 = GAI$ for Z_2's quartiles(top panel) and on $Z_2 = T\_PERS$ for Z_1's quartiles (bottom panel); dashed line = first quartile, solid line = median and dashdot line = third quartile.

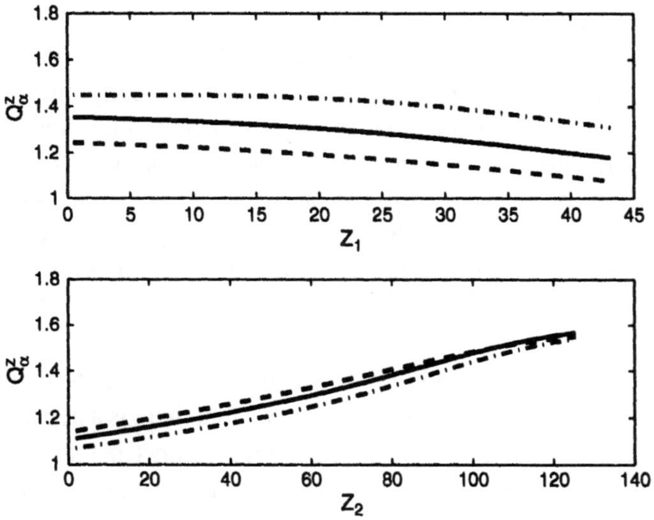

Figure 7.4. Scale and concentration effects on CNR institutes (169 obs). Smoothed nonparametric regression of Q^z_α on $Z_1 = GAI$ for Z_2's quartiles(top panel) and on $Z_2 = T\_PERS$ for Z_1's quartiles (bottom panel); dashed line = first quartile, solid line = median and dashdot line = third quartile.

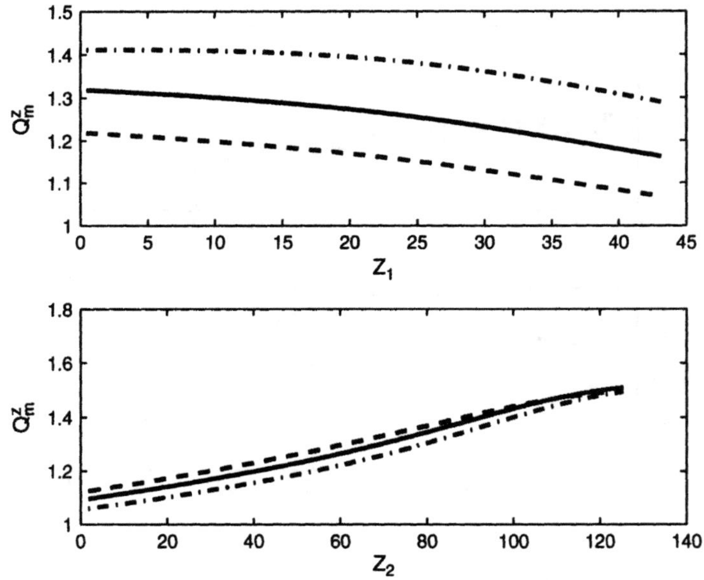

Figure 7.5. Scale and concentration effects on CNR institutes (169 obs). Smoothed nonparametric regression of Q^z_m on $Z_1 = GAI$ for Z_2's quartiles(top panel) and on $Z_2 = T\_PERS$ for Z_1's quartiles (bottom panel); dashed line = first quartile, solid line = median and dashdot line = third quartile.

cycle hypothesis. We do not have longitudinal data on scientists' production and do not assume that younger scientists are monotonically more productive than older ones. Rather, we assume that institutes with higher average age have a lower turnover. They are presumably less able to attract young scientists and are more likely to be isolated from the latest developments in science. As a first approximation we consider the average age of scientists within institutes ($TRES\_AG$). Institutes with higher average age of scientists are old institutes in which the entry of young scientists has not compensated the effect of ageing of incumbents.

Here again, we apply the conditional measures of efficiency to shed empirical light on this interesting aspect. Figure 7.6 shows that there is a negative effect of the average age of researchers on productivity indicators (increasing regression line), although this effect seems to be negligible after the age of 46 years.[40]

The general negative effect of average age on productivity does not necessarily mean that older scientists are less productive in absolute terms. Rather,

[40]Here we set a level of robustness at 10% obtaining a value of $\alpha = 0.98$ and $m = 50$. The number of $K - NN$ provided by our data driven procedure is 48.

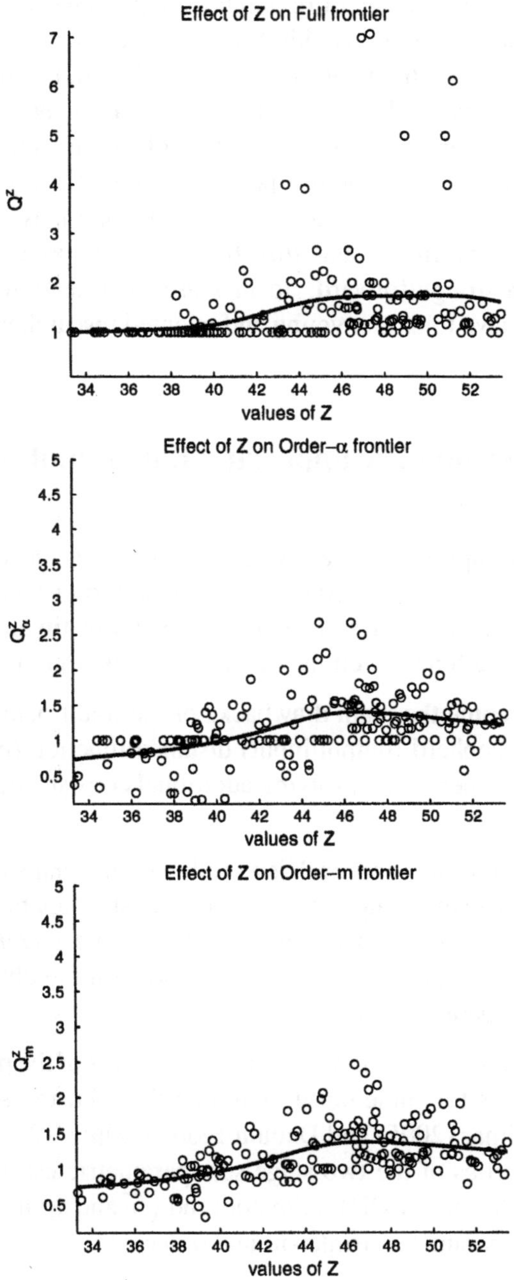

Figure 7.6. Age effects on CNR institutes. FDH (top panel), order-α (middle panel) and order-m (bottom panel) estimates (169 obs). $Z = TRES\_AG$.

institute with higher average age of researchers might have a lower proportion of younger scientists, that they wouldn't or couldn't attract. The average age of an institute reflects its attractiveness and scientific vitality. In fact, the average age of existing personnel is lowered each time a young researcher enters the institute. The higher the scientific prestige of the institute, the resources available for job positions and the prospects for career, the higher the number of young candidates wishing to enter. The average age may be considered a summary statistics for turnover and attractiveness. The policy implication of this finding is then straightforward: to increase their scientific productivity, research institutes have to attract young and talented researchers.

7.5 Robust parametric approximation of multioutput distance function

In this section we apply the recently introduced two stage semi-parametric approach by Florens and Simar (2005) and Daouia, Florens and Simar (2005) and its multivariate extension (described in Chapter 4) to estimate parametrically a multioutput distance function on the Italian CNR research institutes.

It allows to overcome the main drawbacks of the traditional fitting of parametric models of Shephard (output/input) distance function (*e.g.*, Grosskopf, Hayes, Taylor and Weber, 1997), solving additional consistency issues (Coelli, 2000).

The basic idea of this new approach is as follows. In a *first* stage we estimate the efficient frontier using nonparametric and robust nonparametric methods (like FDH, order-m or order-α frontier estimators). In a *second* stage, we fit, by standard OLS, the appropriate parametric model on the obtained nonparametric/or robust nonparametric frontier.

This approach provide much more sensible estimators of the parametric frontier model and allows for some noise by tuning the robustness parameters (α and m). Florens-Simar (2005) and Daouia-Florens-Simar (2005) analyse also the statistical properties of the two-stage semiparametric estimators, and find consistency for full frontier (FDH) estimators and $\sqrt{n}$ and asymptotic normality for partial frontiers parameters (order-m and order-α).

In the application which follows we have chosen a flexible functional form for the output distance function of the CNR institutes, imposing relatively *fewer* a priori restrictions on the structure of production. One such flexible form is the translog form (Christensen, Jorgenson and Lau, 1973), which is a second order-Taylor expansion, usually around the mean, of a generic function, where all variables appear in logarithms.

As we presented in Section 4.7.2, the translog model for $\ln \delta_o(x, y)$ is the following:

$$\ln \delta_o(x,y) \approx \varphi(x,y;\theta) = \alpha_0 + \alpha' \ln x + \beta' \ln y + \frac{1}{2}[\ln x' \ln y']\, \Gamma \begin{bmatrix} \ln x \\ \ln y \end{bmatrix}.$$

where $\Gamma = \Gamma'$ is symmetric. Homogeneity of degree one in y imposes $p+q+1$ constraints:

$$\begin{array}{ll} \beta' i_q = 1, & \text{1 constraint} \\ \Gamma_{12}\, i_q = 0, & p \text{ constraints} \\ \Gamma_{22}\, i_q = 0, & q \text{ constraints} \end{array}$$

$$\text{where } \Gamma = \begin{pmatrix} \Gamma_{11} & \Gamma_{12} \\ \Gamma_{21} & \Gamma_{22} \end{pmatrix}.$$

In the previous section our aim was to analyse the impact of scale and agglomeration, and then of age, on how resources are allocated to CNR institutes (on how their inputs are managed). Therefore, we adopted an input oriented framework. Now we consider the resources allocated to the research institutes as given (as they are not very high compared to other European countries) and we focus on how much the CNR, as a whole, could improve its efficiency in the production of international publications per 100 researchers ($INTPUB100res$) and increasing the services done (including external contracts and other services approximated by the share of funds coming from external sources - P_MARFUN) given the level of cost per 100 employees ($COST100emp$) and the research funds per 100 researchers ($RESFUN100res$) owned by its research institutes. Hence, we adopt an output oriented framework.

The inputs and outputs used in this section are described in Table 7.6. Due to the heterogeneity in the structure of costs and in the publication practices across scientific disciplines, we have normalized all variables dividing by the mean of the scientific areas.

Table 7.6: *Definition of inputs and outputs used for the translog estimation of CNR output distance function.*

VARIABLE	*DEFINITION*
Inputs	
$COST100emp$	*Labour cost per 100 employees (thousands of Euros)*
$RESFUN100res$	*Research funds per 100 researchers (thousands of Euros)*

Table 7.7. Output distance function parameter estimates for CNR research institutes.

Param	Variable	$\widehat{\theta}_{FDH}$	$\widehat{\theta}_{\alpha}$	$\widehat{\theta}_{m}$	$\widehat{\theta}_{COLS}$
α_0	Intercept	-0.6170	-0.4717	-0.4971	-1.4013
α_1	$\ln(x_1)$	-0.3186	-0.1176	-0.1803	0.4965
α_2	$\ln(x_2)$	-0.4687	-0.3798	-0.3975	-0.6711
β_1	$\ln(y_1)$	0.4238	0.4870	0.4622	0.4722
β_2	$\ln(y_2)$	0.5762	0.5130	0.5378	0.5278
$\Gamma_{11.11}$	$\ln(x_1)^2$	0.0957	0.1284	0.1129	0.2122
$\Gamma_{11.12}$	$\ln(x_1)\ln(x_2)$	0.5622	0.4260	0.5172	0.1088
$\Gamma_{11.22}$	$\ln(x_2)^2$	-0.0467	-0.0321	-0.0413	-0.1216
$\Gamma_{12.11}$	$\ln(x_1)\ln(y_1)$	-0.0553	0.0264	-0.0279	-0.2229
$\Gamma_{12.12}$	$\ln(x_1)\ln(y_2)$	0.0553	-0.0264	0.0279	0.2229
$\Gamma_{12.21}$	$\ln(x_2)\ln(y_1)$	0.0655	0.0302	0.0551	0.0449
$\Gamma_{12.22}$	$\ln(x_2)\ln(y_2)$	-0.0655	-0.0302	-0.0551	-0.0449
$\Gamma_{22.11}$	$\ln(y_1)^2$	0.1053	0.1041	0.1079	0.1077
$\Gamma_{22.12}$	$\ln(y_1)\ln(y_2)$	-0.1053	-0.1041	-0.1079	-0.1077
$\Gamma_{22.22}$	$\ln(y_2)^2$	0.1053	0.1041	0.1079	0.1077

Outputs	
$INTPUB100res$	*Number of international publications per 100 researchers*
P_MARFUN	*Percentage of funds raised from the market*

As usually done in empirical works (see *e.g.* Coelli and Perelman 1996, 1999, 2000; Perelman and Santin, 2005; see also Färe and Primont, 1996), we have mean-corrected all variables prior to estimation, *i.e.*, each output and input variable has been divided by its geometric mean. By doing that, the first order coefficients may be interpreted as distance elasticities evaluated at the sample mean.

The empirical results for the estimated model are presented in Table 7.7 in which the parameters are estimated fitting a translog function on the FDH frontier (third column), $\alpha = 0.975$ and $m = 35$ frontiers (respectively fourth and fifth columns), the latter robust at around 10%, and finally the COLS standard approach.

Table 7.8. Bootstrapped confidence intervals for order-α frontier translog approximation. $\alpha = 0.975$.

Param	Variable	$\widehat{\theta}_\alpha$ $\alpha =$ 0.975	Norm low	Norm up	BB low	BB up	Mean boot distrib	Std boot distrib
α_0	Intercept	-0.4717	-0.6207	-0.3226	-0.6706	-0.3785	0.0348	0.0760
α_1	$\ln(x_1)$	-0.1176	-0.2868	0.0517	-0.2776	0.0732	-0.0224	0.0864
α_2	$\ln(x_2)$	-0.3798	-0.5405	-0.2190	-0.4581	-0.1397	-0.0551	0.0820
β_1	$\ln(y_1)$	0.4870	0.3816	0.5924	0.4039	0.5978	-0.0024	0.0538
β_2	$\ln(y_2)$	0.5130	0.4076	0.6184	0.4022	0.5961	0.0024	0.0538
$\Gamma_{11.11}$	$\ln(x_1)^2$	0.1284	-0.0569	0.3137	-0.1320	0.2923	0.0096	0.0945
$\Gamma_{11.12}$	$\ln(x_1)\ln(x_2)$	0.4260	0.1246	0.7275	0.0089	0.6093	0.0945	0.1538
$\Gamma_{11.22}$	$\ln(x_2)^2$	-0.0321	-0.1284	0.0643	-0.1078	0.0886	-0.0258	0.0492
$\Gamma_{12.11}$	$\ln(x_1)\ln(y_1)$	0.0264	-0.1421	0.1948	-0.0545	0.2864	-0.0634	0.0859
$\Gamma_{12.12}$	$\ln(x_1)\ln(y_2)$	-0.0264	-0.1948	0.1421	-0.2864	0.0545	0.0634	0.0859
$\Gamma_{12.21}$	$\ln(x_2)\ln(y_1)$	0.0302	-0.0544	0.1149	-0.0856	0.0843	0.0206	0.0432
$\Gamma_{12.22}$	$\ln(x_2)\ln(y_2)$	-0.0302	-0.1149	0.0544	-0.0843	0.0856	-0.0206	0.0432
$\Gamma_{22.11}$	$\ln(y_1)^2$	0.1041	0.0673	0.1410	0.0599	0.1364	0.0061	0.0188
$\Gamma_{22.12}$	$\ln(y_1)\ln(y_2)$	-0.1041	-0.1410	-0.0673	-0.1364	-0.0599	-0.0061	0.0188
$\Gamma_{22.22}$	$\ln(y_2)^2$	0.1041	0.0673	0.1410	0.0599	0.1364	0.0061	0.0188

Tables 7.8 and 7.9 display the results of our bootstrap exercise, done following the procedure described in Florens and Simar (2005), to build confidence intervals on the estimated parameters (see Chapter 4). Here we set $B = 1000$ bootstrap loops. The covariance matrices used to estimate the normal approximation confidence interval are not reproduced here to save space.

The Scale Elasticity (SE), evaluated at the sample mean, is given by:

$$SE = -\sum_{k=1}^{p} \partial \ln \delta_o(x, y) \,/\partial \ln x_k.$$

It is the negative of the sum of the input elasticities. Therefore, increasing (decreasing) scale economies are indicated by a value of SE greater (less) than one. The scale elasticity, at the approximation point, is equal to the following values, according to the estimator used in the first stage.

$$SE_{FDH} = 0.3186 + 0.4687 \;\; = \;\; 0.7873,$$

Table 7.9. Bootstrapped confidence intervals for order-m frontier translog approximation. $m = 35$.

Param	Variable	$\widehat{\theta}_m$ $m =$ 0.35	Norm low	Norm up	BB low	BB up	Mean boot distrib	Std boot distrib
α_0	Intercept	-0.4971	-0.6370	-0.3573	-0.7159	-0.4440	0.0526	0.0714
α_1	$\ln(x_1)$	-0.1803	-0.3019	-0.0587	-0.3277	-0.0847	0.0175	0.0620
α_2	$\ln(x_2)$	-0.3975	-0.5347	-0.2603	-0.4458	-0.1823	-0.0538	0.0700
β_1	$\ln(y_1)$	0.4622	0.3663	0.5580	0.3600	0.5254	0.0133	0.0489
β_2	$\ln(y_2)$	0.5378	0.4420	0.6337	0.4746	0.6400	-0.0133	0.0489
$\Gamma_{11.11}$	$\ln(x_1)^2$	0.1129	-0.0159	0.2417	0.0293	0.3190	-0.0151	0.0657
$\Gamma_{11.12}$	$\ln(x_1)\ln(x_2)$	0.5172	0.2959	0.7386	0.2474	0.7073	0.0231	0.1129
$\Gamma_{11.22}$	$\ln(x_2)^2$	-0.0413	-0.1176	0.0349	-0.0983	0.0586	-0.0190	0.0389
$\Gamma_{12.11}$	$\ln(x_1)\ln(y_1)$	-0.0279	-0.1370	0.0812	-0.1399	0.0898	-0.0131	0.0557
$\Gamma_{12.12}$	$\ln(x_1)\ln(y_2)$	0.0279	-0.0812	0.1370	-0.0898	0.1399	0.0131	0.0557
$\Gamma_{12.21}$	$\ln(x_2)\ln(y_1)$	0.0551	-0.0115	0.1216	-0.0171	0.1242	-0.0025	0.0340
$\Gamma_{12.22}$	$\ln(x_2)\ln(y_2)$	-0.0551	-0.1216	0.0115	-0.1242	0.0171	0.0025	0.0340
$\Gamma_{22.11}$	$\ln(y_1)^2$	0.1079	0.0825	0.1333	0.0756	0.1298	0.0020	0.0130
$\Gamma_{22.12}$	$\ln(y_1)\ln(y_2)$	-0.1079	-0.1333	-0.0825	-0.1298	-0.0756	-0.0020	0.0130
$\Gamma_{22.22}$	$\ln(y_2)^2$	0.1079	0.0825	0.1333	0.0756	0.1298	0.0020	0.0130

$$\begin{aligned}
SE_{FDH} \in CI^{normapprox} &= [0.6112,\ 0.9633],\\
SE_{FDH} \in CI^{basicboot} &= [0.6090,\ 0.9739];\\
SE_{\alpha=0.975} &= 0.4974;\\
SE_{\alpha=0.975} \in CI^{normapprox} &= [0.2920,\ 0.7027],\\
SE_{\alpha=0.975} \in CI^{basicboot} &= [0.1966,\ 0.5990];\\
SE_{m=35} &= 0.5778,\\
SE_{m=35} \in CI^{normapprox} &= [0.4046,\ 0.7510],\\
SE_{m=35} \in CI^{basicboot} &= [0.3561,\ 0.6948].
\end{aligned}$$

As we explained in Sections 4.6 and 4.7 the COLS estimator (here we obtain a SE of 0.1746) is really a bad choice; the FDH estimator for the first stage may be influenced by outliers, hence it is always useful to compare the previous results with those of partial robust estimators (order-m or order-α).

We observe that all results are of the same order. These results show that in all cases the SE is less than one, indicating the presence of decreasing returns to scale at the mean of the Italian CNR institutes. Hence, it appears that the result of *decreasing returns to scale* for the CNR as a whole seems quite stable for robust and full frontiers estimates.

The inspection of Tables 7.8 and 7.9 show other interesting evidence:

- there is a *positive* and significant interaction between the inputs ($COST$ $100emp$ and $RESFUN100res$), see $\Gamma_{11.12}$ and its related confidence interval.

- there is a significant *trade off* between the research activity (measured by the $INTPUB100RES$) and the external services offered to the market (as measured by P_MARFUN), see the estimations as well as the confidence interval of $\Gamma_{22.12}$.

Nevertheless, these are just a rough approximation of the considered trade-offs as we have not analytically computed elasticities of complementarity and substitution.[41] This computation can be easily handled by applying the standard microeconomic toolbox of partial derivatives and the like (see *e.g.* Mas-Colell, Whinston and Green, 1995; or Varian, 1992) to this distance function framework. It is quite interesting, from an applied perspective, to measure the elasticity of the distance function with respect to inputs and outputs; the rate of substitution between outputs[42], the elasticity of each output with respect to each input, and finally the elasticity between the outputs themselves.

Our main aim in this chapter was to illustrate the powerful application of the new two-stage approach proposed by Florens and Simar (2005), generalised to the multiple output case in Section 4.7 as a better alternative (in terms of statistical inference) than the traditional parametric approaches followed in the literature.

7.6 Conclusions

In the following we report the main findings of the analysis carried out on the Italian CNR research institutes.

A striking result of our analysis is that *size* negatively affects the performance of all CNR institutes. We graphically illustrated that the majority of Italian research institutes operates with decreasing returns to scale.

---

[41]For a comparative detailed review of the elasticities of complementarity and substitution see Cantarelli (2005). On elasticities of substitution and complementarity see also Bertoletti (2005).

[42]See Grosskopf, Margaritis and Valdmanis (1995) for the computation of marginal rates of transformation and Morishima elasticities of substitution among the units of a public system, within a distance function framework.

We did not find a strong support for *agglomeration* effects. The argument that scientific productivity is favoured by the geographical agglomeration of institutes in the same area did not receive empirical support from our data.

Based on detailed evidence at the micro level on research institutes we showed that scientific productivity declines with the average *age* of researchers of the institute. Nevertheless, the key problem is not the declining individual productivity, but rather the fact that as time goes on, it becomes increasingly difficult to create the research climate within scientific institutions that attracts young and talented scientists. The turnover of scientific personnel must be kept high on a permanent basis.

The result on decreasing returns to scale was also confirmed by the robust estimation of the scale elasticity for the average of CNR institutes (around 0.50). By applying the new two step procedure introduced by Florens and Simar (2005), Daouia, Florens and Simar (2005) and extended in Section 4.7, we were able to estimate the confidence intervals for the average scale elasticity of CNR institutes both for order-α and order-m robust estimators. Finally, by doing so, we showed that the parametric approximation of robust and nonparametric frontiers is also feasible in a multi output framework, by estimating robust parameters of a multi output Translog distance function which have better properties than the traditional parametric estimates.

The calculation of elasticities of substitution and of marginal rate of transformation and the like is straightforward and is left to other applications.

Chapter 8

MUTUAL FUNDS PERFORMANCE: EXPLORING THE EFFECTS OF MANAGER TENURE, FUND AGE, AND THEIR INTERACTION

8.1 Introduction

The development of personal finance and the recent movements of retirement planning have renewed the interest on wealth allocation across asset categories and detailed investments. Consequently, mutual fund investment companies have become an increasingly popular way (channel) for capital appreciation and income generation.

However, the identification of superior performing funds remains a controversial topic due to the volatile nature of individual fund performance and the methodological problems that compromise the findings of empirical studies.

There is a growing literature on the evaluation of the performance of mutual funds which deals both on its methodological aspects and on its empirical facets (features).[43]

Recently, several works have applied efficiency and productivity techniques for evaluating the performance of mutual funds. Studies which apply the parametric approach include, for instance: Annaert, van den Broeck and Vennet (1999), Briec and Lesourd (2000). Among the applications of the nonparametric efficiency analysis approach there are: Murthi, Choi and Desai (1997); Morey and Morey (1999); Sengupta (2000); Basso and Funari (2001); Wilkens and Zhu (2001); Daraio and Simar (2004). Indeed the estimation of efficient boundaries arises in portfolio management, as well as in the production framework. In fact, in Capital Assets Pricing Models (CAPM, Markowitz, 1952, 1959) the goal is to study the performance of investment portfolios. Risk (volatility or variance) and average return on a portfolio act like inputs and

[43] Several surveys are available. See *e.g.* Shukla and Trzcinca (1992), Ippolito (1993) Grinblatt and Titman (1995), Cesari and Panetta (2002).

outputs in production models. In these Models, the boundary of the attainable set of portfolios gives a benchmark relative to which the efficiency of a portfolio can be measured. Sengupta (1991) and Sengupta and Park (1993) analyse, from a methodological perspective, the connections between the nonparametric estimation of frontiers and CAPM. For a theoretical analysis of nonparametric efficiency measurement approaches for portfolio selection see Briec, Kerstens and Lesourd, 2004.

Within the nonparametric approach in efficiency analysis, Daraio and Simar (2004) propose a robust nonparametric approach to evaluate and explain the performance of mutual funds. They show how robust nonparametric (order$-m$) frontiers could be useful to address some issues in portfolio performance evaluation. This robust approach adds some new advantages to the traditional advantages of the nonparametric approach (namely: the absence of specification of the functional form for the input-output relationship; the evaluation of performance without the specification of a theoretical model as benchmark; the computation of an efficiency index for each mutual fund; no need to assume the normality of return distribution).

As shown above in Chapter 5, the first advantage is, of course, the *robustness*: as the robust indicators are based on estimators that do not envelop all funds, they are more robust to outliers and extreme values which can strongly influence the nonparametric estimation of portfolio efficiency. The level of robustness can be set by means of the tuning parameters m or α (if order-α frontiers are used). The second advantage is the absence of the curse of dimensionality, that is typical of nonparametric estimators; and the third one is the possibility of comparing samples with different size, in an indirect way, avoiding the sample size bias, of which nonparametric indicators (DEA/FDH) suffer.

Another benefit consists in the possibility of extending the analysis, considering the *conditional influence* of *environmental variables* Z in a robust way as well as decomposing the performance of a firm in an indicator of the *internal* or managerial efficiency, an *externality* index and an *individual* index which measures the firm *intensity* in catching the opportunities or threats by the environment.

In this chapter we develop further the empirical analysis done in Daraio and Simar (2004) on US mutual funds. We apply the comprehensive probabilistic approach described in Chapter 5, and the newly introduced probabilistic efficiency measures, $\widehat{\alpha}(x, y)$ and $\widehat{\alpha}_z(x, y)$, providing new empirical evidence on several interesting issues in the literature of mutual funds performance evaluation.

We base our analysis on a cross-section dataset of US Aggressive Growth funds (annual data for the period June 2001-May 2002). In Daraio (2003) an application of the bootstrap on these data is proposed as well as an analysis of the distribution of efficiency scores. Daraio and Simar (2004) have explored economies of scale and the influence of market risks on these funds and compared with other US mutual funds categories by objective.

In this chapter we focus our empirical investigation on the impact of some new *management variables* on the performance of mutual funds, namely manager tenure and fund age (age from inception date) and their interactions on fund performance.

In particular *manager tenure* is a measure of the manager's survivorship at the job (Golec, 1996). Long tenure implies that the management company finds the manager's ability and performance satisfactory but may also indicate that the manager has few better opportunities because of specialized skills or a modest performance record. Age of fund provides a measure of the fund's longevity or ability to survive in a highly competitive environment. It is simply the number of months that a funds has been in operation.

According to human capital theory, managers with greater human capital (intelligence and so on) should lead to better performance and hence should be paid with an higher compensation. Moreover, performance, risks and fees of mutual funds are all interrelated; consistent with several agency models (see Golec, 1996 and the references cited there) a manager portfolio risk choices will partly depend upon his/her risk taking preferences because the volatility of a manager's pay is influenced by the portfolio's performance.

There is a rich literature on the relation between fund manager tenure and mutual fund performance.

For years, economists have debated whether it is possible for mutual fund managers to "beat the market", either through superior stock selection abilities, or by correctly predicting the timing of overall market advances and declines. Chevalier and Ellison (1999a) examine whether mutual fund performance is related to characteristics of fund managers that may indicate ability, knowledge, or effort. During the time period they study, there is a strong correlation between fund returns and a manager's age, the average SAT score of his or her undergraduate school, and whether he or she holds an MBA. For an interesting analysis of the labour market for mutual fund managers and managers' responses to the implicit incentives created by their career concerns see Chevalier and Ellison(1999b) which find also that managerial turnover is sensitive to a fund's recent performance.

Nevertheless, the evidence is inconclusive regarding manager tenure and performance.

On the one hand, in their study, Lemak and Satish (1996) found that longer-term managers have a tendency to outperform shorter-term fund managers and that longer-term fund managers assemble less risky portfolios. Golec (1996) illustrated that manager tenure is the most significant predictor of performance and found that longer-term managers, with more than seven years tenure, have better risk-adjusted performance. He also showed that performance are positively related to higher management fees and turnover ratios. Khorana (1996) added empirical evidence on the underperformance of fund managers who are replaced or terminated. Furthermore, he showed also that departing managers exhibit higher portfolio turnover rates and higher expenses relative to non-replaced managers.

On the other hand, Porter and Trifts (1998) found that managers with ten-year track records do not perform better than those with shorter track records. On the same line, Detzel and Weigand (1998) and Fortin, Michelson and Wagner (1999) showed that manager tenure is not related to performance.

Summing up, whether mutual fund managers produce greater returns is *controversial* because most studies' funds, sample periods, and the methodological assumptions of the adopted performance measures are not comparable.

We add new empirical evidence on this very interesting and contentious issue using our nonparametric and robust approach. In this chapter, we reduce the extent of fund changes and the *survivorship bias* which affect empirical studies focusing on long time periods, providing a cross-sectional analysis. The chapter unfolds as follows. In the next section we make a description of the data. In the following sections we report the results of our empirical investigation and then we conclude.

8.2 Data description

Our original data consist of the US Mutual Funds universe, collected by the reputed Morningstar and updated at 05-31-2002. Among this universe we selected the Aggressive-Growth (AG) category of Mutual Funds.

According to the description given by Morningstar, *Aggressive Growth*(AG) are *funds that seek rapid growth of capital and that may invest in emerging market growth companies without specifying a market capitalization range.* They often invest in small or emerging growth companies.

We analyse 117 out of the 129 AG funds analysed in Daraio and Simar (2004), for which two new management variables were available: manager tenure and inception date.

The definition of the variables used in the analysis follows.

Total Return is the annual return at the 05-31-2002, expressed in percentage terms. Morningstar calculation of total return is determined each month by taking the change in monthly Net Asset Value (NAV), reinvesting all income and capital-gains distributions during that month, and dividing by the starting NAV. Since most of returns were negative for the analised period, we add 100 to their amounts. We notice also that this transformation does not affect the efficiency analysis that we carry out in an input oriented framework using total return as output.

Risk is the standard deviation of Return, it depicts how widely the returns varied over a certain period of time. It is computed using the trailing monthly total returns for 3 years. All of the monthly standard deviations are then annualized. Standard deviation of return is an absolute measure of volatility. It offers a probable range within which a fund's realized return is likely to deviate from its expected return.

Transaction costs are made by the sum of Expense Ratio, Loads and Turnover Ratio.

Expense Ratio is the percentage of fund assets paid for operating expenses and management fees, including 12b-1 fees (the annual charge deducted from fund assets to pay for distribution and marketing costs), administrative fees, and all other asset-based costs incurred by the fund except brokerage costs. Sales charges are not included in the expense ratio.

Loads have been obtained by summing the Front-End Load and the Deferred Load of each fund. The Front-End Load is the initial sales charge which consists in a one-time deduction from an investment made into the fund. The amount is generally relative to the amount of the investment, so that larger investments incur smaller rates of charge. The sales charge serves as a commission for the broker who sold the fund. The Deferred Loads are also known as back-end sales charges and are imposed when investors redeem shares. The percentage charged, generally declines the longer shares are held.

Turnover ratio is a measure of the fund's trading activity which is computed by taking the lesser of purchases or sales and dividing by average monthly net assets. It gives an indication of trading activity: funds with higher turnover (implying more trading activity) incur greater brokerage fees for affecting the trades. It is also an indication of management strategy: a low turnover figure would indicate a "buy-and-hold strategy"; high turnover would indicate an investment strategy involving "considerable buying and selling" of securities.

Market risks reflects the percentage of a fund's movements that can be explained by movements in its benchmark index. Morningstar compares all equity funds to the S&P 500 index and all fixed-income funds to the Lehman Brothers Aggregate Bond Index. It is calculated on a monthly basis, based on a least-squares regression of the funds returns on the returns of the fund's benchmark index.

Manager tenure is the number of years that the current manager has been the portfolio manager of the fund. For funds with more managers the average tenure is reported.

Fund inception date is the date on which the fund began his operations. We use this information to compute the age in months of mutual funds at April 2002.

As done in previous studies, we adopt an input oriented framework. We use as inputs: Risks (standard deviation of return), Turnover and Expense ratio; as output the Total return, and as External variables: Manager tenure, funds age and their interrelation. We use also as descriptors market risks and fund size (net assets in million of US dollars).

Some descriptive statistics on the inputs, output, external factors and descriptors are offered in Table 8.1, were the average, the standard deviation, the minimum, the maximum and the interquartile range (Iqr) are reported. The latter (Iqr) gives a robust measure of the spread of the data, since it is not affected by changes in the upper and lower 25%; it is given, in fact, by the difference between the 75% and the 25% percentiles of the analysed variable.

Inspection of Table 8.1 shows that the average fund has a risk (standard deviation of return) of 35, has a turnover ratio of 154 with an expense ratio of 1.73; it has a total return of 82 (which is negative, as we added 100 to total return) and an average market risk and fund size of respectively 47 and 469.

Table 8.1. Descriptive statistics on inputs, output, external factors for Aggressive Growth mutual funds (AG117).

Variable	Mean	St. Dev.	Min	Max	Iqr
Risk (Input 1)	34.656	8.827	14.730	81.050	9.765
Turnover (Input 2)	153.479	101.439	15.000	642.000	130.750
Expense Ratio (Input 3)	1.726	1.334	0.480	14.700	0.823
Total Return (Output)	81.766	10.099	40.120	103.760	14.270
Manager tenure (Ex. factor 1)	4.994	3.735	0.513	30.140	3.274
Fund Age (Ex. factor 2)	113.084	103.155	29.103	543.517	48.445
Market risks (Ex. factor 3)	47.402	16.159	6.000	100.000	14.250
Fund size (Ex. factor 4)	468.833	1215.700	0.200	8828.100	215.750

The average fund manager tenure is of around 5 years, while its age is about 113 months from inception date. The range of variation are particularly broad: manager tenure goes from half a year to 30 years, age of fund from 29 to 544 months.[44]

The variables presented in Table 8.1 are highly skewed; this is also confirmed by the scatterplot matrices reported in Figures 8.1 and 8.2 where, along the diagonals of the matrices, are also reported the histograms of all variables. Figure 8.3 shows the scatterplots of Z_1 (manager tenure) and Z_2 (fund age) against the various inputs.

From these plots, it emerges that there are no particular structures or relationships among the variables, and some extreme points are clearly highlighted. This evidence calls for the use of robust methods that we will apply in the following of the chapter to avoid the influence of these outlying points on the efficiency comparisons.

8.3 Impact of mutual fund manager tenure on performance

In the introductory section we have seen that the role of manager tenure on the performance of mutual funds is not a stylised fact but is debated in the literature with contradictory evidences. In this section we apply the methodology described in Chapter 5 to shed light on the role of US Aggressive Growth Mutual funds first globally (*i.e.*, considering the mutual funds as a whole) and then individually, investigating the impact of fund manager on each AG mutual fund, trying to find patterns in the analysed funds.

The following Figure 8.4 illustrates the smoothed nonparametric regression of Q_m^z on manager tenure (Z) (top panel) and of α_{Q^z} on Z (bottom panel). We set the level of $m = 25$ and $\alpha = 0.95$ so that we are robust at 10%. Q_m^z (and α_{Q^z}) are the ratios of conditional on unconditional efficiency measures of order$-m$ (respectively order$-\alpha$) computed in an input oriented framework. We remember that in this framework an increasing nonparametric regression line states a globally negative impact of the external factor, a decreasing nonparametric regression line shows a positive impact on mutual funds performance while a straight line points to an absence of global effect of the factor on the analysed funds. As confirmed also by Figure 8.5 - which shows a zoom on the impact on AG mutual funds which have a manager tenure lower than 13 years, globally speaking, we see that there is no impact of manager tenure on mutual funds performance.

[44] We notice that in order to use the methodology described in Chapter 5 we have made more continuous the last two variables (manager tenure and fund age) by simply adding a small number randomly chosen from the continuous uniform distribution on the interval [-0.499,+0.499]. This transformation does not affect the values and is suitable for our procedure which requires the use of continuous variables.

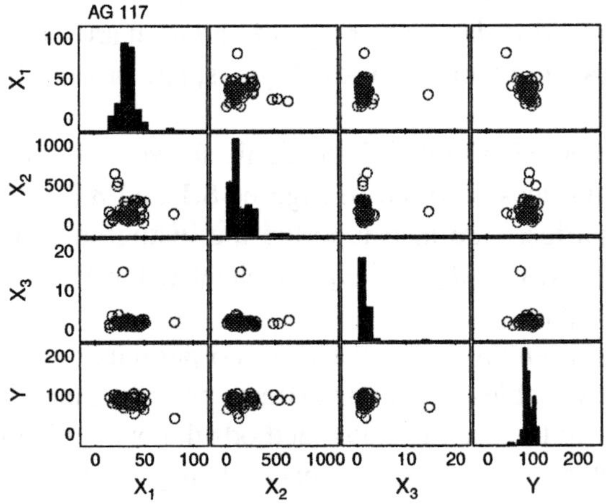

Figure 8.1. Scatterplot matrix of inputs (X) and output (Y) for Aggressive Growth Mutual Funds (AG117).

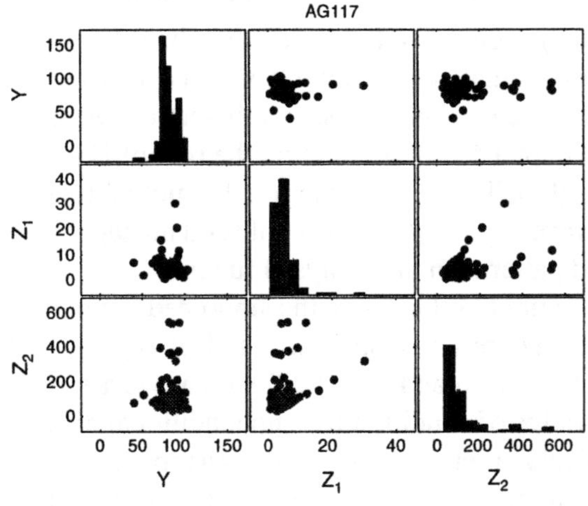

Figure 8.2. Scatterplot matrix of output (Y) and external factors (Z) for Aggressive Growth Mutual Funds (AG117). Z_1 is manager tenure and Z_2 is Fund age in months.

This result supports the findings of Porter and Trifts (1998), Detzel and Weigand (1998) and of Fortin, Michelson and Wagner (1999) who find that longer term manager do not perform better than those with shorter track records. Nevertheless, as we stated in the introduction, it is difficult to compare results of evidence obtained using different dataset, coverage and *in primis* different methods. Most used techniques in empirical finance are ordinary least squares (OLS) with some multi-stage OLS (see *e.g.*, Golec (1996) for a discussion).

On the contrary, our flexible approach, robust and nonparametric, offers the possibility of investigate not only aggregate trends but also single efficiency

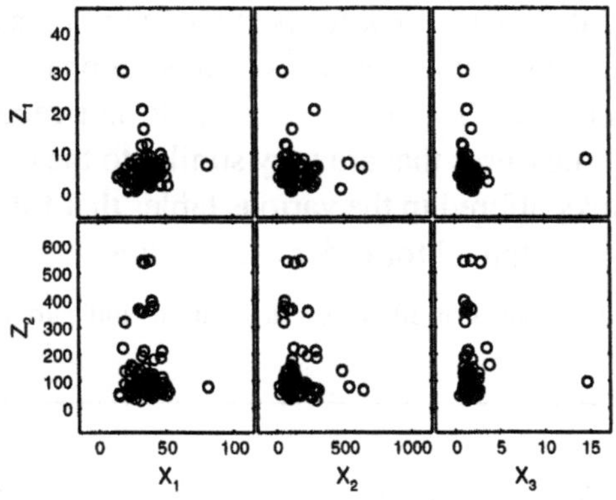

Figure 8.3. Scatterplot matrix of external factors (Z) and Inputs (X) for Aggressive Growth Mutual Funds (AG117).

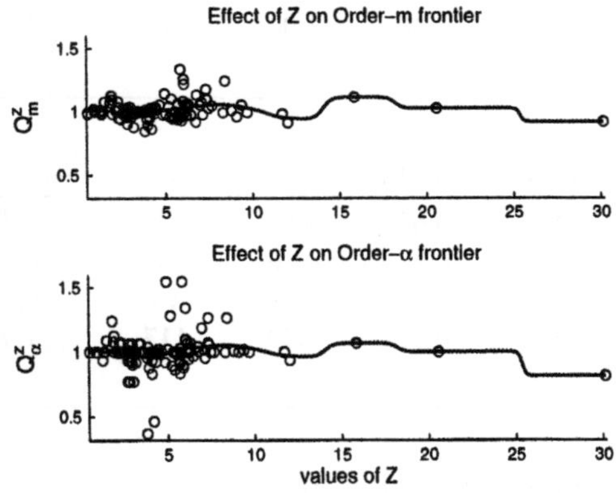

Figure 8.4. Influence of manager tenure on the performance of Aggressive Growth (AG117) Mutual Funds.

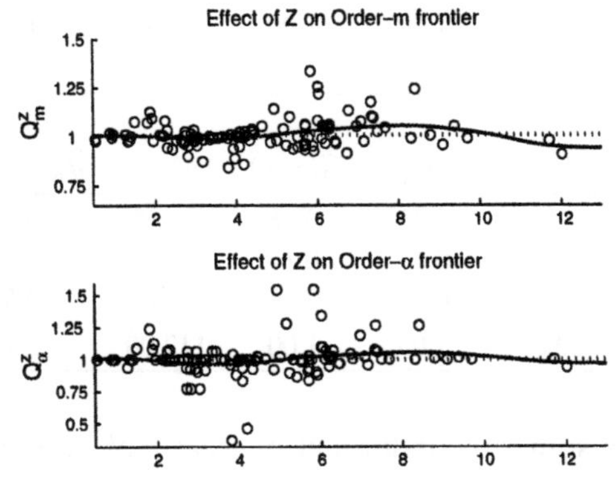

Figure 8.5. Influence of manager tenure on the performance of Aggressive Growth (AG117) Mutual Funds. A zoom on Mutual funds with a manager tenure lower than 13 years.

patterns. These particulars distinct funds are more interesting in empirical finance, where financial analysts look for best outperformers and stars.

In the following we report some descriptive statistics on the various measures of efficiency we computed. To save space we do not report all the results available for order$-\alpha$ measures that are very similar to the order$-m$ ones. We notice that also the ranks offered in the various tables that follow (for order-m) are the same than those obtained for order-α measures.

Table 8.2. Unconditional measures of efficiency, and various indicators, Aggressive Growth Mutual Funds (AG117).

$Q^z_m < 1$					
(15 obs)	N_{point}	$\widehat{\theta}(x,y)$	$\widehat{\alpha}(x,y)$	N_{emp}	$\widehat{\theta}_{m,n}(x,y)$
Mean	1	0.82	0.98	56	1.13
St.dev.	2	0.22	0.03	31	0.42
Min	0	0.51	0.91	14	0.65
Max	6	1.00	1.00	115	2.46
$Q^z_m > 1$					
(26 obs)	N_{point}	$\widehat{\theta}(x,y)$	$\widehat{\alpha}(x,y)$	N_{emp}	$\widehat{\theta}_{m,n}(x,y)$
Mean	15	0.67	0.80	69	0.76
St.dev.	15	0.13	0.16	32	0.13
Min	1	0.51	0.41	13	0.59
Max	56	0.97	0.99	117	1.04
$Q^z_m = 1$					
(76 obs)	N_{point}	$\widehat{\theta}(x,y)$	$\widehat{\alpha}(x,y)$	N_{emp}	$\widehat{\theta}_{m,n}(x,y)$
Mean	7	0.76	0.89	56	0.85
St.dev.	11	0.17	0.13	34	0.15
Min	0	0.47	0.43	1	0.53
Max	60	1.00	1.00	114	1.16
ALL					
(117)	N_{point}	$\widehat{\theta}(x,y)$	$\widehat{\alpha}(x,y)$	N_{emp}	$\widehat{\theta}_{m,n}(x,y)$
Mean	8.31	0.75	0.88	59.05	0.87
St.dev.	12.46	0.17	0.14	33.76	0.23
Min	0.00	0.47	0.41	1.00	0.53
Max	60.00	1.00	1.00	117.00	2.46

Table 8.2 presents some unconditional measures of efficiency and indicators by groups of AG funds which have a different impact or role of manager tenure, namely the 15 mutual funds which have a $Q^z_m < 1$; the 26 funds with $Q^z_m > 1$; the 76 funds with $Q^z_m = 1$ and finally all the 117 funds together.

N_{point} is the number of points which dominates the analysed funds, $\widehat{\theta}(x, y)$ is the FDH input efficiency measure. $\widehat{\alpha}(x, y)$ is the input oriented probabilistic measure introduced in Section 4.3. It is the order$-\alpha$ of the estimated quantile frontier which passes through the unit (x, y). For instance $\widehat{\alpha}(x, y) = 0.98$ means that only 2% of funds with a return at least equal to y are using less inputs than the unit (x, y). Hence, $1 - \widehat{\alpha}(x, y)$ gives an estimates of the probability of unit (x, y) to be dominated, given its level of y. N_{emp} is the number of units used to estimate the distribution function and finally $\widehat{\theta}_{m,n}(x, y)$ is the input order$-m$ efficiency measure where $m = 25$ and is robust at 10%.

Table 8.3 presents some conditional measures of efficiency and indicators for the same groups of AG funds with a different role of manager tenure (given by the values of $Q^z_m >, <, = 1$) as in Table 8.2. ZN_{point} is the number of points which dominates the analysed funds given that $Z = z$, $\widehat{\theta}(x, y|z)$ is the conditional FDH input efficiency measure, $\widehat{\alpha}_z(x, y)$ is the conditional input oriented probabilistic measure introduced in Section 5.2.3. It is the order$-\alpha$ of the estimated conditional quantile frontier which passes through the unit (x, y) given that $Z = z$. Hence, $1 - \widehat{\alpha}_z(x, y)$ gives an estimates of the probability of unit (x, y) to be dominated, given its level of y and the condition $Z = z$. $\widehat{\theta}_{m,n}(x, y|z)$ is the conditional input order-25 efficiency measure and $Q^z_m = \widehat{\theta}_{m,n}(x, y|z)/\widehat{\theta}_{m,n}(x, y)$. $EI^z_m = \widehat{E}(Q^z|Z = z)$ is the externality index defined in Chapter 5, $II^z_m = Q^z \,/\widehat{E}(Q^z|Z = z)$ is the individual index and finally $\alpha_{Q^z} = \widehat{\alpha}_z(x, y)/\widehat{\alpha}(x, y)$.

To characterize the different groups of funds according to the different impact of manager tenure, we provide in Table 8.4 some descriptive statistics which have to be related to the several efficiency measures and indicators presented above.

What do we learn by looking at Tables 8.2 to 8.4

The main aim of the descriptive analysis we reported in Tables 8.2 to 8.4, as we recalled above, is search for individual or group patterns of extremely outperforming funds and characterize their profile. This is particular useful for empirical finance.

It emerges that the profile of AG funds with $Q^z_m < 1$, *i.e.* funds whose efficiency conditioned by the manager tenure is smaller than the unconditional robust efficiency (see the first five lines of Tables 8.2 and 8.3) is characterized by an higher average of manager tenure, around 7 years against a global average of 5, a lower average age of fund, 104 months against the global average of 113 months, a lower average risk (32 against 35), a lower turnover ratio (95 against 153), lower expense ratio (1.48 against 1.73), but an higher level of market risks (56 against 47) and a size of more than twice the average age of the whole sample (net asset values in million of US $ of 1014 against 469).

Table 8.3. Conditional measures of efficiency and various indicators (Z is manager tenure), by groups of Aggressive Growth Mutual Funds (AG117).

$Q^z_m < 1$								
(15 obs)	ZN_{point}	$\widehat{\theta}(x,y\|z)$	$\widehat{\alpha}_z(x,y)$	$\widehat{\theta}_{m,n}(x,y\|z)$	Q^z_m	EI^z_m	II^z_m	α_{Q^z}
Mean	0.93	0.82	0.97	1.03	0.91	1.00	0.92	0.99
St.dev.	1.48	0.22	0.05	0.37	0.03	0.03	0.04	0.02
Min	0.00	0.51	0.85	0.61	0.84	0.92	0.85	0.94
Max	5.00	1.00	1.00	2.25	0.95	1.04	1.00	1.00

$Q^z_m > 1$								
(26 obs)	ZN_{point}	$\widehat{\theta}(x,y\|z)$	$\widehat{\alpha}_z(x,y)$	$\widehat{\theta}_{m,n}(x,y\|z)$	Q^z_m	EI^z_m	II^z_m	α_{Q^z}
Mean	8.12	0.74	0.85	0.85	1.11	1.03	1.08	1.07
St.dev.	9.49	0.17	0.16	0.13	0.07	0.02	0.07	0.05
Min	0.00	0.51	0.46	0.63	1.05	1.00	1.00	0.98
Max	32.00	1.00	1.00	1.11	1.33	1.11	1.30	1.17

$Q^z_m = 1$								
(76 obs)	ZN_{point}	$\widehat{\theta}(x,y\|z)$	$\widehat{\alpha}_z(x,y)$	$\widehat{\theta}_{m,n}(x,y\|z)$	Q^z_m	EI^z_m	II^z_m	α_{Q^z}
Mean	4.91	0.78	0.88	0.85	1.00	1.01	0.99	0.99
St.dev.	6.89	0.17	0.13	0.15	0.02	0.02	0.03	0.04
Min	0.00	0.47	0.42	0.50	0.95	0.95	0.92	0.86
Max	37.00	1.00	1.00	1.11	1.05	1.05	1.05	1.14

ALL								
(117)	ZN_{point}	$\widehat{\theta}(x,y\|z)$	$\widehat{\alpha}_z(x,y)$	$\widehat{\theta}_{m,n}(x,y\|z)$	Q^z_m	EI^z_m	II^z_m	α_{Q^z}
Mean	5.11	0.77	0.88	0.87	1.0	1.01	1.00	1.01
St.dev.	7.44	0.18	0.13	0.20	0.07	0.03	0.07	0.05
Min	0.00	0.47	0.42	0.50	0.84	0.92	0.85	0.86
Max	37.00	1.00	1.00	2.25	1.33	1.11	1.30	1.17

Quite an opposite profile is those of the AG funds with $Q^z_m > 1$, *i.e.* funds which in turn have an efficiency conditioned by manager tenure higher than the unconditional one (see the efficiency measures reported above, from the 6th line from the top to the 10th of Tables 8.2 and 8.3). These funds have a manager tenure of 6 years, market risk, fund age and size are quite the same than the average of the whole sample, but they show a lower average return and higher expense ratio and turnover ratio (182 against 153).

Table 8.4. Some descriptive statistics by group of funds with different impact of manager tenure. Z is manager tenure.

$Q_m^z < 1$ (15 obs)	Risk	Turnover	Expense	T_Return	Mkt risks	Manager Tenure	Fund age	Size
Mean	31.87	95.07	1.48	82.26	56.00	6.53	103.53	1014.48
St.dev.	9.82	71.03	0.75	8.28	18.25	6.71	65.21	2258.49
Min	14.73	15.00	0.48	62.24	20.00	2.00	46.00	2.30
Max	49.71	290.00	2.62	93.08	91.00	30.00	318.00	8828.10

$Q_m^z > 1$ (26 obs)	Risk	Turnover	Expense	T_Return	Mkt risks	Manager Tenure	Fund age	Size
Mean	36.98	182.31	2.18	77.51	47.58	5.88	102.19	571.74
St.dev.	10.94	136.48	2.53	11.35	13.67	2.85	95.42	1292.05
Min	21.07	50.00	0.92	40.12	6.00	1.00	41.00	0.20
Max	81.05	642.00	14.70	93.42	70.00	16.00	544.00	5324.00

$Q_m^z = 1$ (76 obs)	Risk	Turnover	Expense	T_Return	Mkt risks	Manager Tenure	Fund age	Size
Mean	34.41	155.14	1.62	83.13	45.64	4.34	118.75	325.93
St.dev.	7.45	85.89	0.56	9.48	15.85	2.94	110.42	771.33
Min	17.69	44.00	0.90	64.30	8.00	1.00	29.00	0.20
Max	50.22	482.00	3.80	103.76	100.00	21.00	541.00	4914.30

ALL (117 obs)	Risk	Turnover	Expense	T_Return	Mkt risks	Manager Tenure	Fund age	Size
Mean	34.66	153.48	1.73	81.77	47.40	4.97	113.12	468.83
St.dev.	8.79	101.00	1.33	10.06	16.09	3.73	102.70	1210.45
Min	14.73	15.00	0.48	40.12	6.00	1.00	29.00	0.20
Max	81.05	642.00	14.70	103.76	100.00	30.00	544.00	8828.10

Table 8.5. Rank of AG mutual funds with $Q^z_m > 1$ ordered by decreasing INCR = $\widehat{\theta}_{m,n}(x, y|z) - \widehat{\theta}_{m,n}(x, y)$. Z is manager tenure.

Fund Name	$\widehat{\alpha}(x,y)$	$\widehat{\theta}_{m,n}$	$\widehat{\alpha}_z(x,y)$	$\widehat{\theta}^z_{m,n}$	Q^z_m	EI^z_m	II^z_m	α_{Q^z}	$INCR$
1	0.66	0.60	0.77	0.80	1.33	1.03	1.30	1.17	**0.20**
2	0.76	0.68	0.85	0.85	1.26	1.03	1.22	1.12	**0.17**
3	0.85	0.70	0.96	0.87	1.24	1.05	1.18	1.13	**0.17**
4	0.81	0.75	0.90	0.91	1.22	1.03	1.18	1.11	**0.16**
5	0.90	0.84	0.99	0.99	1.18	1.05	1.12	1.09	**0.15**
6	0.87	0.72	0.93	0.82	1.13	1.04	1.09	1.07	**0.10**
7	0.78	0.76	0.82	0.85	1.13	1.00	1.12	1.05	**0.10**
8	0.97	0.92	1.00	1.01	1.10	1.02	1.08	1.03	**0.09**
9	0.81	0.75	0.87	0.83	1.11	1.11	1.00	1.07	**0.08**
10	0.65	0.59	0.74	0.68	1.14	1.01	1.13	1.14	**0.08**
11	0.88	0.79	0.93	0.86	1.10	1.05	1.04	1.06	**0.08**
12	0.99	1.04	1.00	1.11	1.07	1.00	1.07	1.01	**0.08**
13	0.86	0.72	0.96	0.79	1.10	1.05	1.05	1.11	**0.07**
14	0.85	0.88	0.85	0.96	1.08	1.00	1.08	1.01	**0.07**
15	0.92	0.93	1.00	1.00	1.08	1.01	1.07	1.08	**0.07**
16	0.94	0.90	0.96	0.97	1.08	1.05	1.03	1.02	**0.07**
17	0.53	0.61	0.53	0.67	1.09	1.00	1.09	1.02	**0.06**
18	0.73	0.66	0.80	0.72	1.08	1.03	1.05	1.09	**0.05**
19	0.94	0.92	0.95	0.97	1.05	1.03	1.03	1.01	**0.05**
20	0.93	0.91	0.95	0.95	1.05	1.04	1.02	1.02	**0.05**
21	0.91	0.88	0.93	0.93	1.05	1.00	1.05	1.02	**0.05**
22	0.95	0.76	0.97	0.80	1.06	1.03	1.03	1.02	**0.05**
23	0.85	0.75	0.95	0.79	1.05	1.04	1.02	1.12	**0.04**
24	0.41	0.60	0.47	0.64	1.06	1.04	1.02	1.14	**0.04**
25	0.41	0.60	0.46	0.64	1.06	1.03	1.02	1.14	**0.03**
26	0.63	0.60	0.62	0.63	1.05	1.05	1.01	0.98	**0.03**

Funds Name: 1 SunAmerica Foc MultiGr B, 2 SunAmerica Foc MultiGr A, 3 American Heritage Growth, 4 MFS Emerging Growth C, 5 Liberty Contrarian SmCpA, 6 Putnam Voyager II B, 7 Phoenix-Engemann Agg Gr A, 8 Mason Street Ag Gr Stk A, 9 MFS Emerging Growth B, 10 SunAmerica Foc MultiGr II, 11 Putnam Voyager II M, 12 Fidelity Aggressive Grth, 13 Navellier Aggr Growth, 14 Alliance Quasar Instl I, 15 SSgA Aggressive Equity, 16 Vintage Aggr Growth, 17 Atlas Emerging Growth A, 18 Evergreen Sm Co Grth B, 19 Credit Suisse Tr Gl PstVt, 20 Putnam New Opports B, 21 Commerce MidCap Gr Svc, 22 Delaware Trend C, 23 Quaker Aggressive Gr A, 24 Prudential US Emerg Gr C, 25 Prudential US Emerg Gr B, 26 Van Wagoner Emerging Gr.

Table 8.6. Rank of AG mutual funds with $Q_m^z < 1$ ordered by decreasing DECR = $\widehat{\theta}_{m,n}(x, y|z) - \widehat{\theta}_{m,n}(x, y)$. Z is manager tenure.

Fund Name	$\widehat{\alpha}(x, y)$	$\widehat{\theta}_{m,n}$	$\widehat{\alpha}_z(x, y)$	$\widehat{\theta}_{m,n}^z$	Q_m^z	EI_m^z	II_m^z	α_{Q^z}	$DECR$
1	1.00	1.48	1.00	1.25	0.84	0.99	0.85	1.00	**-0.23**
2	1.00	2.46	1.00	2.25	0.91	1.04	0.88	1.00	**-0.21**
3	1.00	1.39	1.00	1.19	0.86	0.99	0.86	1.00	**-0.20**
4	0.99	0.95	0.98	0.83	0.87	0.99	0.88	0.99	**-0.12**
5	1.00	1.20	1.00	1.09	0.91	0.95	0.96	1.00	**-0.11**
6	0.99	0.96	0.98	0.86	0.90	0.99	0.91	0.99	**-0.10**
7	0.98	0.88	0.96	0.78	0.89	0.99	0.90	0.98	**-0.10**
8	1.00	1.13	1.00	1.03	0.92	0.92	1.00	1.00	**-0.10**
9	1.00	1.10	1.00	1.03	0.93	1.03	0.91	1.00	**-0.07**
10	1.00	1.10	1.00	1.03	0.94	1.02	0.92	1.00	**-0.07**
11	0.98	0.90	0.98	0.83	0.93	1.03	0.90	1.00	**-0.07**
12	0.98	1.04	0.97	0.98	0.94	0.99	0.95	0.98	**-0.06**
13	1.00	1.06	1.00	1.00	0.95	1.02	0.93	1.00	**-0.06**
14	0.91	0.65	0.85	0.61	0.94	0.99	0.94	0.94	**-0.04**
15	0.91	0.65	0.86	0.61	0.94	1.00	0.95	0.94	**-0.04**

Funds Name: 1 Goldman Sachs Agg GrStrB, 2 Touchstone Aggr Grth A, 3 GMO Tax-Mgd U.S. Eq III, 4 Scudder Aggressive Gr C, 5 Putnam New Opports A, 6 Scudder Aggressive Gr B, 7 Security Ultra B, 8 Value Line Leveraged Gr, 9 Fidelity Capital Apprec, 10 Janus Olympus, 11 AmCent Vista Inst, 12 Evergreen Sm Co Grth I, 13 Delaware Trend Instl, 14 Alliance Quasar C, 15 Alliance Quasar B.

In order to find out the funds most positively influenced by manager tenure, we report in Table 8.5 the rank of US AG funds, with $Q_m^z > 1$, ordered by decreasing INCR -difference between conditional and unconditional order$-m$ efficiency measure ($= \widehat{\theta}_{m,n}(x, y|z) - \widehat{\theta}_{m,n}(x, y)$) as well as their individual efficiency measures. On the contrary, Table 8.6 reveals the name of AG funds most negatively influenced by manager tenure (with $Q_m^z < 1$), ordered by decreasing DECR ($= \widehat{\theta}_{m,n}(x, y|z) - \widehat{\theta}_{m,n}(x, y)$) as well as their individual efficiency measures.

Hence, we were able to find out the US AG funds that have most been influenced by manager tenure, and analyse their different profiles. Of course, this analysis is not conclusive, because other information would have been useful to complete our understanding of the manager tenure effect, such as age of managers, if they have an MBA, and so on, all information that are not available to us. Nevertheless, this analysis is quite interesting and informative: even if globally speaking, manager tenure does not affect the performance of the analysed funds (see Figures 8.4 and 8.5) our procedure is able to identify the funds which had the major impact (positive or negative) and let us characterize their profile. This is particularly useful in empirical finance to try to understand the management behaviour of stars and best performers.

Another interesting phenomena is the impact of fund age on the performance and its interaction with manager tenure, with which we deal in the next section.

8.4 Interaction between manager tenure and fund age

By using the same technique, we analysed also the impact of fund age on AG mutual funds, and find out that there is no global effect on the performance of the analysed funds. See Figures 8.6 and 8.7.

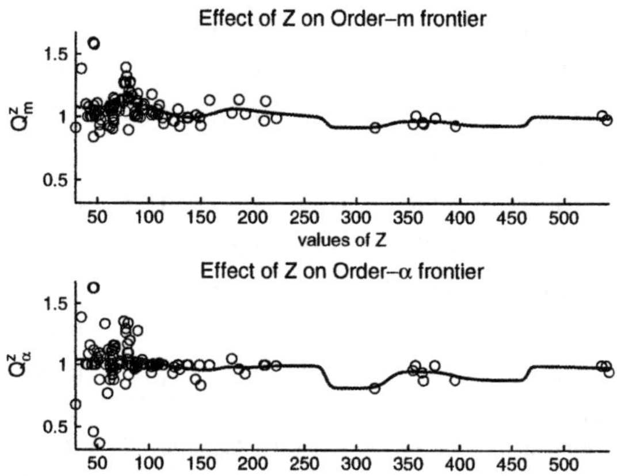

Figure 8.6. Influence of fund age on the performance of Aggressive Growth (AG117) Mutual Funds.

It seems that the ability to survive in a highly competitive environment, as measured by the experience accumulated in a longer number of years in operation, does not affect the performance of the AG mutual funds as a whole. We have also to consider that we analyse a very peculiar time frame: our data spans the terroristic attack of the 11th September 2001 which contributed to the collapse of financial markets in most advanced countries.

Another more interesting question is if in the analysed period there has been interaction between managerial experience (manager tenure) and funds' longevity (measured by fund age), and if this interaction has affected the performance of AG mutual funds. As done below, we analyse the interaction globally, considering a bivariate case for Z, and after that individually (looking at the efficiency of each fund) to point on very peculiar mutual funds which have been particularly influenced (positively or negatively) simultaneously by these factors.

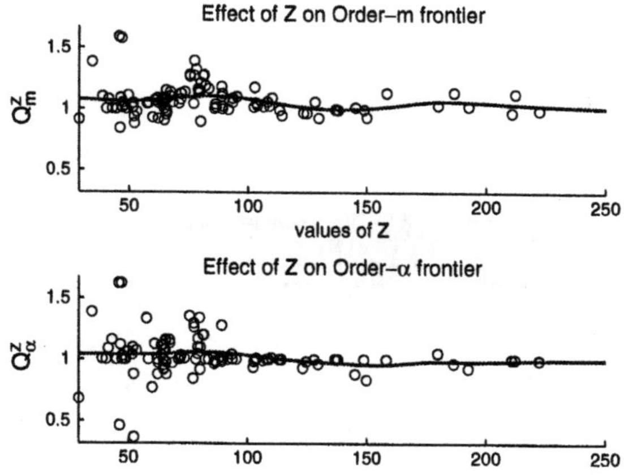

Figure 8.7. Influence of fund age on the performance of Aggressive Growth (AG117) Mutual Funds. A zoom on Mutual funds with a fund age lower than 250 months.

The global impact of manager tenure (Z_1) and fund age (Z_2) on AG funds is shown in Figures 8.8 and 8.9.

We notice that the correlations between manager tenure and fund age is quite low (it is 0.26 although significant at 95%- p. val. $0.004 < 0.05$); the number of $k - NN$ provided by our data driven method (see Chapter 5) is of 55. See Figure 8.10 for the estimation of the density of Z as well as its contour plot.

In particular, Figure 8.8 shows the surface of Q^z_m on Z_1 and Z_2. Figure 8.9 illustrates the smoothed nonparametric regression of Q^z_m on Z_1 (top panel) for Z_2's quartiles; and the smoothed nonparametric regression of Q^z_m on Z_2 (bottom panel) for Z_1's quartiles. The dashed line indicates the first quartile, the solid line the median and the dashdot line the third quartile.

It appears, as we have seen in Figure 8.4, that globally there is no impact of manager tenure till a tenure of around 20 years (note that we only have 3 funds with manager tenure higher than 15 years) and this appears for all quartiles of fund age (top panel of Figure 8.9). By inspecting Figure 8.9 (bottom panel) it seems that fund age does not affect the performance of AG funds if it is conjoint with the first quartile of manager tenure (dashed line), while is seems that for the median of manager tenure (solid line) there is a positive combined effect with an age higher than 400 months, and for longer manager tenure (third quartile, dashdot line) there is a positive effect starting even for funds with age higher than 100 months. Hence, even though there is almost no global effect of manager tenure, our procedure allows to shed lights on the interaction between Z_1 and Z_2. An interpretation of this plot could be that longer and then more experienced manager tenure are better able to exploit the ability/experience of funds in facing highly competitive markets.

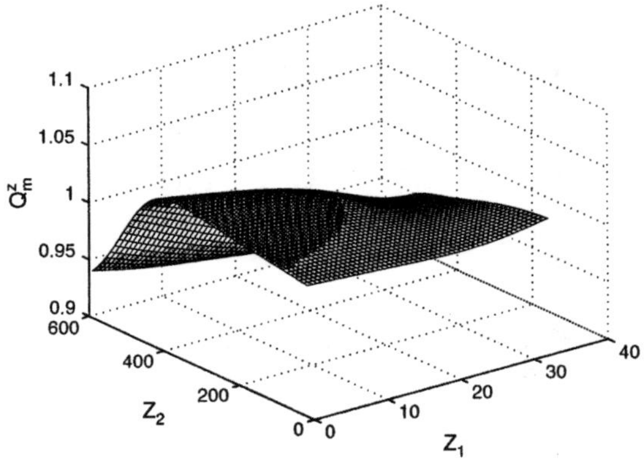

Figure 8.8. Influence of manager tenure and fund age on the performance of Aggressive Growth Mutual Funds (AG117). Surface.

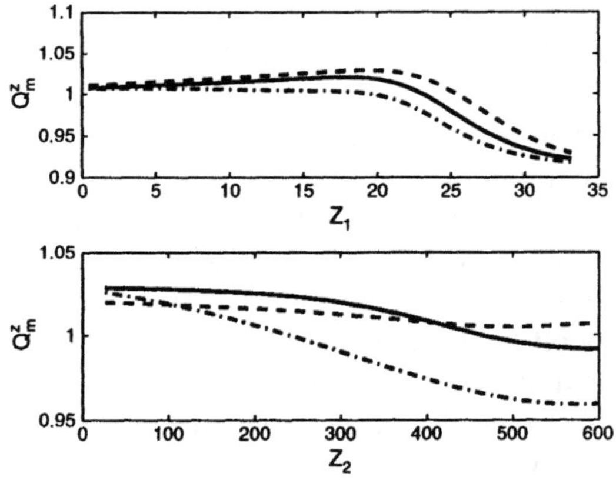

Figure 8.9. Influence of manager tenure (Z_1) and fund age (Z_2) on the performance of Aggressive Growth Mutual Funds (AG117). Plots.

But let examine now the peculiar behaviour of single funds. As in the previous section, Table 8.7 shows some descriptive statistics on efficiency measures and indicators for group of funds that have a different impact of manager tenure jointly considered with fund age. Table 8.8 is useful to characterize the profile of groups of US funds.

Table 8.10 illustrates the rank of US AG funds, with $Q^z_m > 1$, ordered by decreasing INCR -difference between conditional and unconditional order$-m$ efficiency measure ($= \widehat{\theta}_{m,n}(x, y|z) - \widehat{\theta}_{m,n}(x, y)$) as well as their individual efficiency measures. Table 8.9 reveals the name of AG funds with $Q^z_m < 1$, ordered by decreasing DECR ($= \widehat{\theta}_{m,n}(x, y|z) - \widehat{\theta}_{m,n}(x, y)$) as well as their

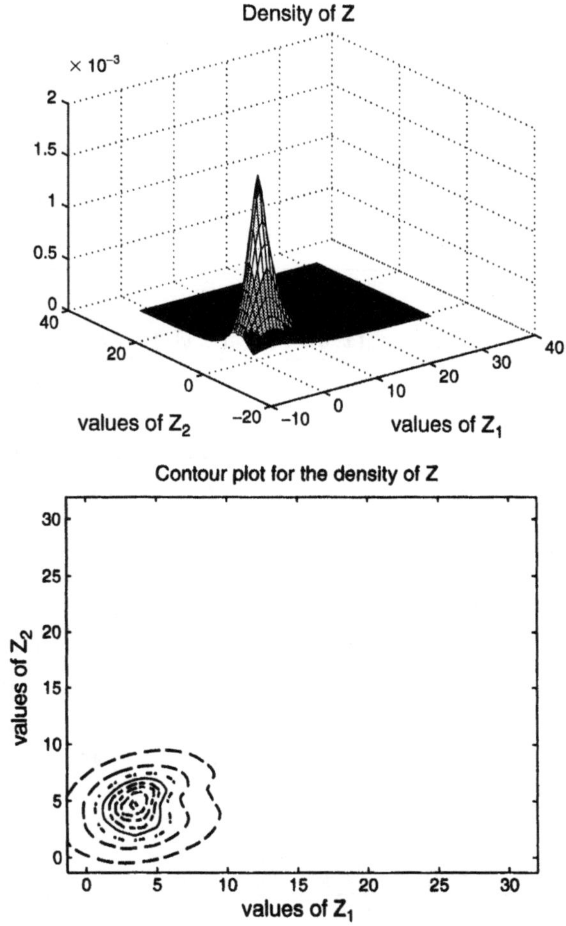

Figure 8.10. Influence of manager tenure (Z_1) and fund age (Z_2) on the performance of Aggressive Growth Mutual Funds (AG117). Density of Z (top panel) and contour plot of the density of Z (bottom panel).

individual efficiency measures. Here we remember that Z is bivariate and is done by manager tenure and fund age. It is also interesting to compare these results with those of the previous section. In particular, there are some funds such as no.1,2,7,12,19,20 and 21 in Table 8.10 that were not listed in Table 8.5; for these funds, manager tenure has an effect only if taking into account conjointly with funds' age. The same holds true for some funds of Table 8.9, such as no. 9, 13, 15, 17 and 18 not listed in Table 8.6.

These considerations are just examples on how to use our approach to shed light on individual pattern of efficiency measures and their explanation. As a matter of fact, we showed that our methodology is very appealing in providing empirical evidence not only on global financial performance of mutual funds, but also on single peculiar profiles.

Table 8.7. Some descriptive statistics on efficiency measures and indicators by group of funds with different impact of manager tenure. Multivariate Z.

$Q^z_m < 1$ (19 obs)	$\widehat{\alpha}(x,y)$	$\widehat{\theta}_{m,n}(x,y)$	$\widehat{\alpha}_z(x,y)$	$\widehat{\theta}_{m,n}(x,y\|z)$	Q^z_m	EI^z_m	II^z_m	α_{Q^z}
Mean	0.96	1.06	0.95	0.95	0.91	1.01	0.90	0.99
St.dev.	0.06	0.40	0.06	0.34	0.04	0.02	0.05	0.02
Min	0.81	0.65	0.82	0.60	0.80	0.93	0.78	0.95
Max	1.00	2.46	1.00	2.16	0.95	1.02	0.98	1.04

$Q^z_m > 1$ (28 obs)	$\widehat{\alpha}(x,y)$	$\widehat{\theta}_{m,n}(x,y)$	$\widehat{\alpha}_z(x,y)$	$\widehat{\theta}_{m,n}(x,y\|z)$	Q^z_m	EI^z_m	II^z_m	α_{Q^z}
Mean	0.75	0.73	0.81	0.82	1.12	1.02	1.10	1.07
St.dev.	0.17	0.12	0.19	0.13	0.10	0.00	0.10	0.06
Min	0.41	0.59	0.42	0.63	1.05	1.01	1.03	0.99
Max	0.97	0.94	1.00	1.01	1.45	1.03	1.43	1.23

$Q^z_m = 1$ (70 obs)	$\widehat{\alpha}(x,y)$	$\widehat{\theta}_{m,n}(x,y)$	$\widehat{\alpha}_z(x,y)$	$\widehat{\theta}_{m,n}(x,y\|z)$	Q^z_m	EI^z_m	II^z_m	α_{Q^z}
Mean	0.91	0.87	0.91	0.87	1.00	1.01	0.99	1.00
St.dev.	0.10	0.14	0.10	0.14	0.02	0.00	0.02	0.04
Min	0.49	0.53	0.53	0.54	0.96	1.00	0.94	0.91
Max	1.00	1.10	1.00	1.08	1.05	1.02	1.04	1.13

ALL (117 obs)	$\widehat{\alpha}(x,y)$	$\widehat{\theta}_{m,n}(x,y)$	$\widehat{\alpha}_z(x,y)$	$\widehat{\theta}_{m,n}(x,y\|z)$	Q^z_m	EI^z_m	II^z_m	α_{Q^z}
Mean	0.88	0.87	0.89	0.87	1.01	1.01	1.00	1.01
St.dev.	0.14	0.23	0.13	0.19	0.09	0.01	0.09	0.05
Min	0.41	0.53	0.42	0.54	0.80	0.93	0.78	0.91
Max	1.00	2.46	1.00	2.16	1.45	1.03	1.43	1.23

Table 8.8. Some descriptive statistics by group of funds with different impact of manager tenure. Bivariate Z.

$Q^z_m < 1$ (19 obs)	Risk	Turn.	Exp.	T_Ret.	Mkt risks	Manager Tenure	Fund age	Size
Mean	33.76	119.84	1.47	81.70	51.74	6.47	111.32	960.77
St.dev.	9.57	97.18	0.69	8.51	18.98	6.04	90.49	2179.79
Min	14.73	15.00	0.48	62.24	20.00	2.00	29.00	2.30
Max	49.71	305.00	2.62	93.08	91.00	30.00	395.00	8828.10

$Q^z_m > 1$ (28 obs)	Risk	Turn.	Exp.	T_Ret.	Mkt risks	Manager Tenure	Fund age	Size
Mean	37.95	165.32	2.19	78.69	46.50	5.71	70.96	382.11
St.dev.	9.94	74.90	2.43	10.80	15.95	2.76	27.02	845.08
Min	26.11	64.00	1.10	40.12	17.00	1.00	35.00	0.20
Max	81.05	305.00	14.70	95.34	72.00	16.00	149.00	3593.00

$Q^z_m = 1$ (70 obs)	Risk	Turn.	Exp.	T_Ret.	Mkt risks	Manager Tenure	Fund age	Size
Mean	33.58	157.87	1.61	83.02	46.59	4.26	130.47	370.00
St.dev.	7.68	108.91	0.59	9.87	15.07	3.00	118.75	891.70
Min	17.69	44.00	0.89	51.61	6.00	1.00	41.00	0.20
Max	50.22	642.00	3.80	103.76	100.00	21.00	544.00	5324.00

ALL (117 obs)	Risk	Turn.	Exp.	T_Ret.	Mkt risks	Manager Tenure	Fund age	Size
Mean	34.66	153.48	1.73	81.77	47.40	4.97	113.12	468.83
St.dev.	8.79	101.00	1.33	10.06	16.09	3.73	102.70	1210.45
Min	14.73	15.00	0.48	40.12	6.00	1.00	29.00	0.20
Max	81.05	642.00	14.70	103.76	100.00	30.00	544.00	8828.10

Table 8.9. Rank of AG mutual funds with $Q^z_m < 1$ ordered by decreasing DECR = $\widehat{\theta}_{m,n}(x,y|z) - \widehat{\theta}_{m,n}(x,y)$.Bivariate Z: Z_1 manager tenure, Z_2 fund age.

Fund Name	$\widehat{\alpha}(x,y)$	$\widehat{\theta}_{m,n}$	$\widehat{\alpha}_z(x,y)$	$\widehat{\theta}^z_{m,n}$	Q^z_m	EI^z_m	II^z_m	α_{Q^z}	$DECR$
1	1.00	2.46	1.00	2.16	0.88	1.02	0.86	1.00	-0.30
2	1.00	1.48	1.00	1.18	0.80	1.02	0.78	1.00	-0.30
3	1.00	1.39	1.00	1.15	0.83	1.02	0.82	1.00	-0.24
4	0.98	0.90	0.96	0.77	0.85	1.02	0.84	0.98	-0.13
5	0.99	0.95	0.98	0.82	0.87	1.01	0.86	0.99	-0.12
6	0.99	0.96	0.98	0.84	0.88	1.01	0.87	0.99	-0.12
7	1.00	1.13	1.00	1.03	0.91	0.93	0.98	1.00	-0.10
8	1.00	1.10	1.00	1.02	0.93	1.02	0.91	1.00	-0.08
9	0.94	0.86	0.92	0.79	0.91	1.02	0.90	0.97	-0.08
10	0.98	1.04	0.96	0.97	0.93	1.02	0.91	0.98	-0.07
11	0.98	0.88	0.96	0.80	0.92	1.01	0.90	0.99	-0.07
12	1.00	1.20	1.00	1.13	0.94	1.02	0.92	1.00	-0.07
13	1.00	1.16	1.00	1.10	0.94	1.01	0.94	1.00	-0.06
14	1.00	1.06	1.00	1.00	0.95	1.02	0.93	1.00	-0.06
15	0.82	0.69	0.85	0.64	0.93	1.02	0.92	1.04	-0.05
16	0.91	0.65	0.86	0.60	0.93	1.01	0.92	0.95	-0.04
17	0.95	0.76	0.93	0.71	0.94	1.02	0.93	0.98	-0.04
18	0.81	0.77	0.82	0.73	0.95	1.02	0.93	1.00	-0.04
19	0.91	0.65	0.87	0.62	0.95	1.01	0.94	0.96	-0.03

Funds Name: 1 Touchstone Aggr Grth A, 2 Goldman Sachs Agg GrStrB, 3 GMO Tax-Mgd U.S. Eq III, 4 AmCent Vista Inst, 5 Scudder Aggressive Gr C, 6 Scudder Aggressive Gr B ,7 Value Line Leveraged Gr, 8 Fidelity Capital Apprec, 9 Prudential US Emerg Gr Z, 10 Evergreen Sm Co Grth I, 11 Security Ultra B, 12 Putnam New Opports A, 13 INVESCO Dynamics Inv, 14 Delaware Trend Instl, 15 AIM Mid Cap Opp A, 16 Alliance Quasar C, 17 Delaware Trend C, 18 Van Kampen Aggr Growth A, 19 Alliance Quasar B.

Table 8.10. Rank of AG mutual funds with $Q^z_m > 1$ ordered by decreasing INCR = $\widehat{\theta}_{m,n}(x,y|z) - \widehat{\theta}_{m,n}(x,y)$.Bivariate Z: Z_1 manager tenure, Z_2 fund age.

Fund Name	$\widehat{\alpha}(x,y)$	$\widehat{\theta}_{m,n}$	$\widehat{\alpha}_z(x,y)$	$\widehat{\theta}^z_{m,n}$	Q^z_m	EI^z_m	II^z_m	α_{Q^z}	$INCR$
1	0.67	0.63	0.80	0.91	1.45	1.02	1.43	1.20	0.28
2	0.70	0.63	0.81	0.89	1.41	1.02	1.38	1.16	0.26
3	0.85	0.70	0.97	0.88	1.27	1.02	1.24	1.15	0.19
4	0.76	0.68	0.88	0.82	1.20	1.02	1.18	1.16	0.14
5	0.81	0.75	0.89	0.87	1.17	1.02	1.15	1.09	0.13
6	0.66	0.60	0.81	0.69	1.16	1.02	1.14	1.23	0.10
7	0.82	0.74	0.90	0.84	1.14	1.01	1.12	1.09	0.10
8	0.63	0.60	0.64	0.68	1.13	1.02	1.11	1.01	0.08
9	0.87	0.72	0.92	0.80	1.11	1.02	1.09	1.06	0.08
10	0.81	0.75	0.89	0.82	1.11	1.03	1.08	1.10	0.08
11	0.85	0.88	0.92	0.97	1.10	1.01	1.09	1.09	0.09
12	0.87	0.72	0.91	0.79	1.10	1.01	1.08	1.04	0.07
13	0.97	0.92	1.00	1.01	1.10	1.02	1.08	1.03	0.09
14	0.88	0.79	0.92	0.86	1.09	1.02	1.07	1.05	0.07
15	0.53	0.61	0.52	0.66	1.08	1.01	1.07	0.99	0.05
16	0.90	0.84	0.94	0.91	1.08	1.02	1.06	1.05	0.07
17	0.92	0.93	1.00	1.00	1.08	1.01	1.06	1.08	0.07
18	0.91	0.88	0.95	0.94	1.07	1.02	1.06	1.03	0.06
19	0.77	0.78	0.76	0.84	1.07	1.02	1.06	0.99	0.06
20	0.43	0.60	0.44	0.65	1.07	1.02	1.05	1.02	0.04
21	0.43	0.60	0.42	0.64	1.07	1.02	1.05	0.99	0.04
22	0.94	0.90	0.97	0.96	1.07	1.02	1.05	1.03	0.06
23	0.65	0.59	0.74	0.63	1.06	1.02	1.04	1.14	0.04
24	0.74	0.66	0.80	0.70	1.06	1.02	1.04	1.08	0.04
25	0.93	0.91	0.95	0.96	1.06	1.02	1.04	1.02	0.05
26	0.41	0.60	0.43	0.63	1.05	1.02	1.04	1.06	0.03
27	0.41	0.60	0.43	0.63	1.05	1.02	1.03	1.06	0.03
28	0.95	0.94	0.97	0.98	1.05	1.02	1.03	1.02	0.05

Fund Names: 1 AIM Small Cap Opp C, 2 AIM Small Cap Opp B, 3 American Heritage Growth, 4 SunAmerica Foc MultiGr A, 5 MFS Emerging Growth C, 6 SunAmerica Foc MultiGr B, 7 Rochdale Alpha, 8 Van Wagoner Emerging Gr, 9 Putnam Voyager II B, 10 MFS Emerging Growth B, 11 Alliance Quasar Instl I, 12 Putnam Voyager II C, 13 Mason Street Ag Gr Stk A, 14 Putnam Voyager II M, 15 Atlas Emerging Growth A, 16 Liberty Contrarian SmCpA, 17 SSgA Aggressive Equity, 18 Commerce MidCap Gr Svc, 19 ABN AMRO/Veredus AggGr N, 20 Van Kampen Aggr Growth B, 21 Van Kampen Aggr Growth C, 22 Vintage Aggr Growth, 23 SunAmerica Foc MultiGr II, 24 Evergreen Sm Co Grth C, 25 Putnam New Opports B, 26 Prudential US Emerg Gr C, 27 Prudential US Emerg Gr B, 28 Putnam New Opports M.

8.5 Conclusions

In this chapter we analysed US Aggressive growth mutual funds and the impact of management variables on their performance, namely manager tenure and fund age.

Considered as a whole, we find that there is almost no impact of manager tenure on mutual funds performance. This result supports the findings of Porter and Trifts (1998), Detzel and Weigand (1998) and of Fortin, Michelson and Wagner (1999) who find that longer term manager do not perform better than those with shorter track records. Nevertheless, as we stated in the introduction, it is difficult to compare results of evidence obtained using different dataset, coverage and *in primis* different methods.

We analysed also the impact of fund age on AG mutual funds, and find that there is no global effect on the performance of the analysed funds. It seems that the ability to survive in a highly competitive environment, as measured by the experience accumulated in a longer number of years in operation, does not affect the performance of the AG mutual funds as a whole. We analysed here a very peculiar time frame: our data span the terroristic attack of the 11th September 2001 which contributed to the collapse of financial markets in most advanced countries.

Finally, we investigated the interaction between managerial experience (manager tenure) and funds' longevity (measured by fund age), and how this interaction affected the performance of AG mutual funds. We found that longer and then more experienced manager tenure are better able to exploit the ability/experience of funds in facing highly competitive markets.

Our flexible approach, robust and nonparametric, offers the possibility of investigate not only aggregate trends but also single efficiency patterns.

By applying the methodology developed in Chapter 5, we were able to find out the US AG funds that have most been influenced by manager tenure and their interaction with fund age, and analyse their different profiles. Our approach is, in fact, able to capture the interaction between the components of the external factors (in this case manager tenure and fund age) at the level of individual funds, even in absence of a global impact of these external factors.

Of course, this analysis is not conclusive, because other information would have been useful to complete our understanding of the manager tenure effect, such has age of managers, if they have an MBA, and so on, all information that were not available to us. Nevertheless, this analysis is quite interesting and informative: even if globally speaking, manager tenure does not affect the performance of the analysed funds our procedure is able to identify the funds which had the major impact (positive or negative) and let us characterize their profile. This is particularly useful in empirical finance to try to understand the management behaviour of stars and best performers.

Chapter 9

CONCLUSIONS

In this book we have provided a state-of-the-art presentation of robust and nonparametric methods in efficiency analysis. We focused our analysis on recent developments which allow the overcoming of some of the most critical drawbacks of traditional nonparametric efficient frontier estimators (DEA/FDH based) and their related efficiency scores.

In addition, this book adds new contributions to the efficiency literature. It presents in a unified way the robust nonparametric measures of efficiency based on partial frontiers (of order-m and of order-α) both unconditional and conditional to external-environmental factors. It develops in a full multivariate case the econometric methodology for the evaluation of the impact of external factors on the performance. A new probabilistic robust measure of efficiency is extended to the conditional case in the Methodology part and operationalized in the Applications part. Another important contribution of the book, from a methodological point of view, is the presentation of the parametric approximations of nonparametric robust frontiers and its extension to the multivariate outputs case.

The simulated examples (with both univariate and multivariate external factors) offer useful guidelines on how to implement the proposed methods in practice. Besides, the applications with real data (presented in Part II) show in details how the proposed techniques could be put in place and give an idea on the rich empirical results that are available from their applications. We provide evidence on some classical topics in Industrial Organization such as economies of scale and economies of scope in various fields (insurance sector, economics of science and financial performance evaluation).

Specifically, from the insurance application we learnt how to reduce the dimensional space to face the curse of dimensionality and the usefulness of partial frontiers in revealing the impact of external factors masked, in the full frontier case, by extreme observations.

In the analysis on the Italian National Research Council institutes we show how to estimate parametric approximation of robust and nonparametric frontiers in a full multivariate framework, by estimating robust parameters of a multi output Translog distance function which have better properties than the traditional parametric estimates.

Finally, the mutual funds application illustrates how the profile of group of funds could be characterized starting from a global analysis of the comparison set towards an even more detailed illustration of single extremely good or bad performers.

These applications clearly demonstrate that the methodological toolbox presented in Part I of this book is built up by methods that are often complementary and help all together to shed light on important aspects of the production process.

By using the real data applications, we have shown that it is always useful to start the analysis by some correlation matrix-plots and some exploratory multivariate techniques (see Härdle and Simar, 2003). After that, according to the kind of data and problem to be analysed an appropriate set of measures has to be selected from the taxonomy we presented in Chapter 2. In a lot of studies, the choice of robust methods presented in Chapters 4 and 5 may be the better solution. The knowledge of the statistical properties of the estimators, presented in Chapter 3 is a basic and fundamental step, in order to be aware of the main problems and limitations of the traditional DEA/FDH approach, and to learn how to bootstrap in this context to allow for a better inference in this setting. A step further is the Chapter 4 where an alternative probabilistic formulation of the activity analysis framework allows us to open the field to a new set of probabilistic efficiency measures which keep a link with the traditional FDH estimator (only asymptotically) while offering a wide range of properties useful under an applied perspective as well as give us the opportunity of parametrically approximate robust multi-output nonparametric frontiers providing better inference also in this setting. In Chapter 5 we use this probabilistic approach to introduce external-environmental factors in this general setting. The econometric methodology we detail and extend to the full multivariate case is particularly useful to shed light on *factors behind the patterns* and for the characterisation of the profile of single DMU and groups of DMUs and not only in providing aggregate or average tendencies.

We hope that the reading of the book has been useful for applied economists who wanted to make use of these recently introduced techniques to evaluate and explain the performance of DMUs in their field or research, without the burden of limitations of traditional methods. Nowadays the implementation of these recent techniques is facilitated by the availability of free software like FEAR (see Wilson, 2005a,b,c).

At this point, the readers should be aware that the performance evaluation is a complex task. A better understanding of the methods described in this book is a necessary step in the performance evaluation. However, a full exploitation of this toolbox is not possible without having a good knowledge of the field of application.

References

[1] Acs, Z. (ed.) (2000), *Regional innovation, knowledge and global change*. London: Pinter.

[2] Adams, J.D. and Griliches, Z. (2000), "Research Productivity in a System of Universities", in Encaoua, D. et al.(eds.), *The Economics and Econometrics of Innovation*, 105-140, Kluwer Academic Publishers, Netherlands.

[3] Afriat, S.N. (1967), "The Construction of Utility Functions from Expenditure Data", *International Economic Review*, 8, 67-77.

[4] Afriat, S.N. (1972), "Efficiency Estimation of Production Functions", *International Economic Review*, 13, 568-598.

[5] Aigner, D.J. and Chu S.F. (1968), "On Estimating the Industry Production Function", *American Economic Review*, 58, 826-839.

[6] Aigner, D.J., Lovell, C.A.K., and Schmidt P. (1977), "Formulation and Estimation of Stochastic frontier Production Function Models", *Journal of Econometrics*, 6, 21-37.

[7] Alchian, A. (1965) "Some economics of Property Rights", *Il Politico* 30:4 (December), 816-829.

[8] Alchian, A., and R. Kessel (1962) "Competition, Monopoly, and the Pursuit of Money", in *Aspects of Labor Economics*. Princeton, NJ: Princeton University Press for National Bureau of Economic Research.

[9] Allen, R., Athanassopoulos, A., Dyson, R.G. and Thanassoulis, E. (1997), "Weights restrictions and value judgements in data envelopment analysis: evolution, development and future directions", *Annals of Operations Research*, 73, 13-34.

[10] Allison, P.D. and Stewart, J.A. (1974), "Productivity differences among scientists: evidence for accumulative advantage", *American Sociological Review*, 39 (4), 596-606.

[11] Amel, D., Barnes C., Panetta F. and Salleo C. (2002), "Consolidation and efficiency in the financial sector:a review of the international evidence", Tema di discussione, Banca d'Italia n. 464.

[12] Andersen, P. and Petersen, N.C. (1993), "A procedure for ranking efficient units in data envelopment analysis", *Management Science*, 39, 1261-1264.

[13] Angulo-Meza, L. and Pereira Estellita Lins M. (2002), "Review of Methods for Increasing Discrimination in Data Envelopment Analysis", *Annals of Operational Research*, 116, 225-242.

[14] Annaert, J., van den Broeck, J., and Vennet R.V., (1999), "Determinants of Mutual Fund Underperformance: A Bayesian Stochastic FrontierApproach", paper presented at the 6EWEPA, Copenhagen, Denmark.

[15] Aragon, Y., A. Daouia and C. Thomas-Agnan (2003), A conditional quantile-based efficiency measure, Discussion paper, GREMAQ et LSP, Université de Toulouse, (http://www.univ-tlse1.fr/GREMAQ/Statistique/mesure.pdf).

[16] Aragon, Y., A. Daouia and C. Thomas-Agnan (2005), Nonparametric frontier estimation: A conditional quantile-based approach, *Econometric Theory*, 21, 358–389.

[17] Audretsch, D.B. and Feldman, M. (1996) "R&D spillovers and the geography of innovation and production", *American Economic Review*, 86(3), 630-640.

[18] Avveduto, S. (2002), "Human resources in science and technology", paper presented to the CISS Moncalieri Workshop, December 11.

[19] Banker, R.D. (1993) "Maximum likelihood, Consistency and Data Envelopment Analysis: A Statistical Foundation", *Management Science*, 39, 10, 1265-1273

[20] Banker, R.D., Chang H., and Cooper W.W. (1996), "Simulation studies of efficiency, returns to scale, and misspecification with nonlinear functions in DEA", *Annals of Operations Research*, 66, 233-253.

[21] Banker, R.D., Charnes, A., and Cooper W.W. (1984), "Some Models for Estimating Technical and scale inefficiencies in DEA", *Management Science*, 32, 1613-1627.

[22] Banker, R.D. and Maindiratta, A. (1988), "Nonparametric Analysis of Technical and Allocative Efficiens in Production", *Econometrica*, 56, 1315-1332.

[23] Banker, R.D. and R.C. Morey (1986a), "Efficiency analysis for exogeneously fixed inputs and outputs", *Operations Research*, 34(4), 513–521.

[24] Banker, R.D. and R.C. Morey (1986b), "The use of categorical variables in Data Envelopment Analysis", *Management Science*, 32 (12), 1613-1627.

[25] Barnett, V. and Lewis T. (1995). *Outliers in Statistical Data*, Chichester, Wiley.

[26] Bartelsman, E.J. and Doms M. (2000), "Understanding productivity: lessons from longitudinal microdata", *Journal of Economic literature*, Vol. XXXVIII, pp.569-594.

[27] Barth, J.R., Nolle D.E. , and Rice T.N. (1997), "Commercial Banking Structure, Regulation, and Performance: An International Comparison", in Papadimmitriou D.B. (ed.), *Modernizing Financial Systems*, New York: Oxford University Press.

[28] Barth, J.R., Dan Brumbaugh, R.Jr., and Wilcox J.A. (2000), "Policy Watch: The Repeal of Glass- Steagall and the Advent of Broad Banking", *Journal of Economic Perspectives* 14, 191-204.

[29] Basso, A., S. Funari, (2001), "A Data Envelopment Analysis Approach to Measure the Mutual Fund Performance", *European Journal of Operational Research*, 135 (3), 477-492.

[30] Berger, A. N., Kashyap A.K., and Scalise J. M. (1995), "The Transformation of the U.S. Banking Industry: What A Long, Strange Trip It's Been," Brookings Papers on Economic Activity, 2, 55-218.

[31] Berger, A.N. and Humphrey, D.B. (1997), "Efficiency of Financial Institutions: International Survey and Directions for Future Research", *European Journal of Operational Research* 98, 175-213.

[32] Berger, A.N., Cummins, J.D. and Weiss, M.A. (1997), "The Coexistence of Multiple Distribution Systems for Financial Services: The Case of Property-Liability Insurance," *Journal of Business* 70, 515-546.

[33] Bergson, A. (1961), *National Income of the Soviet Union since 1928*. Cambridge, MA: Harvard University Press.

[34] Bertoletti P. (2005), "Elasticities of Substitution and Complementarity: A Synthesis", *Journal of Productivity Analysis*, 24(2), 183 - 196.

[35] Bessent, A. and Bessent, W.E. (1980). "Determining the comparative efficiency of schools through DEA", *Educational Administration Quarterly*, 16, 57-75.

[36] Bessent A., Bessent W., Kennington J., and Reagan B. (1982), "An Application of mathematical programming to assess productivity in the Houston independent school district", *Management Science*, 28, 1355-1367.

[37] Bickel, P.J. and Freedman, D.A. (1981), "Some Asymptotic Theory for the Bootstrap", *Annals of Statistics*, 9, 1196-1217.

[38] Bjurek, H. Hjalmarsson, L. and Forsund, F.R. (1990), "Deterministic Parametric and Nonparametric Estimation of Efficiency in Service Production: A Comparison", *Journal of Econometrics*, 46, 213-228.

[39] Bogetoft, P. (2000), "DEA and Activity Planning under Asymmetric Information", *Journal of Productivity Analysis*, 13 (1), 7-48.

[40] Boles, J.N. (1966), "Efficiency Squared-Efficient Computation of Efficiency Indexes", *Proceedings of the Thirty Ninth Annual Meeting of the Western Farm Economics Associations*, 137-142.

[41] Bonaccorsi A. and Daraio, C. (2003a), "A robust nonparametric approach to the analysis of scientific productivity", *Research Evaluation*, 12 (1), 47-69.

[42] Bonaccorsi A. and Daraio, C. (2003b), "Age effects in scientific productivity. The case of the Italian National Research Council (CNR)", *Scientometrics*, 58 (1), 47-88.

[43] Bonaccorsi A. and Daraio, C. (2004), "Econometric approaches to the analysis of productivity of R&D systems. Production functions and production frontiers", in H.F. Moed, W. Glanzel and U. Schmoch (edited by), *Handbook of Quantitative Science and Technology Research*, Kluwer Academic Publishers, 51-74.

[44] Bonaccorsi A. and Daraio, C. (2005), "Exploring size and agglomeration effects on public research productivity", *Scientometrics*, Vol. 63, No. 1, 87-120.

[45] Bonaccorsi, A., Daraio C. and Simar, L. (2006), "Advanced Indicators of Productivity of Universities. An application of Robust Nonparametric Methods to Italian data", *Scientometrics*, Vol. 66, No. 2, 389-410.

[46] Bressler, R.G. (1966), "The Measurement of Productive Efficiency", *Proceedings of the Thirty Ninth Annual Meeting of the Western Farm Economics Associations*, 129-136.

[47] Briec, W., Kerstens, K., and Lesourd J.B., (2004), "Single Period Markowitz Portfolio Selection, Performance Gauging and Duality: A variation on the Luenberger's Shortage Function", *Journal of Optimization Theory and Applications*, 120(1), 1-27.

[48] Briec,W., Kerstens K. and Vanden Eeckaut P.,(2004a), "Non-convex Technologies and Cost Functions: Definitions, Duality and Nonparametric Tests of Convexity", *Journal of Economics*, 81 (2), 155-192.

[49] Briec,W., Kerstens K. and Vanden Eeckaut P.,(2004b), "Nonparametric Disposability Assumptions and A New Approach to Measure Congestion", paper presented at the 21 JMA 2004, Lille.

[50] Briec, W., and Lesourd J.B., (2000), "The Efficiency of Investment Fund Management: An Applied Stochastic Frontier Model, in: C.L. Dunis (ed.), *Advances in Quantitative Asset Management*, Kluwer, Boston, 41-59.

[51] Cantarelli D. (2005), "Elasticities of Complementarity and Substitution in Some Functional Forms. A comparative Review", Working Paper no. 3.157, University of Salerno.

[52] Castells, M. and Hall, P. (1994), *Technopoles of the world. The making of the 21st century industrial complexes*. London: Routledge.

[53] Caves, D.W., Christensen, L.R. and Diewert, W.E. (1982), "The Economic Theory of Index Numbers of the Measurement of Input, Output and Productivity", *Economerica*, 50, 1393-1414.

[54] Cazals, C., Florens, J.P. and Simar, L. (2002), "Nonparametric frontier estimation: a robust approach", *Journal of Econometrics*, 106, 1-25.

[55] Cesari, R. Panetta, F. (2002), "The performance of the Italian equity funds", *Journal of Banking and Finance*, 26, 99-126.

[56] Chambers, R.G., Chung Y. and Färe, R. (1996), "Benefit and distance functions", *Journal of Economic Theory*, 70, 407-419.

[57] Chambers, R. G., and Quiggin J.,(2000), *Uncertainty, Production, Choice and Agency: The State-Contingent Approach*, Cambridge University Press, New York.

[58] Chambers, R. G. (2004), "Productivity Measurement Under Uncertainty", invited paper at the 21 JMA 2004, Lille.

[59] Charnes, A. and Cooper, W.W. (1985), "Preface to Topics in Data Envelopment Analysis", *Annals of Operations Research*, 2, 59-94.

[60] Charnes, A. and Cooper, W.W. (1961), *Management Models and Industrial Applications of Linear Programming*, Wiley, New York.

[61] Charnes, A., Cooper, W.W., Lewin A.Y and Seiford L.M (1994), (edited by), *Data Envelopment Analysis. Theory, Methodology and Applications*, Kluwer Academic Publishers, Norwell USA.

[62] Charnes, A., Cooper, W.W., and Rhodes, E. (1978), "Measuring the Efficiency of Decision Making Units", *European Journal of Operational Research*, 2, 429-444.

[63] Chavas, J.-P. and Cox, T.L. (1988), "A Nonparametric Analysis of Agricultural Technology", *American Journal of Agricultural Economics*, 70, 303-310.

[64] Chavas, J.-P. and Cox, T.L. (1990), "A Non-Parametric Analysis of Productivity: The Case of U.S. and Japanese Manufacturing", *American Economic Review*, 80, 450-464.

[65] Cherchye, L., Kuosmanen T. P., and Post G.T., (2000) "What is the economic meaning of FDH? A replay to Thrall", *Journal of Productivity Analysis*, 13, 263-267.

[66] Cherchye, L., Kuosmanen, T. and Post, G.T. (2001), "Nonparametric Production Analysis under Alternative Price Conditions", CES Discussion Paper 01.05.

[67] Chevalier, J., and Ellison G. (1999a), "Are some Mutual Fund Managers Better Than Others? Cross-sectional Patterns in Behavior and Performance", *Journal of Finance*, 54 (3), 875-898.

[68] Chevalier, J., and Ellison G. (1999b), "Career concerns of Mutual Fund Managers", *The Quarterly Journal of Economics*, 114 (2), 389-432(44).

[69] Christensen L.R., Jorgenson D. W., and Lau L.J., (1973), "Transcendental Logarithmic Production Frontiers", *Review of Economics and Statistics*, 55, 28-45.

[70] Clark, G.L., Feldman M.P. and Gertler M.S., edited by, (2000), *The Oxford Handbook of Economic Geography*, Oxford University Press, NY.

[71] Consiglio Nazionale delle Ricerche (1998), CNR Report 1998. CNR Roma.

[72] Coelli, T. (1996), *Assessing the Performance of Australian Universities using Data Envelopment Analysis*, mimeo, Centre for Efficiency and Productivity Analysis, University of New England.

[73] Coelli, T. (2000), "On the econometric estimation of the distance function representation of a production technology", CORE Discussion Paper 2000-42, Université Catholiqué de Louvain, and CEPA, School of Economic Studies, University of New England.

[74] Coelli, T. and Perelman S., (1996), "Efficiency Measurement, Multiple-output Technologies and Distance Functions: with application to European Railways", CREPP Working Paper no. 96/05, Université de Liege, Belgium.

[75] Coelli, T. and Perelman S., (1999), "A comparison of parametric and nonparametric distance functions: with application to European railways", *European Journal of Operational Research*, 117, 326-339.

[76] Coelli, T. and Perelman S., (2000), "Technical efficiency of European railways: a distance function approach", *Applied Economics*, 32, 1967-1976.

[77] Coelli, T., Rao, D.S.P. and Battese, G.E. (1998), *An Introduction to Efficiency Analysis*, Kluwer Academic Publishers.

[78] Collins, P.M.D. (1991), *Quantitative assessment of Departmental Research*, SEPSU Policy study no. 5, London: The Royal Society.

[79] Cooke, P. and Morgan K. (1998) *The associational economy. Firms, regions and innovation*. Oxford: Oxford University Press.

[80] Cooper, W.W., Li S., Seiford L.M., Tone K., Thrall R.M., and Zhu J. (2001), "Sensitivity and Stability Analysis in DEA: Some Recent Developments", *Journal of Productivity Analysis*, 15, 217-246.

[81] Cooper, W.W., Seiford L.M., and Tone K. (2000), *Data Envelopment Analysis: A Comprehensive Text with Models, Applications, References and DEA-Solver Software*,Kluwer Academic Publishers, Boston.

[82] Cornwell C., Schmidt P., and Sickles R. C. (1990), "Productivity Frontiers with cross sectional and time series variation in efficiency levels", *Journal of Econometrics*, 46, 185-200.

[83] Cummins, J.D., Turchetti, G. and Weiss, M. (1996), "Productivity and Technical Efficiency in the Italian Insurance Industry," Working paper, Wharton Financial Institutions Center, University of Pennsylvania, Philadelphia.

[84] Cummins, J.D. and Weiss, M.A. (2001), "Analyzing Firm Performance in the Insurance Industry Using Frontier Efficiency Methods," in Georges Dionne (ed.), *Handbook of Insurance Economics*, Boston: Kluwer Academic Publishers.

[85] Cummins, J.D., Weiss, M.A., and Zi, H. (1999), "Organizational Form and Efficiency: An Analysis of Stock and Mutual Property-Liability Insurers", *Management Science* 45, 1254-1269.

[86] Daniel, H.D. and Fisch, R. (1990), "Research performance evaluation in the German university sector", *Scientometrics*, Vol. 19 (5-6), 349-361.

[87] Dantzig, G.B. (1963), *Linear Programming and its Extensions*, Princeton University Press, Princeton.

[88] Daouia, A. and L. Simar (2004), Nonparametric Efficiency Analysis: A Multivariate Conditional Quantile Approach, Discussion paper #0419, Institut de Statistique, Université Catholique de Louvain, Louvain-la-Neuve, Belgium, forthcoming in *Journal of Econometrics*.

[89] Daouia, A. and L. Simar (2005), Robust Nonparametric Estimators of Monotone Boundaries, *Journal of Multivariate Analysis*, 96, 311–331.

[90] Daouia, A., J.P. Florens and L. Simar (2005), Functional Convergence of Quantile-type Frontiers with Application to Parametric Approximations, Discussion paper 0538, Institut de Statistique, UCL.

[91] Daraio C. (2003), *Comparative Efficiency and Productivity Analysis based on non-parametric and robust nonparametric methods. Methodology and Applications*, Doctoral dissertation, Scuola Superiore Sant'Anna, Pisa (Italy).

[92] Daraio C., Simar, L. (2004), "A Robust Nonparametric Approach to Evaluate and Explain the Performance of Mutual Funds", Discussion Paper no. 0412, Institut de Statistique, UCL, Belgium, *forthcoming* in *European Journal of Operational Research.*

[93] Daraio C. and Simar, L. (2005a), "Introducing Environmental Variables in Nonparametric Frontier Models: a Probabilistic Approach", *Journal of Productivity Analysis*, 24 (1), pp. 93-121.

[94] Daraio C. and Simar, L. (2005b), "Conditional Nonparametric Frontier Models for Convex and Non Convex Technologies: A unifying Approach", Discussion Paper no. 0502, Institut de Statistique, UCL, Belgium, *forthcoming* in *Journal of Productivity Analysis.*

[95] David, P.A. (1995), "Positive Feedbacks and Research Productivity in Science: Reopening another Black Box", in Granstrand O. (eds), *Economics of Technology*, North-Holland, Amsterdam.

[96] de Alessi, L. (1974) "An economic analysis of government ownership and regulation: theory and the evidence from the electric power industry", *Public Choice*, 19:1, 1-42.

[97] de Alessi, L. (1983) "Property rights, transaction costs, and X-efficiency: an essay in economic theory", *American Economic Review*, 73:1 (March), 64-81.

[98] DEAsoft, software developed and marketed by Performance Improvement Managment Ltd, website: www.deasoftware.co.uk .

[99] Debreu, G. (1951), "The Coefficient of Resource Utilization", *Econometrica*, 19, 273-292.

[100] Deckle, R. (1988), "The Japanese 'Big Bang' financial reforms and marketing implications", *Journal of Asian Economics*, 9, 237-249.

[101] Deprins, D. and Simar, L. (1983), "On Farrel Measures of Technical Efficiency", *Recherches économiques de Louvain*, 49, 123-137.

[102] Deprins, D. and L. Simar (1985), A Note on the Asymptotic Relative Efficiency of the M.L.E. in a Linear Model with Gamma Disturbances, *Journal of Econometrics*, 27, 383–386.

[103] Deprins, D. and Simar, L. (1988), "Mesures d'efficacité de réseaux de chemin de fer", in *Gestion de l' économie et de l'entreprise. L'approche Quantitative*, Edited by CORE, De Boeck-Wesmael, Bruxelles, pp. 321-344.

[104] Deprins, D., Simar L. and Tulkens H. (1984), "Measuring labor-efficiency in post offices", in Marchand, M., Pestieau, P. and Tulkens, H. (eds.) *The Performance of public enterprises - Concepts and Measurement*, Amsterdam, North-Holland, 243-267.

[105] Detzel L.F., R. Weigand (1998), "Explaining Persistence in Mutual Fund Performance", *Financial Services Review*, 7 (1), 45-55.

[106] Diewert, W.E. and Parkan, C. (1983), "Linear Programming Tests of Regularity Conditions for Production Frontiers", in Eichhorn, W., Henn, R., Neumann, K. and Shephard, R.W. (eds.) *Quantitative Studies on Production and Prices*, Wuerzburg and Vienna, Physica-Verlag.

[107] Diewert, W E, (1992), "The Measurement of Productivity", *Bulletin of Economic Research*, vol. 44(3), 163-198.

[108] Dorfman R., Samuelson P. and Solow R. (1958), *Linear Programming and Economic Analysis*, McGraw Hill Text.

[109] Efron, B. (1979), "Bootstrap Methods: another look at the Jackknife", *The Annals of Statistics*, Vol. 7, No.1, 1-26.

[110] Efron, B., and Tibshirani, R.J. (1993), *An introduction to the Bootstrap*, Chapman and Hall, NY.

[111] Emrouznejad A.(2001), "An extensive Bibliogaphy of Data Envelopment Analysis (DEA) Volume I-V", http://www.warwick.ac.uk/ ~ bsrlu.

[112] Färe, R. (1975), "Efficiency and the Production Function", *Zeitschrift fuer Nationaloekonomie*, 35, 317-324.

[113] Färe, R., Grosskopf, S., Lindgren,B. and Roos, P. (1989), "Productivity Developments in Swedish Hospitals: A Malmquist Output Index Approach", in Charnes, A, Cooper, W.W., Lewin, A. and Seiford, L. (eds.), *Data Envelopment Analysys: Theory, Methodology and Applications*, Boston: Kluwer Academic Publishers.

[114] Färe, R., Grosskopf, S. and Lovell, C.A.K. (1985), *The Measurement of Efficiency of Production*, Boston: Kluwer-Nijhoff Publishing.

[115] Färe, R., Grosskopf, S. and Lovell, C.A.K. (1992), "Indirect Productivity Measurement", *Journal of Productivity Analysis*, 2, 283-298.

[116] Färe, R., Grosskopf, S. and Lovell, C.A.K. (1994), *Production Frontiers*, Cambridge University Press, Cambridge.

[117] Färe, R., Grosskopf, S. and Russell, R.R. (1998), *Index Numbers: Essays in Honour of Sten Malmquist*, Boston: Kluwer Academic Publishers.

[118] Färe, R., S. Grosskopf, C.A. K. Lovell and C. Pasurka (1989), "Multilateral Productivity Comparisons when some Outputs are Undesirable: a Nonparametric Approach", *Review of Economics and Statistics* 71 (1), 90-98.

[119] Färe, R., Grosskopf, S. and Weber, W. (1989), "Measuring school district performance", *Public Finance Quarterly*, 17, 409-428.

[120] Färe, R., Grosskopf, S., (2004), *New Directions: Efficiency and Productivity*, Kluwer Academic Publishers.

[121] Färe, R. and Lovell, C.A.K. (1978), "Measuring the Technical Efficiency of Production", *Journal of Economic Theory*, 19, 150-162.

[122] Färe, R. and Primont, D. (1996), "The opportunity cost of duality", *Journal of Productivity Analysis*, 7, 213-224.

[123] Färe, R. and V. Zelenyuk (2003), "On Aggregate Farrell Efficiency Scores", *European Journal of Operations Research* 146:3, 615-620.

[124] Farrell, M.J. (1957), "The measurement of the Productive Efficiency", *Journal of the Royal Statistical Society*, Series A, CXX, Part 3, 253-290.

[125] Farrell, M.J. (1959), "Convexity assumption in theory of competitive markets", *Journal of Political Economy*, 67, 377-391.

[126] Farrell, M.J. and Fieldhouse, M. (1962), "Estimating Efficient Production Functions under Increasing Return to Scale", *Journal of the Royal Statistical Society*, Series A, CXXV, Part 2, 252-267.

[127] Feldman, M.P. (2000), " Location and Innovation: the New Economic Geography of Innovation, Spillovers, and Agglomeration", in Clark, G.L., Feldman M.P. and Gertler M.S., edited by, , *The Oxford Handbook of Economic Geography*, Oxford University Press, NY, 373-394.

[128] Ferrier G.D., and Hirschberg J. G. (1997), "Bootstrapping Confidence Intervals for Linear Programming Efficiency Scores: with an illustration using Italian Bank Data", *The Journal of Productivity Analysis*, 8, 19-33.

[129] Ferrier G.D., and Hirschberg J. G. (1999), "Can we bootstrap DEA scores?", *The Journal of Productivity Analysis*, 11.

[130] Fischer, I. (1922), *The Making of Index Numbers*, Boston: Houghton Mifflin.

[131] Florens, J.P. and Simar, L. (2005), "Parametric Approximations of Nonparametric Frontier", *Journal of Econometrics*, 124, 91-116.

[132] Forsund, F.R., and N. Sarafoglou (2002), "On the origins of Data Envelopment Analysis", *Journal of Productivity Analysis*, 17 (1/2), 23–40.

[133] Fortin R., S. Michelson, and J. Wagner (1999), "Does Mutual Fund Manager Tenure Matter?" *Journal of Financial Planning*, August, 12.

[134] Freedman, D.A. (1981), "Bootstrapping regression models", *Annals of Statistics*, Vol 9, 6, 1218–1228.

[135] Fried, H.O, Lovell, C.A.K. and Schmidt S.S. (1993), edited by, *The measurement of Productive Efficiency. Techniques and Applications*, New York Oxford, Oxford University Press.

[136] Fried, H.O, Lovell, C.A.K. and Schmidt S.S. (2006), edited by, *The Measurement of Productive Efficiency*, 2nd Edition, New York Oxford, Oxford University Press.

[137] Fried, H.O., C.A.K. Lovell, S.S. Schmidt and S. Yaisawarng (2002), "Accounting for environmental effects and statistical noise in Data Envelopment Analysis", *Journal of Productivity Analysis*, 17 (1/2), 157–174.

[138] Fried, H.O., S.S. Schmidt and S. Yaisawarng (1999), "Incorporating the operating environment into a nonparametric measure of technical efficiency", *Journal of Productivity Analysis*, 12, 249–267.

[139] Garfield, E. and Dorof, W.A. (1992), "Citation data: their use as quantitative indicators for science and technology evaluation and policy making", *Science and Public Policy*, 19 (5), 321-327.

[140] Gattoufi, S., M. Oral, and A. Reisman (2004), "Data envelopment analysis literature: A bibliography update (1951-2001)", *Journal of Socio-Economic Planning Sciences*, Vol.38, Issues 2-3, 159-229.

[141] Gijbels, I., Mammen, E., Park, B.U., and Simar L. (1999), "On Estimation of Monotone and Concave Frontier Functions", *Journal of the American Statistical Association*, 94, 220-228.

[142] Girod, O. and Triantis, K. (1999), "The Evaluation of Productive Efficiency Useing a Fuzzy Mathematical Programming Approach: The Case of the Newspaper Preprint Insertion Process", *IEEE Transactions on Engineering Management*, 46, 1-15.

[143] Golec, J. (1996), "The Effects of Mutual Fund Managers' Characteristics on Their Portfolio Performance, Risk and Fees", *Financial Services Review*, 5 (2), 133-148.

[144] Goto, I. (1999), "Japan: The Finalization of the Big Bang," *International Financial Law Review* (July).

[145] Greene, W. H. (1980), "Maximum likelihood estimation of econometric frontier functions", *Journal of Econometrics*, 13 (1), 27–56.

[146] Greene, W.H. (1990), "A Gamma-Distributed Stochastic Frontier Model", *Journal of Econometrics*, 46:1/2, 141-164.

[147] Greene, W.H. (1993),The econometric approach to efficiency analysis, in H. Fried, K. Lovell and S. Schmidt (eds) *The Measurement of Productive Efficiency: Techniques and Applications*, Oxford University Press.

[148] Grinblatt, M. and Titman S. (1995), "Performance Evaluation", in R.Jarrow, V. Maksimovic, W.T. Ziemba (eds.), *Handbooks in OR & MS: Finance*, vol 9, Amsterdam, Elsevier, 581-609.

[149] Grosskopf S., Margaritis D. and Valdmanis V. (1995), "Estimating output substitutability of hospital services: A distance function approach", *European Journal of Operational Research*, 80, 575-587.

[150] Grosskopf, S.(1996), "Statistical Inference and Nonparametric Efficiency: A selective Survey", *The Journal of Productivity Analysis*, 7, 161-176.

[151] Grosskopf, S., Hayes, K., Taylor, L. and Weber, W. (1997), "Budget constrained frontier measures of fiscal equity and efficiency in schooling, *Review of Economics and Statistics*, 79, 116-124.

[152] Grosskopf, S. (2003), "Some Remarks on Productivity and its Decompositions", *Journal of Productivity Analysis*, 20, 459-474.

[153] Grosskopf, S. and Moutray, C. (2001) "Evaluating performance in Chicago public high schools in the wake of decentralization", *Economics of Education Review*, 20, 1-14.

[154] Grosskopf, S., Hayes, K., Taylor L. and Weber W. (1999) "Anticipating the consequences of school reform: a new use of DEA", *Management Science*, 45, 608-620.

[155] Hall, P. and Simar, L. (2002), "Estimating a changepoint, boundary or frontier in the presence of observation error", *Journal of the American Statistical Association*, 97, 523-534.

[156] Halme, M., Joro, T., Korhonen, P., Salo, S. and Wallenius, J. (2000), "Value efficiency analysis for incorporating preference information in DEA", *Management Science*, 45, 103-115.

[157] Hanoch, G. and Rotschild, M. (1972), "Testing the Assumptions of Production Theory: A Nonparametric Approach", *Journal of Political Economy*, 80, 256-275.

[158] Hansmann, H. (1988) "Ownership of the firm", *Journal of Law, Economics and Organization*, 4:2 (Fall), 267-304.

[159] Härdle, W. (1990), *Applied Nonparametric Regression*, Cambridge University Press, Cambridge.

[160] Härdle, W. and L. Simar (2003), *Applied Multivariate Statistical Analysis*, Springer-Verlag, Berlin.

[161] Harker P.T. and S.A. Zenios (2000), edited by, *Performance of Financial institutions. Efficiency, Innovation, Regulation*, Cambridge University Press, UK.

[162] Henderson, D.J. and L. Simar (2005), "A Fully Nonparametric Stochastic Frontier Model for Panel Data", Discussion paper 0525, Institut de Statistique, UCL.

[163] Hess, T. and Trauth, T. (1998), "Towards A Single European Insurance Market", *International Journal of Business* 3, 89-100.

[164] Hicks, J.R. (1935), "The theory of Monopoly: A Survey", *Econometrica*, 3:1 (January), 1-20.

[165] Hogan, A.M.B. (1995), "Regulation of the Single European Insurance Market", *Journal of Insurance Regulation*, 13, 329-358.

[166] Holbrook J.A.D. (1992a), "Basic indicators of scientific and technological performance", *Science and Public Policy*, 19 (5), 267-273.

[167] Holbrook J.A.D. (1992b), "Why measure science? ", *Science and Public Policy*, 19 (5), 262-266.

[168] Holmstrom, B. R., and J. Tirole (1989), "The theory of the firm", in R. Schmalensee and R. D. Willig, eds., *Handbook of Industrial Organization*, Volume I. Amsterdam: Elsevier Science Publishers.

[169] Ippolito, R.A. (1993), "On Studies of Mutual Fund Performance, 1962-1991", *Financial Analysts Journal*, 49 (1), 42-50.

[170] Jaffe, A.B., Trajtenberg M. and Henderson R. (1993) "Geographic localization of knowledge spillovers as evidenced by patent citations", *Quarterly Journal of Economics*, 577-598.

[171] Jeong, S.O. , B. U. Park and L. Simar (2006), "Nonparametric conditional efficiency measures: asymptotic properties". Discussion paper 0604, Institut de Statistique, UCL.

[172] Jeong, S.O. and L. Simar (2005), "Linearly interpolated FDH efficiency score for nonconvex frontiers", Discussion 0501, Institut de Statistique, UCL.

[173] Johnston R. (1994), "Effects of resource concentration on research performance", *Higher Education*, 28, 25-37.

[174] Kao, C. and Liu, S.T. (1999), "Fuzzy Efficiency Measures in Data Envelopment Analysis", *Fuzzy Sets and Systems*, forthcoming.

[175] Khorana, A.(1996) "Top Management Turnover: An Empirical Investigation of Mutual Fund Managers", *Journal of Financial Economics*, 40, 403-427.

[176] King, D. (2004), "The Scientific impact of Nations", *Nature*, 430, 311-316.

[177] Kneip, A. and Simar, L. (1996), "A general framework for frontier estimation with panel data", *The Journal of Productivity Analysis*, 7, 187-212.

[178] Kneip, A., Park B.U. and Simar L. (1998), "A Note on the Convergence of Nonparametric DEA Estimators for Production Efficiency Scores", *Econometric Theory*, 14, 783-793.

[179] Kneip, A., Simar, L. and Wilson, P.W. (2003), "Asymptotics for DEA Estimators in Nonparametric Frontier Models", Discussion Paper no. 0317, Institut de Statistique, UCL.

[180] Koopmans, T.C. (1951), "An Analysis of Production as an Efficient Combination of Activities", in Koopmans T.C. (Ed.), *Activity Analysis of Production and Allocation*, Cowles Commission for Research in Economics, Monograph No. 13, Wiley, New York.

[181] Koopmans, T.C. (1957), *Three Essays on the State of Economic Science*. New York: McGraw Hill.

[182] Korhonen, P., Tainio, R. and Wallenius J. (2001), "Value efficiency analysis of academic research", *European Journal of Operational Research*, 130, 121-132.

[183] Kostoff R.N. (1994), "Performance measures for government-sponsored research: overview and background", *Scientometrics*, Vol. 36, n. 3.

[184] Korostelev, A., Simar L. and Tsybakov A.B. (1995), "Efficient estimation of monotone boundaries", *The Annals of Statistics*, 23, 476-489.

[185] Krugman P. (1991), "Increasing returns and economic geography", *Journal of Political Economy*, 99(3), 483-499.

[186] Kumbhakar S. C., Lovell C.A.K. (2000), *Stochastic Frontier Analysis*, Cambridge University Press, UK.

[187] Kumbhakar, S.C. , Park, B.U., Simar, L. and E.G. Tsionas (2004), "Nonparametric stochastic frontiers: a local likelihood approach", Discussion paper 0417, Institut de Statistique, UCL, forthcoming in *Journal of Econometrics*.

[188] Kuosmanen, T. and Post, G.T. (2001), "Measuring Economic Efficiency with Incomplete Price Information: With an Application to European Commercial Banks", *European Journal of Operational Research*, 134 (1), 43-58.

[189] Land, K.C., Lovell C.A.K., and Thore S. (1993), "Chance- Constrained Data Envelopment Analysis", *Managerial and Decision Economics*, 14 (6), 541-554.

[190] Laredo, P., Mustar P. (eds), (2001), *Research and Innovation policies in the new global economy. An international comparative analysis*, Edward Elgar.

[191] Leibenstein, H. (1966), "Allocative efficiency vs. 'X-efficiency'", *American Economic Review* 56 (3), 392-415.

[192] Leibenstein, H. (1975), "Aspects of the X-efficiency theory of the firm", *Bell Journal of Economics*, 6, 580-606.

[193] Leibenstein, H. (1976), *Beyond economic man*. Cambridge, MA: Harvard University Press.

[194] Leibenstein, H. (1978), "X-Inefficiency exists - Reply to an Xorcist", *American Economic Review* 68 (1), 203-211.

[195] Leibenstein, H. (1987), *Inside the firm*. Cambridge, MA: Harvard University Press.

[196] Lemak D., P. Satish (1996), "Mutual Fund Performance and Managers' Terms of Service: Are There Performance Differences?", *The Journal of Investing*, Winter ,pp. 59-63.

[197] Leontief, W.W. (1941), *The Structure of the American Economy 1919-1939*. New York: Oxford University Press.

[198] Leontief, W.W. (1953), *Studies in the Structure of the American Economy*. New York: Oxford University Press.

[199] Levin, S.G. and P. E. Stephan (1991), "Research productivity over the life cycle: evidence for academic scientists", *American Economic Review*, 81 (1), March, 114-32.

[200] Lewin, A. Y. and Minton J.W. (1986), "Determining Organizational Effectiveness: Another Look and an Agenda for Research", *Management Science*, 32 (5), 514-538.

[201] Lewison, G. (1998), "New bibliometric techniques for the evaluation of medical schools", *Scientometrics*, Vol. 41, 5-16.

[202] Li, X.B. and Reeves, G.R. (1999), "A multiple criteria approach to data envelopment analysis", *European Journal of Operational Research*, 115, 507-517.

[203] Lindsay, C.M. (1976), "A theory of government enterprise", *Journal of Political Economy*, 84, 1061-1077.

[204] Lovell, C.A.K. (1993), "Production Frontiers and Productive Efficiency," in H.O. Fried, C.A.K. Lovell, and S.S. Schmidt, eds., The Measurement of Productive Efficiency, New York, Oxford University Press.

[205] Lovell, C.A.K. (2001), "Future Research Opportunities in Efficiency and Productivity Analysis", in A. Alvarez (ed.), *La Medición de la Eficiencia Productiva*, Pirámide.

[206] Lovell, C.A.K. (2003), "The Decomposition of Malmquist Productivity Indexes", *Journal of Productivity Analysis*, 20, 437-458.

[207] Luenberger, D.G. (1992), "Benefit functions and duality", *Journal of Mathematical Economics*, 21, 461-481.

[208] Luwel, M. (2004),"The Use of Input Data in the Performance Analysis of R&D Systems. Potentialities and Pitfalls", in H.F. Moed, W. Glanzel and U. Schmoch (edited by), *Handbook of Quantitative Science and Technology Research*, Kluwer Academic Publishers, 315-338.

[209] Malmquist, S. (1953), "Index Numbers and Indifference Surfaces", *Trabajos de Estatistica*, 4, 209-242.

[210] Markowitz, H. (1952), "Portfolio Selection", *Journal of Finance*, 77-91.

[211] Markowitz, H. (1959), *Portfolio Selection. Efficiency diversification of investments*, Cowles Foundation for research in Economics at Yale University, John Wiley and sons, Inc.

[212] Martin, B.R. (1996), "The use of multiple indicators in the assessment of basic research", *Scientometrics*, Vol. 36, 343.

[213] Martin, S. (2002), *Advanced industrial economics*, Blackwell Publishers, Malden.

[214] Mas-Colell A., Whinston M.D., Green J.R. (1995) *Microeconomic Theory*, Oxford University Press, USA.

[215] May R. (1993), "The scientific wealth of nations", *Science*, 275, 793-796.

[216] Meeusen, W., Van den Broeck J. (1977), "Efficiency Estimation from Cobb-Douglas Production Functions With Composed Error", *International Economic Review*, 18, 435-444.

[217] Merton, R.K. (1968), "The Matthew effect in science", Science, 159 Jan-Mar, 56-63.

[218] Milgrom P., Roberts J. (1992), *Economics, organization and management*, Prentice Hall, Englewood Cliffs.

[219] Moed H.F., W. Glanzel and U. Schmoch (2004)(edited by), *Handbook of Quantitative Science and Technology Research*, Kluwer Academic Publishers.

[220] Moed, H.F., van Leeuwen T.N. (1996), "Impact factors can mislead", *Nature*, 381:186.

[221] Moorsteen, R.H. (1961), "On measuring Productive Potential and Relative Efficiency", *Quarterly Journal of Economics*, 75 (3), 451-467.

[222] Morey, M.R., Morey, R.C. (1999), "Mutual fund performance appraisals: a multi-horizon perspective with endogenous benchmarking", *Omega, Int. J. Mgmt Sci.*, 27, 241-258.

[223] Morroni, M. (2006), *Knowledge, Scale and Transactions in the Theory of the Firm*, *forthcoming* Cambridge University Press, Cambridge.

[224] Mouchart M., and L. Simar (2002), "Efficiency Analysis of Air Controllers: First Insights", Consulting Report No. 0202, Institut de Statistique, UCL, Belgium.

[225] Mullins N., Snizek W., Oehler K. (1988), The structural analysis of a scientific paper, in Van Raan A.F.J., *Handbook of Quantitative Studies of Science and Technology*, pp. 81-105, North Holland, Amsterdam.

[226] Murthi, B., Choi, Y. and Desai, P. (1997), "Efficiency of Mutual Funds and Portfolio Performance Measurement: a Nonparametric Measurement", *European Journal of Operational Research*, 98, 408-418.

[227] Nadaraya, E.A. (1964), "On estimating regression", *Theory of Probability Applications*, 9, 141-142.

[228] Narin F. (1987), "Bibliometric techniques in the evaluation of research programs", *Science and Public Policy*, Vol. 14, n. 1, pp. 99-106.

[229] Narin, F., Hamilton, K.S. (1996), "Bibliometric performance measures", *Scientometrics*, Vol. 36, 293-310.

[230] Narin F., Olivastro D., Stevens K. A. (1994), "Bibliometrics - Theory, Practice and Problems", *Evaluation Review*, Vol. 18, n. 1.

[231] Niskanen, W.A. Jr. (1971), *Bureaucracy and representative government*. Chicago, Aldine Press.

[232] Okubo Y. (1997), "Bibliometric indicators and analysis of research systems: methods and examples", STI Working Papers 1997/1, OECD, Paris.

[233] Olesen, O.B., and Petersen, N.C. (1995), "Change constrained Efficiency Evaluation", *Management Science*, 41(3), 442-457.

[234] Park, B.U. and Simar, L. (1994), "Efficient Semiparametric Estimation in a Stochastic Frontier Model", *Journal of the American Statistical Association*, 89,no. 427, 929-935.

[235] Park, B.U. Sickles, R.C., and Simar, L. (1998), "Stochastic panel frontiers: A semiparametric approach", *Journal of Econometrics*, 84, 273-301.

[236] Park, B.U., R. Sickles and L. Simar (2003a), "Semiparametric Efficient Estimation of AR(1) Panel Data Models", *Journal of Econometrics*, vol 117, 2, 279-309. Corrigendum to "Semiparametric-efficient estimation of AR(1) panel data models", *Journal of Econometrics*, vol 117, 2, 311.

[237] Park, B.U., R. Sickles and L. Simar (2003b), "Semiparametric Efficient Estimation in Dynamic Panel Data Models", Discussion Paper 0315, Institut de Statistique, UCL, *forthcoming* in *Journal of Econometrics*.

[238] Park, B.U., Simar, L. and Weiner C. (2000), "The FDH Estimator for Productivity Efficiency Scores: Asymptotic Properties", *Econometric Theory*, 16, 855-877.

[239] Park, B.U., L. Simar and V. Zelenyuk (2006), "Local Likelihood Estimation of Truncated Regression and Its Partial Derivatives: Theory and Application". Discussion paper 0606, Institut de Statistique, UCL.

[240] Pedraja-Chaparro, R., Salinas-Jimenes, J., Smith, J. and Smith, P. (1997), "On the role of weight restrictions in DEA", *Journal of Productivity Analysis*, 8, 215-230.

[241] Perelman S., Santin D. (2005), "Measuring educational efficiency at student level with parametric stochastic distance functions: An application to Spanish PISA results", paper presented at the X EWEPA, Brussels, June-July 2005.

[242] Porrini D. (2004), "Information exchange as Collusive Behaviour: Evidence from an Antitrust Intervention in the Italian Insurance Market", *Geneva Papers on Risk and Insurance*, 29 (2), 219-233.

[243] Porter G., J. Trifts, (1998) "Performance Persistence of Experienced Mutual Fund Managers", *Financial Services Review*, 7 (1), 57-68.

[244] Pyke, F. Becattini G., Sengenberger W. (1986), "Industrial districts and inter-firm co-operation in Italy", International Labour Office, Geneve.

[245] Ramsden P. (1994), "Describing and explaining research productivity", *Higher Education*, Vol. 28.

[246] Ray, S.C. and Bhadra D. (1993), "Nonparametric Tests of Cost Minimizing Behavior: A Study of Indian Farms", *American Journal of Agricultural Economics*, 73 (Nov), 990-999.

[247] Ray, S.C. (2004), *Data Envelopment Analysis, Theory and Techniques for Economics and Operations Research*, Cambridge University Press, US.

[248] Richmond, J. (1974), "Estimating the Efficiency of Production", *International Economic Review*, 515-521.

[249] Ritter, C. and Simar, L. (1997), "Pitfalls of Normal-Gamma Stochastic Frontier Models", *Journal of Productivity Analysis*, 8(2), 167-182.

[250] Rosenberg N. (1991), "Critical issues in science policy research", *Science and Public Policy*, Vol. 18, n. 6, pp. 335-346.

[251] Rousseau, S. and Rousseau, R. (1997), "Data Envelopment Analysis as a tool for constructing scientometric indicators", *Scientometrics*, Vol. 40, 45-56.

[252] Rousseau, S. and Rousseau, R. (1998), "The scientific wealth of European nations: taking effectiveness into account", *Scientometrics*, Vol. 42, 75-87.

[253] Russell, RR. (1985), "Measures of Technical Efficiency", *Journal of Economic Theory*, 35 (1), 109-126.

[254] Russell, RR. (1988), "On the Axiomatic Approach to the Measurement of Technical Efficiency", in W. Eichhorn, ed. (1988), *Measurement in Economics: Theory and Applications of Economic Indices*, Heidelberg: Physica-Verlag.

[255] Russell, RR. (1990), "Continuity of Measures of Technical Efficiency", *Journal of Economic Theory*, 51 (2), 255-267.

[256] Samuelson, P.A. (1948), "Consumption Theory in Terms of Revealed Preference", *Economica*, 15, 243-253.

[257] Saxenian A. (1996), *Regional advantage. Culture and competition in Silicon Valley and Route 128*, Boston, Harvard University Press.

[258] Scherer, F.M. (1980), *Industrial market structure and economic performance*, Houghton Mifflin, Boston.

[259] Schmidt, P. (1976), "On the Statistical Estimation of Parametric Frontier Production Functions", *Review of Economics and Statistics*, 58, 238-239.

[260] Schmidt P. and Sickles R. C. (1984), "Productivity Frontiers and Panel Data", *Journal of Business and Economic Statistics*, 2, 367-374.

[261] Schmoch U. (2004), "The Technological Output of Scientific Institutions"; in H.F. Moed, W. Glanzel and U. Schmoch (edited by), *Handbook of Quantitative Science and Technology Research*, Kluwer Academic Publishers.

[262] Schubert A., Braun T. (1993), "Reference standards for citation based assessments", *Scientometrics*, Vol. 26, n. 1, pp. 21-35.

[263] Schubert, A. and Braun, T. (1996), "Cross-field normalization of scientometric indicators", *Scientometrics*, Vol. 36, 311-324.

[264] Schubert A., Glanzel W., Braun T. (1988), "Against absolute methods: relative scientometric indicators and relational charts as evaluation tools", in Van Raan A.F.J., *Handbook of Quantitative Studies of Science and Technology*, pp. 137-176.

[265] Schuster, E.F. (1985), "Incorporating Support Constraints into Nonparametric Estimators of Densities", *Communication in Statistics - Theory and Methods*, 14, 1123-1136.

[266] Scott D. W. (1992), *Multivariate Density Estimation, Theory, Practice and Visualization*, John Wiley & Sons, NY.

[267] Scott, A.J. (ed.) (2001) *Global city-Regions*. Oxford, Oxford University Press.

[268] Seaver, B. and Triantis, K. (1992), "A Fuzzy Clustering Approach Used in Evaluating Technical Efficiency Measures in Manufacturing", *Journal of Productivity Analysis*, 3, 337-363.

[269] Seglen, P.O. (1997), "Why the impact factor of journals should not be used for evaluating research", *BMJ*, 314: 498-502.

[270] Seiford, L.M. (1994), "A DEA bibliography 1978-1992", in Charnes A., Cooper W.W., Lewin A., and Seiford L. (eds.), Data Envelopment Analysis: Theory, Methodology, Applications, Kluwer Academic Publishers, 437-470.

[271] Seiford, L.M. (1996), "Data Envelopment Analysis: The Evolution of the State-of-the-Art (1978-1995)", *Journal of Productivity Analysis*, 7, 99-138.

[272] Seitz J. K.(1966), "Efficiency Measures for Steam-Electric Generating Plants", *Proceedings of the Thirty Ninth Annual Meeting of the Western Farm Economics Associations, 1966*, 143-151.

[273] Seitz J. K.(1971), "Productive Efficiency in the Steam-Electric Generating Industry", *Journal of Political Economy* 79, 878-886.

[274] Sengupta J.K.(1991), "Maximum Probability Dominance and Portfolio Theory", *Journal of Optimization Theory and Applications*, 71, 341-357.

[275] Sengupta, J.K. (1992), "A Fuzzy Systems Approach in Data Envelopment Analysis", *Computers and Mathematical Applications*, 24, 259-266.

[276] Sengupta, J.K., and Park, H.S. (1993), "Portfolio Efficiency tests Based on Stochastic Dominance and Cointegration", *International Journal of Systems Science*, 24, 2135-2158.

[277] Sengupta, J.K. (1994), "Measuring Dynamic Efficiency Under Risk Aversion", *European Journal of Operational Research*, 74, 61-69.

[278] Sengupta, J.K. (1995), *Dynamics of Data Envelopment Analysis. Theory of Systems Efficiency*, Kluwer Academic Publishers, Dordrecht.

[279] Sengupta, J.K. (2000), *Dynamic and Stochastic Efficiency Analysis, Economics of Data Envelopment Analysis*, World Scientific, Singapore.

[280] Sheather S.J., and Jones M.C. (1991), "A relyable data-based bandwidth selection method for kernel density estimation", Journal of the Royal Statistical Society, Series B, 53:3, pp. 683-690.

[281] Shephard, R.W. (1953). *Cost and Production Functions*. Princeton, NJ: Princeton University Press.

[282] Shephard, R.W. (1970). *Theory of Cost and Production Function*. Princeton, NJ: Princeton University Press.

[283] Shephard, R.W. (1974). *Indirect Production Functions*. Princeton, NJ: Princeton University Press.

[284] Shukla, R. and Trzcinca C. (1992), "Performance Measurement of Managed Portfolios", *Financial Markets, Institutions and Instruments*, 1, 1-59.

[285] Sickles R. C. (2005), "Panel estimators and the identification of firm-specific efficiency levels in parametric, semiparametric and nonparametric settings", *Journal of Econometrics*, 126, 305-334.

[286] Silverman, B.W. (1986). *Density Estimation for Statistics and Data Analysis*, Chapman and Hall, London.

[287] Silverman B.W., and Young G.A. (1987), "The Bootstrap: Smooth or Not to Smooth?", *Biometrika*, 74, 469-479.

[288] Simar L., (1992), "Estimating Efficiencies from Frontier Models with Panel Data: A comparison of Parametric, Nonparametric and Semi-parametric Methods with Bootstrapping", *The Journal of Productivity Analysis*, 3, 167-203.

[289] Simar L., (1996) "Aspects of statistical Analysis in DEA-type frontier models", *The Journal of Productivity Analysis*, 7, 177-185.

[290] Simar, L. (2003a), "Detecting outliers in frontier models: a simple approach", *Journal of Productivity Analysis*, 20, 391-424.

[291] Simar, L. (2003b), "How to Improve the Performance of DEA/FDH Estimators in the Presence of Noise?, Discussion Paper 0323, Institut de Statistique, UCL, Belgium.

[292] Simar, L. and Wilson, P.W. (1998), "Sensitivity analysis of efficiency scores: how to bootstrap in nonparametric frontier models", *Management Science*, vol. 44, 1, 49-61.

[293] Simar, L. and Wilson, P.W. (1999a), "Some problems with the Ferrier/Hirschberg Bootstrap Idea", *The Journal of Productivity Analysis*, 11, 67-80.

[294] Simar, L. and Wilson, P.W. (1999b), "Of Course we Can Bootstrap DEA scores! But does it mean anything? Logic Trumps and Wishful Thinking", *The Journal of Productivity Analysis*, 11, 67-80.

[295] Simar, L. and Wilson, P.W. (1999c), "Estimating and Bootstrapping Malmquist Indices", *European Journal of Operational Research*, 115, 459-471.

[296] Simar, L. and Wilson, P.W. (2000a), "Statistical Inference in Nonparametric Frontier Models: The State of the Art", *The Journal of Productivity Analysis*, 13, 49-78.

[297] Simar, L. and Wilson, P.W. (2000b), "A general methodology for bootstrapping in non-parametric frontier models", *Journal of Applied Statistics*, vol.27, 6, 779-802.

[298] Simar, L. and Wilson, P.W. (2001), "Testing restrictions in nonparametric efficiency models", *Communications in Statistics*, 30(1), 159-184.

[299] Simar, L. and Wilson, P.W. (2002), "Nonparametric tests of returns to scale", *European Journal of Operational Research*, 139, 115-132.

[300] Simar, L. and Wilson, P.W. (2003), "Estimation and Inference in Two-stage, Semi-parametric Models of Production Processes", Discussion Paper 0307, Institut de Statistique, UCL, Belgium, *forthcoming* in *Journal of Econometrics*.

[301] Simar, L. and P.W. Wilson (2005), "Estimation and Inference in Cross-Sectional Stochastic Frontier Models", Discussion paper 0524, Institut de Statistique, UCL.

[302] Simar, L. and P.W. Wilson (2006a), "Statistical Inference in Nonparametric Frontier Models: recent Developments and Perspectives", *forthcoming* in *The Measurement of Productive Efficiency*, 2nd Edition, Harold Fried, C.A.Knox Lovell and Shelton Schmidt, editors, Oxford University Press, 2006.

[303] Simar, L. and Wilson, P.W. (2006b), "Efficiency Analysis: The Statistical Approach", Manuscript, Institute of Statistics, UCL, Belgium.

[304] Simar, L. and V. Zelenyuk (2003), "Statistical Inference for Aggregates of Farrell-type Efficiencies", Discussion paper 0324, Institute of Statistics, UCL, Belgium, *forthcoming* in *Journal of Applied Econometrics*.

[305] Simar, L. and V. Zelenyuk (2004), "On Testing Equality of Distributions of Technical Efficiency Scores", Discussion paper 0434, Institute of Statistics, UCL, Belgium.

[306] Simon, H. A. (1955), "A behavioral model of rational choice", *Quarterly Journal of Economics*, 69(1), 99-118.

[307] Simon, H. A. (1957), *Models of Man*, John Wiley and Sons, NY.

[308] Simonoff J.S., (1996), *Smoothing methods in statistics*, Springer series in Statistics, NY.

[309] Sitorius, B.L. (1966), "Productive Efficiency and Redundant Factors of Production in Traditional Agricolture of Underdeveloped Countries", *Proceedings of the Thirty Ninth Annual Meeting of the Western Farm Economics Associations*, 153-158.

[310] Schmidt, P, and R.C. Sickles (1984), Production frontier and panel data, *Journal of Business and Economic Statistics*,3, 171-203.

[311] Stevenson, R.E. (1980), "Likelihood Functions for Generalized Stochastic Frontier Estimation", *Journal of Econometrics*, 13(1), 57-66.

[312] Stigler, G.J. (1976), "The Xistence of X-Efficiency", *American Economic Review*, 66 (1), 213-216.

[313] Swiss Re, (1996), "Deregulation and Liberalization of Market Access: The European Insurance Industry on the Threshold of a New Era in Competition," *Sigma*, no. 7 of 1996.

[314] Swiss Re, (2000a), "Japan's Insurance Markets - A Sea Change," *Sigma*, no. 8 of 2000.

[315] Swiss Re, (2000b), "Europe in Focus: Non-life Markets Undergoing Structural Change," *Sigma*, no. 3 of 2000.

[316] Taubes G. (1993), "Measure for measure in science", *Science*, 14/05/93, Vol. 260, n. 5110, pp. 884-886.

[317] Taveres G. (2002), "A bibliography of Data Envelopment Analysis (1978-2001)". RUTCOR Research Report RRR 01-02, Rutgers University, Piscatway, NJ.

[318] Thanassoulis, E. (2001) *Introduction to the Theory and Application of Data Envelopment Analysis*, Kluwer Academic Publishers, Boston.

[319] Thrall, R.M. (1999), "What is the economic meaning of FDH?", *Journal of Productivity Analysis*, 11, 243-250.

[320] Thursby J.G., and Kemp S. (2002), "Growth and productive efficiency of university intellectual property licensing", *Research Policy*, 31(1), 109-124.

[321] Timmer, C.P. (1971), "Using a Probabilistic Frontier Production Function to Measure Technical Efficiency", *Journal of Political Economy*, 79 (4), 776-794.

[322] Tornqvist, L. (1936), "The Bank of Finland's Consumption Price Index", *Bank of Finland Montly Bullettin*, 10, 1-8.

[323] Treynor, J.L. (1965), "How to Rate Management of Investment funds", *Harvard Business Review*, 43, 63-75.

[324] Triantis, K. and Girod, O. (1998), "A Mathematical Programming Approach for Measuring Technical Efficiency in a Fuzzy Environment", *Journal of Productivity Analysis*, 10, 85-102.

[325] Triantis, K and Vanden Eeckaut P. (2000), "Fuzzy Pair-wise Dominance and Implications for Technical Efficiency Performance Assessment", *Journal of Productivity Analysis*, 13, 207-230.

[326] Tulkens, H. (1993), "On FDH Efficiency Analysis: Some methodological Issues and Applications to Retail Banking, Courts, and Urban Transit", *Journal of Productivity Analysis*, 4 (1/2), 183-210.

[327] Tulkens, H. and Vanden Eeckaut P. (1995a), "Non-frontier measures of efficiency, progress and regress for time series data", *International Journal of Production Economics*, 39, 83-97.

[328] Tulkens, H. and Vanden Eeckaut P. (1995b), "Non-parametric efficiency, progress and regress measures for panel data: methodological aspects", *European Journal of Operational Research*, 80, 474-499.

[329] Turchetti G. and Daraio, C. (2004), "How Deregulation Shapes Market Structure and Industry Efficiency: The case of the Italian Motor Insurance Industry", *Geneva Papers on Risk and Insurance*, 29 (2), 202-218.

[330] van Raan, A.F.J. (1993), "Advanced bibliometric methods to assess research performance and scientific development: basic principles and recent practical applications", *Research Evaluation*, 3:151.

[331] van Raan, A.F.J. (1997), "Scientometrics: state of the art", *Scientometrics*, Vol. 38, 205-218.

[332] van den Broeck J., Koop G., Osiewalski J., and Steel M.F.J. (1994), "Stochastic frontier models: a Bayesian perspective", *Journal of Econometrics*, 61, 273-303.

[333] Vanden Eeckaut, P. (1997), *Free Disposal Hull and Measurement of efficiency: Theory, Application and Software*, PhD Thesis, Faculté des Sciences Economiques, Sociales et Politiques, Nouvelle série (229), Université Catholique de Louvain, Louvain-la-Neuve, Belgium.

[334] Varian, H.R. (1984), "The Non-Parametric Approach to Production Analysis", *Journal of Productivity Analysis*, 52, 279-297.

[335] Varian, H.R. (1985), "Nonparametric Analysis of Optimizing Behaviour with Measurement Error", *Journal of Econometrics*, 30 (1/2), 445-458.

[336] Varian, H.R. (1990), "Goodness-of-Fit in Optimizing Models",in Lewin, A.Y., and Lovell, C.A.K., (eds.) *Frontier Analysis: Parametric and Nonparametric Approaches, Journal of Econometrics*, 46 (1/2).

[337] Varian H.R. (1992) *Microeconomic Analysis*, 3rd edition, W. W. Norton & Company.

[338] Vincent, A. (1968), *La mesure de la productivité*, Dunod, Paris.

[339] Watson, G.S. (1964), "Smooth regression analysis", *Sankhya* Series A, 26, 359-372.

[340] Wilkens, K., J. Zhu (2001), "Portfolio evaluation and benchmark selection: A mathematical programming approach", *Journal of Alternative investments*, 4 (1), 9-20.

[341] Williamson, O.E. (1964), *The Economics of Discretionary Behavior: Managerial Objectives in a Theory of the Firm*, Englewood Cliffs, NJ: Prentice-Hall.

[342] Wilson, P.W. (1995), "Detecting Influential Observations in Data Envelopment Analysis", *Journal of Economics and Business*, 6, 27-46.

[343] Wilson, P. W. (2005a), "FEAR 1.0: A Software Package for Frontier Efficiency Analysis with R", unpublished working paper, Department of Economics, University of Texas, Austin, Texas. Software and working paper downloadable at http://www.eco.utexas.edu/faculty/Wilson/Software/FEAR/ .

[344] Wilson, P. W. (2005b), "FEAR 0.9 Command Reference", Department of Economics, University of Texas, Austin, Texas.

[345] Wilson, P. W. (2005c), "FEAR 0.9 User's Guide", Department of Economics, University of Texas, Austin, Texas.

[346] Zhu, J. (1996), "Data envelopment analysis with preference structure", *Journal of the Operational Research Society*, 47, 136-150.

[347] Zucker L.G., Darby M.R., Armstrong J. (1998), "Geographically localized knowledge: Spillovers or markets?" *Economic Inquiry*, XXXVI, 65-86.

Topic Index

Activity analysis, 21
Age effects, 174
Aggregation of inputs and outputs, 148
Asymptotic results, 47
  consistency, 47
  sampling distributions, 49
Bandwidth selection, 109
  k-Nearest Neighbor method, 109
  empirical rules, 111
  likelihood cross-validation, 109
Bootstrap, 50
  basic, 56
  bias, 55
  bootstrap principle, 54
  bootstrap world, 52
  confidence intervals, 55
  consistent, 56
  empirical distribution, 51
  Monte-Carlo approximation, 51
  sampling distribution, 51–52
  smoothing parameter, 59
  true world, 52
Chance-constrained programming, 39
Conditional efficiency, 96
  decomposition, 113
    externality index, 120
    individual index, 120
    internal or managerial, 120
  full frontiers, 101
  order-α frontiers, 103
    conditional α efficiency, 104
  order-m frontiers, 101
Convexity, 22
Cross-evaluation, 41
Cross-sectional models, 28
Cross-validation, 61
Curse of dimensionality, 48, 65, 78
DEA, 31
DEAsoft, 63
Deterministic frontier approach, 45
Deterministic models, 28
DGP, 50
Economic axioms, 21
Economies of agglomeration, 173
Economies of experience, 163
Economies of scale, 157, 171
Economies of scope, 160
Efficiency, 14
  allocative, 15
  coefficient of resource utilization, 14
  directional, 41
  radial measures, 14
  scale, 15
  structural, 15
  technical, 14, 20
Explaining efficiency, 96
External-environmental factors, 95
FDH, 33
FEAR, 63
Free disposability, 21
Full frontiers, 67
Fund age, 208
Input oriented, 30
Input requirement set, 20
Kernel, 101
  multivariate, 111
  truncated, 112
Malmquist productivity indices, 28
Manager tenure, 199
Multiple objective approach, 41
Nonparametric frontier approach, 30
Nonparametric models, 26
Normal reference rule, 60
Outliers, 79
Output correspondence set, 20
Output oriented, 30
Panel data models, 28
Parametric approaches, 85

Parametric approximations, 86
  bootstrap, 89
  Generalized Cobb-Douglas, 91
  multivariate, 90
  translog, 93, 186
Parametric models, 26
Plug-in principle, 34
Preference structure models, 40
Principal component analysis, 145
Production set, 20
Productivity, 13
  partial, 13
  total factor, 13
Reflection method, 58
Returns to scale, 22
  testing, 151
Robust frontiers, 65
  order-α frontiers, 72
    α efficiency, 75
    computational aspects, 74
    order-α efficiency scores, 73
  order-m frontiers, 68
    computational aspects, 72
    definition, 68
    economic meaning, 71
    order-m efficiency measures, 70
  partial frontiers, 67
  probabilistic formulation, 66
  properties, 77
    advantages, 78
    estimators full frontier, 77
    outliers, 79
    statistical, 77
Robust normal reference rule, 60
Scale elasticity, 189
Shephard distance functions, 24
Slacks, 32
Statistical model, 43
  statistical assumptions, 44
  stochastic elements, 45
Stochastic frontier approach, 30
Stochastic frontier models, 46
Stochastic models, 28
Subsampling techniques, 57
Super efficiency, 41
Taxonomy of efficient frontier models, 25
Two stage methods, 87
Value efficiency analysis, 40
Weight restrictions, 40

Author Index

Acs, Z., 173
Adams, J.D., 168
Afriat, S.N., 17–18, 29
Aigner, D.J., 4, 29, 46
Alchian, A., 18
Allen, R., 40
Allison, P.D., 174
Amel, D., 139
Andersen, P., 41
Angulo-Meza, L., 40
Annaert, J., 193
Aragon, Y., 72, 74–75
Armstrong, J., 174
Athanassopoulos, A., 40
Audretsch, D.B., 174
Avveduto, S., 175
Banker, R.D., 15, 18–19, 31, 47, 98
Barnes, C., 139
Barnett, V., 81
Bartelsman, E.J., 97–98
Barth, J.R., 138
Basso, A., 193
Battese, G.E., 26
Becattini, G., 173
Berger, A.N., 138–139, 143
Bergson, A., 17
Bertoletti, P., 191
Bessent, A., 168
Bhadra, D., 18
Bickel, P.J., 57
Bjurek, H., 16
Bogetoft, P., 41
Boles, J.N., 17
Bonaccorsi, A., 168–170, 176, 184
Braun, T., 169, 178
Bressler, R.G., 17
Briec, W., 41, 193–194
Cantarelli, D., 191
Castells, M., 173
Caves, D.W., 16, 28
Cazals, C., 65–66, 68, 72, 75, 77, 96, 102
Cesari, R., 193
Chambers, R.G., 41
Chang, H., 19
Charnes, A., 2, 14–15, 17, 29, 31, 168
Chavas, J.P., 18
Cherchye, L., 37
Chevalier, J., 195
Choi, B., 193
Christensen, L.R., 16, 28, 186
Chu, S.F., 29
Chung, Y., 41
Clark, G.L., 173
Coelli, T., 26, 90, 92, 168, 186, 188
Collins, P.M.D., 169
Cooke, P., 173
Cooper, W.W., 2, 14–15, 17, 19, 25, 29, 31, 39, 168
Cornwell, C., 29
Cox, T.L., 18
Cummins, J.D., 139, 142–143
Dan Brumbaugh, R.Jr., 138
Daniel, H.D., 169
Dantzig, G.B., 17
Daouia, A., 5, 72, 74–75, 77, 86–88, 91, 94, 96, 103–104, 186, 192
Daraio, C., 6, 65–66, 70–71, 77, 96, 100–102, 113, 122, 144, 168–170, 176, 184, 193–194
Darby, M.R., 174
David, P.A., 175
De Alessi, L., 19
Debreu, G., 2, 14, 16–17, 24
Deckle, R., 138
Deprins, D., 2, 17, 30, 33–34, 86, 145
Desai, P., 193
Detzel, L.F., 196, 200, 216
Diewert, W.E., 16, 18, 28
Doms, M., 97–98
Dorfman, R., 2
Dorof, W.A., 169

Dyson, R.G., 40
Efron, B., 50, 55, 57, 62
Ellison, G., 195
Emrouznejad, A., 25
Farrell, M.J., 2, 14–17, 21, 24, 26, 31, 33
Feldman, M.P., 173–174
Ferrier, G.D., 63
Fieldhouse, M., 17
Fisch, R., 169
Fisher, I., 28
Florens, J.P., 5, 65–66, 68, 72, 75, 77, 85, 87–92, 94, 96, 102, 186, 188, 191–192
Forsund, F.R., 16–17
Fortin, R., 196, 200, 216
Freedman, D.A., 57, 59
Fried, H.O., 6, 29–30, 39, 99
Funari, S., 193
Färe, R., 5, 15–17, 19, 28–29, 32, 41, 98, 168, 188
Garfield, E., 169
Gattoufi, S., 25
Gertler, M.S., 173
Gijbels, I., 49, 56
Girod, O., 40
Glanzel, W., 169
Golec, J., 195, 200
Goto, I., 138
Green, J.R., 191
Greene, W.H., 29, 46, 86
Griliches, Z., 168
Grinblatt, M., 193
Grosskopf, S., 5, 16–17, 19, 28–29, 32, 41, 43, 90, 92, 98, 168, 186, 191
Hall, P., 4, 29, 46, 173
Halme, M., 40
Hamilton, K.S., 169
Hanoch, G., 18
Hansmann, H., 19
Harker, P.T., 139
Hayes, K., 90, 92, 168, 186
Henderson, D.J., 29, 47
Henderson, R., 174
Hess, T., 136, 138
Hicks, J.R., 18
Hirschberg, J.G., 63
Hjalmarsson, L., 16
Hogan, A.M.B., 138
Holbrook, J.A.D., 169
Holmstrom, B.R., 19
Humphrey, D.B., 139
Härdle, W., 114, 145, 218
Ippolito, R.A., 193
Jaffe, A.B., 174
Jeong, S.O., 64, 101
Johnston, R., 168
Jones, M.C., 60, 113
Jorgenson, D.W., 186
Joro, J., 40
Kao, C., 40
Kashayap, A.K., 138
Kemp, S., 168
Kennington, J., 168
Kerstens, K., 41, 194
Kessel, R., 18
Khorana, A., 196
King, D., 169
Kneip, A., 4, 29, 45–46, 48–49, 57
Koopmans, T.C., 2, 14, 16–17
Korhonen, P., 40, 168
Korostelev, A., 48
Kostoff, R.N., 169
Krugman, P., 173
Kumbhakar, S.C., 4, 16, 29, 46, 86, 98
Kuosmanen, T.P., 37
Land, K.C., 39
Laredo, P., 168
Lau, L.J., 186
Leibenstein, H., 19
Lemak, D., 195
Leontief, W.W., 17
Lesourd, J.B., 193–194
Levin, S.G., 170, 175
Lewin, A.Y., 29, 98
Lewis, T., 81
Lewison, G., 169
Li, S., 39
Lindgren, B., 29
Lindsay, C.M., 19
Liu, S.T., 40
Lovell, C.A.K., 4–6, 13–17, 29–30, 32, 39, 46, 86, 97–99
Luenberger, D.G., 41
Luwel, M., 168
Maindiratta, A., 18
Malmquist, S., 16, 28
Mammen, E., 49, 56
Margaritis, D., 191
Markowitz, H., 193
Martin, B.R., 169
Martin, S., 172
Mas-Colell, A., 191
May, R., 169
Meeusen, W., 29, 46
Merton, R.K., 174
Michelson, S., 196, 200, 216
Milgrom, P., 172
Minton, J.W., 98
Moed, H.F., 169, 179
Moorsteen, R.H., 17
Morey, M.R., 193
Morey, R.C., 98, 193
Morgan, K., 173
Morroni, M., 97
Mouchart, M., 148
Moutray, C., 168

Mullins, N., 169
Murthi, A., 193
Mustar, P., 168
Nadaraya, E.A., 114
Narin, F., 169
Niskanen, W.A.Jr., 19
Nolle, D.E., 138
Oehler, K., 169
Okubo, Y., 169
Olesen, O.B., 39
Olivastro, D., 169
Oral, M., 25
Panetta, F., 139, 193
Park, B.U., 4, 29, 45–46, 48–49, 56, 77, 100–101
Park, H.S., 194
Parkan, C., 18
Pasurka, C., 98
Pedraja-Chaparro, R., 40
Pereira Estellita Lins, M., 40
Perelman, S., 188
Petersen, N.C., 39, 41
Porrini, D., 138
Porter, G., 196, 200, 216
Post, G.T., 37
Primont, D., 188
Pyke, F., 173
Quiggin, J., 41
Ramsden, P., 168
Rao, D.S.P., 26
Ray, S.C., 3, 18, 29
Reagan, B., 168
Reisman, A., 25
Rhodes, E., 2, 15, 17, 31, 168
Rice, T.N., 138
Richmond, J., 29
Ritter, C., 46
Roberts, J., 172
Roos, P., 29
Rosenberg, N., 169
Rothschild, M., 18
Rousseau, R., 168
Rousseau, S., 168
Russell, R.R., 15, 28
Salinas-Jimenes, J., 40
Salleo, C., 139
Salo, S., 40
Samuelson, P.A., 2, 18
Santin, D., 188
Sarafoglou, N., 17
Satish, P., 195
Saxenian, A., 173
Scalise, J.M., 138
Scherer, F.M., 172
Schmidt, P., 4, 29, 46
Schmidt, S.S., 6, 29–30, 39, 99
Schmoch, U., 169
Schubert, A., 169, 178
Schuster, E.F., 58
Scott, A.J., 173
Scott, D.W., 57, 110
Seaver, B., 40
Seglen, P.O., 179
Seiford, L.M., 14, 25, 29, 39
Seitz, J.K., 17, 97
Sengenberger, W., 173
Sengupta, J.K., 14–15, 40, 193–194
Sheather, S.J., 60, 113
Shephard, R.W., 2, 16–17, 21, 24, 52
Shukla, R., 193
Sickles, R.C., 29
Silverman, B.W., 58–61, 110
Simar, L., 2, 4–6, 17, 19, 22, 25–26, 29–30, 33–34, 38, 43–46, 48–49, 52, 56–61, 63–66, 68, 70–72, 74–75, 77, 79, 85–92, 94, 96, 99–104, 113, 122, 145, 148, 151–153, 170, 186, 188, 191–194, 218
Simon, H.A., 19, 174
Simonoff, J.S., 57, 110
Sitorius, B.L., 17
Siverman, B.W., 57
Smith, J., 40
Smith, P., 40
Snizek, W., 169
Solow, R., 2
Stephan, P.E., 170, 175
Stevens, K.A., 169
Stevenson, R.E., 46
Stewart, J.A., 174
Stigler, G.J., 19
Tainio, R., 168
Taubes, G., 169
Taveres, G., 25
Taylor, L., 90, 92, 168, 186
Thanassoulis, E., 26, 40
Thomas-Agnan, C., 72, 74–75
Thore, S., 39
Thrall, R.M., 37, 39
Thursby, J.G., 168
Tibshirani, R.J., 50, 55, 57, 62
Timmer, C.P., 17, 97
Tirole, J., 19
Titman, S., 193
Tone, K., 14, 25, 29, 39
Tornqvist, L., 16, 28
Trajtenberg, M., 174
Trauth, T., 136, 138
Triantis, K., 40
Trifts, J., 196, 200, 216
Trzcinca, C., 193
Tsionas, E.G., 4, 29, 46
Tsybakov, A.B., 48
Tulkens, H., 2, 17, 29, 33–35
Turchetti, G., 143–144
Valdmanis, V., 191

Van den Broeck, J., 29, 46, 193
Van Leeuwen, T.N., 179
Van Raan, A.F.J., 169
Vanden Eeckaut, P., 29, 37, 40–41
Varian, H.R., 18, 191
Vennet, R.V., 193
Vincent, A., 13
Wagner, J., 196, 200, 216
Wallenius, J., 40, 168
Watson, G.S., 114
Weber, W., 90, 92, 168, 186
Weigand, R., 196, 200, 216
Weiner, C., 45, 48–49, 77
Weiss, M.A., 139, 142–143
Whinston, M.D., 191
Wilcox, J.A., 138
Wilkens, K., 193
Williamson, O.E., 18
Wilson, P.W., 4, 6, 19, 22, 25–26, 30, 43–46, 49, 52, 57–61, 63–64, 79, 99, 113, 151–153, 218
Yaisawarng, S., 6, 99
Young, G.A., 57
Zelenyuk, V., 16, 63, 100
Zenios, S.A., 139
Zhu, J., 39–40, 193
Zi, H., 143
Zucker, L.G., 174

MIX
Papier aus verantwortungsvollen Quellen
Paper from responsible sources
FSC® C105338

FSC
www.fsc.org

If you have any concerns about our products,
you can contact us on
ProductSafety@springernature.com

In case Publisher is established outside the EU,
the EU authorized representative is:
Springer Nature Customer Service Center GmbH
Europaplatz 3, 69115 Heidelberg, Germany

Printed by Libri Plureos GmbH
in Hamburg, Germany